The Stream of Consciousness

Scientific Investigations into
the Flow of Human Experience

EMOTIONS, PERSONALITY, AND PSYCHOTHERAPY

Series Editors:

Carroll E. Izard • *University of Delaware, Newark, Delaware*

and

Jerome L. Singer • *Yale University, New Haven, Connecticut*

HUMAN EMOTIONS
Carroll E. Izard

THE PERSONAL EXPERIENCE OF TIME
Bernard S. Gorman and Alden E. Wessman, eds.

THE STREAM OF CONSCIOUSNESS: Scientific Investigations into the Flow of Human Experience
Kenneth S. Pope and Jerome L. Singer, eds.

THE POWER OF HUMAN IMAGINATION: New Methods in Psychotherapy
Jerome L. Singer and Kenneth S. Pope, eds.

EMOTIONS IN PERSONALITY AND PSYCHOPATHOLOGY
Carroll E. Izard, ed.

The Stream of Consciousness

Scientific Investigations into the Flow of Human Experience

Edited by

Kenneth S. Pope

Brentwood Veterans Administration Hospital
Los Angeles, California

and

Jerome L. Singer

Yale University

Plenum Press · New York and London

Library of Congress Cataloging in Publication Data

Main entry under title:

The Stream of consciousness.

(Emotions, personality, and psychotherapy)
Includes bibliographies and index.
1. Consciousness. I. Pope, Kenneth S. II. Singer, Jerome L. [DNLM: 1.
Consciousness. BF311 S914]
BF311.S693   153   78-2003
ISBN 0-306-31117-8

© 1978 Plenum Press, New York
A Division of Plenum Publishing Corporation
227 West 17th Street, New York, N.Y. 10011

Printed in the United States of America

To our parents

Kate Sayle and William Kenneth Pope
Yetta and Abraham Singer

Contributors

Paul Bakan • Department of Psychology, Simon Fraser University, Burnaby, British Columbia, Canada

John R. Battista • Department of Psychiatry, University of California, Davis, California

Mihaly Csikszentmihalyi • Department of Human Development, University of Chicago, Chicago, Illinois

Eric Klinger • Division of the Social Sciences, University of Minnesota, Morris, Minnesota

Daniel F. Kripke • San Diego Veterans Administration Hospital; and Department of Psychiatry, University of California, San Diego, California

Kenneth S. Pope • Brentwood Veterans Administration Hospital, Los Angeles, California

Joseph F. Rychlak • Department of Psychological Sciences, Purdue University, West Lafayette, Indiana

Tim Shallice • Department of Psychology, The National Hospital, Queen Square, London, England

Jerome L. Singer • Department of Psychology, Yale University, New Haven, Connecticut

David Sonnenschein • San Diego Veterans Administration Hospital; and Department of Psychiatry, University of California, San Diego, California

Steven Starker • West Haven Veterans Administration Hospital; and Yale University, New Haven, Connecticut. Present Address: Psychology Service, Portland Veterans Hospital and Department of Medical Psychology, University of Oregon School of Medicine, Eugene, Oregon

Jack R. Strange • Department of Psychology, Southern Methodist University, Dallas, Texas

Eugene Taylor • Psychology of Religion and Asian Studies, Harvard Divinity School, Cambridge, Massachusetts

Contents

Chapter 2

Asian Interpretations: Transcending the Stream of Consciousness

Eugene Taylor

Chapter 3

The Science of Consciousness

John R. Battista

Part II • Specific Theoretical Formulations and Links to Basic Research

Chapter 6

Two Streams of Consciousness: A Typological Approach

Paul Bakan

Part III • Experimental Approaches to Studying the Stream of Consciousness

Chapter 7

Experimental Studies of Daydreaming and the Stream of Thought

Jerome L. Singer

Chapter 10

Dreams and Waking Fantasy

Steven Starker

Chapter 11

A Biologic Rhythm in Waking Fantasy

Daniel F. Kripke and David Sonnenschein

Part IV • Implications and Broader Perspectives

Chapter 12

Attention and the Holistic Approach to Behavior

Mihaly Csikszentmihalyi

Introduction: The Flow of Human Experience

Kenneth S. Pope and Jerome L. Singer

The stream of consciousness—that flow of perceptions, purposeful thoughts, fragmentary images, distant recollections, bodily sensations, emotions, plans, wishes, and impossible fantasies—is our experience of life, our own personal life, from its beginning to its end. As scientists, we may approach the subject for the joy of discovering how it works. As clinicians, therapists, and social engineers, we may study it in order to reduce human suffering. But simply as people, we are drawn to it precisely because it is that portion of our being at once most familiar and most mysterious.

How disappointing, then, to search so much of the pyschological literature and find reflected there so little of our day-to-day human experience. How surprising—at least to anyone but a psychologist—that textbooks on thinking (Bourne, Ekstrand, and Duminowski, 1971; Johnson, 1955) can ignore or say little about the stream of consciousness and imagination, that books on personality (Mischel, 1971) or on adolescence (Seidman, 1960) can remain so silent about imagination and fantasy. The recent reawakening of interest in the flow of awareness follows a sleep of nearly half a century. As Roger Brown (1958) put it: "In 1913 John Watson mercifully closed the bloodshot inner eye of American psychology. With great relief the profession trained its exteroceptors on the laboratory animal" (p. 93). Even today, serious exploration of the stream of consciousness involves not only an avoidance of both the self-indulgent mush of uncritical armchair introspection and the self-important trivia of thoughtless laboratory artifice, but also readiness to endure a critical thwack from the most

1

influential psychologist of the century for our "diverting preoccupation with a supposed or real inner life . . ." (Skinner, 1975, p. 46).

While the psychologist stumbled, stuttered, then froze into a paralyzed silence, the artist responded with graceful enthusiasm to the challenge William James 1890/1950 set forth in his chapter "The Stream of Thought." In producing what Edmund Wilson (1922) called "perhaps the most faithful X-ray ever taken of the ordinary human consciousness," James Joyce allowed us to experience the sluggish, mundane, somehow heroic movement of awareness that was Leopold Bloom and the earthy, poignant, willful consciousness of Molly. In the following passage, Molly's consciousness fills mostly with memories of her husband:

> who was the first person in the universe before there was anybody that made it all who ah they dont know that they dont know neither do I so there you are they might as well try to stop the sun from rising tomorrow the sun shines for you he said the day we were lying among the rhododendrons on Howth head in the grey tweed suit and his straw hat the day I got him to propose to me yes first I gave him the bit of seedcake out of my mouth and it was leapyear like now yes 16 years ago my God after that long kiss I nearly lost my breath yes he said I was a flower of the mountain yes so we are flowers all a womans body yes that was one true thing he said in his life and the sun shines for you today yes that was why I liked him because I saw he understood or felt what a woman is and I knew I could always get round him and I gave him all the pleasure I could leading him on till he asked me to say yes . . .I was thinking of so many things he didnt know of Mulvey and Mr Stanhope and Hester and father and old Captain Groves and the sailors playing all birds fly . . . and how he kissed me under the Moorish wall and I thought as well as well him as another and then I asked him with my eyes to ask again yes and then asked me would I say yes to say yes my mountain flower and first I put my arms around him yes and drew him down to me so he could feel my breasts all perfume yes and his heart was going like mad and yes I said yes I will Yes. (Joyce, 1914/1961, pp. 782-783)

Not only in her novels, but also in her critical writings, Virginia Woolf reflected the seriousness with which writers responded to James's insights.

> Examine for a moment an ordinary mind on an ordinary day. The mind receives a myriad impressions—trivial, fantastic, evanescent, or engraved with the sharpness of steel. From all sides they come, an incessant shower of innumerable atoms; and as they fall, as they shape themselves into the life of Monday or Tuesday, the accent falls differently from of old . . . . Life is not a series of gig lamps symmetrically arranged; life is a luminous halo, a semi-transparent envelope surrounding us from the beginning of consciousness to the end . . . . Let us record the atoms as they fall upon the mind in the order in which they fall, let us trace the pattern, however disconnected and incoherent in appearance, which each sight or incident scores upon the consciousness. (Woolf, 1925/1953, pp. 154-155)

While James Joyce, Virginia Woolf, and T. S. Eliot (1950) in his 1919 discussion of the "objective correlative" were seeking ways to convey the stream of consciousness in words, filmmakers like Sergei Eisenstein (1942) discovered moving pictures to be especially well-suited to the flow of experience. Eisenstein developed the "montage" and the "partial representation" to evoke from the viewer the same flow of consciousness occurring in the mind of the artist or one of the film's characters. This effort among artists to represent the stream of consciousness extends into modern works of poetry, fiction, and the visual arts, and—happily—provides us with a touchstone for our own experience with grace, perceptiveness, and humor (Pope and Singer, 1978a).

Only in the last decade or so has consciousness emerged as a legitimate subject for psychological research and discussion. Even thus legitimized, consciousness rarely appears in the scientific literature as that flow of experience so familiar to us all. As researchers, we overlook all too often the possible creative forms that rigorous scientific methodology can assume and instead we limit ourselves to experiments that are easy to set up and control, generally focusing on outcome products of specific directed thinking tasks or on the study of isolated features of thought (e.g., the time it takes to rotate mentally a geometric form; the effectiveness of imagery in paired-associate learning; comparing the size of real or imagined wooden balls). The emergent picture of thought process, therefore, often possesses a quality of organization and rationality that is hard to reconcile with the nature of ongoing thought as it is presented by artists or with our own stream of consciousness if we take the trouble to observe it in its natural course (Pope and Singer, 1978b).

The contributions in this volume represent efforts to study the stream of consciousness with a deep appreciation and respect for its rich diversity, its continuous, often quirky movement, its immediacy in the lives of us all, and ultimately its mystery. We begin with an examination of what various people or groups have meant or mean when they use(d) the term "consciousness," of how they treat it, and to what effects. The chapter by Strange calls our attention to the different meanings of "consciousness' when used by such voices as James, Skinner, Freud, Jung, Sartre, Husserl, Tolman, or Tart. He presents and discusses the evolution of the concept of consciousness within the mainstream of American and other Western views. Of particularly formative influence has been American cognitive psychology (William James, Titchner, the functionalists, and the more recent exponents), the behaviorists (Watson, Tolman, Skinner), and the imported movements (psychoanalysis, phenomenological psychology, and transpersonal approaches).

Taylor's discussion of major Asian psychologies makes vividly clear and explicit their differences not only from the Western psychologies discussed by Strange, but also among themselves in terms of conceptualization and study of the stream of consciousness—differences that are often glossed over or ignored in most popular presentations of "Eastern versus Western" approaches. He presents detailed examination of the treatment of the stream of consciousness by the Taoist psychology of China, the Zen psychology of Japan, the Hindu psychology of India, and the psychology of Indian Buddhism.

Battista moves our focus from formal psychologies to the adjacent sciences—physical, biological, neurophysiological—and their relevance to the study of consciousness. His presentation of the contributions of Magoun, Penfield, Hubel and Wiesel, Olds and Milner, Einstein, Heisenberg, and Wigner lays the groundwork for his discussion of criteria for the development of a scientific theory of consciousness that can accomodate phenomenological, psychological, and empirical data.

In the next three chapters, each author sets forth a carefully articulated conceptualization of the stream of consciousness. The ideas presented are informed by the research of the author as well as others, are comprehensive in scope as well as specific in detail, and—of great importance—are capable of experimental validation or disconfirmation.

Rychlak picks up Battista's discussion of the criteria for a scientific theory of consciousness and moves toward an understanding of the stream of consciousness within a "rigorous humanistic psychology." He emphasizes the active, conceptualizing, telic nature of the stream of consciousness.

Shallice grounds his presentation in the recent, almost startling advances of current cognitive psychology. His information-processing framework stresses the organizing nature of conscious experience, its control function, and particularly its limited capacity.

Bakan presents compelling evidence suggesting two qualitatively different streams of consciousness. One stream is associated with left hemispheric brain function (which has been described by various researchers as symbolic, abstract, linear, rational, focal, conceptual, propositional, secondary process, digital, logical, active, and analytic), the other with the workings of the right hemisphere (described as iconic, concrete, diffuse, perceptual, appositional, primary process, analogue, passive, and holistic). Bakan examines how bias in hemispheric functioning contributes to individual differences in conscious experience.

The contributors of the next section set forth the most current research into the stream of consciousness. Singer focuses on the scientific investigation of daydreams, fantasy, and ongoing imaginative processes—those creative aspects of the stream of consciousness that allow us to do more than sit preoccupied with (or imprisoned in) the present sensory environment or carry out simply plodding, computerlike syllogistic reasoning.

Klinger presents and discusses the various methods currently available for studying the flow of thought. He describes in detail the results of research he and his colleagues have performed regarding important dimensions in the stream of consciousness, and the combinations of motivational and stimulus factors that govern changes in the content of thought from one moment to the next.

Pope presents a series of three studies exploring the influence of posture, solitude, and gender upon normal ongoing thought. These studies suggest that the stream of consciousness seems predominantly oriented toward long-term memory or future fantasy, but physical movement or presence of others lead to greater discontinuity and also more focusing upon the present situation.

Starker discusses three studies of night dreams and waking fantasies. He finds striking stylistic consistencies in the "structure" of fantasy, rather than the "content," that transcend the individual's state of arousal.

Kirpke and Sonnenschein investigate the biological rhythm in waking fantasy. They report two experiments, one in a rigidly controlled laboratory and the other in a normal social environment, that demonstrate cyclicality in both waking mental functions and their physiological correlates. The authors discuss possible endogenous biological origins for these approximately 90-minute fantasy cycles.

In the concluding chapter, Csikszentmihalyi draws on a wide body of research, including his own, to set forth a broad holistic conceptualization of the flow of experience with special emphasis on the economy of attention. He views the stream of consciousness in its relationship to the development of both individual human beings and social systems.

References

Bourne, L. E., Ekstrand, B. R., and Duminowski, R. L. *The psychology of thinking.* Englewood Cliffs, N.J.: Prentice-Hall, 1971.

Brown, R. W. *Words and things.* Glencoe, Ill.: The Free Press, 1958.

Eisenstein, S. *The film sense.* New York: Harcourt, Brace, 1942.

Eliot, T. S. Hamlet and his problems. In *Selected essays.* New York: Harcourt, Brace, 1950.

James, W. *The principles of psychology*. New York: Dover, 1890/1950.

Johnson, D. M. *The psychology of thought and judgment*. New York: Harper, 1955.

Joyce, J. *Ulysses*. New York: Random House, 1914/1961.

Mischel, W. *Introduction to personality*. New York: Holt, Rinehart, and Winston, 1971.

Pope, K. S., and Singer, J. L. Regulation of the stream of consciousness: Toward a theory of ongoing thought. In G. E. Schwartz and D. Shapiro (Eds.) *Consciousness and self-regulation: Advances in research*. Vol. 2. New York: Plenum Press, 1978a.

Pope, K. S., and Singer, J. L. The waking stream of consciousness. In J. M. Davidson, R. J. Davidson, and G. E. Schwartz (Eds.) *Human consciousness and its transformations: A psychobiological perspective*. New York: Plenum Press, 1978b.

Seidman, J. M. *The adolescent, a book of readings, revised*. New York: Holt, Rinehart, and Winston, 1960.

Skinner, B. F. The steep and thorny way to a science of behavior. *American Psychologist*, 1975, **30**, 42–49.

Wilson, E. Ulysses. *New Republic*, 1922, **31**, 164.

Woolf, V. Modern fiction. In V. Woolf, *The common reader*. New York: Harcourt, Brace, 1925/1953.

PART I

Historical, Cultural, and Interdisciplinary Perspectives

1

A Search for the Sources of the Stream of Consciousness

Jack R. Strange

After a behavioristic hiatus of over half a century, American psychologists in the 1960s began, at first tentatively, to return consciousness to its former central position of concern. Because of this long period during which the use of the term was not allowed, we lost contact with the historical roots of the several different, but legitimate, definitions of consciousness. Today, we find psychologists of a wide variety of orientations using this word and assuming that its meaning is the same for others as it is for them. As William James pointed out in his *Pragmatism* (1907), many interminable quarrels continue because a key word in the dispute has two meanings that are incompatible. In most cases this incompatibility is quite real, for, as James says, the "practical consequences" may be entirely different according to which meaning is followed.

Most of us realize that we are not all talking about the same thing when we use the term "consciousness." We are not always certain, however, of just what differences are involved. It may be instructive at this point to give a few examples of present usage.

awareness is not included

> Human consciousness, the subtle interplay of fleeting images, perceptions of the immediate environment, memories of long gone events, and daydreams of future or impossible prospects, all carried along the stream of thought, represent a true miracle of our experience of being. (Singer, 1974, p.1)

> It requires a special verbal environment to impose consciousness on

Jack R. Strange • Department of Psychology, Southern Methodist University, Dallas, Texas.

behavior by inducing a person to respond to his own body while he is behaving. If consciousness seems to have a causal effect, it is the effect of the special environment which induces self-observation. (Skinner, 1974, p. 153)

Consciousness is like a surface or a skin upon a vast unconscious area of unknown extent. (Jung, 1968, p. 7)

Sanskrit has about twenty nouns which we translate into "consciousness" or "mind" in English because we do not have the vocabulary to specify the different shades of meaning in these words. (Tart, 1969, p. 3)

We shall see that each of the foregoing conceptualizations has its own history which allows us to trace its development from its unique set of presuppositions.

1. Roots of the Concept of Consciousness in American Cognitive Psychology

Most contemporary psychologists trace consciousness and stream of consciousness back to William James, often without realizing that with his broad philosophical background James was able to use and keep straight several different definitions of consciousness. To understand James, we must be familiar with the history and usage of consciousness that preceded him, both in America and in Europe. We find that from the beginnings of modern philosophy in the early seventeenth century psychology was the study of cognition—how we come to know and be aware (conscious) of the world.

1.1. Consciousness in Philosophical Psychology

By 1700, the rational philosophy of René Descartes and the empirical philosophy of John Locke were being studied in American colleges. Locke's approach was especially appealing in this country, and Bishop Berkeley's modification of Locke was known firsthand in 1729-31 at which time Berkeley was in America in an unsuccessful attempt to found a college in Rhode Island (Boring, 1950). Samuel Johnson (1696-1772), who was already versed in Locke, came under Berkeley's personal influence, and as president of King's College (later Columbia University) wrote *Elementa Philosophica*, which was published in 1752 by Benjamin Franklin. In this first American philosophy textbook, Johnson gives us the following definition of consciousness:

By consciousness is meant our perception of ojbects *ab extra*, or from reflecting or turning the eye of our mind inward, and observing what passeth within itself; whereby we know that we perceive all those sensible

objects and their connections, and all the pleasures and pains attending
them, and all the powers and faculties of our minds employed about them.
(Fay, 1939, pp. 31–32)

This definition follows Locke's dictum that what is in consciousness
was first in the senses. Johnson also shows his familiarity with the
Scottish philosophy of the period in his use of the phrase "faculties of
our minds."

A contemporary of Johnson's, Jonathan Edwards (1703–1758), also
followed Lockean empiricism in his psychology. The following quotation from Edwards is a historical precedent for James's later view that
each consciousness is personal: "Well might Mr. Locke say, that
identity of *person* consisted in identity of consciousness; for he might
have said that identity of *spirit*, too, consisted in the same consciousness; for a mind or spirit is nothing else but consciousness, and what
is included in it" (Fay, 1939, p. 26). It is also interesting that Edwards
reduces the concepts of both mind and spirit to that of consciousness,
which was not a metaphysical substance or entity, but was simply
what was going on in personal awareness. This reduction was not
typical of early American psychology, which tended to follow Descartes' separation of mind and body into two separate, concrete
substances, both equally real.

For a period of 150 years, philosophical psychology in America
was an amalgam of British empiricism, the Scottish school, and the
Cartesian rational separation of mind and body. Psychology was the
self-conscious or introspective study of mental processes, such as
perceiving, reasoning, feeling, and willing. Because of the tendency to
think of these processes as mental faculties, a truly functional study of
mental activities did not develop. For example, President James
McCosh of Princeton University, in his 1886 textbook, *Psychology: The
Cognitive Powers,*follows the old amalgam just four years before James's
Principles was to revolutionize the teaching of psychology.

McCosh's book opens with: "Psychology is the science of the
soul . . . By soul is meant that self of which everyone is conscious . . .
Psychology should have as its province the operations of the conscious
self, leaving to Physiology the structure of the organism" (McCosh,
1886, pp. 1–4). This attempt to hold on to the old philosophical
psychology was made a decade after the establishment of physiological psychology courses by James at Harvard and by Wundt at Leipzig.

1.2. William James's Views of Consciousness

It has been said with much truth that any isolated quotation from
William James (1842–1910) is bound to be unreliable. A few isolated

references to consciousness by James will illustrate this point and the problems it presents for current psychology.

> By states of consciousness are meant such things as sensations, desires, emotions, cognitions, reasonings, decisions, volitions and the like. (James, 1892, p. 1)

> It is that our normal waking consciousness, rational consciousness as we call it, is but one special type of consciousness, whilst all about it, parted from it by the filmiest of screens, there lie potential forms of consciousness entirely different. (James, 1958, p. 298)

> . . . consciousness is at all times primarily *a selective agency*. . . . The item emphasized is always in close connection with some *interest* felt by consciousness to be paramount at the time. (James, 1890, I, p. 139)

> The expressions "affection of the soul" [and] "modification of the ego," are clumsy, like "state of consciousness," and they implicitly assert theories which it is not well to embody in terminology before they have been openly discussed and approved. . . . *My own partiality is for either FEELING or THOUGHT.* (James, 1890, I, p. 186)

> For twenty years past I have mistrusted "consciousness" as an entity; for seven or eight years past I have suggested its non-existence to my students and tried to give them its pragmatic equivalent in realities of experience. It seems to me that the hour is ripe for it to be openly and universally discarded. (James, 1912, p. 3)

In these five quotations James equates consciousness with:

1. Mental activities
2. Regions of the spirit
3. A self or ego function
4. Feeling or thought
5. Something that does not exist

We see in these examples that James used several different definitions of consciousness. As a philosopher, he was aware of these differences and used the meaning that he needed to make his point in a specific context.

1.2.1. Consciousness in James's Principles. In his *Principles of Psychology* (1890), James defined consciousness as mental activities that interact with brain and other body functioning. Although as a philosopher he never preferred an interactionism, he chose it for the principles because it allowed him to present effectively both the biological and the mental facts that made up the new physiological psychology. His dualism was a commonsense one that enabled him to get on with his psychology and leave to the future his working out a consistent metaphysical position.

The *Principles* begins with: "Psychology is the Science of Mental

Life . . . " (James, 1890, I, p. 1). For James our mental life is made up of activities: " . . . such things as we call feelings, desires, cognitions, reasonings, decisions, and the like . . . " (James, 1890, I, p. 1). As we have seen in a foregoing quotation, he preferred the word *thought* to that of *consciousness*: "The first fact for us, then, as psychologists, is that thinking of some sort goes on" (James, 1890, I, p. 224). For what has come to be called "stream of consciousness," James chose "Stream of Thought" and used this phrase as the title of Chapter IX in the *Principles*. He preferred *thought* because it has a verb form *thinking* that emphasizes activity, whereas *consciousness* does not.

James's stream of thought metaphor permitted him to focus on mental activities and avoid the sterile trap of the structuralists (Wundt and Titchener), who analyzed the discrete contents of consciousness. He admits that it may be "convenient" to think of mental activities as being

> built out of unchanging simple ideas . . . [but] a permanently existing "idea" or "Vorstellung" which makes its appearance before the footlights of consciousness at periodical intervals, is as mythological an entity as the Jack of Spades. (James, 1890, I, p. 236)

The stream of thought is personal (it belongs to a particular person), is always changing, is continuous, deals with objects independent of itself, and is selective, choosing what objects to welcome or reject. Very important among the objects selected are the feelings of relations: "We ought to say a feeling of *and*, a feeling of *if*, a feeling of *but*, and a feeling of *by*, quite as readily as we say a feeling of *blue* or a feeling of *cold*" (James, 1890, I, pp. 245–46). Such feelings (and all the other aspects of the stream of thought) are not *things* but are mental activities that allow us to perceive and conceive of objects and things. For example, as contemporary cognitive psychologists now realize, images are not copies of things stored in memory, but are constructed by mental processes from stored information " . . . just as stimulus information is used in the act of perception" (Neisser, 1967, p. 279).

Part of present-day confusion about consciousness stems from pushing the stream analogy too far. James's stream is a temporal one, not a spatial one. Mental activities occur continuously from moment to moment. James is not concerned with the metaphysical question of a concrete place where the activities occur, as in a *soul*, or a *mind*, or a *consciousness*. Of course, if one presupposes a place, one has a right to talk about such a place so long as one is logically consistent within the framework of presuppositions.

It is not necessary, however, to make consciousness a stream in which mental activities swim as minnows do in a creek, Psychologists who feel this imperative are in the position of early physicists who, on learning that light travels in waveform (electromagnetic vibrations), were certain that it had to have a medium in which to vibrate, as sound waves vibrate in air. When they could not discover a medium, they invented a fictitious "ether" to be the hypothetical medium. After a great search for the real ether, they found that electromagnetic vibrations, unlike sound, do not need a medium. Then, the use of the concept and the term "ether" were quietly dropped by physicists.

1.2.2. Consciousness in James's Other Works. Much of the confusion about James's view of consciousness can be attributed to the way he used the term in his *Psychology: Briefer Course* (1892). James was busy with philosophy and was reluctant to return to psychology in order to abridge the *Principles* into one volume. He did the abridgment grudgingly and hurriedly, as Perry points out: "His motives were quite frankly commercial . . . " (Perry, 1954, p. 20). He changed his definition of psychology to " . . . the description and explanation of states of consciousness as such" (James, 1892, p. 1). He also changed the chapter title from "Stream of Thought" to "Stream of Consciousness." In neither of these changes did he define consciousness or clarify the situation by placing the new usage in the light of that of the *Principles*.

Further confusion stems from his *The Varieties of Religious Experience* (1902). This book grew out of a series of lectures on religion that he gave at the University of Edinburgh. His openness and broadmindedness, coupled with his talent for free and creative philosophical speculation, made these lectures a brilliant *tour de force*—an intelligent, informed, and very human insight into this category of experiences—but not a source of precise philosophical thinking and definition.

For the best thinking James was capable of, we must turn to his posthumously published *Essays in Radical Empiricism* (1912). Here we find that James moved from the dualism of the *Principles* to a position of Berkeleyan idealism, which eliminated the material world and made consciousness the only reality. After all, implicit in Locke and all the empiricists who followed him is that the world we know through our senses is not known directly, but only as it appears in our consciousness of it. Berkeley took this implication and used it to rule out the material world. Hume, following Berkeley, carried this implication to its *reductio ad absurdum*, that all we know is a "flux of impressions," where they come from and where they are, we can never know (Peters, 1953).

Building on these earlier empiricists, James formulated his "radical empiricism." Just as Berkeley denied the existence of material (body), James denied the existence of both material and consciousness (mind):

> To deny plumply that "consciousness" exists seems so absurd on the face of it—for undeniably thoughts do exist. . . . Let me then immediately explain that I mean only to deny that the word stands for an entity, but to insist most emphatically that it does stand for a function. (James, 1912, p. 3)

James formulated a monism in which "there is only one primal stuff . . . of which everything is composed" (James, 1912, p. 4). He called this "stuff" "pure experience," which is prior to either material objects or consciousness. At this point he has made explicit the core of Lockean empiricism.

Thus, James contributes the basic definition of consciousness to the mainstream of American functional, cognitive psychology—consciousness is thought, which includes all the mental activities, such as feeling, imagining, reasoning, knowing, perceiving, conceiving, remembering, and all the rest. Consciousness, according to him, is not a substance, nor a place, nor any *thing*, except a stream of thought that results from pure experiencing. It is true that in the *Varieties* James was open to the possibility that other entirely different definitions of consciousness might be as useful to other individuals as his was to him, but it is egregiously gratuitous to claim that he, in fact, espoused these other views.

1.3.   E. B. Titchener's Views of Consciousness

Wundt's approach to psychology was represented in America by E. B. Titchener (1867–1927), who gave it the name "structuralism." For Titchener: "All human knowledge is derived from human experience . . . and there can be no essential difference between the raw materials of physics and the raw materials of psychology" (Titchener, 1909, p. 6). Although he called it psychological parallelism, this view is in fact a double-aspect monism and is not for practical purposes different from James's view. Nor is Titchener's definition of consciousness fundamentally different:

> Consciousness is identified with mind, and "conscious" with "mental." So long as mental processes are going on, consciousness is present, as soon as mental processes are in abeyance, unconsciousness sets in. (Titchener, 1909, 18)

The important difference between James and Titchener is James's use of the "stream of consciousness" metaphor to emphasize that the mental processes (activities and functions) are what psychologists are to study. Following Wundt's lead, Titchener used introspection to study the structure of slices of consciousness that attempted to freeze a single moment or thin cross-section of the stream. They believed that they, like chemists, should search for the elements or basic building blocks of the structure of consciousness. As every history of psychology details, this search proved unproductive, and the mainstream of American psychology, flowing from James's conceptions, passed them by.

Apart from his search for the chimerical elements, however, Titchener pursued a number of research directions that are of interest to cognitive psychologists today. We have only to mention, for example, his involvement in the "Perky phenomenon," from which much recent research in imagery has been generated. Another example is the current interest in pre-attentive processes (Broadbent, 1977), which were studied by Titchener as a passive or involuntary first phase of attention (Titchener, 1909, p. 268). It is not an unreasonable prediction to say that Titchener's overall contribution to psychology will be favorably reevaluated in the light of our contemporary concern with consciousness.

1.4. Functionalist Views of Consciousness

Contemporary with Titchener's structuralism was Angell's functionalism, which had developed out of Wiliam James's approach to psychology. In his textbook, *Psychology*, J. R. Angell (1867–1949) defines psychology as the "science of consciousness." Of this subject matter he states:

> Consciousness we can only define in terms of itself. Sensations, ideas, pains, pleasures, acts of memory, imagination, and will—these may serve to illustrate the experiences we mean to indicate by the term; and our best endeavour to construct a successful definition results in some such list, of which we can only say: "These taken together are what I mean by consciousness." (Angell, 1908, p. 1)

As was James, Angell and the other functionalists were greatly influenced by Darwin's theory of evolution. In the light of this theory they held that consciousness, because it has survival value, has evolved as an adaptive mechanism just as physical characteristics have. According to Lloyd Morgan's theory of emergent evolution, consciousness emerged as a natural property of the high level of organization attained in evolution by the human organism, including, of course, the very complex structure of the brain. Therefore, for functionalists, consciousness is not an anemic, acausal epiphenomenon; rather, it is a determining force, an equal to the physical body.

Their evolutionary view tended to make functionalists either interactionists or proponents of a double-aspect view. In the later section on mind-body, we shall see that an emergent-properties, double-aspect theory has recently been proposed (Holt, 1972, p. 8) as the best solution for cognitive psychologists doing research in imagery.

As an eminent historian (Boring, 1950) has said, all American psychologists tend to be functionalists by temperament, regardless of the label they take for themselves. The reason for this pervasiveness is that functionalism is a practical, commonsense approach that most Americans prefer. Common sense seems to affirm that consciousness exists and makes a difference in a person's everyday life. It also seems to interact with the physical, material world, which common sense also affirms.

1.5. Present Status of Consciousness in Cognitive Psychology

We shall conclude this section on the roots of consciousness in traditional American cognitive psychology with a brief word about where we are today. In the last dozen or so years many psychologists have felt free to leave the confines of behaviorism. A book on cognitive psychology can begin: " . . . the world of experience is produced by the man who experiences it" (Neisser, 1967, p. 3). The core topics are again sensation, perception, memory, and attention still set before the backdrop of consciousness and stream of consciousness, but discussed in terms of information theory and systems analysis.

Another present-day concern is with imagery, which behaviorists ignored. Again the work of Wundt and Titchener is important, and their method of introspection is being reexamined (McKeller in Sheehan, 1972). Long neglected in academic psychology, a return to the study of daydreams and their imagery has been made (Singer, 1974, 1975). These concerns and other current cognitive ones are natural extensions of the history that stretches from Johnson and Edwards to James, Titchener, and Angell, and over the long behavioristic break, down to the present.

2. Background of the Behaviorist View of Consciousness

Thus far, discussion of the behavioristic hiatus has been in the past tense, where it belongs. This was not meant to imply, however, that the study of behavior is unimportant or that it is not legitimate. The problem was that pure behaviorists gained the field and ruled out the study of other important concerns of psychology, such as consciousness. The purpose of this section is to examine the behaviorist view of consciousness and trace the roots of this view.

Materialism, which is the philosophical position of most behaviorists, was given its modern impetus by La Mettrie (1709–1751) in France in the early eighteenth centruy. La Mettrie denied the existence of soul and mind, believing that the brain is the "organ of thought." His was a mechanistic view of man as a machine. The development of this materialist position coincided with the rise of modern science. The early scientists tended to be naive realists, whose common sense told them that all that existed was the observable, material world. By the nineteenth century science was entrenched in a mechanistic, deterministic, materialistic "world of reality."

John B. Watson (1878–1958) founded behaviorism in 1912–13 and defined psychology as a natural science that studied behavior, not consciousness, by observation and experimentation. In the beginning, Watson treated consciousness as an epiphenomenon but he later stated: "Behaviorism claims that 'consciousness' is neither a definable nor a usable concept; that it is merely another word for the 'soul' of more ancient times. The old psychology is thus dominated by a kind of subtle religious philosophy" (Watson, 1924, p. 3).

2.1. Tolman's Definition of Consciousness

Giving full allegiance to Watson, most behaviorists simply dropped consciousness from their lexicon. One of the few to attempt a behavioristic definition of consciousness was E. C. Tolman (1886–1959), that rather remarkable sign-Gestalt, purposive behaviorist. At the height of the behaviorist takeover, he wrote:

> . . . wherever an organism at a given moment of stimulation shifts then and there from being ready to respond in some relatively less differentiated way to being ready to respond in some more differentiated way, there is consciousness. (Tolman, 1927, p. 435)

As might be expected of a behaviorist, he formulated his definition to fit the behavior of even the most lowly organism, defining conscious activity in terms of the barest ability to react adaptively to the environment.

2.2. Skinner's Definition of Consciousness

With the resurgence of cognitive psychology, behaviorists have been stirred to account for the concept of consciousness. As the current leader and philosopher of behaviorism, B. F. Skinner has attempted to clarify his position. In *About Behaviorism* (1974), he points out that to say a person is conscious of "states or events in his body" is simply to say that he is under the control of internal stimuli:

> A boxer who has been 'knocked unconscious' is not responding to current stimuli. . . . A person becomes conscious in a different sense when a verbal community arranges contingencies under which he not only sees an object but sees that he is seeing it. In this special sense, consciousness or awareness is a social product (Skinner, 1974, pp. 219–220).

Concerning his belief in the acausal nature of consciousness, he says: "If consciousness seems to have a causal effect, it is the effect of the special environment which induces self-observation" (Skinner, 1974, 153). His emphasis on acausality stems from his view of consciousness as an unimportant epiphenomenon.

A purely "materialist psychology" is a contradiction of terms. Given the dualism of mind-body, material is synonymous with body and is studied in physics and the other side of the dualism (soul or mind or consciousness) is studied in psychology. Both physicists and psychologists are often quite interested in what relationships, if any, exist between mind and body. In this traditional dualistic frame of reference, behaviorism may be a physical or a biological or other natural science, but it cannot be psychology. W. S. Hunter (1930) realized this fact many years ago and proposed that we call the study of the human organism, *anthroponomy* (a different kind of study of *anthropos* has preempted the better word, anthropology). Hunter wanted to avoid the dualism entirely and focus on the total behavior of the organism. In the later section on the history of mind-body, we shall see that his approach is a form of monism.

3. Views of Consciousness from Abroad

Cognitive psychology has been a part of the mainstream of American psychology since Colonial times and behaviorism is an indigenous twentieth-century American phenomenon. Other important psychologies with distinctive approaches to consciousness originated abroad and were brought over in this century. These psychologies include the psychoanalytic, the phenomenological, and the transpersonal.

3.1. Consciousness in Psychoanalysis

Although behaviorism was dominant in academic psychology in the period between the two world wars, it was challenged in the latter part of this period by the importation of Freud's psychoanalysis. Earlier, literary and artistic America had accepted a Freudian view of mankind, just as they had embraced James's concept of stream and consciousness. Until the relatively recent advent of humanistic, cognitive approaches to psychology, behaviorism and psychoanalysis struggled with each other for the center of the stage.

In the *Project for a Scientific Psychology* in 1895, Freud made his first attempt to conceptualize consciousness. He saw it as more than an epiphenomenon, but, nevertheless, connected with the workings of the central nervous system. From the beginning, he held that it was not the whole psychical apparatus: " . . . consciousness is the subjective side of a *part* of the physical processes in the neuronic system— namely, of the perceptual processes . . . " (Freud, 1954, p. 373). As his psychological insights increased, Freud gave up the attempt to explain consciousness in terms of neuronal activity in the brain, for he felt that neurological science was not advanced enough to handle the complex psychical events that he was uncovering. He left to the future of that science such explanations.

Although he was reluctant to become involved in philosophical speculation, Freud admitted that his later theories were based on a kind of psychophysical parallelism, which like Titchener's view had elements of double aspectism. What he did in fact was to work out a purely psychical theory, with the hope that someday the physical side of the theory would fit in. Libido, for example, was psychic sexual energy, it was different from physical energy and Freud made no attempt to reconcile the two.

More important than consciousness in psychoanalytic theory is the unconscious:

> Unconsciousness is a regular and inevitable phase in the processes constituting our mental activity; every mental act begins as an unconscious one, and it may either remain so or go on developing into consciousness, according as it meets with resistance or not. (Freud, 1957, p. 51)

To illustrate his conception of the unconscious, Freud cites experiments using posthypnotic suggestion and his analytic work with hysterics.

For Freud the unconscious mental processes are older "primary processes," which follow the pleasure principle of *Lust-Unlust* and serve to satisfy inner needs. Since external reality must be involved in such satisfaction, the "reality principle" evolved and a secondary process of thinking developed to handle logically the demands of reality.

Under the rule of the pleasure principle, consciousness had been only an awareness that some things in the world bring pleasure and others cause pain.

> The increased significance of external reality heightened the significance also of the sense-organs directed towards that outer world, and of the *consciousness* attached to them; the latter now learned to comprehend the qualities of sense in addition to the qualities of pleasure and pain which hitherto had alone been of interest to it. (Freud, 1951, 320)

Thus, with the advent of the reality principle consciousness expanded to be aware of and take into account the manifold aspects of the world that can be perceived. At the same time memory became important as a depository of the activity of consciousness.

Also with the coming of the reality principle there is a flow of energy outward (object cathexis), which can be wasteful unless the objects must be attended to. Thus, all cathected ideas in unconscious thought do not become conscious unless they are given additional cathexis (investment of psychic energy), which is called *attention cathexis* or *hypercathexis*. The development of language also served consciousness in that words are attention cathected. The preconscious develops as a reservoir for words and other hypercathected ideas that can flow into consciousness. "The idea which is not put into words or the psychic act which has not received hypercathexis then remains in the unconscious in a state of repression" (p. 327).

In 1909, Freud made his only visit to the United States in order to give a series of lectures in honor of the twentieth anniversary of the founding of Clark University. When these lectures were published (*A General Introduction to Psychoanalysis*, 1920), G. S. Hall, president of Clark, wrote the preface to the American edition. Hall and James, among other American psychologists, showed an interest in Freud's ideas about the unconscious. James died in 1910 and, unfortunately, was not able to follow up his interest. Soon after Freud's visit, behaviorism swept all other approaches out of American colleges and universities. Therefore, the early influence of Freud was in the popular areas of the arts and journalism and in the practice of psychoanalysis, mainly by members of the medical profession.

An American pioneer in the study of the unconscious was Morton Prince, who founded the Harvard Psychological Clinic. In 1914, he published *The Unconscious* in which he presented his views as independently arrived at and not a part of Freudian psychology. He takes his definitions of consciousness and stream of consciousness from James and contributes a term of his own, *coconsciousness*: " . . . a coexisting dissociated consciousness or coconsciousness of which the personal consciousness is not aware, i.e., of which it is 'unconscious' " (Prince, 1914, p. 249). His work is important in that it shows that a concept of the unconscious could be developed within the framework of American functional psychology. In time, however, Prince's original work on the unconscious was eclipsed by the ascendance of the psychoanalytic view.

3.2. Consciousness in Phenomenological Psychology

Although Husserl founded the phenomenological movement in philosophy around 1900, a phenomenological approach, broadly defined, has been a part of psychology since the descriptions of mental phenomena by Aristotle. Goethe in the eighteenth century, for example, described his many observations of color phenomena. Sensory psychology of the early nineteenth century was based on the meticulous observations of tones, colors, and images by such pioneers as Purkinje, Weber, and Fechner (Boring, 1950).

Husserl's philosophy was centered on immediate conscious experience. His was a systematic, logical attempt to discover the "essences" of consciousness. He did not deny the ojbective world, but held that it is known to us through the phenomena of consciousness that are "intentional." For Husserl " . . . intentionality refers to the fact that all consciousness is consciousness of something that is not consciousness itself" (Georgi, 1970). His method was descriptive, making a qualitative analysis of the phenomena of consciousness. This description was to be made with as little theoretical bias as possible.

American psychology was introduced to the descriptive method of phenomenology by the Gestalt psychologists during the 1920s. The Gestalt method is the qualitative analysis of mental phenomena, as they appear in consciousness. They study immediate experience, stressing its wholeness. Instead of using scientific analytic methods and experimentation, they rely on what Boring (1950) has called the *experimentum crucis*, the crucial experience that illustrates how perception or learning occurs. The careful description of such an experience produces the facts of Gestalt psychology. They are parallelists in their effort to show the correlation (*isomorphism*) between brain states and conscious experiences.

Existential psychology also has its roots in phenomenology. According to Sartre, "Consciousness is a being such that in its being, its being is in question in so far as this being implies a being other than itself" (Sartre, 1956, p. 629). Although, as this quotation shows, existentialists accept Husserl's view of consciousness, they are not pure phenomenological psychologists. They also have roots in Kierkegaard's writings on existence, which give them their aim of defining authentic existence and human freedom, rather than making qualitative analyses of the variety of conscious phenomena as the Gestaltists do.

In the last two decades a pure form of phenomenological psychology has developed in the United States. Starting with Husserl's definition of consciousness, phenomenological psychologists describe conscious phenomena in an effort to clarify human experience. The importance for the history of the stream of consciousness is that these psychologists define psychology as, not the study of behavior, but the study of the flow of experience.

3.3. Transpersonal Views of Consciousness

Transpersonal psychology in America is an outgrowth of the humanistic psychology movement, which Maslow in the 1950s called the "third force" that would balance behaviorism and psychoanalysis. The transpersonal approach also has roots in Far Eastern philosophies (see Taylor's chapter in this volume).

Where traditional American psychologists focus attention on the external, physical world, transpersonal psychologists focus on an inner, spiritual realm. Their distinctive method is intuitive exploration of what they call the dimensions of consciousness, which they seem to define as inclusive of all the aspects of awareness already covered in this paper plus aspects foreign to most Western thought. Illustrative of the breadth of their definition are the many topics covered in White (1972). In his book, *The Highest State of Consciousness*, states of consciousness include normal waking, sleeping, dreaming, hypnagogic, hypnopompic, rapturous, meditative, hypnotic, daydreaming, comatose, expanded-conscious, and many others.

Ring (1974) in an article, "A Transpersonal View of Consciousness," gives us a survey of the vast spiritual realm of consciousness by mapping "inner space." In concentric rings around waking consciousness, he maps the following consciousnesses: preconscious, psychodynamic, autogenetic, transindividual, phylogenetic, extraterrestrial, and superconsciousness; all of these rings are surrounded by the void.

In discussing each of these regions of consciousness, Ring draws heavily on the LSD research of Grof (1972). We find that each region is itself divided into many subregions. Phylogenetic consciousness, for example, includes the following consciousnesses: cellular, tissue, organ, plant, animal, inorganic matter, and planetary. Knowledge of these regions has come from such sources as reports of drug and mystic experiences.

A caution about the transpersonal uses of consciousness is given by Singer:

> The question I raise, however, is whether this new interest in exploring our own consciousness has taken on excessively mystical or "gimmicky" characteristics. . . . Despite our impressive information now on the complexities of EEG patterns and associated autonomic and motor states during sleep, we have very little clear evidence of the existence of true altered states of consciousness. What we do know is that people report different kinds of thoughts and fantasies and imagery under different kinds of experimental sets or with different degrees of reduction of external stimulation. They also bring different histories to each of these situations, and, as a result, are more or less prepared for particular kinds of imagery trips. (Singer, 1974, p. 215)

In reply to this criticism transpersonal psychologists might point out that inner exploration is not limited to "imagery trips." In fact, in their scheme of consciousness reaching from waking to the void, an inner exploration that reaches the void may not only be without imagery, but might be a most remarkable "pure consciousness of pure consciousness itself!" We must keep in mind that the differences between transpersonal and other psychologies constitute a matter of different presuppositions about the basic nature of the universe.

4.   The Mind–Body Problem

From the time of Plato on, the tendency in Western civilization has been toward a *dualism* of mind and body. This tendency reached its full form in Christian doctrines, and was formally stated in modern philosophy by René Descartes (1596–1650). His famous *cogito ergo sum* (I think; therefore, I am) implies that personal consciousness is the only sure knowledge that an individual has. Consciousness itself he identified with mind (soul), which to him was a substance as real and as concrete as the substance he called body (matter). In his dichotomy of mind–body, Descartes defined body as extended (space-filling), physical material and defined mind as "thinking thing" (*res cogitans*), which was unextended (did not take up space) and was not made of any physical material, but was purely spiritual. He also posited that these two substances mutually affect each other, giving the name *interactionism* to his position.

We have already seen that James took an interactionist position in his *Principles*. A contemporary statement concerning interactionism is found in Wilder Penfield's book, *The Mystery of the Mind* (1975). Penfield tells how he was at last brought face to face with his dualistic belief. He states that for over 50 years he " . . . worked as a scientist trying to prove that the brain accounted for the mind . . . " (p. 113).

The persistent problems involved, however, in trying to account for consciousness led him finally to admit:

> In the end I conclude that there is no good evidence, in spite of new methods, such as the employment of stimulating electrodes, the study of conscious patients and the analysis of epileptic attacks, that the brain alone can carry out the work that the mind does. I conclude that it is easier to rationalize man's being on the basis of two elements than on the basis of one. (p. 114).

In Penfield's view mind is like a programmer and the brain is like a computer. They work together in producing the behavior of the human organism.

After Descartes's interactionism was formulated, a number of other solutions to the mind-body problem were prepared. G. W. Leibnitz (1646–1716) worked out a position called *psychophysical parallelism*, in which the two substances, mind and body, are perfectly correlated but do not interact or in any way influence each other. He made the metaphysical assumption that God had set the world up this way. Wundt took this position as the official one for his physiological psychology; he did not, however, emphasize the metaphysical nature of mind-body. He was interested only in the fact that consciousness and the workings of the body are perfectly correlated.

Another form of dualism is the *epiphenomenalism* of Skinner. In this position the primary substance is material, which in its activity generates consciousness. This consciousness is ephemeral and acausal and completely dependent on the workings of the body. For practical purposes epiphenomenalism reduces to materialism.

If a person begins with the Cartesian dualism and attempts to discard one of the two, a kind of *monism* results. We see this in the positions of both *materialism* (body only) and *idealism* (mind only). For example, although Watson admitted that he had a personal consciousness, he took the official position that only the material world exists (an objective monism). Berkeley accepted the material world, but since he proved that we cannot know it directly, he took an idealist position (a subjective monism).

Double-aspectism is also a kind of monism in which the dualism is accepted, but is explained as two different views of the same thing. Pure monisms are nearly impossible in a culture with a long dualistic tradition such as ours. In some Far Eastern cultures, however, a truly monistic idealism is autochthonous and everything in the universe is accepted as a manifestation of pure spirit.

Early psychologists who were well versed in philosophy, like James, Wundt, and Titchener, understood and tried to take into account the metaphysical problems involved in the mind–body dualism. After behaviorism's emphasis on natural science, however, American psychologists tended to avoid philosophy as an alien study. Nevertheless, since a position on mind–body is essential to any system of psychology (McGeoch, 1933), they took commonsense positions concerning the dualism. They accepted the subjective fact that they are conscious and the fact of the objective world. They made no metaphysical assumptions about substances or reality. Instead, if they felt that in their experience consciousness and objects mutually affect each other, they operated as commonsense interactionists. Most seemed to be comfortable with a simple correlation of brain (and other bodily functions) with consciousness and were commonsense parallelists. Some of these parallelists were epiphenomenalists, but others gave full equality to the two sides of the dichotomy.

In recent times the old fear of philosophy has abated, and we see renewed attempts to face and solve or resolve the mind–body problem (see Battista's chapter in this volume). One of these attempts has arisen out of Lloyd Morgan's (1923) emergent evolution (Holt, 1972). In this view what we call consciousness and what we call a complex brain are both characteristic of the high level of organization that human beings have evolved. They are both emergent aspects of the total organism in the environment. This view, however, is more than a double-aspect or even a multi-aspect one. In a full psychological study of a human being " . . . we are viewing the organism *at once* as

TABLE I. Positions on the Mind–Body Problem

Commonsense dualism (metaphysical assumptions ignored):
1. Interactionism: Consciousness and bodily actions affect each other.
2. Parallelism: Consciousness and brain activity are perfectly correlated.
3. Epiphenomenalism: Consciousness is an acausal by-product of brain functioning.

Metaphysical dualism (metaphysical assumptions made about the reality of two basic substances—spiritual and material):
1. Interactionism (Descartes).
2. Parallelism (Leibnitz).

Monism (reduced from dualism):
1. Materialism (only the objective world exists).
2. Idealism (only the subjective world exists).

Monism (only one basic substance or principle):
1. Double-aspectism (identity hypothesis): Mind and body are two aspects of one basic substance or principle.
2. Emergent evolutionism: Consciousness and brain function (and other levels of bodily activity) are emergent properties of the complex nature of the human organism.
3. Spiritual (as certain Far Eastern views).

physical, behavioral, mental, and transpersonal" (Strange and Taylor, 1978). We may confine our study, for convenience, to any one of these aspects, in which case we are operating at a given level of analysis. These levels ascending from least to most complex in terms of emergent characteristics are the physical-biological level, the behavioral level, the mental (conscious/unconscious) level, and the transpersonal (transcendental experience) level (Strange and Taylor, 1978).

The problem with taking a commonsense position on mind–body is that assumptions are ignored, but are, nevertheless, present and important. Psychologists today are returning to a more philosophically sophisticated approach to psychology and are beginning to bring their basic presuppositions out into the open. We cannot hope that all of us will be able to agree on a single set of assumptions; we can hope, however, that each of us will know his or her own presuppositions and those of each different approach.

Table I gives a summary of the several commonsense and metaphysical positions on mind–body.

5. Historical Definitions of Consciousness

To be conscious is to be aware, and consciousness is the state of being aware. In Tolman's use of the term, we saw that even lower animals may have consciousness, defined as their being able to react to the environment. (In the case of human beings, the basic definition usually includes the awareness of being aware, or self-consciousness.) Freud also preferred a simple consciousness that attends to the environment and is aware of sensory information; for him, to perceive is to be conscious.

Consciousness for Titchener is subjective experience and our awareness of it. This is also the basic phenomenological definition. James emphasized mental activity in his definition and stressed the dynamic quality of the activity in his stream-of-consciousness metaphor. Epiphenomenalists, like Skinner, and parallelists, like Wundt, see consciousness as a matter of the subjective correlates of objective brain functioning.

Differing qualitatively from all the foregoing are those who follow Descartes' lead and see consciousness as an aspect of a substantial soul or mind, in which a variety of consciousness may exist. Even more different are the transpersonal psychologists who take a Far Eastern type of monistic view of consciousness as a pervading aspect of the whole universe, inorganic as well as organic, physical as well as spiritual (since these terms only describe aspects of the oneness).

6.   Concluding Statement

We end our search for the sources of the stream of consciousness back in the ocean of the present. Each of the many tributaries that we explored have contributed to one or more of the views of consciousness held today. Each definition of consciousness follows from its own unique, historically established set of presuppositions. We see that, if such basic assumptions are *in toto* mutually exclusive, the different definitions that derive from them are incompatible. In such cases we are talking about entirely different things and can engage in no logical argument, nor meaningful dialogue, but can only quarrel.

Thus, according to which assumptions we make, the stream of consciousness is one of the following:

1. A complex of mental activities changing and flowing in time.
2. A succession of states, each real, yet different in quality and kind from each other (not just different combinations of mental activities).
3. A personal participation in universal (cosmic) consciousness.
4. A flow of personal experience.
5. An epiphenomenal by-product of continuous brain functioning.
6. A matter of schedules of reinforcement provided by our social environment.
7. Subjective awareness correlated with brain functioning.
8. A set of emergent properties or characteristics.

Since each human being makes sense of the universe within the frame of reference of a given set of presuppositions, each of the foregoing views is legitimate. What we ultimately know about the stream of consciousness will be the total of what all the different approaches find out. No one view, however, can disprove the findings of another, nor prove that its findings are the Truth, even though all are in part true (with a small *t*). If we take the trouble to know and make known our assumptions, we can understand not only our own findings, but we can also understand and appreciate what others are discovering about the stream of consciousness.

References

Angell, J. R. *Psychology*. New York: Henry Holt, 1908.
Broadbent, D. E. The Hidden Preattentive Processes. *American Psychologist*, 1977, 32, 109–118.

Boring, E. G. *A history of experimental psychology* (2nd Ed.). New York: Appleton-Century-Crofts, 1950.

Fay, J. W. *American psychology before William James.* New Brunswick, New Jersey: Rutgers University Press, 1939.

Freud, S. *A general introduction to psychoanalysis.* London: Boni and Liveright, 1920.

Freud, S. Formulations regarding the two principles in mental functioning. *Organization and pathology of thought.* New York: Columbia University Press, 1951.

Freud, S. *The origins of psycho-analysis.* New York: Basic Books, 1954.

Freud, S. *A general selection from the works of Sigmund Freud.* New York: Doubleday Anchor, 1957.

Georgi, A. *Psychology as a human science.* New York: Harper & Row, 1970.

Grof, S. Varieties of transpersonal experiences: Observations from LSD psychotherapy. *Journal of Transpersonal Psychology,* 1972, *4,* 45-80.

Holt, R. R. On the nature and generality of mental imagery. In P. W. Sheehan (Ed.), *The function and nature of imagery.* New York: Academic Press, 1972.

Hunter, W. S. Anthroponomy and psychology. In C. Murchison, *Psychologies of 1930.* Worcester, Massachusetts: Clark University Press, 1930.

James, W. *The principles of psychology.* New York: Henry Holt, 1890.

James, W. *Psychology (briefer course).* New York, Henry Holt, 1892.

James, W. *Pragmatism.* New York: Longmans, Green, 1907.

James, W. *Essays in radical empiricism.* New York: Longmans, Green, 1912.

James, W. *The varieties of religious experience.* New York: Mentor Books, 1958.

Jung, C. *Analytical psychology, its theory and practice.* New York: Vintage, 1968.

McCosh, J. *Psychology: The cognitive Powers.* New York: Charles Scribner's Sons, 1886.

McGeoch, J. The formal criteria of a systematic psychology. *Psychological Review,* 1933, *40,* 1-12.

McKeller, P. Imagery from the standpoint of introspection. In P. W. Sheehan (Ed.), *The function and nature of imagery.* New York: Academic Press, 1972.

Morgan, L. *Emergent evolution.* London: Williams and Norgate, 1923.

Neisser, U. *Cognitive psychology.* New York: Appleton-Century-Crofts, 1967.

Penfield, W. *The mystery of the mind.* Princeton, New Jersey: Princeton University Press, 1975.

Perry, R. B. *The thought and character of William James.* New York: George Braziller, 1954.

Peters, R. S. *Brett's history of psychology.* London: George Allen and Unwin, 1953.

Prince, M. *The unconscious.* New York: Macmillan, 1914.

Ring, K. A transpersonal view of consciousness. *Journal of Transpersonal Psychology,* 1974, *6,* 125-156.

Sartre, J. P. *Being and nothingness.* New York: Philosophical Library, 1956.

Singer, J. L. *Imagery and daydream methods in psychotherapy and behavior modification.* New York: Academic Press, 1974.

Singer, J. *The inner world of daydreaming.* New York: Harper Colophon, 1975.

Skinner, B. F. *About behaviorism.* New York: Knopf, 1974.

Strange, J., and Taylor, E. A model of integrative levels useful in curriculum planning. (In preparation), 1978.

Tart, C. T. *Altered states of consciousness.* New York: Wiley, 1969.

Titchener, E. B. *A text-book of psychology.* New York: Macmillan, 1909.

Tolman, E. C. A behaviorist's definition of consciousness. *Psychological Review,* 1927, *34,* 433-439.

Watson, J. B. *Behaviorism.* New York: Norton, 1924.

White, J. *The highest state of consciousness.* New York: Doubleday-Anchor, 1972

2

Asian Interpretations: Transcending the Stream of Consciousness

Eugene Taylor

1. Introduction

An examination of the historical roots of American psychology reveals that we have a variety of different frames of reference within which to regard the phenomena of consciousness. There is, first of all, cognitive psychology—what we would call the mainstream of the present-day scientific, academic orientation. Secondly, there is the interpretive framework of the psychoanalytic tradition, which emphasizes dynamics of the unconscious, and most currently, its relation to adaptive functioning of the ego. Thirdly, we have the experiential orientation of the Humanistic movement, advocates of which tend to focus on the creative relationship between consciousness and the unconscious, chiefly through the visualization of preconscious mental processes. Finally, there is the relatively new expression called *Transpersonal Psychology*, which focuses on inner exploration, and the actualization of "ultimate states" of consciousness (Sutich, 1976) achieved through the practice of personal disciplines.

Each of these historical traditions in its own way contributes a unique perspective to understanding the phenomena of consciousness. Yet, we must raise the question as to whether or not any of these are in and of themselves sufficient interpretive frames of reference for an adequate understanding of Asian notions concerning the same

Eugene Taylor • Psychology of Religion and Asian Studies, Harvard Divinity School, Cambridge, Massachusetts.

phenomena. The answer must in every case be an emphatic, No. Cognitive psychologists, and their behavioristic predecessors, have tended to reduce the rich variety of definitions for the notion of consciousness to specified, measurable constructs. Asian definitions are thus only admissible when they have been cast into the framework of the scientific method, the presuppositions of which some analysts claim are surprisingly protestant in character (Bakan, 1967). In other words, Asian concepts of consciousness are dealt with only when they have been "made Western." The psychoanalytic tradition, on the other hand, has attempted to interpret Asian notions by translating them into Freudian terms (Alexander, 1931), while humanistic and transpersonal psychologists have relied more on their own phenomenological definitions, or the definition of one single Asian spiritual text or teacher only. In all cases, no one has sought to bring together in a very broad way knowledge of how the various classical psychologies of Asia have, themselves, comparatively defined the term.

Perhaps the one significant attempt to do this that still remains unequalled—perhaps also because he has yet to be completely understood—is in the psychology of C. G. Jung. Jung, particularly, was well versed in the traditional philosophies of Asia. Yet, he remained to the last true to the roots of his own Western heritage, claiming, in the same way that Emerson had read the Asian scriptures for the "lustre" they produced, that he studied Asia to become more Jung, rather than to become Asian.

How then do we as Westerners even presume to have a sensible comprehension of consciousness according to the way the Asian traditions understand it, especially when attempting to comprehend such a thing is at best a hazardous proposition, full of innumerable pitfalls arising from our mutual cultural biases, readily liable to misinterpretation because of radically different philosophical presuppositions, not to mention linguistic barriers, incomparability of basic sources, and the sheer absence of documented material? One means however, may be suggested that has been relatively unexplored by contemporary psychologists, although none other than William James himself was aware of it through his relationship with the famous Harvard Orientalist, Charles Rockwell Lanman (Lanman, in Lyall, 1899). This is the wealth of psychological constructs objectively documented by a tradition of Western scholarship in the scientific study of comparative religion and philosophy.

The basic data of this effort deals with material covering more than three thousand years, including primary translations of significant texts from the original languages, as well as literally thousands of secondary references in the scholarly periodical literature. For our purposes here, however, we will restrict ourselves only to those periods of major selected traditions that can be considered "classical" in a psychological sense (see Fig. 1), that is, productive of distinct psychological systems (Murphy, 1968), or of significantly formative insights into the nature and dynamics of consciousness and the ultimate transformation of personality. Out of these traditions we further intend to focus on some major constructs relating to the stream of consciousness *per se*, namely, expressions from Chinese Taoism according to Lao-tzu; from Japanese Zen, especially in the tradition of Hui-neng; from the orthodox Hindu school of Samkhya-Yoga; and from early Madhyamika thought in Indian Mahayana Buddhism.

2.   Taoist *Wu-wei:* "Noninterference" with the Stream

While William James suggests that because of the current state of our psychology we must content ourselves with an examination of only the personal aspects of the stream of consciousness (1958, p. 28), classical Chinese Taoism has described it more broadly as the unrealized dimension of all of life. This personal aspect of the stream, James called the "me," or empirical ego, which appears to be made up of different subcomponents, such as the biological, the material, the social, and the spiritual. In Taoism this is expressed as *tao* (pronounced "d" as in "dow," which rhymes with "how"), transliterated into English with a smaller case letter "t." It is their designation for the individual flow the stream of consciousness. The pure sense of "I," on the other hand—that enigmatic illuminating character of consciousness in James's terms—is called *Tao*, transliterated with a capitol "T." It refers simply to that flow of all of life—the passage of time, the change of the seasons, the entire milieu of history and evolution; in short, everything that we in the West define as what the individual flow of consciousness is *not*.

In Taoism the individual flow of consciousness and the flow of all of life are continually, at every moment, seen to mutually interpenetrate one another. The reason, according to Lao-tzu, legendary author of the *Tao te Ching*, that we have inner conflicts, problems in relationship, and evil in society, is because of the inability of the normal personality to understand that certain definite laws of change govern both the flow of consciousness and life in the same way. People thus act *as if* the stream of their thoughts and feelings did not have the far-reaching consequences that inevitably they must produce. Such ignorance artificially creates interference with the stream, and

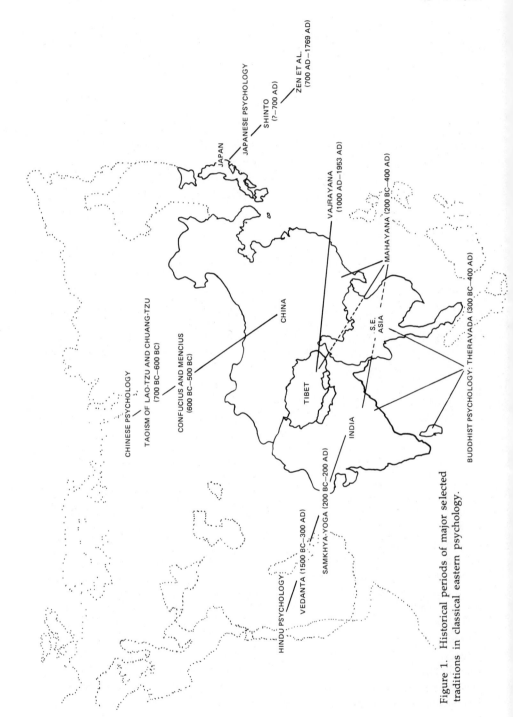

Figure 1. Historical periods of major selected traditions in classical eastern psychology.

the result is neuroticism, psychosomatic conversion reactions, unful-filled relationships, and the like.

Te, however, is the Taoist notion that expresses the power or energy of things to interpenetrate and change into each other. It is the very principle of transformation itself. Specifically, it means "to plant" in the sense of "potential," a latent power or virtue inherent in something. Psychologically, it means "a power over the outside world undreamt of by those who pit themselves against matter while still in its thralls" (Waley, 1958, p. 46). *Te* is the power not seen by those who are so caught up in the context of the stream of their thoughts and feelings that they fail to see the influences of the *process* of cognitive thought on their current state of physical, emotional, and psychologi-cal well-being.

An individual develops *te*, or the power to change the inner conditions of mental ill-health, by comprehending the paradoxical law that governs the flow of the stream, that the Tao in motion is constantly reversing itself. In other words, consciousness is cyclic, that everything is at some point always changing into its opposite. Thus, it is poetically said of *Tao*:

> The coldest day of winter
> Is the first day of spring.

And so of *te*:

> To beget
> To nourish
> To beget but not to cherish
> To achieve but not to claim
> This is called the Mystic Virtue(*te*).

But how, might we ask, does one acquire *te*? Two answers that the Taoists give are behavioral, through the practice of Chinese forms of Yoga and meditation; and mental, by developing the attitude of *wu*, literally "no-thing," which means transcending the unconscious influ-ences of the stream through spontaneous noninterference with it.

More correctly, however, the technical term is not just *wu*, but *wu-wei*, or the "magical passivity of inward quietness." *Wu* should be taken to mean "no-thing" in the sense of nothing obscuring the clarity or lucidity of the stream of awareness. On the other hand, *wei* means "obscure because of being so small or dark" (Waley, 1958, p. 187). It refers to the subtlety of things that are normally unconscious, particu-larly our inability to see that the stream of both consciousness and the unconscious are perpetually changing into one another. *Wu-wei* thus means that by inward quietness, or by not interfering with the natural course of things, these fundamental changes of life are revealed.

Wu-wei has been variously translated to mean noninterference, non-doing, the secret of action without deeds, or actionless activity. The Taoists, however, did not mean that one should never act, but that one should be fluid and changing enough to always know how to adjust one's self to circumstances. But how to make circumstances work for us? Through *non*interference with the natural course of events. It is a negatively stated expression about an essentially positive condition. It does not mean negative in the sense of bad or pessimistic, but rather, is used in terms of "opposite," as in "looking in the opposite place from where you would expect to find the answer." This is why it is said:

> What is of all things most yielding (water)
> Can overwhelm that which is of all things most hard(rock).
> Being substanceless it can enter even where there is no space.
> That is how I know the value of action that is actionless.
> But that there can be teaching without words,
> Value in action that is actionless,
> Few indeed can understand. (Waley, 1958, p. 197)

In adopting the attitude of *wu*, the realized man thus harmonizes with the stream, sees into its inner meaning, transcending it through noninterference. He blends with it by becoming completely still and so paradoxically transforms consciousness through his inaction.

3.   *Wu-nien*: "No-Thought" of the Stream in Zen

While the Zen tradition in Japan is essentially Buddhist in origin, it may be considered as distinctly different from its Indian counterparts (which we will discuss shortly), principally because of its historical antecedents in Chinese soil. Zen in many respects must therefore claim a closer affinity with the general spirit of Taoism. This we see in the Zen expression of *wu-nien*. As with Taoist *wu-wei*, *wu-nien* means not repression, nor forcefully stopping thought, but rather, nonattachment and consequently nonreinforcement of the stream of thoughts and feelings.

In the work of Hui-neng, legendary founder of the Zen tradition in China as it later developed in Japan, *wu-nien* had its greatest expression as "no-thought-ness." It was Hui-neng who said, "No-thought is not to think, even when involved in thought." Paraphrasing his own translation of Hui-neng, the scholar Yampolski writes:

> Thoughts are conceived as advancing in progression from past to present to future, in an unending chain of successive thoughts. Attachment to one instant of thought leads to attachment to a succession of thoughts, and thus to bondage. But by cutting off attachment to one instant of thought, one may . . . cut off attachment to a succession of thoughts and thus attain to no-thought, which is a state of enlightenment. (Yampolski, 1967, p. 116)

No-thought thus means watching a thought go by without identifying with it emotionally or cognitively with more thoughts and feelings. One then sees a thought arise, burst forth into the field of conscious awareness, reach its zenith, and then begin to degenerate, decay, and finally disappear. Thoughts come and go without any consequence. They have not produced any associated thoughts. No words have been spoken as a result of attaching one's self to them, nor have any behaviors been initiated.

Hui-neng further taught that as soon as one instant of thought is cast off the person awakens into a completely different state. This is because when one becomes aware of the field of consciousness after quieting the flow of thoughts and feelings, consciousness itself is seen to change. In other words, consciousness of what is normally unconscious causes both consciousness and the unconscious to become something else. The two no longer are the same that they were before because both were defined in relation to each other. What they both become is just *wu*— awareness with no conceptual thought. Under the proper instruction of a Zen master, this leads to what is called in Zen the experience of *satori*, or "a breakthrough into the reality of one's own true nature," a deep inner state where one is a witness to that which is "pure, genuine, vast, and illuminating" about one's self (Chang, 1959, p. 80).

Of all of the different traditions, Zen has been explored the most with regard to its direct relationship to psychotherapy. In this regard, a most significant bibliography has been compiled by Lesh (1970). Throughout this literature, the concept of *wu-nien*, "no-thought," or "no-mind," has played a central role. As early as 1958, Van Dusen pointed out the importance of this notion as an effective psychotherapeutic orientation in developing spontaneous techniques uniquely suited to each patient.

Van Dusen's claim was that different kinds of pathology exhibited different reactions to moments of mental blankness, loss of memory, failure at concentration, or loss of meaning. Of importance is the way this void is perceived. It can be totally destructive as in chronic schizophrenia or it can be productive, as in the so-called therapeutic regression in service of the ego. In fact, however, the feared empty space is a fertile void, and exploring it instead of fleeing from it is a turning point toward therapeutic change.

An example of *wu-nien* in Zen psychiatry is recounted in an anecdote by the Western therapist, Jack Huber:

> A Zen Buddhist nun had been sent from the nunnery in the country side of Japan to do shopping in the nearby large city. She had never been in a large city before. Her buying accomplished, she returned to the nunnery. In a short time the other nuns noticed her behaving strangely, and when she became acutely disturbed she was put to bed. The major symptom was her terror at the snakes she saw crawling over her body. Physicians and then psychologists and psychiatrists were brought in to see her but they could do nothing. Finally, a Zen psychiatrist, famed in the big city, was brought in. He was in her room for only five minutes. "What is the trouble?" He asked, "The snakes, the snakes crawl over my body and frighten me." Perhaps she let out a scream as a snake crawled over her. The psychiatrist thought a bit and then said, "I must leave now, but I shall come back to see you in a week. While I am gone, I want you to do two things. First, complain to no one. Say nothing of this matter to anyone. And second, observe the snakes very carefully so that when I return you will be able to describe their movements accurately to me." In seven days he returned and found the nun out of bed and doing the duties she had been assigned before her illness. He greeted her and then asked, "Did you follow my instructions?" "Indeed," she answered, "I complained to no one. And then I centered my attention on the snakes, but alas, I saw them no more, for when I observed them carefully they were gone. (Huber, 1965, p. 3)

Here, the psychiatrist penetrated deeply into the nun's mental confusion by seeing that she was afraid to let go of her fear of entering that fertile, creative void, while from the nun's standpoint, her hallucinations disappeared when she looked directly at them with no thought of attachment. This in both cases is the psychotherapeutic value of *wu-nien*.

Such notions have also been explored extensively in scientific experiments. Large numbers of EEG studies on Zen monks in meditation, for instance, have long been cited in the literature (Okeima, Koga, Ikeda, and Suguyama, 1957; Kasamatsu, Okuma, Takenska, Koga, Ikeda, and Suguyama, 1957; Hirai, Izawa, and Koga, 1958; Hirai, 1960). One interesting aspect of this work with regard to "no-thought" is the phenomena of habituation. Here, repeated presentation of the same stimulus, usually a click, at first produces a strong response, but then less and less of one, until finally no response is recorded on the EEG in normal subjects. Meditating Zen masters who were exposed to the same clicks, however, did not show the customary habituation (Ornstein, 1972, p. 131). Rather, they responded to the last click just as strongly as the first and also recovered their original undisturbed state just as quickly (Kasamatsu and Hirai, 1969). This is why it is said, "In Zen, there are no distractions, *everything* is an appropriate object of meditation." Such then is the nature of *wu-nien*, or "no-thought" of the stream.

4. *Nirodha* : A "Burning Out" of the Stream in Yoga

Yoga, being a Sanskrit word derived from the root *yuj* (discipline) means to join or yoke, as in "yoking" the wandering train of our thoughts by concentrating on them, collecting the normally scattered rays of the mind and joining them in one-pointed concentration with the body, integrating mind and body so that both are transcended. This "yoking" or taming of the mind is generally described as the purification of consciousness by promoting inward calmness. This is a process of transcending the stream that is technically called *nirodha*, a "burning out" of undesirable characteristics of mental life through the practice of inner examination and self-control, both of which are essential to produce the conditions necessary for insight.

Nirodha first refers to a quieting of the flow of waking conscious impressions. This is expressed in the famous phrase, "yoga is the restriction of the fluctuations of mental activity." Restriction in this sense is a condition brought about through extended practice in detaching the senses from their attachment to objects in the external material world. Thus, like Taoist *wu*, or *wu-nien* in Zen, it is not a form of repression, the automatic blocking out of contents from consciousness, nor is it to be termed supression, the willful, active, and directed disregard of conscious contents, therefore, forcing them into the unconscious. Rather, restriction refers to a relaxed, natural cutting off of the immediate influx of sense impressions, and so also to their lack of influence in stimulating cognitive perceptual thought processes. More subtly, however, *nirodha* refers to a "burning out" of the unconscious determinants of conscious thoughts, a "burning up" of the seeds of waking conscious impressions.

To understand this it is important to examine the meaning of consciousness *per se* in Yoga. The technical term for consciousness is *citta* (pronounced "ch" as in "church") which appears in the normal field of awareness in the form of changing cognitive thoughts (*vritti*) and simultaneously in the unconscious as "latent impressions" (*samskaras*). Every waking cognitive impression that we have, according to Yoga, psychology, is accompanied by a corresponding unconscious impression, or "seed" that lies dormant in the unconscious, ripening like a piece of fruit until it is then ready to sprout forth into the field of awareness to produce more cognitive thoughts under the appropriate future conditions. Hence, we have memories, visual pictures, emotions, and the like, associated with a thought in the field of awareness or accompanying it as a "penumbra" in James's terms, that peripheral tinge to the passing of each cognitive impression. Note here the similarity of this notion of "unconscious seed" to Freud's description of the spontaneous eruption of unconscious repressions into consciousness (Freud, 1951) and to Tolman's famous experiments demonstrating the phenomena of latent learning (Tolman, 1957).

All thought, whether conscious or unconscious, in Yoga is classified as to whether it hinders or helps in the process of self-realization. Hindered mental activities include such things as what we in the West would call factual knowledge, all types of verbal communication, misconceptions, delusions, sleep, and memory, especially that aspect of memory called forgetting. Those that are unhindered, or liberating, include good thoughts, insights, and inner realizations. Unhindered kinds of thoughts tend to balance or neutralize the influence of hindered thoughts, and so need to be actively cultivated in the beginning. Eventually, however, Yoga means restricting both hindered and unhindered thought, good thoughts as well as bad, since even the "thought of enlightenment" can become another limiting preconceived idea, and so be for the unwary just another diabolical mental game.

Transcending the stream thus means not only quieting the flow of thoughts on the surface of the mind, but also eliminating the possibility that any thought will sprout forth from the unconscious. How to accomplish this is perhaps one of the most interesting aspects of Yoga psychology and involves the active cultivation of insight into one's own inner thought processes through the practice of personal discipline.

4.1. *Sadhana*: Personal Discipline

The stream of *citta* is quieted and then "burnt out" through the cultivation of a graded set of practices beginning with purification of the body, which then supports purification of the mind. Practices such as keeping the body clean, eating pure foods, becoming knowledgeable about the techniques of Yoga—practicing the physical postures (*asana*), learning to regulate breathing, and to detach the senses from their attachment to objects in the external material world—all are referred to as "external aids" in Yoga. They are cultivated in preparation for developing the "inner aids," a combined tool for intensive concentration referred to as *samyama*, a tool for cultivating complete restraint, or self-control. *Samyama* is composed of attention (*dharana*), meditation (*dhyana*), and concentration (*samadhi*).

Attention (*dharana*), we might say, refers to a free-floating state of readiness to respond, nonspecifically, much like what James describes as the period between thinking a thought and then verbalizing it. In Yoga, however, an object, perhaps a thought or a sense preception, can be before the mind, with the mind paying attention to it, but where the mind, itself, has not yet labeled what it is looking at. Attention in this sense is the suspension of labeling, like Husserl's method of bracketing. Attention is the extension of this nonspecific state of readiness to respond, and is preparation for meditation proper.

Meditation (*dhyana*) is the "even flow of thought round about an object." This means that the object of perception is not just simply labeled and then ignored in favor of whatever else comes into the mind. Rather, the mind fixes on an object, and without labeling it, proceeds to examine it from every angle, becoming aware of all the manifold ways in which it *could* be defined, yet not attaching itself to any of them.

Concentration, or *samadhi*, is simply extended meditation, but may be said to differ from meditation, in that while meditation examines the object from all angles, concentration (*samadhi*) clearly focuses, undisturbed, on the object itself, seeing it only for what it is. This kind of concentration in Yoga is said to produce intuitive insight (*prajna*). Insight through concentration is the revelation of normally unconscious contents—repressions, past memories, complexes, etc.— while remaining unattached to the emergence of such material. Insight in this sense means a clear discrimination (*viveka-khyati*) among the object one perceives, the cognitive knowledge one has about that object, and the consciousness, itself, that is aware of what is being perceived. To reveal and then focus on only this conscious awareness itself is the aim of concentrated insight.

Developing *samyama*, the threefold tool of attention, meditation, and concentration thus produces insight into any object of perception. But it must be remembered that the point of doing this in Yoga is to purify consciousness, to distill only it from any realization. The effect then of separating the object itself, from our cognitive knowledge, about it, from the consciousness that is aware of both of these, produces insight that transforms consciousness from one state into another. One is then led from considering the gross, material aspects of the object as something to concentrate on, to its very fine and subtle characteristics that we would normally overlook. This leads in Yoga to concentration on the sense organs and the neuro-anatomical structures (Do we see the real object? Or do we see only its isomorphic analogy in our nervous system?), and finally to the mind itself and its ongoing functions of registering, discriminating, and recording. Attention is thus drawn to the stream of one's own consciousness as an appropriate object of contemplation. Each of these—gross objects, their subtle characteristics, the body, and the mind, itself—are all to be transcended through concentrated insight and discriminative discernment into what is really consciousness and what is not.

This last, or "transcendence of the mind itself," is the most complex of the definitions for the stream of consciousness in Yoga. It deserves our final comment, because here lies the essence of *nirodha*, a "burning out" of the stream.

4.2. The Continuously Flowing Stream of Insight

While we in the West consider only the flow of cognitive thoughts and feelings to be what streams onward—a phenomenon over which we have little control—in Yoga psychology, as we have suggested, the normal flow of waking conscious impressions can be naturally quieted through practice in sense-detachment. By concentrating on making the surface of the mind calm, we can promote insight, which is the liberation of heretofore unconscious or unknown contents into the field of awareness. In Yoga we thus deliberately set the conditions for the latent seeds of past impressions to be called forth—in order to eradicate them—to "burn them out—so that they no longer have the potential of ever sprouting forth again. (Note, here, the very close analogy to a psychoanalytic definition of catharsis (Freud and Breuer, 1966), and certain similarities to Wolpe's technique of desensitization (Wolpe, 1958).) In Yoga, as we noted earlier, this "burning out" is effected through insight.

When we consider the healthy psychotherapeutic effects of insight stressed in the history of Western psychology (Brill, 1929; Allport, 1937; Rogers, 1942; Kohler, 1947; Fromm-Reichman, 1950; Maslow, 1954; and Angyal, 1965), it becomes easier to see its significance in Yoga for the ultimate transformation of consciousness, and thus personality. The importance of this phenomena is that insight may not only be promoted but that under the proper circumstances can be sustained for long periods. By setting the stage for its occurrence—inward calmness via a cessation of external sensory stimulation, and eliminating all obstacles to its maintainence, such as analytic thought or emotional attachments—we create the conditions where insight produces inner calm, which increases the probability of the onset of more insight, which in turn produces more calmness, and more insight, until it is possible, because there are no inner obstructions, to experience a continuously flowing stream of insights into the world of all objects.

A seemingly insignificant realization, for example, is often discovered in a moment of quiet reverie. Normally a person would see things "click" together that he had not seen before, perhaps a solution to some minor problem. He makes only a minor adjustment. Seeing the new connection right away, perhaps giving a small chuckle or "Ah ha!" to himself, he then goes back to some previous train of thought, to watching television, or to physical work—whatever was happening before.

The Yogi, however, would not attach himself to this single, momentary realization, but would just become aware of its illuminating quality. It is like the old saying, "Find one truth and immediately nearby, others will surely be discovered." By focusing only on the illuminating quality of the realization, which is sustained through the practice of techniques in personal discipline (*sadhana*), more insights are promoted. This is why in Vedanta Yoga insight also may be called the "inner guide." Eventually what the Yogi is aiming for, however, is called technically *samprajnatasamadhi*, literally, "concentration on the highest wisdom," defined psychologically as a continuously flowing stream of insights into the world of objects (Woods, 1972, p. 96). Knowledge of what James would call the personal "me"—material, biological, social, and spiritual—reaches its peak in this experience. Thus, this state is also called the "Raincloud of Knowable Things," or a "showering of the blessings of self-realization."

Returning to our example, it would be as if one were to experience not only the minor readjustment to a passing insight, but to experience one "Ah ha!" and then another, and another, and another, in rapid succession. In the mind's eye, however, images are not coming sequentially, like a normal logical thought train, but simultaneously, revealing themselves all at once, as pieces in a puzzle that suddenly spring forth into the whole picture at a certain instant. In the same manner, it was Mozart who saw the entire symphony at once from start to finish in his mind (Ghiselin, 1952, p. 45). It is revelation at once of all aspects of the stream of consciousness.

All of this can be compared with James, where he describes our normal perception of the stream:

> In most of our concrete states of consciousness, sensations, memories, feelings, desires, determinations of will—all of these different classes of ingredients are found simultaneously present to some degree, though the relative proportion they bear to one another is very shifting. (James, 1958, p. 29)

In the *samadhi* that is a continuously flowing stream of insights, however, all of these aspects of the stream, normally in shifting proportion to each other, are revealed at one time, multidimensionally as a whole, complete gestalt.

This is, however, not the highest experience in Yoga. The highest experience is transcending or going beyond this continuously flowing stream. Such a feat is accomplished by simply focusing not on the content of realizations themselves, but on the consciousness that is aware of those realizations! Then, as at every other level of concentration, consciousness "passes purely into itself," abiding solely in itself as "pure self-shining intelligence," the highest *samadhi*, a state described as the total *non*consciousness of all objects (*Asamprajnatasamadhi*). Not unconsciousness, but purified consciousness.

According to James:

> (These) are states of insight into depths of truth unplumbed by the discursive intellect. . . , illuminations, revelations, full of significance and importance, all inarticulate though they remain; . . . as a rule carry with them a curious sense of authority for all after-time, . . . susceptible (also) to continuous development in what is felt as inner richness and importance. (James, 1928, p. 381)

This is *nirodha*, a 'burning out' of the stream.

5. *Sunyata*: The "Emptiness" of the Stream in Indian Buddhism

When they talked about the stream of consciousness, the early Buddhist schools took great pains to analyze it as *the* conditioned reality to be transcended. Because attachment to the stream brought only pain and suffering (*dukkha*), it was to be abandoned in favor of *Nirvana*, a psychological state described as the "cessation of great hatred and ignorance," a complete annihilation or "extinguishing of the flame" of sense-desire. Later Buddhist schools, on the other hand, taught that "all things are empty." What this meant was that the stream was not an illusion to be abandoned in favor of *Nirvana*, but that enlightenment meant to live more vitally and dynamically in the *midst* of the stream while being free.

The technical notion of a "stream" *per se* in early Buddhism is *samtana* or *samtati*. Etymologically, these allied Sanskrit terms mean a spreading or extending of influence, as in the extension of a lasting sense of sameness in personal identity over a lifetime or in the appearance of continuity in consciousness from moment to moment. The Buddhist notion of simply "consciousness," on the other hand, can be applied to a broad spectrum of states, from psychotic, to normal (but underdeveloped), and finally to heightened, transcendent states of awareness. This last is perhaps emphasized the most, particularly where some schools have developed clearly defined stages (*bhumis*) or subtle grades of consciousness (*jhana*) on the path to enlightenment (Goleman, 1975).

The two most common terms associated with the normal flow of thoughts and feelings, as well as the sense of personal identity, however, are *samjna* and *vijnana*. *Samjna* refers to "consciousness" of data coming in exclusively from the sense organs. Historically, it was further subdivided into "eye-consciousness," "ear-consciousness," "taste-consciousness," etc., with a different technical term associated with each sense organ and its respective field of operation, ending in that proverbial sixth-sense, the mind, whose field is defined as all of the sense organs and their fields taken collectively. *Vijnana* is used to refer to the general faculty of conscious awareness, not only of sense-data (*samjna*), but also feelings, the body, and the unconscious.

The situation is further complicated, however, by the use of other terms that give additional shades of meaning for "body-consciousness." This can be compared to the general notion of body language in the field of kinesics (Birdwhistell, 1970), to "passive volition" in biofeedback studies (Green and Green, 1972), and to such notions as character armor in Reichian-Gestalt body work (Fadiman and Frager, 1976).

Additionally, the Buddhists also recognized different aspects of "perceptual consciousness," such as attending, receiving, examining, determining, cognizing, and registering. According to early theories of perception (Sarathchandra, 1930), each of these activities was considered in its own right as a separate and distinct "state" of consciousness.

Generally, *samjna* and *vijnana* refer to the stream of individual thoughts and feelings as we would define it in Western cognitive psychology (cf. Battista's chapter on the distinction between perception and cognition), and are used by the Buddhists to define the nature of the normal personality. As such, they play a major role in defining the apparent continuity of consciousness from moment to moment, and, in turn, give the impression that there is a lasting sense of sameness about personal identity.

5.1. The Sense of Personal Identity

When James suggested that the necessary purposes of psychology are served by attributing intelligence only to the pulsations of consciousness from one moment to the next in the individual personality, instead of to some eternal "soul" or "spirit" (James, 1893, p. 203), he was echoing one of the primary tenets of Buddhist thought, namely, that there is no underlying soul or self that constitutes the permanent identity of individual personality. Personal identity and consciousness are for the Buddhists momentary and perpetually changing; they are simply a function of momentary conditions in a constant state of flux, and therefore "nothing to cling to."

The early Buddhist schools referred to personal identity as *skandha*, literally, "heap" or momentary "conglomeration" of conditions. Technically, this sense of our normal personality is analyzed into (1) the physical body (*rupa*), (2) sense organ stimulation and emotional reactions (*vedana*), (3) cognitive perceptual identification of sense-data (*samjna*), (4) the unconscious "seeds" (cf. Yoga) of everyday waking conscious thought (*samskara*), and (5) the general faculty of awareness (*vijnana*) that mediates between the body, the senses and emotions, perceptions, and unconscious "seeds."

Our sense of personal identity, the Buddhists claim, is a function of the way these separate conditions of personality only appear to relate themselves to one another. Personality is thus a function of the way in which we perceive it. The sense of sameness about identity is something that human consciousness projects upon itself, and is not necessarily the way things "really are." According to such an interpretation, therefore, the nature of personality, consciousness, and the stream was for the Buddhists, conditioned.

When we think of conditioning in Western psychology, we generally interpret it in terms of either classical, reflexive, "Pavlovian" learning, or in terms of Skinnerian reinforcement contingencies. In either case, what is being expressed is the way the organism is attached behaviorally to stimuli in the external environment. For the Buddhists, conditioning means nearly the same thing, but is viewed essentially from the *inner* standpoint of how to free one's self from it. To be conditioned thus means not only that one is attached to objects as well as their cognitive and behavioral consequences, but also that such attachment is what impedes inner exploration and prevents the liberating experience of higher states of consciousness.

Our conditioning, according to Buddhist psychology, creates the illusion that "something" lasts permanently from one moment to the next. Actually, what endures is only the conditioned consequences of our attachment, and those only last until we break the illusion of thinking and acting *as if* the stream of consciousness and our sense of personal identity had an absolute reality apart from our ideas of permanency about them. Our conditioning is thus at the very heart of illusion.

5.2. The Formula of Conditioning

The conditioned nature of the stream of consciousness is expressed in Buddhist psychology by the mnemonic formula to be contemplated in meditation called conditioned-coproduction (*pratitya-samutpada*). Broadly speaking, conditioned coproduction refers to the interdependent relationship of all phenomena to each other. This is expressed in the idea that nothing has an independent identity, but that everything conditions or is linked to everything else in some way. John Donne said this when he wrote, "No man is an island unto himself," and Charles Darwin alluded to it in *The Origin of Species* (1859), when he suggested that if man goes on selecting, and thus augmenting, any peculiarity, he will almost certainly unconsciously modify other parts of the structure, owing to the mysterious law of correlation of growth.

The Buddhist notion of conditioned coproduction is both a philosophical statement on causality and a psychological statement on the stream of conditioning. Philosophically, it says that causes do not determine effects in a predetermined past-present-and-future sense. Rather, what we call effects are in reality a part of the conditions of the "cause," and in fact, support the coming into existence of the latter. Causes and effects are thus said to arise codependently. Psychologically, it means that there can be no objective, independent reality to a "stream of consciousness" apart from our phenomenal conception of it.

Interpreting this notion, a Zen Buddhist from Korea once remarked that Western scientific determinism in its most rigid Newtonian sense sees things in linear, external terms, while some scholars, both East and West, understand the more subtle interpretation of causality implied by the multidimensional notion of conditioned coproduction. A true Buddhist, however, would go one step further and point out that conditioned coproduction is not merely an interesting philosophical or psychological notion that describes something that happens "out there" somewhere where the scientists and scholars can observe it, somehow independent of the very act of observation. Rather, it must be understood from the standpoint that whatever is observed is dependent upon the inner ongoing thought processes of the observer's *own* stream of consciousness, as much as it is conditioned by external determinates.

Perhaps the most cogent statements in Western psychology today on this very point are made by such investigators as Kuhn (1970), Rosenthal (1966), Bakan (1967), and Tart (1975). Kuhn, for instance, discusses the perception of incongruity among scientists who adhere to models, or paradigms, that do not explain anomalies appearing in their investigations, anomalies that turn out to be the "stock in trade" of later scientific revolutions guided by newer models. The implications, of course, are that definitions in psychology cannot be divorced from the mind-set of the scientific observer.

This has been aptly pointed out by Rosenthal in his famous studies on experimenter bias, where he empirically demonstrates that an experimenter's preconceived expectations can unconsciously influence experimental outcome in terms of errors of observation, in the misrecording of data, and in the selective interpretation of results.

Finally, there is an allusion to this from James, himself, where he notes the "questionability of assuming that a world of matter exists altogether independently of the perceiving mind" (1893, p. 2).

Conditioned coproduction, when used by the Buddhists to explain the apparent continuity of the stream of consciousness, is described in terms of the twelve links (*nidana*) in the matrix of causation: ignorance, unconscious seeds, ego-consciousness, name-and-form, the six sense fields, contact of sense organs and objects with consciousness, feelings, craving, grasping, becoming, birth, and decay and death. Accordingly, their analysis of the stream thus might look something like the following.

Because the normal personality is underdeveloped, and therefore ignorant of the transitory, impermanent nature of the stream of existence, the conditions are established for the person to become the victim of his own unconscious desires, not recognizing that they arise only because of habitual sense-attachment. This produces a false dichotomy between consciousness and the unconscious, because while consciousness is preoccupied with its own sense of self-importance, placing security in what it thinks is the absolute nature of its thoughts and feelings, unconscious forces are continually sweeping them away. Since consciousness is always orienting itself toward external material reality, searching for the answers to life's questions "somewhere out there" and forever ignoring the paradox of the unconscious, a kind of normal neurosis is the result. This in turn makes it even more difficult to change ingrained, unconscious habit patterns.

The more objects "out there" that are perceived and identified, the more the senses become activated, and the more thoughts and feelings arise from the unconscious. Contact with the external material world then increases disproportionately with awareness of inner events. More feelings of pleasure and pain are experienced, which creates more desires, reinforces more grasping for objects, and the continual enlargement and extension (*samtana* or *samtati*) of personality. Through the collection and projection of such attachments, we have the process called "becoming," which is our perpetual condition from birth to death. Attachment to the stream thus produces more attachment, blindly reproducing itself by becoming evermore deeply imbedded in the unconscious, while consciousness, on the other hand, continues to reduce itself through greater extension out into the external world, ignoring the unconscious in the belief that only what is properly real is what we logically and apparently can see, hear, feel, taste, touch, and smell.

But what then for the Buddhists is the ultimate nature of this stream? The early schools claimed variously that "concepts, ideas, and objects are artificial cuts in an uninterrupted flow of moments," or that it is an "impersonal process of perpetual change where the point-instants following upon one another according to causal laws may be arbitrarily united in a series (*samtana*) which receives names" (Stcherbatsky, 1962, p. 190). The most famous analogy, however, refers simply to a string of pearls:

> The Buddhists reject a "self" which runs like a single thread through a string of pearls. There are only the pearls, and no thread to hold them together. But the collection of pearls is one and the same, because strictly continuous, i.e., each pearl sticks to the one before and the one behind, without any interval between. (Conze, 1967, p. 132).

Compare this with James, where he says:

> . . . if from the point of view I am one self, from another I am quite as truly many. Similarly of the attitude of continuity; it gives to the self the unity of mere connectedness, or unbrokenness, a perfectly definite phenomenal thing--but it gives not a jot or tittle more. (1893, p. 202)

Because of this the Buddhists avoided such questions as "Are the world and soul eternal or not?" "Is the soul different from the body?" "Where and when did the stream of existence begin, and where does it end?" Such things were avoided because they were false questions. Nothing "began" a long time ago and "continues on" without alteration into the future. Personality does not just begin at birth and end at death, nor does the stream "begin" or "end" anywhere. Rather, our illusions about the absolute reality of the stream of consciousness and personal identity are being created anew each minute. For the Buddhists, *everything* appears and disappears from moment to moment, only apparently attached by the conditioned consequences of each moment's proximity to the next.

Listen again to James:

> In our waking hours, though each pulse of consciousness dies away
> and is replaced by another, yet that other, among the things that it knows,
> knows its own predecessor, and finding it "warm" in the way we have
> described greets it saying: "Thou art mine, and part of the same self with
> me." Each later thought, knowing and including thus the thoughts that
> went before, is the final receptacle—and appropriating them is the final
> owner—of all that they contain and own. As Kant says, it as if elastic balls
> were to have not only motion but knowledge of it, and a first ball were to
> transmit both its motion and its consciousness to a second, which took up
> both into *its* consciousness and passed them to a third. . . . It is this trick
> which nascent thought has of immediately taking up the expiring thought
> and "adopting" it, which leads to the appropriation of the remoter
> constituents of the self. (1893, pp. 204-205)

These individual pulsations are what the Buddhists have referred
to as the individual pearls in such close proximity that they *appear* to
be united, so that one *assumes* an underlying thread. The parallels
between James and the early Buddhist schools in this regard are really
quite remarkable. James, however, attributes a definite functional
reality to the individual pulsations, while later Buddhist schools,
particularly the Madhyamika, claimed that, according to their analysis
of personality, consciousness, and the individual pulsations of the
stream, "all things are empty."

5.3. Emptiness: The Ultimate Nature of the Stream

The term "Emptiness," or *sunyata*, ("empty" or "void,") can be
interpreted to mean "found wanting" in the sense of what worldly
attachments lack. The Buddhist writers stress, however, that it is not
to be construed as an absolute nothing, to mean the nonexistence of
everything or the denial of reality. Rather, it means emptying the
mind of particular ideas for the purpose of realizing moments of deep
inner quiet and implies the possibility of experiencing one of those
heightened states described in terms of its "surpassingly pure and
unsurpassable emptiness."

One of the most important statements on emptiness in the Indian
Mahayana Buddhist tradition is to be found in the *Madhyamikakarikas*,
or Verses on the Middle Way, attributed to the teacher, Nagarjuna,
who lived approximately A.D. 200 (Murti, 1955; Robinson, 1967; and
Streng, 1967). Basically the work is a criticism of theoretical reasoning,
and presents a method of demonstrating both the relativity and
ultimate emptiness of all mental constructions. This method is called
prasanga, and is a negative dialectic leading to the dissolution of

attachment to all of our so-called truth statements, thus promoting what the Buddhists call *prajnaparamita*, or the "perfection of wisdom."

A verbal description of the cartography of this method is quite simple: Any statement made as an absolute assertion about the nature of ultimate reality can never be completely true, because such statements can be made only in terms of similar statements that are opposite in meaning. (Compare this with Kelly's theory of personal constructs (1955), where the opposite of every "belief" statement is always implicitly subsumed in the unconscious.) If its opposite, however, is the case, then the original assertion, while still perhaps being true, cannot be taken as absolutely true, but must be taken as relative. It is only relatively true because it can have existence only in relation to its opposite.

Since this must hold true for all phenomena, then all things are empty of any absolute nature, because all phenomena exist, come into being, and are produced codependently, including all arguments based on theoretical reasoning. Such statements are constructed mental fabrications, even, Nagarjuna points out, our notions of "emptiness." Consequently we have the famous statement, "Emptiness is also empty of itself." The result is that all arguments are not proved wrong, but are more wisely averted. This is the meaning of *Madhyamika,* or middle way, the experience of transcending both negation *and* assertion.

Perhaps the most significant and far-reaching contribution of this school, one that has profoundly influenced Mahayana Buddhist thought throughout Asia for almost two thousand years, is the notion that conditioned coproduction and emptiness are the same. We do not escape from suffering into enlightenment, but rather, become enlightened when we realize that the world of suffering and the world of enlightenment are but two perspectives for looking at the same ultimate reality. All phenomena can therefore be described in terms of both their limiting and liberating aspects. Psychologically, this translates as our statement that the "stream of consciousness is empty." It means that attachment to individual thoughts and feelings, and especially concern with the mental construction of the stream, is limited and conditioned by the state of consciousness of the person defining it. It also means that whatever the stream of consciousness really is, it cannot have an absolute reality apart from our unavoidably transient, consensually validated mental fabrications about it. Enlightenment or the highest wisdom, then, comes from not necessarily abandoning words and concepts "about" reality of the stream, but in more wisely using them because one understands their ultimate relativity.

One who sees thought as empty is, therefore, not lacking in thought, but has an overabundance of it in all of its forms of mental activity. This is because highest knowledge and the perfection of wisdom, while from an absolute standpoint are a "wordless teaching," from the standpoint of conventional reality can only be expressed in terms of limiting constructs, which, themselves, however, are the very vehicles for their own transcendence. As such, they form a part of a religious teaching that for those who understand the subtlety of it

Figure 2. Mandala motif similar to those used throughout Asia as a meditative technique to both reveal and transcend the stream of consciousness. Sit in a relaxed position and hold the mandala a little less than arm's length away from the eyes. Fixate on the interlocking rings in the center and, without disturbing your gaze, become aware of your breathing. Begin counting each single cycle of your inhalation and exhalation. Count to 25. Concentrate on simply looking at the center and counting. Nothing else. If you loose count, begin again at 1. Note the number of times you are distracted. Try to see the blankness that precedes each wandering. Try to count successfully to 25.

provides a vision of "how to walk" amid the difficulties of existence, a notion that upon closer examination we find to be entirely commensurate with the highest ideals of our own scientific enterprise. This then is the ultimate meaning of *Sunyata*, the "emptiness" of the stream.

References

Alexander, F. Buddhistic training as an artificial catatonia. *Psychoanalytic Review*, 1931, *18*, 129-145.

Allport, G. W. *Personality; A psychological interpretation*. New York: Henry Holt, 1937.

Angyal, A. *Neurosis and treatment: A holistic theory*. New York: John Wiley, 1965.

Bakan, D. *On method*. San Francisco: Josey-Bass, 1967.

Berger, E. M. Zen Buddhism, general psychology, and counseling psychology. *Journal of Counseling Psychology*, 1962, *9*, 122-127.

Birdwhistell, R. L. *Kinesics and context: Essays on body motion communication*. New York: Ballantine, 1970.

Brill, A. A. Unconscious insight: Some of its manifestations. *International Journal of Psycho-Analysis*, 1929, *10*, 145-161.

Capra, F. *The Tao of physics*. Berkeley: Shambhala, 1975.

Chang, G. C. C. *The practice of Zen*. New York: Harper & Row, 1970.

Conze, E. *Buddhist thought in India*. Michigan: University of Michigan Press, 1967.

Dai, B. Zen and psychotherapy. *Voices*. Fall-Winter, 1969, 118-124.

Darwin, C. *The origin of species*. Philadelphia: University of Pennsylvania Press, 1959.

Fadiman, J., and Frager, R. *Personality and personal growth*. New York: Harper & Row, 1976.

Freud, S. *Psychopathology of everyday life*. New York: New American Library, 1951.

Freud, S., and Breuer, J. *Studies on hysteria*. New York: Avon, 1966.

Fromm-Reichmann, F. *Principles of intensive psychotherapy*. Chicago: University of Chicago, Press, 1950.

Ghiselin, B. *The creative process*. New York: New American Library, 1952.

Goleman, D. The Buddha on meditation and states of consciousness. In Tart, C. T. (Ed.), *Transpersonal psychologies*. New York: Harper & Row, 1975.

Green, E., and Green, A. Biofeedback training and Yoga. Address presented at the conference of Psychic and Self-Healing: The Transcendent Human Potential. San Francisco, California, May 6, 1972.

Hirai, T. Electroencephalographic study on the Zen meditation (Zazen): EEG changes during the concentrated relaxation. *Psychiatrica et Neurologia Japonica*. 1960, *62*, 76-105.

Hirai, T., Izawa, S., and Koga, E. EEG and Zen Buddhism: EEG changes in the course of meditation. *EEG Clinical Neurological Supplement*, 1959, *18*, 52.

Huber, J. *Through an Eastern window*. New York: Bantam, 1965.

James, W. *The principles of psychology*. 2 vols. New York: Holt & Co., 1890.

James, W. *Psychology: the briefer course*. New York: Henry Holt, 1893.

James, W. *The varieties of religious experience*. New York: Longmans, Green & Co., 1928.

James, W. *Talks to teachers on psychology*. New York: Norton, 1958.

Jung, C. G. *The practice of psychotherapy*. New York: Random House, 1966.

Kasamatsu, A., and Hirai, T. An electroencephalographic study on the Zen meditation (Zazen). In Tart, C. T. (Ed.), *Altered states of consciousness*. New York: Wiley, 1969, 489-501.

Kasamatsu, A., Okuma, T., Lakenska, S., Koga, E., Ikeda, K., and Suguyama, H. The EEG of Zen and Yoga practitioners. *Electroencephalography and Clinical Neurophysiology,* 1957, *9*, 51-52.

Kelly, G. A. *The psychology of personal constructs.* Vol. 1. New York: Norton, 1955.

Kohler, W. *Gestalt psychology.* New York: Liveright, 1947.

Kuhn, T. S. *The structure of scientific revolutions.* Chicago: University of Chicago Press, 1970.

Lanman, C. R. Handwritten facsimile. In Lyall, A. C., *Asiatic studies: Religious and social.* London: John Murray, 1899.

Lesh, T. V. Zen and psychotherapy: A partially annotated bibliography. *Journal of Humanistic Psychology.* 1970, *10*, 1, 75-83.

Maslow, A. *Motivation and personality.* New York: Harper and Row, 1954.

Murphy, G., and Murphy, L. *Asian psychology.* New York: Basic Books, 1968.

Murti, T. R. V. *The central philosophy of Buddhism: A study of the Madhyamika system.* London: Allen and Urwin, 1955.

Okeima, T., Koga, E., Ikeda, K., and Suguyama, H. The EEG of Zen and Yoga practitioners. *Electroencephalography and Clinical Neurophysiology,* 1957, *9*, 51.

Ornstein, R. E. *The psychology of consciousness.* San Francisco : W. H. Freeman, 1972.

Robinson, R. H. *Early Madhyamika in India and China.* Madison: University of Wisconsin Press, 1967.

Rogers, C. R. *Counseling and psychotherapy.* Cambridge, Massachusetts: Riverside Press, 1942.

Rosenthal, R. *Experimenter effects in behavioral research.* New York: Appleton-Century-Crofts, 1966.

Sarathandra, E. R. *Buddhist psychology of perception.* Colombo: Ceylon University Press, 1958.

Stcherbatsky, T. *Buddhist logic.* Vol. 2. New York: Dover, 1962.

Streng, F. J. *Emptiness: A study in religious meaning.* New York: Abingdon Press, 1967.

Sutich, A. J. *The founding of humanistic and transpersonal psychology: A personal account.* Unpublished doctoral dissertation. San Francisco, California: Humanistic Psychology Institute, 1976.

Tart, C. T. *Transpersonal psychologies.* New York: Harper & Row, 1975.

Tolman, E. C. *Purposive Behavior in Animals and Men.* New York: Century Co., 1957.

Van Dusen, W. Wu-wei, no-mind, and the fertile void in psychotherapy. *Psychologia,* 1958, *1*, 253-56.

Waley, A. *The way and its power.* New York: Grove Press, 1958.

Wolpe, J. *Psychotherapy by reciprocal inhibition.* Stanford, California: Stanford University Press, 1958.

Woods, J. H. *The Yoga-system of Patanjali.* Harvard Oriental Series, Delhi: Motilal Banarsidas, 1972.

Yampolski, P. B. *The platform sutra of the sixth patriarch.* New York: Columbia University Press, 1967.

3

The Science of Consciousness

John R. Battista

1. Science and Consciousness

Most people consider science to be the study of the objective, physical world that exists independent of our awareness of it. From this perspective, it seems impossible to develop a scientific theory of consciousness because consciousness is a subjective experience that is outside the realm of the phenomena explained by science.

However, a number of findings in twentieth century physics have forced a fundamental reconsideration of this dualistic attitude toward science and reality and have begun to bring the relationship between science and consciousness into a new light. First, Einstein's theory of relativity revealed that matter, energy, space, and time are not fixed and immutable characteristics of the universe but rather relativistic constructs that involve the unique perspective of the observer. Thus, two observers traveling at different velocities near the speed of light may observe the same event to occur at different times and to differ in mass and length. Furthermore, Heisenberg's uncertainty principle revealed that the process of observation makes it impossible to know both the position and momentum of an object being observed with complete certainty. Physics was therefore limited to formulating probability connections between the outcomes of observations, and could not make statements about what was actually occurring in the unobserved physical world. Thus, quantum physics, the most basic and all-

John R. Battista • Department of Psychiatry, University of California, Davis, California.

encompassing form of physics, does not found itself on presumed space–time realities but anchors itself in sensory experience (Stapp, 1972; Wigner, 1969).

This recognition of physics' concern with conscious experience breaks the dualistic view of science and reality and legitimatizes the development of a scientific theory of consciousness. In fact, the development of such a theory appears to be central to the continued advancement of physics, psychology, and neurophysiology.

For example, there is a great controversy in contemporary physics about the nature of physical reality and its relationship to consciousness (Walker, 1972; Jammer, 1974). Some theoreticians such as Popper (1956) continue to believe in a single, objective reality while others such as Everett (1957) argue for the existence of multiple, simultaneous realities. Alternately, Stapp (1975) suggests that we can never know the ultimate nature of physical reality and must be content with theories that explain how such a reality is revealed to us. Some physicists such as Wigner (1972) contend that consciousness causes physical reality to take on a particular form. This contention is supported by the empirical verification of Bell's Theorem (Stapp, 1975), which shows the existence of nonlocal causality (faster than light information transfer) and implies that how a physicist decides to do an experiment may partially determine the results found by another physicist in a spatially disconnected area of the universe! Regardless of the validity of any of these particular points of view, it seems clear that the development of a scientific theory of consciousness would help physicists to better formulate the nature of reality.

Similarly, the relationship between consciousness and physical reality is central to psychology and neurophysiology. Rubenstein (1965), for example, has convincingly argued that psychology needs to be formulated in such a way that it is consistent with neurophysiology if it is ever to become a fully developed science. Similarly, neurophysiologists such as Pribram (1971) have begun to recognize the need to utilize conscious psychological constructs in order to fully account for the functioning of the human brain.

Thus, the breakdown of the dualistic world-view during this century challenges science to reconceptualize the relationship between consciousness and reality. The development of a scientific theory of consciousness is central to this undertaking and holds the potential of unifying the physical, biological, and psychological sciences within a holistic and unified view of reality (Battista, 1977).

2. Methodology for the Development of a Scientific Theory of Consciousness

Given that the development of a scientific theory of consciousness is a legitimate and significant field of inquiry for science, we can now consider how the scientific method provides us with a procedure for developing such a theory. There are five main steps in the development of a scientific theory according to the scientific method. First, define the phenomenon that is to be explained. Second, collect all the available data about this phenomenon. Third, evaluate the ability of existing theories to explain these data. Fourth, develop a new theory to explain the data if none of the existing theories are capable of doing so. Fifth, test the theory by evaluating its predictions about the phenomena to be emphasized under unknown and previously untested situations. The following sections will apply this procedure to the development of a scientific theory of consciousness.

3. Defining the Term "Consciousness"

The first step in the development of a scientific theory of consciousness is to define what we mean by the term "consciousness." Basically the term has been used in three distinct ways. First, as a theoretical construct referring to the system by which an individual becomes aware; second, to refer to reflective awareness, an awareness of being aware; third, as a general term encompassing all forms of awareness.

The use of consciousness as a theoretical construct is confusing because the term is so commonly used to refer to experience rather than the means of explaining it. Restricting the term to reflective awareness also causes difficulties because it excludes early childhood experiences that occur before the development of reflective awareness and adult experiences such as dreaming and ecstasy that occur without reflective awareness from being considered conscious. Thus, consciousness is best utilized as a general term referring to all forms of experience or awareness.

4. Three Kinds of Data about Consciousness

The second step in the development of a general theory of consciousness is to collect all of the available data about consciousness. There are three kinds of data about consciousness—phenomenological, psychological, and empirical—each of which arises from its own distinct method for investigating consciousness—introspection, observation, and measurement.

Introspection emphasizes the study of consciousness through direct experience. Meditation, free-association, and active imagination are examples of introspective techniques that can be utilized for the phenomenological investigation of consciousness. This method results in data about the experience of consciousness: phenomenological data about consciousness.

Observation emphasizes the use of the investigator's own consciousness to understand the experiences of another individual. The position of the therapist in conducting psychotherapy and the psychologist in studying the development of cognition in children are examples of this psychological method of understanding consciousness. This method results in data about the condition under which individuals will be in a particular state of consciousness: psychological data about consciousness.

Measurement emphasizes understanding consciousness through making measurements on the physical variables associated with it. The study of the level of central nervous system neurotransmitters associated with depression and the EEG patterns associated with meditation are examples of the empirical approach to the investigation of consciousness. This process results in data about the relationship between consciousness and physical variables: empirical data about consciousness.

These three kinds of data about consciousness are the main source of difficulty in resolving the perennial mind–body problem. It is difficult to see how any theory could simultaneously account for phenomenological data about the experience of consciousness and empirical data about the physical basis of consciousness, and yet this is exactly what the scientific method would demand of any potential general scientific theory of consciousness.

Let us then explore these three kinds of data in more depth in order to establish specific criteria that any general theory of consciousness must be able to explain. Such a general theory would be considered scientific if its hypothesis were developed in such a way that they could be tested and verified independent of the phenomena they are being used to explain.

4.1. Phenomenological Data about Consciousness

Phenomenological data about consciousness stem from a consideration of the direct experience of consciousness. Such considerations have resulted in data about the nature of human consciousness as well as the range of conscious experience.

Phenomenological data about the nature of human consciousness are frequently contradictory and difficult to explicate in a way that could serve as useful criteria for a general theory of consciousness. Thus, rather than attempt to review the extensive body of introspective literature, this discussion will be limited to three essential points that stand out across investigators: the primacy of conscious experience, consciousness as a field, and the stream of consciousness.

The primacy of consciousness refers to the fact that consciousness is the basis of all knowledge. Consciousness exists as an experience that transcends the split between the knower and the known by relating them. This is what James (1890) means when he states that consciousness is neither physical nor psychological and is what the phenomenologists (Koestenbaum, 1962) call the intentional nature of consciousness. (For a more detailed presentation of James's work, see the chapter by Strange in this volume.)

The concept of consciousness as a field (Gurwitsch, 1964) refers to the fact that consciousness is experienced as a whole that unifies a multitude of perceptions, emotions, and thoughts. Consciousness is not composed of different bits and pieces but is gestalt with some aspects attended to more than others (James, 1890). Thus, we are not aware of just one thing at a time, but rather a unified field whose parts are perceived with varying degrees of intensity.

The stream of consciousness (James, 1890) refers to the ongoing and ever-changing nature of experience. Consciousness is a unified flow of experience analogous to a stream rather than a series of disconnected and unrelated events.

An introspective investigation of the states of consciousness has always fascinated mankind and served as the source of data for the construction of taxonomies of the forms of conscious experience and their hierarchical relationship to one another. Such taxonomies have always been an integral part of Eastern culture (Taimni, 1961; Green and Green, 1971; Golemann, 1972) and have recently been developing in the West (Kripner, 1972; Ring, 1974; Wilbur, 1975) based on Tart's (1972) pioneering work pointing out the existence of a variety of specific states of consciousness. I have not attempted to explicate a complete and exhaustive taxonomy of consciousness in this section but rather to delineate the relationship among eight main forms of consciousness (sensation, perception, emotion, affect, cognition, intuition, self-awareness, and unition—an experience of oneness or unification with everything) in an attempt to generate some basic phenomenological criteria that can be utilized in the development of a general theory of consciousness.

Sensations are physiological reactions to stimuli interacting with the nervous system. Sensations are generally considered to constitute the unconscious physical basis of consciousness rather than the most fundamental form of consciousness. However, this seems to be an arbitrary and confusing distinction. No doubt most adults rarely if ever experience sensations. However, fetuses and infants probably experience many sensations that are only slowly organized into perceptions during the process of development. Furthermore, a number of Yogis such as Sri Aurobindo (see Satprem, 1968) have described the experience of a physical or sensory realm of consciousness that is more fundamental than perception. Finally, a number of psychophysics experiments (Stevens, 1975) have shown that individuals can experience sensations of something long before they form a definite perception of it. Thus, we can think of sensations as raw, physical experience that constitutes the foundation of perception and the more complex forms of consciousness.

Perceptions result from our awareness of sensations and serve as the contents of conscious experience. We distinguish the perceptions of sight, sound, touch, smell, pain, and position through cognition.

It is important to distinguish perception from cognition just as we must distinguish perception from sensation. Cognition refers to the reflective awareness of perceptions in much the same way that perception constitutes an awareness of sensations. Thus, perception exists independent of any cognitive process. Many people find this to be a confusing concept because they have come to accept cognition as their only form of consciousness and thus consider all consciousness to be cognitive. However, infants certainly perceive faces, for example, and yet we know from the work of Inhelder and Piaget (1958) that they are incapable of generating constructs that would let them know that they are looking at a face. Perception thus constitutes a distinct form of consciousness that is more complex than sensation but less complex than cognition.

Emotions are experiences that arise in response to perceptions or sensations. Emotions thus constitute a more complex form of consciousness than either perception or sensation. We recognize a wide range of emotions through cognition: hunger, sexuality, anger, grief, love, etc. However, emotions can exist independently of cognition. For example, emotions can frequently be observed to occur in people who are unaware of them, and many people engaged in introspective processes such as psychotherapy frequently discover emotions that have been outside of their cognitive awareness.

Affects constitute positive or negative reactions to emotions so that emotions take on a pleasurable, unpleasurable, or anxiety-colored tone. Affects are certainly distinct from emotions, as shown by the fact that sexual excitement can be experienced as pleasurable and exciting in one circumstance and threatening and anxiety-provoking in another.

Cognition is the most common form of adult human consciousness. Cognition is the state of consciousness involved in conceptualization or reflection upon experience and is thus more complex than sensory, perceptual, emotional, or affective consciousness. The ability to conceptualize develops throughout childhood and generally does not reach its most abstract form at least until the time of puberty (Inhelder and Piaget, 1958). Conceptualization is predicated on a subject-object split that involves a linear, sequential, and rational process.

Perhaps the most interesting aspect of cognition is the experience of free will, the ability to make choices that determine actions and result in consequences that alter our perceptions of the world. The issue of free will is thus of central importance to any general scientific theory of consciousness.

Intuition and other nonrational states of consciousness such as daydreaming, hypnotic states, and dreams constitute an alternative to the cognitive means of relating to experience. Instead of treating experience in a logical, sequential manner, it is grasped directly and holistically.

In my own opinion these nonrational states of consciousness are complementary to cognitive consciousness at the same general level of complexity. However, Western culture has generally tended to consider nonrational states of consciousness as inferior to and more primitive than cognitive consciousness, whereas Eastern culture has tended to elevate some of them such as intuition (Buddhi) above cognition.

Self-awareness is an awareness of one's own style of relating to experience and provides a sense of self or person. Undoubtedly many individuals would consider this state to be an abstract form of cognition, but I experience it as a more complex form of consciousness than either cognition or intuition (see Taylor's discussion in this volume on *samprajnatasamadhi*).

Union or unitive consciousness is the final and most complex form of consciousness that we shall consider. The term "unition" was coined to refer to a state of consciousness in which a whole and boundless relationship with everything is experienced. The subject-object dichotomy is transcended and an omnidimensional experience of oneness comes into being that unifies all of the other forms of consciousness. Thus, the term unition is utilized to imply the same experience that others have described as *samadhi, satori,* peak experience, mystic experience, or transcendental state (see Taylor's section in this volume on *asamprajnatasamadhi*).

4.2. Psychological Data about Consciousness

Psychological data about consciousness emerge from an investigator's observation of the conditions under which particular states of consciousness occur in other individuals. This process has been extensively applied to perception, emotion, affects, cognitions, and dreams. A few of the basic findings of this work will be discussed in this section in order to generate some preliminary psychological criteria for evaluating and developing a general scientific theory of consciousness.

Psychological investigations of perception have revealed that perception involves the interpretation of sensory input in such a way as to construct an experience that is understandable and conforms to expectations. For example, individuals will misperceive cards in which the color and suit are mismatched as being correctly matched when a few of these cards are placed within a deck of regular playing cards (Bruner, 1973). Similarly, Hastorf and Cantril (1954) have shown that individuals will tend to perceive sporting events in a way that conforms to their own hopes and expectations about the event. Finally, Pribram (1971) has reviewed a series of experiments in which individuals who have been given glasses that make the world appear upside down spontaneously alter their perceptions in such a way that the world continues to appear in its expected manner after only a two-week period! Thus, psychological experiments reveal that perception is a constructive process that involves interpreting sensory data along expected and pragmatic dimensions.

Psychological investigations of emotion have revealed that emotions result from an interaction of internal arousal and perceptions. The more arousal that occurs the more intense the emotional reaction (Schacter and Wheeler, 1962). However, the particular emotion that is experienced is a function of the perceptual environment within which the arousal takes place. For example, Schacter and Singer (1962) showed that joy and anger could easily be manipulated by social cues when a state of sympathetic arousal was initiated in an individual without a clear explanation of its cause.

Psychological data about affects are commonly known and easily recognized. Under situations of high and increasing uncertainty about the future we tend to experience anxiety. Alternately, situations that lead to uncertainty reduction are associated with a positive affect. We have all had the experience of having a positive affect in response to getting an insight into a problem we have been working on and developing anxiety in response to discovering yet another difficulty associated with such a problem. Previous work about the development of meaning in life (Battista and Almond, 1973) revealed that the degree of meaning that an individual experiences is a function of the rate with which an individual can reduce the uncertainty associated with developing and satisfying life goals.

There thus seems to be an overall relationship among emotions, affects, and uncertainty. Emotions result from the specific way in which uncertainty about the meaning of a state of arousal is reduced utilizing perceptions. Affects result from the rate with which this uncertainty reduction does or does not take place. Increasing levels of uncertainty are experienced as a negative affect while decreasing levels of anxiety are experienced as a positive affect. Affects can thus be thought of as the first derivative of the process of uncertainty reduction that is associated with the experience of emotions.

Psychological data about the conditions of cognitive consciousness have generally been cast in terms of the unconscious. The unconscious is used in this context to refer to actions, emotions, or perceptions that tend to occur without reflective awareness.

There are two basic conditions under which people tend to be unconscious in this sense. First, unconscious acts tends to occur in highly learned, repetitive situations. For example, an experienced typist is unaware of skipping one space after words and two spaces after sentences. Second, perceptions or emotions that conflict with our hopes, beliefs, or self-image tend to remain unconscious. This finding has come from a wide variety of experiments in support of Festinger's (1957) theory of cognitive dissonance as well as observations from the psychotherapeutic setting. For example, Brehm, Back, and Bogdonoff (1969) showed that subjects who had already missed two meals and who reported being hungry and then voluntarily committed themselves to miss another meal for few explicit reasons and no money (i.e., a high dissonance group) subsequently reported themselves to be less hungry, ordered fewer items of food in a free meal following the experiment, and had lower free fatty acids than a low dissonance control group who were given good theoretical and financial justification for missing an additional meal. Thus, people not only tend to be unaware of input that conflicts with their world view but actually alter their physiology to match their cognitive set!

An overall relationship between cognition and uncertainty thus begins to become clear. Unconsciousness tends to occur under situations of high or low uncertainty while cognition occurs in situations of moderate uncertainty. This suggests a bell type of curve representing the relationship between consciousness and uncertainty.

Psychological investigations of dreams have revealed that dreams represent perceptions that have not been successfully integrated into cognitive consciousness. This failure of integration may result from the subliminal exposure to the material as shown by Pötzl (1960) or may be the result of psychodynamic reasons as shown by Malamud (1934) and Breger, Hunter, and Lane (1971). This work thus supports our previous hypothesis that nonrational states of consciousness such as dreams, daydreams, and intuition function to complement cognition.

4.3. Empirical Data about Consciousness

Empirical data about consciousness stem from an investigation of the physical variables that are associated with specific conscious states. The physical basis of consciousness has always fascinated mankind, but the contemporary approach to the investigation of consciousness stemmed from Wundt and the earliest physiological psychologists (see Strange in this volume).

Penfield's (1950) finding of specific cortical sites for sensations and memory traces in combination with the clinical finding that discrete neurological deficits are associated with specific focal anatomical lesions combined to suggest a discrete, localized, and specialized neuronal basis for consciousness. This idea was reinforced by Magoun's (1954) finding that consciousness is dependent on the functioning of the reticular activating system in the brainstem, and Olds and Milner's (1954) work showing the existence of localized pleasure and pain centers in the brain. Finally, Hubel and Wiesel's (1959) discovery of single-cell analyzers of sensory input was heralded as the uncovering of the "gnostic units" within the brain (Konorski, 1967).

However, these findings of the discrete organization of the brain were challenged by Lashley (see Pribram, 1971) and a number of studies that were more directly concerned with consciousness. For example, Sokolov (1960) found that a cortical evoked response would occur to the discontinuation or modification of habituated stimuli, thus showing that habituation was not the result of neuronal "tiring" caused by repeated stimulation but resulted from an active process in which a particular spatio-temporal sensory response was "expected." Similarly, Libet's (1966) finding that direct cortical stimulation takes between 0.5 and 1.0 seconds to result in conscious experience gave strong evidence against the "light-bulb model of consciousness" that had been prevalent before that time. Pribram (1971) has reviewed much of the literature that shows the functional as well as the discrete organization of the brain.

The role of neurotransmitters in the regulation of affects, and the relationship between patterns of cortical electrical activity and particular states of consciousness are two of the many focuses of current neurophysiological research on the physical basis of consciousness. Our discussion will be limited to a few of the basic conclusions of this research in an attempt to show the kind of data that any general theory of consciousness must be able to account for.

The initial interest in the relationship between neurotransmitters and affects arose from the clinical finding that a number of drugs that decrease the level of catecholamine and indoleamine neurotransmitters in the brain, e.g., reserpine, alpha-methyl dopa, were found to cause depression, while antidepressant drugs such as amphetamine and the tricyclics were known to increase the levels of these same neurotransmitters. Furthermore, lithium carbonate, which is effective in the treatment of mania, is now known (Weil-Malherbe, 1976) to work through decreasing the level of neurotransmitters in the synaptic cleft within the central nervous system. Measurements of the breakdown products of these neurotransmitters in the urine and cerebral spinal fluid of individuals with affective disturbances have been difficult to interpret but generally have confirmed the hypothesis of an association between decreased levels of indoleamine (serotonin) or catecholamine (norepinephrine and dopamine) and depression (Akisal and McKinney, 1975). Finally, the treatment of depression with the precursors of the depleted neurotransmitters has given confusing but basically confirmatory evidence for the hypothesis that neurotransmitters control the affect state of individuals (Weil-Malherbe, 1976). The most current theory of the relationship between neurotransmitters and affects (Kety, 1971; Prange, Wilson, Lynn, Alltop, Stikeleather 1974) suggests that serotonin controls the stability of the affect system while the level of catecholamine controls the positive or negative form of the affect.

Data about the cortical activity of the brain in sensation, perception, cognition, intuition, and unitive states of consciousness are now available in the neurophysiological literature. Average cortical evoked response data (John, 1976) suggests that sensation involves the action of discrete neurons while perception entails changes in the spatiotemporal patterns of a set of neurons that respond differently to sensory stimuli depending on the context within which they occur.

Data on the localization of cortical processes involved in the

cognitive and intuitive modes of consciousness have emerged from
the study of split-brain subjects. This work is now widely known and
has been well reviewed by Galin (1974). Suffice it to say that this
research suggests that cognition and intuition represent two distinct
modes of information processing that are localized to some extent in
the dominant and nondominant hemispheres. The dominant hemisphere operates in a linear, sequential manner that is probably
concerned with language-dependent cognitive consciousness. Alternately, the nondominant hemisphere operates in a holistic, symbolic
manner that is probably concerned with nonrational states of consciousness such as intuition.

The unitive state of consciousness has been investigated in a
number of EEG studies (Banquet, 1973; Gellhorn and Kiely, 1972;
Domash, 1976) with surprisingly similar results. Each of these studies
has concluded that the unitive state of consciousness is involved in
very fast beta activity that probably represents the synchronization of
the entire cerebral cortex.

5.   Criteria for a General Scientific Theory of Consciousness

The phenomenological, psychological, and empirical data reviewed in the last three sections place constraints on a general theory
of consciousness and can be used as criteria for evaluating potential
general theories of consciousness. We may thus conclude that any
general scientific theory of consciousness must be able to:

1. Define consciousness by its hypotheses in such a way as to
answer the questions, What is consciousness? and What are the
conditions under which it will occur?

2. Account for the primacy of consciousness by explaining how
consciousness transcends the subject-object dichotomy and relates the
knower with that which is known.

3. Define sensation and account for the data that suggest that
sensation involves the firing of discrete and specific sets of neurons.

4. Define perception and account for the data about the relationship between perception and habituation; repeated stimulation will
not be perceived but the discontinuation or alteration of an habituated
stimulus will result in perception.

5. Account for cortical evoked response data that show that
perception is involved with alterations in the spatio-temporal pattern
of a set of neurons that interpret the context of sensory stimuli, and

psychological data that show that perception is a constructive and interpretive process.

6. Define emotion and account for the finding that different emotional states can be derived from the same state of physiological arousal depending on the context within which it occurs.

7. Define affects and explain how positive and negative affects are related to increases and decreases in the rate of uncertainty reduction and are correlated with alterations in the level of central nervous system neurotransmitters.

8. Define cognition and explain how it tends to occur only under situations of moderate uncertainty reduction.

9. Define the nonrational states of consciousness such as intuition and dreaming, and show how they tend to complement the cognitive processes; i.e., perceptions or emotions that are not processed cognitively will tend to occur in nonrational states; cognitive and intuitive processes are somewhat lateralized to different cerebral hemispheres.

10. Define self-awareness and show its hierarchical relationship to the other states of consciousness.

11. Define unition and account for the finding that unitive states occurring during meditation involve the synchronization of the entire cerebral cortex.

12. Account for the experience of consciousness as a field that has an ongoing streamlike quality.

13. Account for the experience of free will.

6.   Theoretical Approaches to Consciousness

There are three main theoretical approaches to consciousness: dualistic, monistic, and holistic. Dualistic approaches emphasize that mental states and physical states are totally distinct from one another. Monistic approaches argue that there are only mental or physical states. Holistic approaches contend that mental and physical states constitute different aspects or hierarchical levels of a single unified reality.

Each of the three main theoretical approaches to consciousness is further subdivided into distinct theoretical positions. Thus, there are concrete and abstract forms of dualism, subjective and objective forms of monism, and relativistic, emergent, and informational forms of holism. These seven theoretical approaches to consciousness will be discussed in terms of their ability to meet the preliminary criteria for a general scientific theory of consciousness.

6.1. Concrete Dualism

Concrete dualism is based on the belief that the mind and body are totally distinct entities. The body is believed to have a real physical existence that is subject to the laws of the spatio-temporal world. The mind is seen as free of spatio-temporal constraints but subject to its own set of laws. Frequently, an ego is postulated to account for the nature of subjective experience.

Concrete dualistic interactionists such as Descartes (see Ryle, 1949) and Eccles (1976) argue that the mind and body are able to mutually influence one another while concrete dualistic parallelists such as Liebnitz (see Ryle, 1949) argue that mind and body unfold in a parallel but causally unconnected manner.

Most concrete dualists do not attempt to present a theoretical explanation of consciousness but rather limit themselves to a discussion of the basis for their beliefs. The most notable exception to this generality is the psychoanalytic theory of consciousness (Barr and Langs, 1972) as it developed from the work of Freud (1895/1954, 1900/1953).

Freud's earliest work concerned with consciousness (1895/1954), "Project for a Scientific Psychology," uses the term "consciousness" to refer to a special group of neurons that invest energy in a stimulus resulting in an awareness of it. However, Freud abandoned this neurological approach to consciousness for a purely mental model. In *The Interpretation of Dreams,* Freud (1900/1953) considers consciousness to be the sense organ of the mental apparatus. It is the mental system that is utilized for attending to the qualities of stimuli. Conscious experiences result from investing (cathecting) a stimulus with hyper-cathexes, a quantitatively limited amount of freely mobile psychic energy that can be blocked by the anticathexes involved in defensive operations.

Ego psychologists such as Klein (1959) and Rapaport (1960) then went on to define consciousness as the energy-dispensing function of the ego. The ego is hypothesized to dispense attention cathexes, a kind of psychic energy that is neutralized from the drive energies. Conscious experience results when the attention cathexes attracted by a stimulus within the mental apparatus exceed a certain threshold amount. These basic ideas have been applied to altered states of consciousness by Tart (1975, 1976).

The dualistic nature of psychoanalytic metapsychology is frequently overlooked because many analytic theoreticians speak about psychic energy as if it is derived from physical energy and can be discharged through the body. However, the psychoanalytic theory of consciousness is dualistic because the concept of psychic energy upon which it rests is vitalistic and totally incompatible with physical energy (Holt, 1967; Rosenblatt and Thickstun, 1970; Peterfreund, 1971; Schafer, 1973). There are not different kinds of physical energy. Physical energy cannot impart qualities to objects. Physical energy is not a thing that can be separated from matter to be channeled, pooled, or blocked.

Similarly, there have been many critiques of psychoanalytic theory because of the mechanistic conceptualization of mind that it employs. Ryle (1949) has pointed out that all dualistic theories treat the mind as if it is an object, but of a different class of objects than physical objects. He calls this a "category mistake" and sees the fallacy as analogous to mistaking a university for one of the buildings that partially comprise it.

However, the real problem with classical dualism is not vitalism or mechanism *per se*. The point is not so much that vitalistic thinking is false, but rather that it constitutes a metaphor or descriptive analogy rather than a scientific explanation. To say that conscious experience results from energy being dispensed to a stimulus and that this energy may be blocked or displaced is considered to be a useful clinical model by some therapists. However, this model is descriptive rather than explanatory (Rubenstein, 1965).

None of the theoretical constructs have any meaning independent of the phenomena that they are used to explain. Thus, they do not explain anything. This is the basis for Ryle's (1949) famous critique of dualistic explanation as a "ghost in the machine." Thus, although concrete dualistic approaches to consciousness may serve as helpful clinical metaphors, they cannot serve as the foundation for a general scientific theory of consciousness because they cannot be utilized to explain empirical data and do not explain in a scientifically acceptable manner.

6.2. Abstract Dualism

The inadequacy of concrete dualism does not necessarily imply the inherent fallacy of a dualistic approach to the mind-body problem. A hidden variable theory of consciousness based on quantum mechanics has been explicated as providing a contemporary and valid form of dualism (Walker, 1970).

Hidden variables are real, nonphysical variables whose existence was postulated in order to explain the indeterminacy limits of classical quantum mechanics. According to classical quantum mechanics, the world is inherently indeterminant at the quantum level as per Heisenberg's uncertainty principle. Given information about the state of a particle, one can generate a probability distribution for its state at a future time through the Schrödinger wave equation but cannot determine which state will actually occur.

Einstein was one of the most vocal critics of this position, and Einstein, Podolsky, and Rosen (1935) were able to show that classical quantum mechanics is not a complete theory. This gave impetus for a number of theoreticians, led by Bohm (1952), to propose the existence of hidden variables that determine which of the states predicted by the Schrödinger wave equation will actually occur. Walker (1970) then went on to equate these hidden variables with consciousness.

Although such an approach may appear to be more appealing than classical dualism, it still retains the same essential problem. A hidden variable interpretation of consciousness makes consciousness undefinable except through experience and precludes the explanation of different forms of consciousness and the conditions under which they occur.

Walker (1970) recognized these difficulties and attempted to resolve them by arguing that the hidden variables are related to the physical variables of the nervous system through a single quantum mechanical operator. He argues that consciousness is dependent upon a certain rate of synaptic transmission and information processing. Although such ideas are quite interesting, they are extraneous to a hidden variable theory of consciousness and can be understood as a form of informational holism.

6.3. Subjective Monism

Subjective monism is commonly associated with the idealistic philosophy of Berkeley (Cowan, 1975) and the Yogic philosophy of Patanjali (Taimni, 1961). Subjective monism argues that the physical world does not have an existence independent of either an individual or universal consciousness and thus absorbs physical reality into a consciousness-based monism.

This position has some credence in light of findings in psychology and physics that show that what is observed is a function of the properties of the observer. Although such data imply that knowledge of the physical world and the form it takes is based on a conscious individual, they do not imply that the existence of the physical world is dependent upon conscious experience.

Subjective monism suffers from the same essential problem as concrete and abstract dualism. It does not provide a verifiable answer to the question, What is consciousness? and precludes an explanation of the forms and conditions for conscious and unconscious phenomena.

6.4. Objective Monism

Objective monism takes the opposite approach to consciousness as subjective monism. It argues that consciousness is a material entity and absorbs subjective experience into a physical monism. Thus, the excitation of particular neurons or sets of neurons is taken to be equivalent to particular forms of consciousness (Wooldridge, 1968; Konorski, 1967).

Objective monism does have a distinct advantage over the preceding three approaches. It defines consciousness in a way that is independent of experience, and is thus capable of discriminating the forms of consciousness and the conditions under which they will occur.

However, there are at least two serious problems associated with objective monism. First, consciousness is not identical with neurophysiological states, even if they are invariably associated. That would make consciousness an exclusively objective phenomena when it is also an inherently subjective experience (Place, 1962). Thus, objective monism defines away the problem of subjectivity rather than resolving it.

Second, to say that consciousness is a neurophysiological state is an empirical statement about consciousness but not a theoretical explanation of it. It allows one to generalize that a particular neurophysiological state is associated with a particular form of consciousness in human beings but cannot be utilized to determine if computers, plants, and animals are conscious (Walker, 1970). Thus, objective monism is an empirical description of consciousness rather than a theoretical scientific explanation of it.

6.5. Emergent Theories

The first four approaches to consciousness reveal a paradox. If consciousness is conceptualized as inherently nonphysical, empirical data cannot be explained. Alternately, if consciousness is conceptualized as physical, phenomenological data cannot be explained. The emergent, relativistic, and informational approaches to consciousness attempt to resolve this paradox by three different holistic means.

Emergent theories consider consciousness to develop from physical interactions. Epiphenomenalism (Huxley, 1893) was the earliest form of an emergent theory and conceptualized consciousness as a simple by-product of physical interactions.

Later, field theories (Köhler, 1940) were developed within Gestalt psychology as a second form of emergent theory. Field theories consider consciousness to be an electromagnetic field around the brain that results from the integration of the neurophysiological states that comprise it.

Finally, Sperry's (1969, 1976) emergent interactionism constitutes a third form of emergent theory. Sperry considers consciousness to be a higher-order, molar property of the brain that is able to control lower-level neurophysiological phenomena. He argues that consciousness exists in the same relationship to neuronal events as water does to the atoms that comprise it. He states that this molar property is the result of the functional organization of the cerebral cortex rather than a spatio-temporal phenomenon such as a field. As such his view is consistent with the hierarchical nature of systems (Battista, 1977).

Dewan (1976), in a provocative article attempting to support Sperry's position from the standpoint of control system theory, argues that consciousness is analogous to the operation of a virtual governor by mutual entrainment. According to this principle, individual units within a system become interrelated in such a way as to maintain certain molar properties of the system as a whole and thus act as if they are being governed although no actual physical governor is present.

Emergent theories of consciousness are intuitively appealing. They do not deny the significance of brain operations and yet do not reduce consciousness to them. Alternately, they do not deny subjectivity and free will and yet do not drift off into disembodied abstractions.

The main difficulty with emergent theories in general, and Sperry's in particular (Bindra, 1970), is that they are too vague and nonspecific to be critically tested. It is appealing to believe that consciousness is an emergent holistic property of the brain, but what do these properties specifically refer to, and what distinguishes conscious from unconscious aspects of these processes?

The electromagnetic field theory form of emergent theory is more specific but still inadequate. This stems from the fact that no criteria are given to differentiate the different types of conscious experience or to differentiate conscious from unconscious field.

Holding this argument aside, a general electromagnetic field theory of consciousness is probably false. Attempts to verify a general field theory of consciousness (Lashley, Chow, and Semmes, 1951; Pribram, 1971) by mechanically disrupting this field and looking for alterations in phenomena such as pattern discrimination performance assumed to be associated with consciousness have all been negative. Furthermore, as pointed out by Walker (1970), if consciousness is associated with an electromagnetic field around the brain it should be significantly affected by strong electromagnetic radiation such as that emitted near a radio transmitter. There does not appear to be any empirical data in support of this although it is known that strong electromagnetic changes such as those resulting from sun spots may affect psychological states (Friedman, Becker, and Bachman, 1965). Thus, consciousness probably is not associated with a general electromagnetic field around the brain but may well be associated with local and discrete fields (Pribram, 1971; Brenner and Kaufman, 1975).

Therefore, although emergent theories of consciousness are not currently developed enough to provide testable hypotheses about consciousness, they may provide a suitable framework within which a general theory of consciousness could be developed. In fact, informational holism, which is consistent with emergent theory, does appear to provide the basis for a general theory of consciousness.

6.6. Relativistic Theories

Relativistic approaches attempt to resolve the paradox of consciousness by theorizing that subjectivity and objectivity are complementary processes that result from the relativistic way in which brain phenomena are comprehended. James's (1907) early version of this approach, known as neutral monism (what Strange calls radical empiricism elsewhere in this volume, argues that mind and matter are both part of a more fundamental and basic unity. With the advent of quantum mechanics, a complementarity or double-aspect theory of consciousness was developed based on Heisenberg's uncertainty principle. Globus's (1973, 1974) work is one of the most sophisticated forms of this theoretical approach.

Globus, following Feigl (1967), replaces the mind-body problem with the question, What is the difference between subjective, mental events and objective, neuronal events? Globus (1974) sees no difference but argues that it is impossible to simultaneously experience and observe the same brain event because representing an event being experienced necessitates changing its physical state. He then argues that consciousness is identical with "neurally emobodied events" ("pure events") and asserts that subjectivity refers to the events themselves while objectivity constitutes representations of these events.

Although such a position makes sense, it does come to terms with the core issue for a general theory of consciousness. Globus recognizes this when he asks the question, Are all pure events conscious or just some of them? The answer to this question is the crux of a relativistic approach to a general theory of consciousness, and yet any answer would have to go beyond the theoretical position outlined so far.

Globus (1974), recognizing this fact, argues that all pure events are conscious but are divided into two groups. Representation events provide the content of consciousness and are synonymous with analogical, interneuronal, postsynaptic potentials that comprise the junctional microstructure and constitute the basis for the EEG (Pribram, 1971). Processing events provide the context of consciousness and are synonymous with digital, intraneuronal events. These hypotheses are useful in that they allow a correlation between the operational and discrete aspects of the brain and the contents and context of consciousness. However, they do not explain the conditions and intensity of conscious and unconscious phenomena.

Globus (1974) argues that unconscious phenomena are either processing events that constitute the context of consciousness or unrealized potentials that do not occur because the system does not process data in that way. He explains the intensity and duration of consciousness in terms of the duration and strength of the junctional microstructure.

Globus (1974) is thus on the verge of equating the existence and intensity of consciousness with the amount of energy in the junctional microstructure. He therefore presents a physical version of the classical psychoanalytic theory of consciousness by equating consciousness with the discharge of physical energy through the neuronal apparatus.

However, as pointed out by Bateson (1972), neurons are not like billiard balls that transfer energy from one to the other. Energy is not "dammed up" in the junctional microstructure when it is not processed. Rather, neurons operate primarily on their own energy derived from physiological sources and fire as the result of information transmitted from one to another. Although information transmission in the nervous system requires reciprocal energy changes, it does not necessarily require energy transmission and is certainly not synonymous with such transmissions. Furthermore, Holt (1967) has pointed out that any energy explanation of consciousness incorrectly utilizes energy as an explanatory concept. Thus, although the complementarity approach to consciousness may provide the basis for a general theory of consciousness, Globus's attempt to explain the existence and intensity of conscious phenomena in terms of the amount of energy in the junctional microstructure is fallacious.

6.7.   Informational Holism

If conscious and unconscious neuronal events do not meaningfully differ from one another in terms of the amount of energy they contain, in what way(s) can they be differentiated? Informational holism argues that they differ in terms of the amount of information they represent, and explains the existence and intensity of conscious phenomena in terms of an amount of information.

Similar information theories of consciousness have been independently developed by Roy John (1976) and the author. However, the idea of representing consciousness as information is implied by, or latent within, a relatively large number of works (Tomkins, 1962; MacKay, 1966; Pribram, 1971, 1976; Shallice, 1972; Tiller, 1972; Sarfatti, 1975).

Informational holism defines consciousness as information. The different forms of consciousness refer to different hierarchical levels of information. Events are conscious at a particular level of consciousness when they contain the threshold amount of information for that level. If they do not they will be unconscious. This theoretical position thus meets the first criteria for a general theory of consciousness, an ability to define consciousness and explain the conditions under which it will occur.

This theoretical approach is also consistent with introspective data about the primacy of conscious experience. Consciousness forms the basis of all knowledge of the world: It transcends the subject-object dichotomy by relating the knower with that which is known. This experience of consciousness is consistent with the theory that consciousness is information because information is inherently relational; it results from an interaction of a receiver with some source of data and cannot be reduced to either.

Information is often thought of as an entity that is carried by a signal and exists independently of some measuring process. This is false. Information is knowledge and can be measured in terms of the amount of uncertainty reduction that a particular signal or stimulus provides the receiver. Any input that reduces the possible states of the receiving system by 50% is defined as representing one "bit" of information for the system (MacKay, 1969).

For example, although we can mathematically represent the maximum amount of information that a particular book might carry, the actual amount of information it contains can only be understood in relationship to a particular reader. For an individual who can not read the language the book is written in or who already has mastered the material within the book, it will carry a relatively small amount of information. For the individual who is full of questions about the subject matter of the book, it will contain a relatively large amount of information.

Informational holism has a unique approach to the mind–body problem. Although consciousness is carried by physical variables, it is not reducible to these variables because the same physical state may carry different amounts of information depending on its probability of occurrence in relation to the states of the system as a whole. This follows from the fact that the uncertainty within a system is a function of the probability distribution of the entire system (Khinchin, 1957), including the universe.

Informational holism is like the emergent theories of consciousness in that information is a hierarchically ordered, holistic phenomena that emerges from the states that carry it. Alternately, informational holism is consistent with the relativistic approach to the mind–body problem. Pure neuronal events can be understood as containing a particular amount of information that may or may not be conscious. There is no objective way to find out about these events without measuring them. This will necessarily change the events but yield a certain amount of information about them.

Therefore, an information theory of consciousness is based on a relativistic, hierarchical, and holistic approach to the mind–body problem. Mind and body are conceptualized as hierarchically ordered aspects of the same unified system.

Accounting for the psychological and empirical data about each of the forms of consciousness is a complex task that can only be preliminarily outlined at present. The purpose of this presentation is to show the capacity of information theory to account for this data rather than defending a formalized general theory of consciousness. Many of the hypotheses presented in this section are thus highly speculative, but should stimulate both empirical attempts to test them as well as attempts at further theory development.

Physical interactions define a basic level of information, info 1, by determining a particular physical state from all of the potential states of a system. Sensation refers to this first level of information. All physical interactions can be characterized by a particular amount of sensation using this model. Particular neurons in the central nervous system are programmed to respond to particular stimuli in a fixed manner and thus constitute sensory information about the physical environment. This is the basis of all of the neurophysiological work that has shown the discrete organization of the brain.

Perception refers to a second level of information, info 2, information about the first level of information. This can be understood conceptually as the meaning of the info 1 (sensation) to the organism. It results from the representation of a sensation or set of sensations in terms of some innate or learned frame of reference.

The mathematical representations of this level of information involves the change in the uncertainty of one set of variables given that a second set of variables is in a particular state (Khinchin, 1957). This is a higher order concept of information than info 1 because each of the variables that comprise the state of the second set of variables involved in info 2 represents a certain amount of info 1.

Assuming that each of these variables refers to a neuron or set of neurons, the ability to generate into 2 is dependent on a much more complex nervous system than info 1. It requires the ability to represent something as well as react to it. Perception would thus be predicted as limited to those organisms whose nervous system is developed at least to this level. This position is consistent with John's (1976) conclusion that perception is mediated by alterations in the average temporal firing patterns of an ensemble of sets of neurons.

This theory of perception is also capable of explaining the empirical data (Sokolov, 1960) about habituation. When a stimulus first occurs it is novel and unexpected and therefore carries a relatively large amount of information (i.e., it will tend to be conscious). However, with repeated stimulation its novelty wears off, its probability of occurrence increases, and the amount of information it carries decreases so that it will tend to become unconscious. When the stimulation is fully expected (i.e., the subject is habituated), the failure of the stimulus to occur is now unexpected, has a low probability of occurrence, carries a relatively large amount of information, and will tend to become conscious.

The constructive and interpretive nature of perception is also consistent with this information theory of perception. The set of neurons that constitutes the basis for perception is characterized by a certain probability distribution for each of its potential combinations. This probability distribution reflects the readiness of each neuron to respond to a particular sensory input as the result of learned experience. The entire ensemble of neurons thus constitutes a template or schemata for the interpretation of sensations that is predisposed to interpret sensations in a particular manner. It is this predisposition or expectation of the ensemble that accounts for the constructive nature of perception and explains the misinterpretation of sensory data in terms of expected or biased directions.

Emotions are hypothesized to refer to a third hierarchical level of information: information about info 2, i.e, information about the meaning of a sensation. This can be thought of as an evaluation of a sensation in light of the perceptions with which it is associated, or as an evaluation of the meaning of a perception in light of the innate and learned needs of the organism. This process results in different forms of a third level of information that we experience as emotions.

This theory of emotions is consistent with Schacter and Singer's (1962) finding that a particular state of physiological arousal is compatible with a number of different emotions depending on the context within which it occurs. This theory of emotions does not involve an awareness of info 3 and is thus consistent with the clinical finding that emotional states can be observed in individuals who are cognitively unaware of their occurrence.

Previous research (Battista and Almond, 1973) showing a relationship between the rate of uncertainty reduction and positive and negative affect states suggests that affects refer to the first derivative of emotions (info 3). Positive affects result from increases in the rate of info 2 uncertainty reduction while negative affects would result from increasing uncertainty associated with info 2.

This hypothesis is consistent with the data about the relationship between central nervous system neurotransmitters and affects. Neurotransmitters can be expected to control the rate of information processing by altering the rate of synaptic transmission. Thus, processes that alter the level of synaptic neurotransmitters or their rate of turnover can be expected to alter the affect state because such changes will alter the rate with which information transmission (uncertainty reduction) takes place.

So far informational holism has been able to account for sensations, perceptions, emotions, and affects. Perceptions constitute information about sensations. Emotions serve the function of orienting ourselves to perceptions, while affects serve to reinforce particular patterns of information processing. Awareness is the result of information about these contents of consciousness and thus constitutes a fourth level of information.

There are two complementary ways of generating this information. The first is to treat the contents of consciousness as objects and evaluate them in a logical, sequential manner in terms of learned categories or constructs. This process that creates a subject-object dichotomy is cognition and results in thought. Alternately, the contents of consciousness can be related to one another in a noncausal, holistic way that is assumed to result in the nonrational states of consciousness such as intuition. Cognition and intuition are thus hypothesized to refer to complementary forms of a fourth level of information. Empirical findings showing that dreams tend to occur when the perception of the sensations associated with these events is not processed cognitively support the idea that the intuitive mode of information processing serves to complement and supplement cognition.

Sirac (1975), of the Physics-Consciousness Research Group in San Francisco, has suggested that these two modes of information processing can be conceptualized mathematically in terms of the two possible matrix structures of a four-member group. He argues that the Klein Group may constitute the structure of logic and the Transformation Group, the structure of intuition. Sirac further goes on to suggest that the left cerebral cortex may process information (info 4) predominantly according to the Klein Group while the right cerebral cortex may process information (info 4) predominantly according to the Transformation Group. This hypothesis could account for the data suggesting a relationship between lateral specialization and mode of information processing.

Self-awareness results from the process of evaluating subjective experience. Self-awareness is thus hypothesized to refer to a fifth level of information. It involves an understanding of the particular way in which one processes subjective experience (i.e., cognitively or nonrationally).

The sixth and final level of consciousness refers to information about the process of self-awareness itself. It is an awareness of the process of being aware. This experience is hypothesized to constitute unition and refers to a sixth level of information. The EEG data and descriptions of the process of self-realization (Taimni, 1961) make it appealing to imagine this state to involve the synchronization of the entire brain. If this hypothesis is true, split-brain subjects should be incapable of experiencing unitive states. As suggested by Domash (1976) the brain in such a synchronized state could be likened to a superfluid and respond as a totality to any incoming stimulus. The recent finding of nonlocal (faster than light) modes of information transmission (Sarfatti, 1975; Stapp, 1975) might suggest how an individual can experience unification with the entire universe during such a state.

We are now in a position to understand how an information theory of consciousness is capable of handling the phenomenological data that show that consciousness is a field that has the quality of a stream. James (1890) argued that consciousness is not experienced as composed of distinct and separate perceptions that are somehow brought together in a conscious experience. Rather, consciousness constitutes a whole field or gestalt within which particular elements may be more prominent than others. This analysis of consciousness is totally consistent with the nature of subjective experience referring to the fourth level of information. At this level, percepts, emotions, and affects are all unified into a gestalt but each will be differentiated by the amount of information that it carries. Thus, although consciousness at this level constitutes a given whole field, particular elements will be emphasized more than others.

The stream of consciousness stems from an understanding of the nature of the human nervous system. The great diversity of potential neuronal states makes uncertainty an inherent feature of the human brain. This uncertainty is motivating because decreases in uncertainty result in positive affects while increases in uncertainty are generally experienced negatively. The human being is thus inherently motivated, as observation of children or the electrical examination of the resting brain will show. The brain does not just respond to stimuli, it seeks information and continuously attempts to process the information it already possesses. It is this ongoing and never-ending information processing that gives consciousness its ongoing and never-ending streamlike quality.

The final issue to be considered is free will. Free will is understandable at the level of self-awareness (info 5). Reflection on the experience of cognition reveals that a number of potential possibilities are available with which to resolve uncertainty associated with the contents of consciousness. If this uncertainty did not exist, cognition itself would not occur. The individual is capable of imagining himself to respond in a variety of ways and in fact decides which way to respond in terms of the perceived consequences of that decision. However, the individual has learned to evaluate that decision in a particular way, so that his action will be both understandable and predictable by another individual. Free will exists for the individual at the same time he appears to be determined. The individual is free because there is no compulsion to act in a particular manner. However, how an individual does act is determined by the way in which information about the environment is processed. This process is predictable and thus appears to be determined.

7. Informational Holism as a General Scientific Theory of Consciousness

Informational holism is based on three fundamental hypotheses:

1. Consciousness is information.
2. The different forms of consciousness refer to different hierarchical levels of information.

3. The intensity of a particular state of consciousness is a function of the amount of information it represents.

The preceding section showed how informational holism could be utilized to account for each of the criteria for a scientific general theory of consciousness. The primacy of consciousness is a direct result of considering consciousness to be information. Information is knowledge. It is impossible to have knowledge without information. Information, like consciousness, is the source of all that we know.

Sensation refers to the basic level of information. The particular form and amount of sensation that an object experiences is a function of the structure of the object. Thus, the remarkable array of human sensory experience is a direct result of the discrete and complex way in which the human brain is structured.

Perception refers to a second level of information, information about sensations. This involves the interpretation of sensation in order to construct perceptions and is therefore consistent with psychological and empirical data that show the interpretive and constructive nature of perception. This hypothesis is also consistent with the data about habituation because the amount of information that results from the repetition and discontinuation of a stimulation parallels the experience of perceptual habituation.

Emotions refer to a third level of information that involves the interpretation of the meaning of a sensation. This hypothesis is consistent with the psychological data showing that a particular state of physiological arousal is compatible with a variety of emotional states depending on the context within which it occurs.

Affects refer to the rate with which uncertainty associated with the second level of information is altered (i.e., the first derivative of info 3). This hypothesis is consistent with the psychological findings that negative affects are associated with increasing amounts of uncertainty while positive affects are associated with decreasing amounts of uncertainty. This position is also consistent with the empirical data about the relationship between neurotransmitters and affects because neurotransmitters control the rate of uncertainty reduction occurring in the central nervous system.

Cognition and the nonrational forms of consciousness such as intuition and daydreams refer to complementary aspects of a fourth level of information. This hypothesis is consistent with empirical data about hemispheric specialization and psychological data showing that perceptions and sensations that are not cognitively processed will tend to occur in nonrational forms. This approach is also consistent with the psychological finding that cognition tends to occur only under situations of moderate uncertainty reduction because no information is generated without uncertainty or when uncertainty levels are too high to allow that uncertainty to be processed into cognitive information.

The fourth level of information provides awareness of the three lower levels of consciousness (sensation, perception, emotions) and thus unifies them into an experience that we commonly refer to as consciousness. This unification accounts for the phenomenological data about consciousness as a field.

Self-awareness refers to a fifth level of information. The hierarchical relationship between self-awareness and cognition explains the experience of free will. Free will exists from the perspective of self-awareness because a number of different alternatives for responding to a given situation exist. However, an individual will appear to be predictable and determined because he has learned to respond to a situation in a particular manner.

Unition refers to a sixth level of information that involves an awareness of the process of being aware. This is hypothesized to involve the synchronization of the entire cerebral cortex, as is suggested by EEG studies of this state of consciousness.

Informational holism thus provides the basis for a general theory of consciousness because it can meet all the criteria we established to define such a theory. Furthermore, the fact that it is possible to measure the amount of information in the brain makes this approach scientific because its basic hypothesis can be tested and verified.

8. Implications of Informational Holism for Our View of Man and the Universe

In this section we shall discuss the implications of informational holism for three fundamental questions:

1. Does consciousness exist apart from human beings?
2. What is the nature of reality?
3. What is the relationship of man with the universe?

According to informational holism, consciousness is information. Information is certainly not restricted to human beings and informational holism thus predicts the existence of nonhuman consciousness.

Sensation refers to the basic level of information that exists in all physical interactions. Informational holism thus predicts that the entire physical universe experiences sensory consciousness. However, the degree of sensory consciousness is predicted to be a function of the amount of information represented by the state of a particular object. This amount varies tremendously between inanimate and animate objects and among plants and animals.

Inanimate objects do not significantly alter their structure in response to a wide variety of environmental circumstances and thus extract little information from them. For example, a rock does not significantly change if a car goes by or someone speaks to it. Alternately, as we ascend the phylogenetic scale, living matter becomes more and more capable of responding to and distinguishing a large number of environmental states. While the amoeba may "sense" only that something is in touch with it, animals with a nervous system are capable of differentiating a remarkable array of stimuli. It is thus easy to see that although the entire universe experiences sensory consciousness, this experience is much more developed and intense in plants and animals higher up the phylogenetic scale.

Clearly, consciousness in nonhuman beings is not limited to sensation only. For example, all animals with even a rudimentary nervous system will form percepts (info 2). Furthermore, computers would be predicted to have perceptual consciousness according to informational holism. In fact, informational holism could be utilized to make predictions about the level of consciousness of all nonhuman objects.

An even more interesting prediction emerges from applying informational holism to objects such as groups and institutions that transcend traditional physical boundaries and are defined by their information-processing structures. Informational holism would clearly predict that groups have consciousness, thus giving credence to thinking of the mind and vitality of social organizations.

From my own perspective, the most interesting prediction of informational holism comes from attempting to apply it to the universe as a whole. It is impossible to develop a complete understanding of the universe as a whole because each individual is a part of it and any attempt to understand it will modify it. However, even given this limitation it is quite clear that it would make sense to talk about a seventh level of information that would involve the universe's experience as a whole and refer to the interaction and coordination of all of the lower levels of information. The implications of informational holism for spirituality and transpersonal consciousness is thus a very exciting area for further investigation.

Informational holism also has a number of exciting implications for the nature of reality. First, reality is neither singular nor objective. Rather, the universe is a unified whole that is hierarchically ordered into different levels of reality, each referring to a particular level of information. Information is inherently relational and involves the interaction of two structures, one serving as the source of data and the other as the receiver. Information is neither subjective nor objective. Subjectivity and objectivity refer to the relative hierarchical relationships between two interacting structures. A lower-level structure will appear objective, the structure interacting with that lower level will be experienced subjectively.

Thus, informational holism is holistic. It is neither dualistic nor monistic. Both dualism and monism are accepted as aspects of an integrated and unified system. There is no mind–body problem. Mind and body refer to different hierarchical levels of the same unified system. Many readers will recognize the relationship between informational holism and general system theory. In fact informational holism is based on the holistic paradigm that underlies general system theory (Battista, 1977). Informational holism can thus be considered to be a part of a unified general system theory of the universe.

Finally, let us consider the implications of informational holism for our view of man and his relationship to the universe. First, the lack of a sharp distinction between physical and conscious reality reveals that man is not separated from the world but is an integral part of it. Second, information theory reveals that the universe is structured so that it is constrained both from the bottom up as well as from the top down. This implies that man is both free and determined. Self-consciousness provides both freedom and choice at the same time it makes us aware of our determinism and finiteness. Furthermore, informational holism provides justification and meaning for concepts like the self and person. It allows us to develop a unified, holistic theory of man and our universe. I hope that you will join with me in attempting to explore the potentialities of this challenge.

References

Akisal, H. S., and McKinney, W. T. Overview of recent research in depression. *Archives of General Psychiatry*, 1975, *32*, 285–305.

Banquet, J. Spectral analysis of the EEG in meditation. *Electroencephalography and Clinical Neurophysiology*, 1973, *35*, 143–151.

Barr, H., and Langs, R. The psychoanalytic theory of consciousness. In *LSD: Personality and experience*. New York: Wiley-Interscience, 1972.

Bateson, G. *Steps to an ecology of mind*. New York: Ballantine Books, 1972.

Battista, J., The holistic paradigm and general system theory. *General Systems*, 1977, *22*, 65–71.

Battista, J., and Almond, R. The development of meaning in life. *Psychiatry*, 1973, *36*, 409–427.

Bindra, D. The problem of subjective experience. *Psychological Review*, 1970, *77*, 581–584.

Bohm, D. A suggested interpretation of the quantum theory in terms of "hidden variables." *Physical Review,* 1952, *85,* 166-179.

Breger, L., Hunter, I., and Lane, R. The effect of stress on dreams. In H. J. Schlesinger (Ed.), *Psychological Issues,* Vol. 7, New York: International Universities Press, 1971.

Brehm, M., Back, K., and Bogdonoff, M. A physiological effect of cognitive dissonance under food deprivation. In P. Zimbardo (Ed.), *The cognitive control of motivation.* Glenview, Ill.: Scott, Foresman and Company, 1969.

Brenner, D., and Kaufman, L. Visually evoked magnetic fields of the human brain. *Science,* 1975, *190,* 480-482.

Bruner, J. S. *Beyond the information given: Studies in the psychology of knowing.* New York: W. W. Norton, 1973.

Cowan, D. *Mind underlies spacetime.* San Mateo, Ca.: Joseph Publishing Company, 1975.

Dewan, E. Consciousness as an emergent causal agent in the context of control system theory. In G. Globus (Ed.), *Brain and conscious experience.* New York: Plenum Press, 1976.

Domash, C. The transcendental meditation technique and quantum physics. In. D. Orme-Johnson (Ed.), *Scientific research on transcendental meditation.* Vol. 1. Weggis, Switzerland: Maharishi European Research University Press, 1976.

Eccles, J. Brain and free will. In G. Globus (Ed.), *Brain and conscious experience.* New York: Plenum Press, 1976.

Einstein, A., Podolsky, B. and Rosen, N. Can quantum-mechanical description of physical reality be considered complete? *Physical Review,* 1935, *47,* 777-780.

Everett, H. Relative state formulation of quantum mechanics. *Review of Modern Physics,* 1957, *29,* 454-462.

Festinger, L. *A theory of cognitive dissonance.* Stanford, Ca.: Stanford University Press, 1957.

Feigl, H. *The mental and the physical.* Minneapolis: University of Minnesota Press, 1967.

Freud, S. The interpretation of dreams (1900). In J. Strachey (Ed.), *Standard edition.* Vols. 4 and 5. London: Hogarth Press, 1953.

Freud, S. Project for a scientific psychology. In M. Bonaparte, A. Freud, and E. Kais (Eds.), *The origins of psychoanalysis: Letters to Wilhelm Fliess, drafts and notes, 1887-1902.* New York: Basic Books, 1954.

Friedman, H., Becker R., and Bachman, C. Psychiatric ward behavior and geophysical parameters. *Nature,* 1965, *205,* 1050-1052.

Galin, D. Implications for psychiatry of left and right cerebral specialization. *Archives of General Psychiatry,* 1974, *31,* 572-583.

Gellhorn, E., and Kiely, W. Mystical states of consciousness: neurophysiological and clinical aspects. *Journal of Nervous and Mental Disease,* 1972, *154,* 399-405.

Globus, G. Consciousness and brain. *Archives of General Psychiatry,* 1973, *29,* 153-160.

Globus, G. The problem of consciousness. *Psychoanalysis and Contemporary Science,* 1974, *3,* 40-69.

Goleman, D. The buddha on meditation and states of consciousness. *Journal of Transpersonal Psychology,* 1972, *4,* 1-44.

Green, E. E., and Green, A. M. On the meaning of transpersonal: some metaphysical perspectives. *Journal of Transpersonal Psychology,* 191, *3,* 27-46.

Gurwitsch, A. *The field of consciousness.* Pittsburg: Duquesne University Press, 1964.

Hastorf, A., and Cantril, H. They saw a game: a case study. *Journal of Abnormal Social Psychology,* 1954, *49,* 129-134.

Holt, R. Beyond vitalism and mechnism: Freud's concept of psychic energy. *Science and Psychoanalysis,* 1967, *11,* 1-40.

Hubel, D. H., and Wiesel, T. N. Receptive fields of single neurons in the rat's striate cortex. *Journal of Physiology,* 1959, *148,* 574-591.

Huxley, T. *Evolution and ethics, and other essays.* New York: Appleton-Century-Crofts, 1893.

Inhelder, B., and Piaget, J. *The growth of logical thinking from childhood to adolescence.* New York: Basic Books, 1958.

James, W. *Pragmatism.* London: Longmans, 1907.

James, W. *The principles of psychology (1890).* Vol. 1. New York: Dover, 1950.

Jammer, M. *The philosophy of quantum mechanics.* New York: John Wiley and Sons, 1974.

John, R. A model of consciousness. In G. Schwartz and D. Shapiro (Eds.), *Consciousness and self-regulation.* New York: Plenum Press, 1976.

Kety, S. S. Brain amines and affective disorders. In B. T. Ho and W. M. McIssac (Eds.), *Brain chemistry and mental disease.* New York: Plenum Press, 1971.

Khinchin, A. *Mathematical foundations of information theory.* New York: Dover, 1957.

Klein, G. Consciousness in psychoanalytic theory. *Journal of the American Psychoanalytic Association,* 1959, *7,* 5–34.

Koestenbaum, P. The sense of subjectivity. *Review of Existential Psychology,* 1962, *2,* 47–65.

Köhler, W. *Dynamics in Psychology.* New York: Liveright, 1940.

Konorski, J. *Integrative activity of the brain.* Chicago: University of Chicago Press, 1967.

Kripner, S. Altered states of consciousness. In J. White (Ed.), *The highest state of consciousness.* New York: Doubleday, 1972.

Lashley, K., Chow, K., and Semmes, J. An examination of the electrical field theory of cerebral integration. *Psychological Review,* 1951, *58,* 123–136.

Libet, B. Brain stimulation and conscious experience. In J. Eccles (Ed.), *Brain and conscious experience.* New York: Springer-Verlag, 1966.

MacKay, D. Cerebral organization and the conscious control of action. In J. Eccles (Ed.), *Brain and conscious experience.* New York: Springer-Verlag, 1966.

MacKay, D. *Information, mechanism and meaning.* Cambridge: MIT Press, 1969.

Magoun, H. W. The ascending reticular system and wakefulness. In J. F. Delafresnage (Ed.), *Brain mechanism and consciousness.* Springfield, Ill.: Charles C. Thomas, 1954, 1–20.

Malamud, W. Dream analysis. *Archives of Neurology and Psychiatry,* 1934, *31,* 356–372.

Olds, J., and Milner, P. Positive reinforcement produced by electrical stimulation of the septal area and other regions of the rat brain. *Journal of Comprehensive Physiological Psychology,* 1954, *47,* 419–427.

Penfield, W., and Rasmussen, T. *The cerebral cortex of man: a clinical study of localization of function.* New York: MacMillan, 1950.

Peterfreund, E. Information, systems and psychoanalysis. *Psychological Issues.* New York: International Universities Press, 1971.

Place, U. Is consciousness a brain process? In V. Chappel (Ed.), *The philosophy of mind.* Englewood Cliffs, N. J.: Prentice-Hall, 1962.

Popper, K. R. Three views concerning human knowledge. In H. D. Lewis (Ed.), *Contemporary British philosophy.* London: G. Allen and Unwin, 1956.

Pötzl, O. Preconscious stimulation in dreams, associations, and images. *Psychological Issues.* Vol. 2. New York: International Universities Press, 1960.

Prange, A., Wilson, I, Lynn, C. W., Alltop, L. B., and Stikeleather, R. A. L-tryptophan in mania: Contribution to the permissive hypothesis of affective disorders: *Archives of General Psychiatry,* 1974, *30,* 56–62.

Pribram, K. *Languages of the brain.* Englewood Cliffs, N. J.: Prentice-Hall, 1971.

Pribram, K. Problems concerning the structure of consciousness. In G. Globus (Ed.), *Brain and conscious experience.* New York: Plenum Press, 1976.

Rapaport, D. On the psychoanalytic theory of motivation. In R. Jones (Ed.), *Nebraska symposium on motivation.* Lincoln: University of Nebraska Press, 1960.

Ring, K. A transpersonal view of consciousness: A mapping of farther regions of inner space. *Journal of Transpersonal Psychology*, 1974, *6*, 125–256.

Rosenblatt, A., and Thickstun, J. A study of the concept of psychic energy. *International Journal of Psychoanalysis*, 1970, *51*, 265–278.

Rubenstein, B. Psychoanalytic theory and the mind-body problem. In N. Greenfield, and W. Lewis (Eds.), *Psychoanalysis and current biological thought*. Madison: University of Wisconsin Press, 1965.

Ryle, G. *The concept of mind*. New York: Barnes & Noble, 1949.

Sarfatti, J. The physical roots of consciousness. In J. Mishlove (Ed.), *The roots of consciousness*. New York: Random House, 1975.

Satprem. *Sri Aurobindo or the adventure of consciousness*. New York: Harper & Row, 1968.

Schacter, S., and Singer, J. Cognitive, social and physiological determinants of emotional state. *Psychological Review*, 1962, *69*, 379–399.

Schacter, S., and Wheeler, L. Epinephrine, chlorpromazine and amusement. *Journal of Abnormal Social Psychology*, 1962, *65*, 121–128.

Schafer, R. Action: its place in psychoanalytic interpretation and theory. *Annals of Psychoanalysis*, 1973, *1*, 159–196.

Shallice, T. Dual functions of consciousness. *Psychological Review*, 1972, *79*, 383–393.

Sirac, S. P. The structure of consciousness. *Lecture given at Langley Porter Neuropsychiatric Institute*, 1975.

Sokolov, E. N. Neuronal models and the orienting reflex. In M. A. Brazier (Ed.), *The central nervous system and behavior*. New York: Josiah Macy Jr. Foundation, 1960.

Sperry, R. A modified concept of consciousness. *Psychological Review*, 1969, *76*, 532–536.

Sperry, R. Mental phenomena as causal determinants in brain function. In G. Globus (Ed.), *Brain and conscious experience*. New York: Plenum Press, 1976.

Stapp, H. P. The Copenhagen interpretation and the nature of space-time. *American Journal of Physics*, 1972, *40*, 1098–1115.

Stapp, H. P. Bell's theorem and world process. *Il Nuovo Cimento*, 1975, *29*, 270–276.

Stevens, S. S. *Psychophysics*. New York: John Wiley and Sons, 1975.

Taimni, I. *The science of Yoga*. Madras: Theoretical Society Press, 1961.

Tart, C. States of consciousness and state-specific science. *Science, 1972, 176*, 1203–1210.

Tart, C. *States of consciousness*. New York: Dutton, 1975.

Tart, C. The basic nature of altered states of consciousness: a systems approach. *Journal of Transpersonal Psychology*, 1976, *8*, 45–64.

Tiller, W. Consciousness, radiation and the developing sensory system. In *The dimensions of healing*. Los Altos, Ca.: Academy of Parapsychology and Medicine, 1972.

Tomkins, S. *Affect, imagery and consciousness*. Vol. 1. New York: Springer, 1962.

Walker, E. The nature of consciousness. *Mathematical Biosciences*, 1970, *7*, 131–178.

Walker, E. Consciousness in the quantum theory of measurement. *Journal for the Study of Consciousness*, 1972, *5*, 46–63.

Weil-Malherbe, H. The biochemistry of affective disorders. In R. Grenell and S. Gabay (Eds.), *Biological foundations of psychiatry*. New York: Raven Press, 1976.

Wigner, E. P. Epistomology of quantum mechanics. *Psychological Issues*, 1969, *6*, 22–36.

Wigner, E. P. The place of consciousness in modern physics. In C. Muses and A. Young (Eds.), *Consciousness and reality*. New York: Avon, 1972, 132–141.

Wilbur, K. Psychologia perenis: the spectrum of consciousness. *Journal of Transpersonal Psychology*, 1975, *7*, 105–132.

Wooldridge, D. *Mechanical man: the physical basis of intelligent life*. New York: McGraw-Hill, 1968.

PART II

Specific Theoretical Formulations and Links to Basic Research

4

The Stream of Consciousness: Implications for a Humanistic Psychological Theory

Joseph F. Rychlak

1. Introduction

The first time I read anything by William James was in an undergraduate philosophy course, where we were assigned selections from *Pragmatism* (James, 1907). He was never incorporated into my general psychology courses, but in time I did elect to take a history course and then read Boring (1950) to learn something about James as an historical figure. I had, of course, heard of him by way of the popular media and soon undertook to read his *The Varieties of Religious Experience* (James, 1928), which was then and still is prominently displayed on the popular bookshelves. By the time I was completing my undergraduate education, I had the impression of James as a remarkably insightful person, a man who was marvelously in touch with the human condition, but whose impact on the theoretical models then being advanced in psychology (*circa* 1953) was amazingly absent.

This was all the more surprising because if one read outside of strictly psychological sources James was continually being cited. His masterpiece, the *Principles of Psychology* (James, 1890) was included in the Great Books collection put together by Robert Maynard Hutchins (James, 1952, the edition to which we will henceforth refer). I was

Joseph F. Rychlak • Department of Psychological Sciences, Purdue University, West Lafayette, Indiana.

already out of graduate school when I tried to study this volume. It took me years to get through the book, reading off and on. Why this was true I cannot say, except of course that I had the modernist's prejudice that more recent research evidence had discredited his accounts of behavior. But, then, I was really not looking for research evidence in coming back to James repeatedly. I was looking for a—not new, but—different image of the human being than what psychology seemed to be committed to, an image that though implied throughout his writings is never specifically tied up and named in the way that he named the tough-minded versus the tender-minded types of psychologists. I was developing into a humanistic psychologist, and "knew in my heart" or in what James might have called the fringes of my understanding, that he too was such a psychologist. And I think I resented the fact that he had seemingly left the psychological context for philosophy without establishing a clear "school" of humanistic psychology that might have countered the functionalistic-behavioristic line then emerging in psychology.

Let me temper this slightly irrational annoyance by hastily adding that I was fully aware of his defense of a nonmechanical image of the person. His analysis of determinism and willingness to entertain a free-will hypothesis (see, e.g., James, 1965) clearly places him on the humanistic side of the ledger. But these efforts were primarily of a philosophical nature and hence no effort was given to actually applying such theory to a scientific research test. I had the nagging belief that even in his theoretical developments in the *Principles* (James, 1952) James was too ready to submerge his explanations in the biological underpinnings of the physical organism, although he rejected the reductive, molecular-model form of thinking in other contexts. It took me some years before I realized that biological formulations *per se* do not necessarily contradict a telic image of the person.

In time, with maturity, I began to appreciate that James was theorizing at the border regions between what have traditionally been called philosophical topics on the one hand and psychological topics on the other. He wanted a balance of the two, a comprehensive picture of the human situation, as did Wilhelm Wundt, for that matter (see Rychlak, 1977, chap. 3). It is now my view that due to its subtle catholicity Jamesian theory failed to capture the imagination of the experimentalists, who found it much easier to translate a narrowly mechanistic image of the person into their research designs. Actually, the direction here was the reverse (Rychlak, 1977, chap. 4). James had a conception of the human being *first* and he considered the research context to be something that followed, or that studied some aspect of this person but did not speak for all of him "at once." In other words, Jamesian thought is always cognizant of the difference between what is *theory* (metaphysical assumptions, etc.) and what is *method* (how such assumptions are tested). It is of extreme importance to recall that James understood and appreciated the views of Ernst Mach, and even cultivated a friendship with this prime mover of the "new physics" that was to culminate in Einstein's brilliant innovations (see Feuer, 1974, p. 41).

As Oppenheimer (1956) once told psychologists directly, modern physical theory is far more in tune with a telic, purposive image of the person than the Newtonian form of theorizing on which most of rigorous psychology is based. Rather than first analyzing the assumptions on the basis of which they then characterized "behavior," the psychologists of the first half of this century put their hopes on the scientific method to provide them not only empirical evidence but also a frame of reference—what has amounted to a metaphysics—within which to assess the merits of that which they presume to be "discovering." Thanks to their rejection of anything smacking of philosophical examination, the naive realism that has resulted from this behavioristic ideology has actually served to hold psychology back as a scientific discipline (Rychlak, 1977). Most psychologists today are embarrassingly unschooled in the fine points of theory construction. If only they had followed the example of William James!

It was my study of this new physics, the philosophy of science that stands behind it as assumptive grounds (Rychlak, 1968), that rekindled my interest in James. I can now see definite parallels between what I have been trying to do and what he was pointing toward, as an image of the person. Although I could not be said to have based my humanistic *logical learning theory* (Rychlak, 1977, chap. 8) on Jamesian principles knowingly, there can be no doubt that I have often been paddling in his wake. In a true sense, I have tried to test empirically some of the central points James was advancing concerning the nature of human mentation. There is no better example of his views on mentation than Chapter IX of the *Principles* (James, 1952), dealing with the stream of thought or consciousness. I would like to focus on the arguments of this chapter before surveying the major tenets of logical learning theory and some research evidence in its support. The drift of Jamesian thought can be seen most clearly in my work by following this line of presentation. First, however, we need to take up some theory-construction issues so that we can appreciate more clearly the humanistic polemic that James was advancing.

2. Some Theory-Construction Considerations

There are four interrelated but distinctive aspects of theory construction that we must first get in mind before analyzing the stream of consciousness conception: theory versus method, the nature of causation, the nature of meaning, and the Lockean versus Kantian models.

2.1. Theory versus Method

It may seem odd for a paper on theory to take up the question of method, particularly since we have already implied that methodological considerations are themselves predicated on metaphysical (i.e., theoretical) assumptions. Does this not mean that theory is uppermost, the foundation of all else, and hence that it can be discussed at its own level and without regard for method? I do not subscribe to this view, because I know that what we speculate on theoretically is enlarged *or not* based on the kind of methodological test that we put to our speculations. Although theory and method are two somewhat different conceptual activities, they *always* must be considered in preliminary fashion before setting one or the other aside for didactic purposes. And we must be cognizant of the interplay between these dual aspects of the scientific effort.

A *theory* is the stipulated, implied, hypothesized, "believed-in," etc., relationship existing between two or more conceptions (constructions, abstractions, terms, labels, etc.). Psychologists are prone to get very technical about this term, putting down all sorts of restrictions on what it means to theorize "scientifically," but I identify this process with thought itself. As Conant (1952) once noted, the habits of thought used by the scientist are really no different than the habits employed by the caveman (p. 40). These are logical habits, in which thought is predicated by assumptions that tie "this" item (clouds) to "that" item (rain) and arrive thereby at a theoretical hypothesis (rain follows when certain types of clouds assemble).

But, now, it is in the putting to test of such theoretical hunches that we specifically delineate what a scientist does in addition to what all men do, every day. A *method* is the means or manner by which we submit our theoretical hunches to test. The most usual method is purely cognitive or conceptual, involving the plausibilities of common sense or procedural evidence (Rychlak, 1968, p. 75). We all must proceed on the basis of what seems plausible to us, what meets our overall grasp of experience. We went on procedural evidence when we believed the world to be flat. This met our everyday understanding most sensibly, and hence it seemed a preposterous stretch of imagination to claim the earth was spherical. We also employ procedural evidence in the tautological proofs we make of mathematical derivations. Logical consistency or the coherence theory of truth is also a manifestation of procedural evidence. Ultimately, procedural evidence is what we mean by metaphysical assumptions, arguments from definition, or even "theoretical proofs" of a proposition.

Science was to add a more strict criterion of proof in its research method, employing validating evidence. To validate we put down a prescribed succession of events, through so-called control and prediction manipulations, and then see if the outcome is as we have said it would be, based on some criterion measurement (Rychlak, 1968, p. 77). This places an additional burden on the scientific theoretician, because now he cannot argue to what is plausible and coherent, but must design an experiment, a "trial run" in which his claims on reality must correspond to the empirically observed outcome (sometimes called a correspondence theory of truth). Saying that "redheads are hotheads" based on a tautological inference between red fire and hotheadedness is one thing; proving it is another! But, as any laboratory experimenter knows, it is frequently difficult to think up a design to prove something that everyone already knows to be true. The two activities, theorizing and methodologizing, lean in slightly different directions even though they are anchored in the same soil.

2.2. The Nature of Causation

Our next theory-construction issue gets more specifically to the way in which we explain anything. Explanation involves description, and it is essential that in describing something we relate it to something else (as per our definition of theory, above). As Meyerson (1930) has shown most clearly, the theoretical description encompassing an explanation invariably comes down to a relation of identity between that which one takes as a standard, principle, or assumption and that which one is attempting to explain. Today, thanks in large measure to Kuhn (1970), we call this predicating standard a paradigm, but other terms such as model, schemata, construct, etc., are also used to describe this descriptive process.

Probably the oldest set of theoretical paradigms against which other things and events were to be explained is Aristotle's theory of the *four* causes. He did not "think up" these causes, because they were presaged in the theories of earlier philosophers. But he formalized what was already in use and pulled together what I consider to be the most powerful theory of knowledge ever formulated. In another context, I have organized and tabulated the major constructs of over one hundred thinkers across history, subsuming them under one or more of the Aristotelian causes (see Rychlak, 1977, chap. 1).

What are these four causes? First, there is the *material* cause, a substance conception that, when acting as grounds against which to theoretically account for something else we have an emphasis given to the "stuff" of which things are made. Genetic, biological, and physiological theories place heavy emphasis on the material cause. Next, there is the *efficient* cause, which gets at the obvious fact that things are organized, moved along, constructed, and so on, by some thrust or impetus over time. A weather pattern is made to happen thanks to differential atmospheric pressures, an organism grows thanks to energic expenditures, and a house gets built by the manipulation of certain objects brought together into a sum total.

A third cause is the *formal*, by which Aristotle captured the fact that we know things through the form they take on. Humans have certain forms and animals have others. Even a windstorm, whipped by efficient causes into a certain level, can be seen taking the well-known form of a funnel cloud and hence we know at this point that a tornado is upon us. The last cause that can act as a principle of explanation is the *final*, by which Aristotle meant "that, for the sake of which" a thing exists or an event takes place. The "that" in this case may be thought of as the purpose or intention. When we employ the final cause we frame a teleological (or telic) theory of whatever it is we are attempting to explain (*telos* is from the Greek, meaning the end or reason involved with objects or events).

2.3. The Nature of Meaning

In speaking of how we theoretically describe something by relating it to a precedent "given," we have already touched on what the meaning of meaning is. Meanings are by their nature relational ties. In fact, *to mean* has Anglo-Saxon roots that convey "to intend," so that something has meaning if it reaches purposively for—symbolizes—a relational tie to something else. This symbolical conception of meaning is clearly telic. Of course, our psychological models today do not hold to this symbolical, expressive interpretation of meaning. They take philosophical precedents from British empiricism, which utilizes a principle of association (based on frequency and contiguity considerations) to account for meaning and meaningfulness in purely mechanical terms, as a sign function rather than a symbolical expression (Langer, 1948, p. 46). According to this view, an item has meaningfulness depending on how many other items to which it has been associated, and the specific meanings taken on depend on which other items have been bonded to it in this purely efficient-cause (i.e., nontelic) process of being attached or hooked-up via frequency and contiguity factors.

Now, it is right here that a major distinction in meaning can be made. Are words or images as meaningful items *always* and *only* unipolar referent points, becoming tied to other unipolar referent points in some fashion (either automatically or intentionally, as the case may be), or are certain meanings *already* bipolar in designation once framed by a reasoning intellect? Just where a theorist stands on this question stamps him as either *demonstrative* or *dialectical* in outlook. Demonstrative theoreticians lean in the direction of unipolarity and dialecticians view (at least certain) meanings to be bipolar in nature (Rychlak, 1976). It was Aristotle who drew this distinction between the two styles of approaching meaning, and he did so in order to undermine the theory of knowledge that Socrates and Plato had held to before him. This theory suggested that all knowledge was united by the oppositionality of meanings so that it was possible to work one's way over from one side to another by following a dialectical process of "questions and answers," as exemplified in the Socratic dialogues. Beginning our line of investigation in error, we could come to know truth, because ultimately as opposites truth and error were intrinsically related (one and many thesis).

Aristotle considered such verbal exchanges as Socrates carried out to be mere exchanges of opinion. His theory of knowledge stressed beginning a line of discourse in the known truth, based on what he called "primary and true" propositions, tautologies or the hard facts of observation, as the case may be (see Rychlak, 1968, chap. IX). One cannot begin a line of study in error and come to know truth. Error breeds only error. Rather than believing that all meanings are ultimately interrelated, the demonstrative reasoner seeks to delineate the true from the false according to a discrimination between unipolarities. He follows the so-called law of contradiction (A is not not-A) rather than the one and many thesis.

It is important to note that Aristotle was talking about how *all* human beings reason (think, theorize, etc.), so that he never intended to say that anyone could reason exclusively demonstratively or dialectically. Human beings reason both ways, but if they wish to be rigorously correct in their understanding they have to regularly move from dialectical machinations—reasoning by opposites—to the more ironclad, unidirectional procedures of demonstrative reasoning.

2.4. Lockean versus Kantian Models

It is possible to pull together the causes and interpretations of meaning into two contrasting models, using John Locke and Immanuael Kant as prototype historical figures to name these stylized outlooks (see Rychlak, 1973, pp. 10–11 for a schematization). The men or their specific philosophies are not what are important. We could use other historical figures, such as Democritus for Locke and Plato for Kant, and it is even possible to see this contrast in outlook in Eastern philosophies such as the comparison between Confucius and Mo Ti (see Rychlak, 1976, 1977, for many such examples). What is important is the general style of conceptualization and resultant explanation achieved through use of these models.

The *Lockean* model is a constitutive formulation, seeing things as being made up of smaller units into bigger units in a simple-to-complex fashion. Meanings are combined in this fashion as well, so that they always accrue from below. What something means depends upon what goes to make it up as a fabric of unipolarities brought together into a connected totality. Often this totality is viewed in quasi-mathematical fashion, as calculated or at least calculable. The unipolar (atomic) building blocks of Lockeanism for behavioral description are always material and/or efficient causes. Any over-riding patterns (formal causes) to be observed in behavior are *in principle* reducible to underlying associative ties of an efficient-cause nature (typical stimulus–response conception of "lawfulness"). The pattern *qua* pattern is not an essential ingredient of the explanation. We must reduce the "constituted" pattern to its underlying "true" determinants.

The Lockean model is framed from a third person or *extraspective* theoretical perspective, so that in accounting for behavior we speak about influences on "that, over there," rather than on "me, I, self," and so on. The source of direction on the organism is always placed unidirectionally (demonstratively) from an antecedent in the environment (including biological and genetic factors) *to* the organism's mental processes *to* a consequent output or response of some type. In other words, there is no self-direction or true choice of alternatives on this model. The Lockean model is a nontelic formulation of events. In the recent trend to "cognitive" psychology we supposedly get a self-direction type of theory based on the organism's capacity to mediate, organize, and encode (see Neisser, 1967). However, there is no fundamental change in the theory under espousal from what had been developed earlier by Tolman and others. Locke (1952) himself discussed how the *tabula rasa* intellect is first given (efficiently-caused) inputs from early experience and then probabilistically uses these earlier experiences to modify later behaviors according to a principle of frequency (p. 369). Hence, it makes no difference whether we speak of current stimulus–response (S–R) connections forming demonstratively to send an organism along life's way, or we refer to earlier connections of this sort now acting as mediators (including feedback mechanisms). The fundamentally unidirectional, antecendent-to-consequent thrust of events over time is still the characteristic mechanism of a Lockean model.

The *Kantian* model is a conceptual formulation in which the organism is said to behave "for the sake of" a predicating assumption or schemata (categories of the understanding). Rather than *tabula rasa* the mentation of this organism is *pro forma,* selectively organizing that which it knows by actively bringing cognition to bear. This thrusts our attention to a first-person or *introspective* theoretical perspective, for as theorists we are now describing things from the viewpoint of an "I" or "me" that behaves in what is clearly a telic fashion. As such, the Kantian formulation places great emphasis on the formal and final causes. It is not the antecedent stimulus or the input that efficiently causes the organism to behave, but rather the patterning (formal cause) of the conceptual categories that organize sensory stimulations and endow them with the meanings for the sake of which (final cause) the organism then intends its behavioral line.

The organism *must* play an active, conceptualizing role in experience because much of the experiential input from the environment is framed within bipolar meanings. This requires the conceptualizing organism to "take a position" on the nature of its perceived reality rather than simply responding to it. Reality is not to be understood in "one" way but rather has "many" ways to be grasped. This is a predicating and not a mediating mentality. And even when a position is taken vis-à-vis reality this mentality is cognizant of the reverse stand, as an implication, possibility, or potential alternative. There is a self-reflexivity involved in mentation, so that the organism can reason dialectically from what is to what is not, and in this manner transcend the unidirectional (material and efficient) causes of experience in hopes of turning things around to its *intended* aims, aims that are not "in reality" but that might truly be created by a telic intelligence working toward its chosen ends.

3. The Stream of Consciousness as a Humanistic Model of the Person

We can now review Chapter IX of the *Principles* (James, 1952) in light of our theory-construction rubrics. In doing so, I specifically hope to show how James draws out a telic, humanistic image of the person by employing the implied outlines of a dialectical conception even as he skirts a direct reference to this important heuristic schemata (Rychlak, 1976).

James (1952) begins Chapter IX by challenging the belief that mental ideas are composed of sensations (p. 146). Sensations just do not occur as singular items, so we cannot believe that they have a constitutive role to play in the formation of ideas. He goes on in an introspective and idiographic vein to emphasize that thoughts and feelings are always had by individual selves. Psychology has no right to question the existence of personal selves (p. 147). This question of whether a person can bring to bear some form of (Kantian) influence onto his line of behavior, or, whether he is strictly an environmentally controlled mechanism is still very much with us, as witnessed in the recent exchange between Bowers (1973) and Mischel (1973). James (1952) is clearly challenging the assumptions of a Lockean model, and in the next few paragraphs he even names Locke (p. 150) to show how this model's presumption that the bodily sensations that supposedly summate as ideas is open to severe criticism.

Ideas are not simply constituted of bodily sensations in building-block fashion, since they take on variegated forms in expression. They do not step *"before the footlights"* (James, 1952, p. 153) of consciousness at periodical intervals, but are clothed in different verbal attires and enacted from altering perspectives without losing their identity in meaning expression. This discussion is also remarkably modern, for one can read Neisser (1967) today on the new approaches in cognitive psychology and find him advancing a comparable argument as well as referring to James in support of it (p. 94).

Continuing his attack on what we would consider a demonstrative theory of behavior, James (1952) next observes that consciousness is not best described as a series of bits and pieces, aligned in a unidirectional row akin to a "chain" or a "train" of mental events (p. 155). Borrowing from the Heraclitian metaphor (p. 151), he then proposes to speak of consciousness or thought as a stream (p. 155). And here, we suggest, is the first clear borrowing from the dialectical heritage. Heraclitus was a dialectician, who in suggesting that we never step into the same river twice was actually voicing the one and many thesis (refer above). His point was that, as with the ideas before the footlights, though a river changes its constituent nature at any given point of reference from moment to moment (many), it retains the *identity* of a river (one) at all times. We never fail to recognize the river *qua* river amidst the changing circumstances of its nature.

Even though the dialectical metaconstruct adapts well to those psychological characterizations that James took an interest in, such as free will (see Rychlak, 1977, p. 64 and p. 91), the sophistry that he perceived in dialectical philosophical arguments like those of the Hegelians (James, 1952, p. 107) and others seems to have turned him away from this theory-construction alternative. We cannot even call James a purely Kantian theorist, for there are many Lockean themes in his writings (see, e.g., his treatment of free will, James, 1952, p. 819). In pragmatism we find a philosophy closely aligned with British empiricism. We might sum it up by calling James a Yankee philosopher, who sought to frame things as simply and clearly as possible, without that complexity of German idealism so typical of the Continental philosophies that kept the dialectic alive. We would therefore consider James a mixed-model, Lockean-Kantian theoretician, as was Freud (see Rychlak, 1973, chap. 4, for a discussion of mixed models). Even so, there are striking dialectical formulations in the chapter under review, as when James next speaks of the experiencing of thunder:

> Into the awareness of the thunder itself the awareness of the previous silence creeps and continues; for what we hear when the thunder crashes is not thunder *pure,* but thunder-breaking-upon-silence-and-contrasting-with-it. (James, 1952, p. 156)

James's (1952) next metaphor for the activity of thought is that of a bird, which flits about, alternating between flights and perchings (p. 158). For centuries, dialecticians had characterized thought in this fashion, as moving from thesis-point to antithetical-point and thence to a synopsis or synthesis-point, but of course James was not being influenced by this theoretical precedent. The view of thought as moving from periods of action to stopping places along its course had been expressed by Charles S. Peirce in 1878 and Henri Bergson in 1889 (Simon, 1970, p. 69 and p. 72), and since these men are both admitted sources of influence on James we can presume that this is the line from which he took direction.

James (1952) next goes on to distinguish between the sensationalists and the intellectualists. The sensationalist theorists tend to remove feelings (emotions) from mind, as in the example of Bain, who had limited the flow of thought to ideas and the relations between ideas (p. 159). The intellectualist theorists have also taken the position that feelings do not enter into mentation, if indeed they exist at all. But, for James, feeling relations are central to the course of thought. And here we observe a tendency that I think all humanists share, that is, to ascribe meaningful significance to something called emotion, feeling, or affection in human affairs. These are not simply "drive" or "motivational" terms to the humanist, who views the idiosyncratic and even subjective mood of the individual as a major aspect of life. People live within an aura of their personalized feeling tones that introduces an element to their behavior having no direct, efficient-cause tie to environmental input. They have a uniquely personal commentary to make on what happens to them, a physiological appraisal as Arnold (1970, p. 174) has called the emotion, which may or *may not* go along unidirectionally with the valences of environmental input. For example, some individuals are offended by displays of consideration from others so that what is a positive reinforcement on commonsense grounds may be an aversive stimulation granting the emotive uniqueness of the individual who is receiving this attention. And offended parties can pretend otherwise, covering up (dialectically) their negative evaluation of the actions aimed at "positively reinforcing" them.

James (1952) next builds on his fixed-fluid description of thought by using a kaleidoscope metaphor. The brain is said to pulse and exchange levels of tension at nonuniform rates, much as the patternings of the multicolored glass in a kaleidoscope shift abruptly and unpredictably with each slight turn of the visual screen. The fixed points ("bird perchings," to mix metaphors) James called substantive and the flow of movement ("bird flights") he termed transitive states. The brain is therefore always in a state of change and differentially so in different regions (pp. 159–160).

Though I do not recall seeing it drawn before, there is a striking parallel between the Jamesian effort to conceptualize abrupt shifts from given points to given points in thought, and Niels Bohr's efforts to account for the fact that the particular orbit that an electron takes around the nucleus of an atom is similarly abrupt in changing and totally unpredictable. The electron clearly does not follow an efficiently caused, unidirectional course but jumps from one orbit to another—and avoids others altogether!—in what is truly a kaleidoscopic manner. As is well known, Bohr (1934) proposed his stationary state theory of subatomic particles to deal with this otherwise inexplicable phenomenon (p. 108), focusing on the altering patterns (formal causes) and de-emphasizing thereby the processes of uniform change (efficient causes) that Newtonian physics had so relied on. In fact, as if to underscore the arbitrariness with which these particles seemed to "behave," Bohr even suggested the following:

> We are here so far removed from a[n] [efficient-] causal description that an atom in a stationary state may in general even be said to possess a free choice between various possible transitions to other stationary states. (Bohr, 1934, p. 109)

Now, the fascinating thing about Bohr's theorizing is that he apparently relied (at least in part) on a Kierkegaardian *dialectical* conception of change to ground his explanations. Kierkegaard had rejected the typical natural science explanation of change as inadequate to account for human (psychic) development. Rather than moving through life by unidirectional change, being impelled along by a uniform progression of efficient causation, Kierkegaard held that life moves from one fixed *stadia* to another by way of abrupt changes, due to the operation of a qualitative dialectic that altered the patterns (formal causes) for the sake of which (final causes) human beings anchored their existence. Feuer (1974) has shown how Bohr's teacher and friend, Harøld Höffding, deflected this dialectical conception of change into the former's thinking, culminating in that peculiar type of explanation now employed in subatomic physics (p. 135). Once again, we have a clear example of how Jamesian thought meshes beautifully with dialectical formulations, so long as we are cognizant of the subtleties in theory construction. (For a more thorough discussion of Kierkegaardian change see Rychlak, 1977, chap. 6).

The reference from Bohr on free will is apropos, because after making some further criticisms of the Lockean constitutive model James (1952) now begins to reveal the telic propensities of his theorizing. He says that we all have this "feeling" of what direction our thoughts are taking (p. 165), a faint brain process that he calls a psychic overtone, suffusion, or *fringe* (p. 167) that gives us knowledge about objects or events rather than mere acquaintance with them. James then moves on to a discussion of meaning, something that all teleo-humanistic theorists place great emphasis on. Meaning, he says, is the topic of a thought or the conclusion arrived at during the substantive parts of the stream's progress (p. 168). Note that in this theoretical development emphasis is being put on the *end* of thought rather than on its instrumental processes.

By "end" I mean the given meanings that one arrives at during the stopping places, and for the sake of which behavior is then enacted. I would like to describe this as a predicating rather than a mediating conception of mentation. Whether we arrive at our predicating points logically or illogically, according to a unidirectional progression of implications or a flighty and inconsistent derivation, the point of importance is what something *means* given that a predication has been affirmed rather than the way in which this meaningful "conclusion" has been arrived at. Meaning is a (formal-final) cause of what is to occur after it has been framed or affirmed, because that is how a predicating (premising) intellect "works."

Psychology after James put its emphasis on the Newtonian concern with *process*, often voiced as "it is not *why* things occur (i.e., meaning) but *how* they occur that the scientist must account for." As we noted in our theory-construction discussion above, the mediational models of today do not require that meanings play a unique role in the course of behavior. Meanings are signs, fed into the organism's processing equipment as (efficient-cause) *effects*. They are never truly originating sources of control because it is impossible for the organism to lend *new* meaning to what is input. Cybernetic reasoning is not creative reasoning because there are no truly symbolical alternatives open to the succession of events termed "behavior."

Having now put meaning forward as a central construct, James returns to his other humanistic emphasis—that is, mental feelings—to argue that certain psychic overtones are emotive in nature (James, 1952, p. 171). Feelings provide a continuing context within which words take on altered significations. Some thoughts are more fringed with emotion than others (p. 175). Thinking is like a special algebra, in which the relationship between terms (formal cause) is more important than what is specifically put down as a symbol system. In addition, human thinking is self-reflexive, so that knowing that he knows the person tends to play the role of psychologist on himself (p. 177). Here again, a dialectical rationale would have aided the Jamesian development, since the ability to turn back on what one is thinking and realize that one could be thinking otherwise is a basic tenet of the Kantian notion of transcendence (by way of the transcendental dialectic in reason).

In playing the psychologist we are likely to commit the *psychologist's fallacy* (James, 1952, p. 180), which involves making up explanations of, for example, what thinking "must be" like rather than introspectively capturing what our thought is without such presumptive bias. Pretty soon, rather than focusing on the original thought, we are voicing thoughts about this thought, and introducing conceptions that have nothing to do with the original mentation. Hence: "What a thought *is*, and what it may be developed into, or explained to stand for, and be equivalent to, are two things not one" (pp. 180–181). This tendency to criticize psychological analyses of phenomenal events by characterizing them in some preconceived, arbitrary fashion that then robs them of their spontaneous and essential nature I have called the *purity* criticism (Rychlak, 1968, p. 390). Humanistic psychologists are especially prone to level purity criticisms at mechanistic formulations (see Rychlak, 1973, chap. 12).

An especially galling form of the psychologist's fallacy is made today by a large proportion of the experimentalists who claim to speak for rigorous psychology. This has to do with what we mentioned in the introduction above as the tendency to confound what is a theoretical with what is a methodological activity. It so happens that the scientific method of manipulating an independent variable (IV) to watch its relational "effects" on a dependent variable (DV), given that extraneous factors (control variables) are frozen out of the picture, assumes the superficial appearance of an efficient-cause determination. In actuality, the IV–DV relationship is a purely mathematical one—a formal cause!—introduced by way of Leibniz's function construct and later refined by Dirichlet (Rychlak, 1977, chap. 1). It does not speak to the nature of the causal tie that might *actually* account for an observed, lawful relationship between the two variables. However, thanks to generations of identifying the IV with the stimulus (S) and the DV with the response (R), psychologists have routinely equated these two conceptions and even defined them synonymously (see English and English, 1958, p. 578).

The upshot is that even if a humanistic psychologist formulates his theory in terms of an empirical test, designs an experiment to give it proper evaluation, and then finds empirical evidence *in support of* his telic construct he is trapped into the S–R theorist's language. The assumption is that he has found an S–R regularity or S–R law, because he found an IV–DV regularity. Actually, to speak of S–R laws is to confound language, because lawfulness is best thought of as methodological terminology and the S–R construct is simply one of several theories that might account for the observed IV–DV regularity. The confounding of S–R with IV–DV is made possible because of the efficient-cause metaconception that subsumes both regularities in the minds of too many modern psychologists. If we had followed James's admonition in the psychologist's fallacy we would not have been so likely to slip our arbitrary theoretical templets (S–R) over our observed experimental regularities (IV–DV) and read the latter as reflecting *only* the former, thereby effectively negating all chances of capturing the spontaneously *telic* nature of most human behavior.

James (1952) goes on to underscore the importance of choice in thought (p. 185). Mentation is selective and preferential, so that to reason is to break up the total into various parts and then to pick out from among the many those that in our particular life circumstance lead to the most helpful, proper conclusion (p. 186). Although not mentioned in this chapter, James was to refer to the "cash value" of ideas. This again suggests a more Kantian, bringing-to-bear of predicate assumptions (conclusions) that have value for the person as he "behaves for the sake" of them. Perception is more like noticing what is there for the noticing than it is receiving that which is automatically input. Another important feature of mentality underscored by James is the fact that it is constantly alive to possibilities by way of alternatives (p. 187). He ends Chapter IX on this note, stressing that each individual conceptualizes the world somewhat differently (arbitrarily), and that even though there is considerable agreement among people as to what has value and what does not, the fundamental (dialectical?) splitting of experience into *me* and *not-me* ensures that idiographic (subjective) differences will occur, because: "Each of us dichotomizes the Kosmos in a different place" (p. 187).

4. Logical Learning Theory and the Jamesian Tradition

As noted in the introduction, I have for some time now been developing a view of behavior termed "logical learning theory" in which I employ both dialectical and demonstrative formulations to sketch a more Kantian human image than is currently available in extant learning theories. Since I submit my teleological conceptions to empirical test, I have termed this a "rigorous humanistic psychology" (Rychlak, 1977). Furthermore, I now suggest that logical learning theory meets William James's polemical recommendations, that it takes his stream-of-consciousness view of mentation seriously, and if we are prepared to acknowledge the unnamed dialectical features of his Chapter IX documented above, that we have here one variation of Jamesian psychology "alive and kicking" today. I would next like to list the basic tenets of logical learning theory, elaborating on them to some extent, and then move on to the closing section in which we briefly survey the research evidence in support of this view.

1. *Human mentation is pro forma and not tabula rasa.* As James appreciates, the essence of meaning is that it involves an organization of relations into pattern. Indeed, even so-called "lawful behavior" is a patterning of actions into meaning. Due to its Lockeanism, modern psychology places the directing origin of all such behavioral patterning in the environment (situation, learning context, etc.), which etches a determination on the initially *tabula rasa* intellect. In time the human being can use some of these early etchings as mediational aides. Logical learning theory contends that human behavior is predicated by inborn and hence unlearned capacities to pattern experience (see point 6). The mind predicates rather than mediates, behaving in a *pro forma* fashion to lend and extend meanings to experience rather than simply process them in an input–output fashion.

2. *Human behavior is not only responsive, but also telosponsive.* By restricting human actions to the concept of "response(s)," psychology

has prejudiced the case in favor of efficient causation. The stimulus–response theoretical construct, including such variations as input–output or antecedent–consequent, is the *sine qua non* of efficient causality. As an antidote to this prejudicial terminology, which is so frequently confounded with the language of method (refer above), logical learning theory proposes the construct of telosponsivity in human affairs. A *telosponse* is the person's taking on of (i.e., premising, predicating) a meaningful item (image, word[s], judgmental comparison, etc.) relating to a referent acting as a purpose for the sake of which behavior is then intended (Rychlak, 1977, p. 283). Thus, in describing how a subject would leave a room, rather than speaking of his responses made to a door stimulus, logical learning theory would suggest that the door (item) is predicated meaningfully (doors as concepts have a certain purpose) and then this meaning is intended in the behavioral patterning to follow of "leaving the room."

3. *Premises are affirmed precedently, and the meaning predicated thereby is brought forward sequaciously.* The term "precedent" refers to being first in order without consideration given to the supposed passage of time. This holds true in syllogistic reasoning, for example, where the major premise is precedent to both the minor premise and the conclusion without therefore requiring that the passage of time in any way influences the succession of meaning-extension along the way. Time passage (efficient causality) is irrelevant to a logical patterning (formal causality). The term "sequacious" means that what follows in meaning-extension is "slavishly compliant" upon what has gone before in the predication. Hence, in telosponsivity mentation is seen to occur in the form of granting *this* (precedent) *that* necessarily follows (sequaciously). As James pointed out, what is important in the flow of thought is the predication arrived at—he called this a conclusion—because the meaning-extension carried out in behavior depends upon this rather than how it was framed initially (refer above). Even an illogical predication, impulsively arrived at, can have cash value in the behavior to follow.

4. *Thought is arbitrary, thanks to its dialectical nature.* As already suggested above, it is our view that the stream metaphor is compatible with a dialectical formulation of the thought process. Whereas James emphasized the transitive (fluid) aspect of mentation, logical learning theory emphasizes the more substantive aspects of this admittedly dynamic process (Rychlak, 1977, chap. 8). It seems to us that as basically telic phenomena thoughts fix a *given*—an end the Greeks called it or James's so-called conclusion—in what the individual affirms as that believed-in or preferred or hoped for. Mind serves a conservative role by ordering life experience in this fashion. Of

course, new circumstances force thoughts to consider new items but always in terms of the already known (fixed) meanings. Furthermore, since the thinker can dialectically alter the grounds for the sake of which behavior is intended, it is possible for behavior to be arbitrarily grounded. This takes us to our next point:

5. *Free will is not only possible but a necessary aspect of human behavior.* Free will is a nontechnical or popular way of referring to the capacity that telosponding organisms have dialectically to alter the meanings that they affirm as premises in the course of behavior (meaning-extension). We are free organisms to the extent that we can rearrange the grounds for the sake of which we are determined. Grounds are patterned organizations taken on precedently. Before affirmation of a grounds we can speak of freedom, and after affirmation we can speak of will(-power) in the meaning-extension to follow sequaciously. Free will is therefore a necessary outcome of the bipolarity in meaning, and the fact that predications can be and often are arbitrary. James did not treat free will in this fashion due to his disdain for the dialectic, but his recognition of thought's self-reflexive nature waited only on such dialectical rephrasing in order to be brought into line with the present interpretation. Note that in the sequacious conception we have a form of necessity ascribed to behavior, a *telic determinism* to parallel the determinations of mechanistic psychology. Mechanistic determinisms are "blind" because they are *not* predicated. Hence, teleology is not inconsistent with scientific determinism so long as we are prepared to extend our deterministic conception to other than efficient causes. What determines the course of a cloud in the sky is not solely what determines the course of a person, though both cloud and person are determined natural objects.

6. *Affection must be distinguished from emotion.* Here we have another deviation from strict Jamesian terminology, although the difference I believe is more apparent than real. As we have seen, James insisted that emotions or feelings entered into the relational ties of thought that created meaning. Logical learning theory finds it instructive to distinguish between *affections* or affective assessments, which are transcendent telosponses (i.e., self-reflexive acts that put sensory experience and even telosponsivity itself to preferential evaluation) and *emotions*, which are bodily based feelings. It is our view that much of what James considered to be "felt meanings" were in fact affective assessments, purely mental organizations of thoughts according to what seemed good or liked or even "right" to incline toward at the fringes of consciousness.

This mental inclination is more akin to "feeling" one's way along a darkened passageway than it is to literally "feeling" a bodily process, which can no more "step before the footlights" as a discrete entity than can ideas. Such bodily processes (feelings, emotions) are undoubtedly active at all times in behavior, but what we incline toward intuitively or prefer to further is something occurring totally within mind. There is a telic capacity to judge the preferred direction, hence to choose one type of meaningful organization over another for furthering (meaning-extension), which does not wait on bodily sensations *per se*. As noted under 1. above, this is not something that is learned by the individual. We are born with this telic capacity to put experience to affective assessment, and further thereby one direction of meaning-extension more readily than another.

Emotional promptings are never arbitrary once active, even though we may name them arbitrarily depending upon what situation we are in or how we see things falling into place as an emotion is upon us. As the James-Lange theory actually expressed it, first we react bodily and *then* we sense the emotion (James, 1952, p. 743). Emotions "have us" rather than vice versa. Even a supposedly positive emotion such as sexual arousal can be evaluated by some individuals as negative (improper, frightening, etc.) based on precedent affective attitudes. We have essentially a mind-body issue here, with affection on the side of the former and emotion on the side of the latter. It goes without saying that *both* affection and emotion are highly important to behavior.

7. *The course of precedent-sequacious meaning-extension follows a principle of tautology*. Psychology has so far overlooked an important principle of learning in banking as it has exclusively on the frequency and contiguity principles of the Lockean model. Though statistics as all logic ultimately reduces to the patterned consistency of a tautology, psychologists have grossly underestimated the importance of this way of learning (or not learning) more about what we know, i.e, of extending what we predicate to sequaciously understand what we then experience. Thus, the *tautology* is a (meaningful) relation of identity between items considered either (a) extraspectively as redundant (e.g., "a rose is a rose"), or, (b) introspectively as the premised meaning being extended from what is known to what can be known (e.g., "that has a rose quality about it").

Examples of the tautology range from the repetitive rigidity of the stereotype to the partial identities of analogy, metaphor, allegory, and synechdoche. Even more complexly, pure dialectical relations are tautological since one pole of the meaning necessarily enters into the definition of the opposite pole (one and many thesis). Hence, logical learning theory rests solidly on the fact that tautologies as patterned relations enter into all of human understanding and put it to fixed order. The brain seems to be such an organizing, patterning organ that also attains a certain hemispheric organization in time (Sperry, 1966).

James (1952) also recognized that human beings think by way of a tautological process in which "*a* is *a, b, b*" (p. 299). He termed this the "sense of sameness" but employed the concept with the idea that, although the verbal expression might be different in one part of the stream of thought than another, the successive portions of this mental stream: *"can know that they mean the same matters which the other portions meant"* (p. 299). The mind can always intend, and know when it intends, to think of the same conception. Indeed, the mind also constructs permanent conceptions that it employs repeatedly (p. 300). In logical learning theory we view this as the most distinctive role played by mind, emphasizing the continuity and singularity (the *one*) of conceptualization rather than the changes (the *many*) that take place in time due to meaning-extensions of an analogical or metaphorical type. It must never be forgotten that analogies and metaphors are relations of *partial identity*, thus having both a tautological side (the direct parallel drawn) plus a dialectical opposition in what contrasts to the identity. As such they too participate in that mental sense of sameness that James properly alluded to.

5. Empirical Validation of Logical Learning Theory

When we turned to the methodological context in order to validate our line of theorizing, we referred to the operationalized measure of affective assessment as *reinforcement value* (in the interests of space, specific experiments will not be cited; see Rychlak, 1977, chaps. 9 and 10 for a review of the more than 50 experiments that have been conducted). This is a judgment made by subjects of whether they like or dislike materials that they are subsequently asked to memorize, recognize, or otherwise deal with in an experimental task. The like-dislike decision is viewed as the result of dialectical processes in which certain items are organized one way and others another way. A differential idiographic meaning is generated based upon the affective assessment of the person. Ratings are taken from subjects twice, with from several minutes to several days lapsing between testings. Although we have studied the ambivalent ratings of learnable items, most of our work has dealt with materials that have been reliably liked and/or disliked (i.e., rated in the same direction on both occasions).

The first prediction we needed to make was: Which meanings would be more readily extended in a learning task, the liked or disliked? Logical learning theory contends that it depends on what has been predicated in the task at hand. If the task consists of materials that are positive in reinforcement value, then these should be extended more readily than disliked, and vice versa. Since it was impossible to say globally what consonant-vowel-consonant trigrams (nonsense syllables) referred to—that is, they could not be said to circumscribe some one body of meaning such as baseball, or Italian cooking, or Biblical stories—we surmised that the individual would use a self-evaluation as grounds for the sake of which the idiographically unique meanings of the trigrams would be extended. Since we presumed that most people liked themselves, the earliest experiments predicted that liked trigrams would be learned more readily than disliked trigrams. This was established in paired-associates and free-recall formats without a hitch, and readily extended to lists of unrelated words (i.e., words that also did not refer clearly to a global realm of understanding). The tautology in this instance might be put into the formula, LIKED (self) = LIKED (trigrams).

But if this were true then the reverse formula of DISLIKED (self) = DISLIKED (trigrams) should also hold. Our next group of studies was conducted on both hospitalized abnormals (primarily schizophrenic diagnoses) and normals with weak self-images as determined by empirical testing. As logical learning theory predicts, we found that abnormals and normals with weak self-images did indeed narrow the "positive reinforcement-value effect" in learning, or reverse it entirely. We were in time to suggest a view of abnormality in which the maladjusted person is pictured as premising more and more of his life negatively relative to the extension of positive meaningfulness, functioning according to a quasi-Malthusian principle. The normal has a reverse style of coming to know experience, whereby liked predications follow a geometric progression and the disliked meanings expand at an algebraic rate (speaking figuratively, of course).

The clearest test of this view of abnormality came when we had the *same* subjects learn words relating to two circumscribed realms of meaning, either close interpersonal relations with peers *or* relations with authority figures. These subjects had indicated a problem ("hang-up") in one of these areas and a sense of complete confidence in the other. After making reinforcement-value ratings of these words they learned some of them in a free-recall format (i.e., they rated many words from among which lists were constructed for memorization). It was found that subjects learned along positive reinforcement value in their competency area but that they *reversed* in their problem area and actually reached criterion more readily for disliked than liked words. It made no difference which of the areas was a strength and which was a weakness. This study established for the first time that predication and not just self-evaluation was involved in the affective learning process.

We also found that even if a subject dislikes being a subject in an experiment, this negative predication of the situation can be reflected in the meaning-extensions of his learning style. Subjects who volunteer and enjoy the experience extend along the positive, and nonvolunteers who expressly try to avoid it learn along the negative. The nature of the task can also have an influence. Thus, if subjects are given a negative reinforcement (as sounding a chime) when they fail to recall the second member of a paired-associates couplet, as opposed to being positively reinforced like this when they *do* correctly recall it, the line of meaning-extension goes according to predictions. Disliked materials are extended more readily under conditions of negative reinforcement and vice versa for liked materials. It is obvious that "external reinforcers" are no more relevant here than the "internal evaluation" contributed by the subject. To account for such findings traditional theories must fall back on a patchwork of mediation theorizing. They have to suggest that the past "reinforcement history" of a subject is what serves to discriminate when a negative reinforcement will be more or less negative—and vice versa for positive reinforcements. Logical learning theory speaks directly to what is observed and measured. It does not require a theoretical elaboration of what is *unobserved* in order to retain its descriptive integrity.

When findings on reinforcement value are presented to what James called the tough-minded critic they are always explained away through efforts to "reduce" them to underlying frequency and contiguity factors of one type or another. For example, the claim is made that people learn what they are familiar with more readily than what they are unfamiliar with. Hence, if a subject rates something as liked and then grasps it more readily in a task than something disliked, this just means that he has sorted things out into easy–hard based on past familiarity (the reinforcement history again!). The advocates of logical learning theory spent years conducting over one dozen experiments, including cross-validating factor analyses, to show that reinforcement-value ratings *cannot* be reduced to or accounted for by the typical verbal-learning measures of meaningfulness such as familiarity, ratings of wordlikeness, frequency in the standing language structure, pronounceability, imagery, or even straightforward ratings of easy versus hard to learn (see Rychlak, 1977, chap. 9). I do not think we changed any minds in the tough-minded group. As James pointed out, it is just plain impossible for many psychologists to believe that mentation receives an influence from affection (or is it emotion?) that is not itself a product of some mechanistic underpinning. I sometimes think that they have confused their scientific role with that of being a "sound" person generally. Since emotional people often are impulsive and unreliable, a science that admits emotions (we would say affections) to the mind will of necessity be tender-mindedly unreasoned and intemperate. This seems to be their attitude.

The question of predication or grounding has always been important in our researches. In one study we had subjects first rate a number of life situations for reinforcement value, such as getting up in the morning, setting out on a long driving trip, going to the beach, and so on. Later, we asked these subjects to write a short story with these scenes framed as topic sentences. It was found as predicted that when subjects liked a situation they wrote stories that were judged by blind raters to be generally positive in tone and vice versa for disliked situations. We also hypothesized that a subject's general personality style should act as a grounding for the meaning of various words relating to his personality. We in fact found that when dominant subjects learn dominant word meanings they reach criterion on their liked dominant words more rapidly than their disliked, but that there is no such positive reinforcement-value effect to be seen in their learning of submissive words. And there is a reverse finding for submissive subjects, who partial out their learning on submissive words according to the positive reinforcement-value effect, but who do not do so when learning dominant words.

We have found that learning disliked verbal materials previous to liked materials results in significant (nonspecific) *positive* transfer taking place across tasks, but that reversing the order and moving from a liked to a disliked task results in little positive or actual *negative* (nonspecific) transfer occurring. I have even wondered whether the theories of formal discipline that James's former student, Thorndike, thoroughly discredited were not in fact covert reflections of affective assessment. Assuming that most students disliked Greek or Latin more than they did history, mathematics, or literature the observed improvements taking place from the former to the latter could be due to affection. Logical learning theory would suggest that the premise for the academic task has shifted here, from "disliked task [hard to do]" to "liked task [easier to do]" and therefore the overall effectiveness of meaning-extension is different. Rather than furthering *error* (disliked meanings) more readily than accuracy as in the study of Greek, the students would be "learning" accurately in those studies such as history or mathematics that they favor. I have found over the years that students often equate courses that are easy with courses that they like, and that they really are unable to say "why" this is the case or what makes a course likable. If we take the meaningfulness afforded by affection seriously, it does not matter "why" something is liked or disliked. As with James's talk of coming to a conclusion (refer above), it really does not matter what the grounds are for making the affective assessment, just so that it *is* made.

There is another point here concerning the concept of reinforcement. Logical learning theory views this as primarily a methodological term, where it is relatively easy to "operationally define" a reinforcement in terms of sounding chimes or saying "uh humm" following a subject's actions. Explaining what this term means theoretically is another matter, and a highly confused one in modern psychology. Even so, in a neo-Jamesian spirit we can define reinforcement theoretically as occurring when the learner's predicated affirmations are successfully extended. Positive reinforcements further meanings that are rooted in positive premises, and negative reinforcements further meanings that are rooted in negative premises. To paraphrase James, reinforcement is the cash value of a predication, paid in positive or negative coin! This means that human beings do *learn error*. The error variance is just as much predicated as the central tendency. The stream of consciousness is not a demonstrative process in which "to learn" means only "to learn as the instructor would have you learn." It is a highly personalized dynamic of learning according to what is uniquely predicated and the affective process enters into this—*not* acquisition, but—extension of meanings in both a positive and a negative (telic) direction.

There are some fascinating ethnic and social-class differences to be noted. Black subjects and Mexican-Americans, as well as lower socioeconomic subjects of any ethnic identity, are more likely to fall back on affection in their learning styles than control groups composed respectively of whites, Anglo-Americans, or middle-class subjects. Our explanation of these findings rests on the question of identity. To the extent that a subject feels outside of the main thrust of a society—or, put another way, removed from ready identification with the values of that society—to that extent will he fall back on the purely innate ability he has to order experience affectively and learn in this completely natural (i.e., unlearned, innate) fashion rather than according to the intellectualized discriminants of the broader verbal community.

It should not be thought that our work has been limited to the more contrived and removed designs of the laboratory. In one instance we made a movie of quasi-IQ subtests based on the format of the Wechsler Intelligence Scale for Children [WISC], and then had seventh and eighth grade children rate these for reinforcement value in the typical fashion. We found that the children scored roughly five IQ points higher on a prorated WISC for liked than for disliked subtests. Of course, once again, to the typical laboratory psychologist this can only mean that these children were more motivated to do well on liked than disliked tests, that they tried harder and paid better attention to the former than the latter, and so on, all of which boils down to our familiar frequency-contiguity account of behavior. Since we have dozens of studies proving that the reinforcement-value variable *cannot* be accounted for by such factors, I am no longer impressed by these stylized, tired disclaimers of a legitimate role for affection in learning.

No, I would rather step back across the decades and read William James, a psychologist of human nature whose lead was not followed into this century, but whose example is still there for us to ground our understanding in terms of. It is my personal hope that the present volume will not only rekindle interest in James, but that his example will strengthen the confidence of psychologists who might be willing to begin thinking about behavior in telic fashion. We do not have to agree with every theoretical concept that James put forward in order to take inspiration from his work. As he frequently noted, even though our specific concepts may differ across our respective streams of thought, an identity is possible in that we might share a common intellectual tradition. It is in this sense of sameness that we all *do* step into the *same* Heraclitian river, again and again.

References

Arnold, M. B. (Ed.), *Feelings and emotions*. New York: Academic Press, 1970.

Bohr, N. *Atomic theory and the description of nature*. Cambridge: The University Press, 1934.

Boring, E. G. *A history of experimental psychology*. 2nd ed. New York: Appleton-Century-Crofts, 1950.

Bowers, K. S. Situationism in psychology: An analysis and a critique. *Psychological Review*, 1973, *80*, 307–336.

Conant, J. B. *Modern science and modern man*. Garden City, N. Y.: Doubleday Anchor, 1952.

English, H. B., and English, A. C. *A comprehensive dictionary of psychological and psychoanalytic terms*. London: Longmans, Green and Co., 1958.

Feuer, L. S. *Einstein and the generations of science*. New York: Basic Books, 1974.

James, W. *Pragmatism: A new name for some old ways of thinking*. New York: Longmans, Green & Co., 1907.

James, W. *The varieties of religious experience*. New York: Longmans Green & Co., 1928.

James, W. *The principles of psychology*. New York: Holt, 1890. Also in R. M. Hutchins (Ed.), *Great books of the Western world*. Vol. 53. Chicago: Encyclopedia Britannica, 1952.

James, W. The dilemma of determinism. In D. Browning (Ed.), *Philosophers of process*. New York: Random House, 1965.

Kuhn, T. S. *The structure of scientific revolutions*. 2nd ed. Chicago: The University of Chicago Press, 1970.

Langer, S. K. *Philosophy in a new key*. New York: Penguin Books, 1948.

Locke, J. *An essay concerning human understanding*. In R. M. Hutchins (Ed.), *Great books of the Western world*. Vol. 35. Chicago: Encyclopedia Britannica, 1952.

Meyerson, E. *Identity and reality*. New York: Macmillan, 1930.

Mischel, W. Toward a cognitive social learning reconceptualization of personality. *Psychological Review*, 1973, *80*, 252–283.

Neisser, U. *Cognitive psychology*. New York: Appleton-Century-Crofts, 1967.

Oppenheimer, R. Analogy in science. *American Psychologist*, 1956, *11*, 127–135.

Rychlak, J. F. *A philosophy of science for personality theory*. Boston: Houghton Mifflin Co., 1968.

Rychlak, J. F. *Introduction to personality and psychotherapy: A theory-construction approach*. Boston: Houghton Mifflin Co., 1973.

Rychlak, J. F. (Ed.), *Dialectic: Humanistic rationale for behavior and development*. Basel, Switzerland: S. Karger AG, 1976.

Rychlak, J. F. *The psychology of rigorous humanism*. New York: Wiley-Interscience, 1977.

Simon, Y. *The great dialogue of nature and space*. Albany, New York: Magi Books, Inc., 1970.

Sperry, R. W. Brain bisection and mechanisms of consciousness. In J. C. Eccles (Ed.), *Brain and conscious experience*. New York: Springer-Verlag, 1966.

5

The Dominant Action System: An Information-Processing Approach to Consciousness

Tim Shallice

1. Introduction

For 50 years theory in hard-core areas of Anglo-American psychology remained frozen into behaviorist and neo-behaviorist paradigms. In the thaw of the last 10 to 15 years the explanation of the existence and properties of consciousness has reemerged as an acceptable and important problem for cognitive theory. A wide diversity of views has been put forward but those cognitive psychologists who have discussed these issues have almost all accepted a materialist position and attempted to explain consciousness and its properties by using information-processing theories of human cognition (e.g., Miller, 1962; Hochberg, 1970; Atkinson and Shiffrin, 1971; Shallice, 1972; Posner and Klein, 1973; Mandler, 1975).

The theories put forward by cognitive psychologists in recent years have tended to contain three core concepts: the organized nature of conscious experience, its limited capacity, and its control function. These are intuitively appealing concepts as they correspond firstly to the organized nature of perceptual experience—for instance, as exemplified in the ideas of the Gestalt school—secondly, to the relatively limited nature of the contents of focal awareness when loosely contrasted with the multitude of processes occurring at any time in the

Tim Shallice • Department of Psychology, The National Hospital, Queen Square, London, England.

nervous system, and thirdly, to the way that this conscious "tip of the iceberg" seems related to the most important events occurring around one and to the crucial actions one is carrying out.

Theorists may be classified according to which of these properties they see as most central, the other properties being in some sense deducible from it. Thus, the first property is central, for instance, to Hochberg (1970), Turvey (1974), Allport (1977), and Marcel and Patterson (1977). They argue that conscious perception is dependent upon the successful matching of a constructed model of the world with a trace of the "passively processed" sensory input. In Turvey's terms the operation of hierarchically organized banks of perceptual analyzers, operating in a cascade mode as in Pandemonium (Selfridge, 1959), provides only "tacit knowledge." "Explicit knowledge" depends on a constructive process and a successful match with the stored tacit knowledge. The artificial intelligence literature provides strong theoretical reasons for assuming that such matching processes are important in perception (e.g., Sutherland 1973). Yet, as Kahneman (1973) has pointed out, one is normally aware of mismatches with expectations, not with matches. We hear the clock stop, but habituate to its continuing ticking. The relation between such matching processes and consciousness is therefore at best problematic. I will return to this point later.

The limited capacity notion has been most obviously applied in the ideas of such theorists as Atkinson and Shiffrin (1971) and Erdelyi (1974) that consciousness corresponds to the contents of a short-term memory (STM) system of limited capacity. In some versions, such as Mandler's (1975) approach to STM as an attentional process, the concept of control follows from the limited capacity short-term memory system being an all-purpose one analogous to Broadbent's (1971) "address register" used in all high-level cognitive operations. For reasons developed elsewhere (Shallice, 1975, 1978), I consider that the evidence from memory experiments put forward in support of such a high-level system is better explained in terms of a number of relatively peripheral specific purpose short-term memory stores. The most crucial evidence is neuropsychological. Severe damage to a short-term memory system can occur without major cognitive impairment (Shallice and Warrington, 1970, 1977b). If one assumes that short-term memory stores are relatively peripheral systems, there is no particular reason to assume that they have important control functions. In addition, neither input nor storage of information in such short-term memory systems need produce a conscious experience, as testified by the ability to answer questions to which one had not originally attended, experimentally corroborated (at a very peripheral level) by

Eriksen and Johnson (1964) and by the insensitivity of incidental, auditory-verbal, short-term memory capacity to the difficulty of a secondary task (Bartz and Salehi, 1970; Shallice, 1975). However, it will be argued later that this approach captures certain of the aspects of consciousness in that the contents of short-term memory stores form part of what William James (1890) described as "the background of consciousness."

An alternative limited-capacity approach has been adopted by Posner and Klein (1973) and Posner and Snyder (1975), who have argued that consciousness reflects the use of a high-level, limited-capacity processing system. As this approach has much in common with the following one, it will not be separately discussed.

The final approach, adopted by me in a previous paper (Shallice, 1972), is to begin with the concept of control, not organization or limited capacity. The unitary aspect of conscious experience is then derived from the control aspect, the organizational aspect being seen as a general property of nervous system organization orthogonal to the problem of consciousness. Consciousness is presumed to arise as an evolutionary answer to the problem of ensuring that at least one action or thought process has control of all the musculature and mental machinery it requires in order to be successfully carried out.

My earlier paper had the aim of constructing a relatively simple model that would enable the conceptual problem of the relation between phenomenological and information-processing theories to be concretized. Since the relevance of conscious experience as a problem for information-processing theory is now widely accepted, this chapter will be concerned with elaborating the original model to deal more adequately with empirical phenomena. The theory will be developed dealing first with action, then with cognition, and finally with perception. Empirical evidence will then be considered. Finally, more detailed phenomenological correspondences will be discussed.

2. Dominance among Action-Systems

2.1. Competition between Potential Actions

It is now standardly accepted that the multitude of our potential actions are controlled by a complex multilevel system with the higher-levels controlling the operation of the action over larger intervals of time and space than do the lower levels (e.g., Pew, 1974; Turvey, 1977). The higher level contains a more abstract representation of the action and does not predict the exact consequences of any instruction sent to the lower levels, the particular way in which its instructions are executed being "unknown" to it. Thus, the systems involved in the highest level control of skilled piano playing would contain no quantitative information of the signals actually sent to the finger and arm muscles, the principle of "executive ignorance," to use Turvey's term.

It is now also widely accepted that control does not operate entirely hierarchically; it is obvious that many feedback circuits exist (e.g., Gibbs, 1970). However, the cybernetic problem of the control of multiple simultaneous actions is made more difficult not less by the presence of feedback, so this chapter will be concerned merely with simple hierarchical systems.

The highest level of control of skill is now thought to be mediated by a set of motor schemas or motor programs that can be executed with a wide variety of initial limb positions and local environments; thus, one's signature looks much the same however or wherever written. In Bernstein's (1967) terms such high level programs are concerned much more with the spatial pattern of the movement than with its metric properties. I will term them action-systems; they receive input from perceptual systems and send output to effector systems; damage to them would give rise to the higher forms of apraxia such as ideational apraxia.

What would happen if two incompatible actions are motivated by separate aspects of the world? An obvious example is that of talking and eating. A slightly more complicated one is that of a relatively inexperienced driver in an old-fashioned car who has to cope with a situation in which both changing gear and signaling by means of hand signals are roughly equally induced. The two actions require different and conflicting movements to be made with each hand. One action must be executed in its entirety or neither action can be carried out. What must be avoided at all costs is for the two hands to be controlled by separate action-systems. The nervous system does indeed avoid it. As Bullock and Horridge (1965) point out, "The most careful observation of animal behaviour has repeatedly emphasised the lack of such maladaptive cancellation and the reality of a unity of action at any moment." The standard physiological mechanism proposed to ensure this is reciprocal inhibition, but at what level does it need to operate?

If the selection were to be carried out at the higher level alone, then this would require either that only one action could be carried out at a time or that the full specification of the potential effector requirements of each action-system be available to ascertain which potential actions were compatible. Since we frequently carry out more than one action—we can walk and talk—provided that neither is too difficult, the former alternative can be ruled out. The latter, besides breaking Turvey's principle of "executive ignorance," would produce severe overload especially when many actions are available or when the effector systems used by an action-system change rapidly.

The alternative of selection occurring at the lower level seems practicable provided some way of assessing the importance (and practicability) of obtaining the goal of each action is available to the lower level of each system. One obvious means is available, namely for the "strength" of the signal transmitted to the lower level to be a measure of its importance, with the lower level obeying only the stronger signal. This would be analogous for the motor system to the way that the rate of firing of a cortical cell in the perceptual system is dependent on the similarity between the stimulus and the cell's "trigger feature." Yet, if two tasks were roughly equally important then either there would be a mutually inhibitory stand-off or, given noisy transmission, the stronger input to two lower-level systems could derive from different action-systems that would lead to chaotic responding.

It seems therefore that selection needs to occur at both levels. The danger of roughly equally strong signals being transmitted from the higher level can be resolved by ensuring that in normal circumstances one action-system is much more strongly activated than all others; that action-system is then described as being "dominant." A less strongly activated action-system can then control effector-systems presumably less efficiently provided that there is no conflict of its requirements with those of the dominant system.

That this cybernetic problem is not just theoretical is shown by the split-brain organism. In the first few weeks after surgery, patients who have received a sectioning of the corpus callosum for relief of epilepsy can produce conflicting movements. Smith and Akelaitis (1942) report two such cases. One patient "performed curious antagonistic reactions, such as attempting to put on an article of clothing with the right hand and pulling it off with the left." The other "displayed persistent movement antagonisms for a short period after the operation, such as picking up a deck of cards, putting it down and picking it up." Related observations have been made by Gazzaniga, Bogen, and Sperry (1962) and by Logue, Durward, Pratt, Piercy, and Nixon (1968). Double-volitional activity has also been shown in split-brain animals (Trevarthen, 1965). Thus, subcortical structures, by themselves, do not ensure coherence of action; this must be produced cortically, where the suggested dominance property would be mediated.

This split-brain difficulty recedes a few weeks or months after the operation, but at a considerable cost, as the patient appears unable to maintain reasonable levels of activation in both hemispheres (Trevarthen, 1974; Kinsbourne, 1974). It appears that the subcortical systems that control the general levels of activation of the hemispheres are limiting activation to one or other hemisphere; activation is not spread between both. The unity of volitional activity is then retained, but cognitive flexibility is much reduced.

2.2. Competition between Central Processes

The standard position in modern neuropsychology is that cognitive processes are carried out by a large number of anatomically distinct units each of which has a definite microfunction. Thus, units involved in spatial, arithmetic, higher-level visual-perceptual, short-term memory and language functions are all dissociable. Moreover, many are internally differentiable. For instance, performance on the Block Design subtest of the WAIS can be impaired at a central level by both right parietal and left parietal damage, the former mediating the spatial mapping aspects of the task and the latter, possibly, the executive aspects (Warrington, 1969).

In addition, it is possible to model relatively overlearned cognitive tasks as the operation of cognitive programs—say, as Newall and Simon's (1972) production systems—that utilize fixed special-purpose units (e.g., Newall, Shaw, and Simon, 1958; Miller, Galanter, and Pribram, 1960; Newall and Simon, 1972). For instance, one such unit, the auditory-verbal short-term memory store, can be used in language comprehension programs (Baddeley, 1976; Saffran and Marin, 1975; Shallice and Warrington, 1977b), as a maintenance store in rote rehearsal routines (Craik and Watkins, 1973; Shallice, 1975), or for arithmetic operations (Baddeley and Hitch, 1974).

At the higher level, then, an analogous cybernetic problem to that of competing actions can arise if more than one action-system—as cognitive programs will also be called—requires the use of the same special-purpose cognitive unit. Thus, arguments for a dominance relation between action-systems carry over directly from skills to thought.

2.3. Competing Percepts

The dominance situation concerning competing percepts has both similarities to and differences from that of competing thoughts and actions. Treisman, Sykes, and Gelade (1977) have, in fact, already put foward a somewhat related argument for perception. They point out that there is now much evidence that at the more peripheral levels of the perceptual system, different attributes or dimensions of the stimulus are processed in parallel by different analyzers (e.g., Hawkins, 1969; Saraga and Shallice, 1973; Garner, 1974). How, then, if two stimuli are presented having different values on more than one dimension, do the appropriate values become reintegrated in the final percept? How, for instance, do we perceive a green square and a red triangle as such and not as a red square and a green triangle? These authors suggest that such stimuli are processed serially so as to ensure perceptual coherence and not because of any limitation on the number of elementary analyzers. Their experimental findings support the view that when searching for a multidimensionally defined target that cannot be discriminated from all other stimuli using any single dimension, that processing is (spatially) serial. Such seriality of perceptual processing, it could be argued, arises out of the need to prevent illusory detection of targets when their component dimensions are physically present in spatially distinct nontarget stimuli.

Strong supporting evidence that seriality of processing over stimuli in different spatial locations arises from an active process comes from a neuropsychological source, namely, the syndrome of "attentional dyslexia" (Shallice and Warrington 1977a). When more than one word is presented simultaneously, patients with this difficulty are apt to make visual Spoonerisms. Parts of words are actually "seen" in the corresponding parts of other words. This is most plausibly interpreted as due to a failure to ensure active inhibition of the results of the lower-level processing of stimuli other than that being identified at that instant. Similar segmentation errors occur in normal subjects when identifying words under pattern masking (Allport, 1977; Shallice and McGill, 1978), which suggests that the normal inhibitory process takes time to operate.

In action and cognition it is necessary for reasons both of flexibility and of integrating separate subskills that seriality be partial not absolute. There is an even more obvious reason why strict (spatial) seriality would be inappropriate for the higher levels of the perceptual system, namely, the need to ensure that "interrupts" by newly occurring highly salient stimuli are possible.

I will therefore adopt a view of parallel processing in perception based on the ideas of Laberge (1975) and Treisman, Sykes, and Gelade (1977). Lower levels of the perception system are assumed to operate spatially in parallel. At a somewhat higher level, the level of the shape classification units damaged with right parietal lesions (Warrington and Taylor 1973), the amount of attentional selection a unit requires will be assumed to depend upon both its familiarity and complexity. Stimuli such as letters may, at this level, be processed in parallel, as suggested both by the findings of Egeth, Jonides, and Wall (1972) on the invariance of the speed of discriminating a number from a background of letters and by the existence of segmentation errors. However, for stimuli as complex as faces or words, mainly serial processing seems more likely. Higher levels still, where meaningful identification of the percept occurs, and which are impaired in associative agnosia (Lissauer, 1890; Warrington, 1975) will be assumed to operate according to the dominance principle, namely that only one "recognition unit" can be strongly activated at any time. This fits with the position of Treisman et al.; it will be justified further later. If identification of spatially distinct stimuli is predominantly sequential, an attenuating filter (Treisman, 1960) becomes important to prevent confusing overload of the identification unit.

2.4. The Creation of Dominance

It has been argued that both actions and cognitions result from the operation of a highly flexible set of programs (termed action-systems) on a large but limited set of effector devices and cognitive units. The coherence of thought and action, it has been claimed, requires the dominance principle, namely, that only one action-system should be strongly activated at a time. The function of ensuring dominance could be allocated to a specific system separate from the action-systems as, for instance, Laberge's (1975) attention center or Kahneman's (1973) effort system. Alternatively, the function could be performed by the action-systems themselves as in my approach (Shallice, 1972) and that of Walley and Weiden (1973). There are, in fact, two systems anatomically distinct from action-systems that have some claim to carry out "attention-center" functions: subcortical structures often conceived of as mediating attention (e.g., Milner, 1970) and frontal lobe systems considered to mediate planning (Luria, 1966; Shallice and Evans, 1978). There is, though, a problem about how two such systems would interact.

Whatever system performs this function, how would it carry it out? One possibility would be for a (necessarily separate) system to order action-systems in order of the priority of their use at any instant and then allocate to the compatible ones of highest priority the effector and cognitive systems they require. Yet, if such priority ordering were performed serially, given the large number of action-systems a human must have available, reordering of priorities would be far too slow to cope with the frequent, sudden, and crucial changes that can occur in an environment.

A relatively simple parallel system is, though, available. If the importance of each action-system operating (together with its practicability) can be measured by a single variable, its salience, then it is necessary to ensure that a mapping of salience on to activation is achieved that makes the most salient action-system much more activated than any other; in other words, that it is dominant. This is the type of problem described by Maruyama (1963) as the "Second Cybernetics," namely, the problem of magnifying potentially small differences.

From study of sensory systems (e.g., Ratliff, 1965) mutual inhibition is well known to increase contrast. It has been used at higher levels as the basis for explaining focal attention in the closely related models of myself (Shallice, 1972) and of Walley and Weiden (1973). In my approach, dominance is ensured by following Maruyama's general prescription for difference—amplifying systems, namely, by incorporating positive feedback. It is assumed in line with cell assembly theory (Hebb, 1949; Milner, 1957) that the salience of action-systems is mediated by the firing of a particular assembly, which is internally self-exciting; if it alone is stimulated at above a certain rate, its cells will fire at an increasing rate to maximum firing. If, however, all the assemblies mutually inhibit each other and inhibition is less powerful than activation at low levels of activation and more so at high, then the dominance property can be shown to follow mathematically, given certain simple mathematical assumptions (see Shallice, 1972).

There are problems with this very simple model (see Appendix). However, it can be adapted so that at any instant only one system is strongly activated and some others are weakly activated; the stronger the dominant system is activated, the weaker the other ones would be. The dominant system controls all of the effector units it requires. The weakly activated ones can control any other effector or cognitive units. Moreover, if it be assumed along with Kahneman's (1973) notions of effort, that the more complex and unfamiliar a skill then the more highly activated an action-system needs to be to control it, then it will follow that subdominantly operated action-systems can only mediate simple or highly overlearned tasks.

2.5. Empirical Evidence for the Dominance Mechanism

A model of this generality, whose subcomponents are not operationally defined, is clearly not simply falsifiable. Theoretically one would need to compare single and dual task performance on two tasks of which one has complete models of the subject's performance; the tasks themselves would need to require totally different cognitive and effector units and to operate at different levels of difficulty. Even this would not necessarily allow a satisfactory test of the overall model. For instance, different levels of effort (Kahneman, 1973) may operate in the single and dual task situation. Such a prescription is, in any case, impracticable. Instead, the model's plausibility will be examined on two levels, the relevance of activation and reciprocal inhibition as psychological constructs and the general suitability of the dominance model for explaining the control of competing actions and thoughts.

That activation and inhibition are relevant concepts on the physiological level is too obvious to require support. Yet, at least two types of evidence show that these physiological concepts have psychological relevance. Hillyard, Hink, Schwent, and Picton (1973) showed that if observers are attending to a particular ear, the N_1 wave of the evoked potential to a tone in that ear was 30 to 40% larger than if they were attending to the other ear. This strongly supports the position taken earlier that attenuation filtering (Treisman, 1960) occurs in attention and that this involves a reduction in activation above a certain point in the perceptual system. Moreover, another part of the evoked potential, namely, the P_3 wave occurring 300 to 400 msec after stimulus onset, is larger when the stimulus is a target stimulus, when it is unexpected and obtrusive, when it provides knowledge of results, or when the stimulus has to be compared with another stimulus (Hillyard and Picton, 1977). Activation in some high-level system, measured physiologically, correlates with a psychologically relevant variable. Indeed, Posner (1974) has argued that the P_3 wave is a correlate of conscious experience. Hillyard and Picton (1977), more conservatively, regard it as a correlate of target identification under what Broadbent (1971) has described as "response set." It would follow from the arguments on consciousness advanced in a later section that these are isomorphic descriptions, provided the subject's task requires dominant action-system control.

A second way in which activation as a physiological concept is psychologically relevant derives from Kinsbourne's (1975) experiments on the way priming a particular hemisphere by a cognitive operation, that is primarily mediated by it, improves visual discrimination based on the appropriate half-field. Thus, a secondary speech task, primarily mediated by the left hemisphere, leads to better gap discrimination in the right than in the left half-field. This is most plausibly explained in terms of a general activation of left hemisphere systems.

If we turn to the complementary roles of activation and reciprocal inhibition as means of selecting the most activated action-system, the suggested mechanism has a close analogy in MacKay's (1970) model for the production of low-level speech errors. He argues that speech motor units at both syllabic and phonemic levels are preprimed for a phrase and output results when a broad-band scanning device activates further the units that are due to be produced at about that time. Singleness of response is ensured by reciprocal inhibition between units. From the model a number of the properties of Spoonerisms and of stutterers' errors can be explained. For instance, the tendency for phonetically similar phonemes to interchange can be explained as resulting from the way by which activated units corresponding to similar phonemes also tend to activate each other by a spread of activation principle. So the chance that a similar phoneme occurring later in the word is produced by mistake is greater than for a nonsimilar phoneme, since its unit is activated both by being already somewhat preprimed and by the activation of the unit corresponding to the phoneme that should be produced then.

At a somewhat higher level, a very similar explanation can be given for the greater-than-chance occurrence of mixed errors (Shallice and McGill, 1978), errors in which a word both semantically and phonologically similar to the target word is produced, such as "Finchley" (a part of London) for "Finsbury" (another part). Again it is presupposed that prior to production, units corresponding to the target are activated at both semantic and phonological levels and so activate units corresponding to the error. The phonological unit corresponding to the error is therefore activated both from its own semantic unit and from the phonological unit corresponding to the target. If, by chance, it becomes the most strongly activated its activation will increase rapidly. Reciprocal inhibition again ensures that only one word is actually produced. That a much more specific subsystem, that controlling speech production, appears to utilize mechanisms of activation and reciprocal inhibition is indirect support for their operation as a general cortical mechanism for selecting between alternatives from a specific finite set.*

Turning to the model of action-system dominance itself, inhibitory effects appear to occur as an action-system becomes dominant. Posner and Snyder (1975) have attempted to show that conscious processing of a signal has such inhibitory effects. In their experiment a prime occurs at varying intervals of time (0–500 msec) before a trial on which two letters are presented, the subject having to decide whether the letters are the same or different. They find that if a different letter is used as the prime then reaction time is slowed when compared with

---

* A related approach has been suggested for choice reaction tasks (see Rabbitt and Rodgers, 1977).

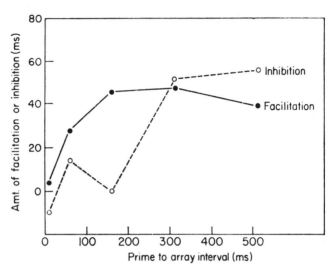

Figure 1. Posner and Snyder's estimates of the time course of facilitation (from when prime is identical to the "same" letter pair) and inhibition (prime different from "same" letter pair) obtained by comparisons with the effect of neutral primes. Facilitation is held not to be dependent upon consciousness. (From Posner and Snyder, 1975.)

the use of a neutral prime (a cross), provided that at least 300 msec (an interval comparable to that of the P_3 wave) intervenes between the prime and the letter pair. However, since the effect mainly occurs in a condition when the letter prime is the same as the matching letters on 80% of the trials on which it occurs, the effect could be reinterpreted as concerning the speed with which one can bias letter identification as a result of prior information. Hence it is not clear whether their effect is an automatic inhibitory effect due to the conscious processing of a signal on the processing of other signals or due to an optional strategy on the part of the subject.

The model presented earlier is compatible with two related and widely held generalizations about the thought process, that the mainstream of thought is normally sequentially organized and that high-level control of skill is subject to limited capacity constraints. The assumption that only one action-system can be strongly activated at any time, and that conscious experience is related only to this dominant system means that a serially organized mainstream of thought should exist. This is a standard assumption of computer simulation theories of problem-solving such as that of Newall and Simon (1972). It is strongly supported by examination of subjects' protocols in complex problem-solving tasks. Thus, De Groot (1965) in his very detailed examination of the thought processes of chess masters playing chess, concluded: "The more microscopically we examine the phase structure, the more we come across automatic processes and sequences that must be governed by an extensive series of fixed linkages" (p. 274). Yet, even he is forced to acknowledge that seriality of processing is not absolute: "In both thought processes (in two different protocols) we are concerned with "calculational serendipity," that is, during routine calculations there may be a sudden coincidentally evoked means-abstraction with respect to the main goal" (p. 278). This "calculational serendipity" or to use the more familiar term "insight," being unrelated to the previous mainstream of thought and interrupting it, implies that seriality cannot be absolute. Dominance theory allows for these nonserial aspects, as a secondary component of the thought processes.

More direct evidence of both the high-level limited capacity and of the partial parallelity involved in cognition and action is derived from standard dual task paradigms where interference between two simultaneously performed tasks occurs (e.g., Broadbent, 1971; Kahneman, 1973). A problem in assessing this whole literature is that two tasks may involve at some level the same effector or cognitive units producing so-called structural interference. It has even been claimed, for instance, by Allport, Antonis, and Reynolds (1972), that all fundamental interference between tasks results from an overload of specific-purpose units such as effector or cognitive units. However, this is a most implausible position, as demonstrated in the excellent review by Kahneman (1973). For instance, long-term memory performance for word lists is severely affected by simultaneously performing motor skills with no episodic memory component (e.g., Murdock, 1965; Baddeley, Scott, Drynan, and Smith, 1969; Bartz and Salehi, 1970).

However, recent experiments have shown that under certain circumstances two quite complex tasks can be performed simultaneously relatively satisfactorily (e.g., Allport et al. 1972; Shaffer, 1975; Spelke, Hirst, and Neisser, 1976). In the Allport et al. experiment subjects had to sight-read music and shadow prose at the same time. By the second session they showed little evidence of interference. Moreover, there was no evidence of any rapid switching from one task to the other; interword intervals in shadowing with the concurrent task were distributed quite normally. Such experiments present a real difficulty for the present theory, where only relatively simple tasks should be possible in conjunction with a dominant task. It is typical of such experiments, though, that the combination of skills used is highly practiced. The Allport et al. subjects had a lengthy practice session and two experimental sessions. Moreover, the tasks were both relatively easy for their subjects with error rates for the most difficult

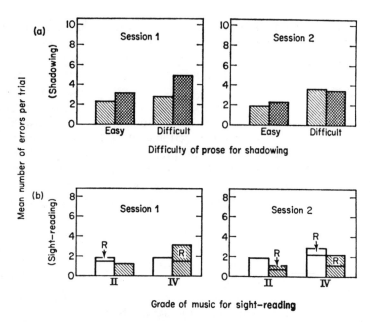

Figure 2. Accuracy of one task at different levels of difficulty of the other from the Allport *et al.* experiment. In (a) the singly hatched columns refer to the easy concurrent sight-reading condition and the cross-hatched columns to the more difficult condition. In (b) the blank columns refer to an undivided attention sight-reading condition and the hatched ones to concurrent auditory shadowing. *R* refers to rhythm or timing errors. (From Allport, Antonis, and Reynolds, 1972.)

version of the two tasks being roughly 1% and 2% respectively. Therefore, the results are compatible with the assumption that at least one of the tasks was operating at an activation level below dominance but above that normally found for a subdominant action-system. It is possible that the function of practice with a pair of skills is to enable the subject to learn to over-ride the strong tendency for the destabilizing of activation levels that dominance produces, so as to maintain both action-systems at roughly the same activation levels. It will be assumed that such activation control in the performance of specific pairs of tasks is a function of frontal planning systems, distinct from action-systems.

The investigations of Reason (1976) into "action-lapses" support the view that well-learned relatively simple actions are, in fact, often carried out under low levels of activation. Action-lapses are those bizarre, inappropriate behaviors, often said to result from "absent-mindedness," but perhaps better termed "other-mindedness," such as undressing and getting into bed when going upstairs to change. Reason shows that they result from excessive concentration on some alternative cognitively more demanding task. The rarity of such lapses highlights the way that we are normally able to carry out a routine task while concentrating on something else. Moreover, we must have no awareness of carrying the routine task out, as when an action-lapse occurs we often continue for some time on the wrong action plan before noticing the error. Thus, lack of awareness and low levels of activation appear to be related.

If the action-system controlling the correct secondary task such as changing, in the example given above, has too little activation, then a situation analogous to a mixed-error in speech can occur. The action-system controlling undressing being also a subroutine of the action-system involved in going to bed will tend to activate that action-system too. If the stimulus situation also tends to activate the incorrect action-system, it can become more strongly activated than the one controlling changing clothes, and so begin to control that aspect of behavior. If, instead, the action-system controlling changing had been dominant, the small amount of extra activation produced by the stimulus situation would have been insufficient to switch control. So the theory predicts that action-lapses should occur only in the nondominant mode.

It should be noted that the prediction that the more strongly the dominant action-system is activated, the weaker are nondominant systems activated is closely related to Easterbrook's (1959) theory that increased arousal reduces the range of cues utilized by the organism, a view that has received much support (see Kahneman, 1973). For instance, Hockey (1970) showed that the greater the level of arousal the less a subject detects in the more rarely stimulated parts of the visual field. A mechanism to produce this type of effect has been suggested by Walley and Weiden (1973) who present evidence to show that the effect of increased arousal is to facilitate inhibitory cortical interneurones.

Evidence has therefore been presented of the usefulness of activation and reciprocal inhibition as theoretical constructs in psychological models as well as physiological ones, and for the plausibility of the dominance relation holding between action-systems. The exceptions involve well-learned combinations of highly practiced skills in which it is argued that frontal planning mechanisms counteract the dominance-inducing positive feedback tendencies.

2.6. The Selection of the Dominant Action-System

The hierarchy of control systems that are simultaneously in operation range from those that control muscle contraction at the lowest level to very high-level ones such as those that mediate the attainment of life-goals. Where in this range is the dominant action-system of the moment located? It may be roughly defined as the lowest level of control that cannot operate simultaneously with any equally well-learned program of similar complexity with which it has no structural interference. This is an equivalent criterion to that given by Posner and Klein (1973) that conscious processes interfere with other processes that too need to be conscious.

How is this dominant action-system selected? There appear to be four distinct ways. Relatively primitive systems such as those that control the orienting response must on the above criterion presumably be considered action-systems since they interfere with other ongoing cognitive activity. They would appear to be capable of being called-in by relatively primitive subcortical systems such as those involving the reticular system and the thalamus. Mechanisms for biasing of the organism toward, say, reception of stimuli or response preparation, described by Hamilton, Hockey, and Rejman (1977) as the "control of activation space," would operate at this level. Selection by these systems would be involuntary (see Posner, Nissen, Ogden, and Davidson, 1975).

That such primitive systems can actually select an action-system of the complex skill or thought type for dominance as opposed to biasing selection toward a type of system seems unlikely. Other means of selection, though, obviously can do this. The language system can call in a particular action-system, as in the response to a command or a request; in other words, when it operates in a "slave" mode. This "slave response" is, however, always under the potential control of other systems (except under hypnosis when it appears to be relatively autonomous (Miller, Galanter, and Pribram 1960)). Thus, like all high-level means of selection it is "voluntary."

Very frequently, dominant action-systems will be called in by higher-level action-systems as subroutines. Thus, the action-system controlling a well-learned even though complex task such as performing a statistical calculation or cleaning a room will call in many other action-systems such as those concerned with looking up statistical tables and division in the one case and emptying a vacuum cleaner and moving furniture in the other. The higher-level systems remain subdominant until the lower-level system has achieved its goal. After, this control is transferred back and the higher-level system becomes briefly dominant before calling in yet another lower-level action-system. Goals may, however, be set up without an obvious means of attaining them being available. This implies both that there must be systems for the production of aims and mechanisms that can revitalize them when a solution eventually becomes practicable. As shown, for instance, by Newall and Simon (1972), the production of aims can itself be undertaken by routine programs, the working-back method to achieve what they term "difference goals" that describe "either difficulties to be surmounted or gaps in information and specification to be filled." However, the ability to take up an unrealized aim again at an appropriate time implies that monitors must be capable of being set up that will reactivate the action-system when an appropriate stimulus or internal state occurs. The monitoring system must enable an appropriate recognition unit to transmit its own activation in a multiplicative fashion to activate the relevant "dormant" action-system.

Finally, there are many occasions when a task is presented, for which no appropriate higher-level action-system exists. In such situations potentially appropriate action-systems cannot be called in directly by another action-system. It is assumed that potentially appropriate action-systems are called in by planning systems, to be discussed later. The multiplicity of these selection systems therefore suggests that ultimate control must be within the action-systems themselves, presumably by mutual inhibition. The activation level of an action-system would therefore depend on the activating input received from various sources, and on the activation level of other action-systems (see Appendix).

3. Consciousness and the Operation of the Dominant Action-System

3.1. The Selector Input

To assume that the continual flux of conscious experience is directly related to changes in dominance between action-systems still leaves the nature of the relation between phenomenological and information-processing concepts open. In the previous version of this theory it was argued that a particular type of input to the dominant action-system called the selector input activates it, sets its goal, is stored in episodic memory, and is capable of being spoken about. The multiple and central roles of this input lead to the whole information-processing system when attempting to "understand" and "describe" itself, developing a concept that corresponds to the input, namely "consciousness." So it was argued that "consciousness" in phenomenological language becomes isomorphic to "selector input to the dominant action-system" in information-processing terms.

The selector-input to the dominant action-system was defined in contrast to the so-called specific input using an analogy between the variables set when control was passed to a subroutine and the further input called up by the routine after control has been passed to it. This was held to correspond to the differentiation made by Bernstein (1967) for motor skills between the perceptual inputs that lead to a skilled action being triggered—say, the sight of an apple when hungry—and the visual and kinesthetic input, which provide estimates of the difference between the position of the hand and apple when reaching for it. Conceptually they may be loosely distinguished by whether or not they can be easily modeled in an *analogue* simulation of the skill.

A recent neuropsychological discovery seems highly pertinent to this identification of consciousness with the selector input to the dominant action-system rather than the specific input. This is the phenomenon of "blind-sight" arising from occipital lobe damage (Weiskrantz, Warrington, Sanders, and Marshall, 1974). Damage to primary visual cortex leads to field defects (scotomas), which can be so dense that the patient is unable to perceive anything in the affected part of the visual field. This was the case for patient DB, who had received an extensive right occipital lobectomy to remove an arterio-venous malformation. When a spot of light was presented in his left visual field he could not perceive it. Yet, when asked to guess where the spot of light was he could point to it very accurately. Some discriminations could even be made in the consciously blind half-field, such as distinguishing horizontal from vertical, green from red, and a cross from a circle. When the patient made these discriminations they were not subjectively based on visual experience. Thus, when asked about the last of these discriminations, he said he saw nothing but perhaps had a "feeling" that it was "smooth" (the O) or "jagged" (the X). He was astonished when shown a video of his own performance.

The phenomenon cannot be explained in terms of greatly reduced normal vision since acuity as measured by the fineness of a grating that could be discriminated as being horizontal or vertical was nearly as good for the left (blind) visual field as for the right (sighted) field. Moreover, the dissociation between the abilities lost and preserved is entirely compatible with those of monkeys with bilateral occipital lobe removal who presumably have to rely on the so-called second visual system involving the subcortical structures, superior colliculus and pulvinar (Humphrey and Weiskrantz, 1967; Humphrey, 1970).

This phenomenon supports the view that the input used to direct the arm in reaching is not "available" to consciousness. It fits with old introspective studies on simple reaction time that found that observers could report very little about the interval between a stimulus and a

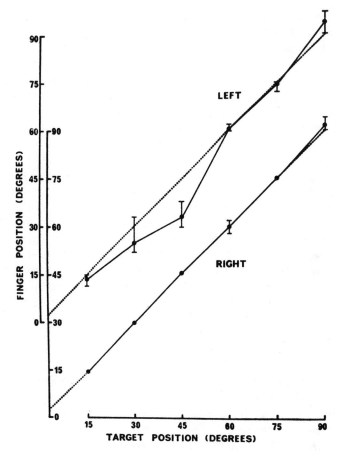

Figure 3. Finger-reaching responses for blind-sight patient, DB, for spot targets of a given eccentricity. Stimuli in the right (sighted) and left (blind) half fields were randomly interspersed. (From Weiskrantz, Warrington, Sanders, and Marshall, 1974.)

response (Cattell, 1886; Ach, 1905; Watt, 1905) and with the study of Fehrer and Raab (1962), who found that preventing a visual stimulus being perceived by means of metacontrast did not increase reaction time to it. In both cases the action-system had been set up in the preparation period; the stimulus merely triggered the preset response.

However, this distinction between "selector" and "specific" input is unnecessarily complicated. Consider simple reaction-time to a faint stimulus. "Sensory set" becomes essential rather than "motor set" (see Woodworth and Schlosberg, 1954) and one is aware of the stimulus before the response is produced. Even if the initiation of such a response depends upon higher-level perceptual processing, why should one be aware of the stimulus prior to responding when one is not aware of it when "motor set" is operating? The "selector input" concept provides no answer. The situation becomes more comprehensible if one assumes that under motor set, all processes between stimulus occurrence and the response are controlled by effector units whose operation has been preset by an action-system that remains dominant throughout. By contrast, the action-system involved in sensory set must contain two lower-level action-systems. The first, set up by the warning signal, maximizes perceptual sensitivity appropriately for the expected stimulus. The second, selected by activation of the appropriate perceptual units, sends an output to the effector system. On this view "sensory set" involves a qualitatively more complex action-system than "motor set."

This would suggest that the distinction between selector and specific input is more simply expressed as the distinction between input to a dominant action-system *on its own level* and input to a concurrently operating lower-level system such as an effector system. The "analogue/nonanalogue" distinction between specific and selector inputs would now refer to models appropriate for different levels of the total system.

3.2. The Identification of Action-Systems and Productions

The concept of the input utilized by a dominant action-system on its own level seems vague. It can, however, be made more precise. Consider, for example, one of the most comprehensive theories of problem-solving at present available in psychology, that of Newall and Simon (1972). Their theory incorporates, in addition to long-term memory systems, short-term memory systems and external memories (written material potentially perceived with foveal vision), a set of production-systems. A production-system is a way of organizing a program. As a very simple example, the simplified production-system for the subsection of driving behavior appropriate at traffic lights is shown in Table I.

Each production in a production-system is a condition, action-sequence pair. If the condition is satisfied, then the action-sequence is produced with the action-sequence itself, if necessary, being another production-system. After each action-sequence is complete control checks through the conditions sequentially until one is found to be satisfied, when its action sequence is carried out. The advantages of this sort of system is not only that it mimics subjects' protocols in certain complex cognitive tasks well. Each production is independent of the others so that new ones can easily be added, and is a

TABLE I. Highly Simplified Production-System for Driving
Behavior Controlled by Traffic Lights[a]

Condition			
Light	Distance	Car movement	Action sequence
Red	Distant	Moving	Slow, prepare to stop
R	Close	M	Stop
R	C	Stopped	—
Green	D	M	Continue in third gear
G	C	M	Continue
G	C	S	Start

[a] Consideration of more stimulus situations would be dealt with by adding to the six productions listed.

meaningful component of the total problem and is basically very simple, almost an S-R system, as Newall and Simon (1972) point out.

Action-systems and production-systems perform similar functions in different conceptual systems. If one considers them as different ways of representing the same basic process, then one problem for production-systems is resolved but another is created.

While production-systems can simulate human cognition well in many situations, their adequacy as a component part of a model of the human thought process is limited by the requirement that the conditions of each production are checked sequentially, which (as discussed in an earlier section) is inappropriate for the rapid selection of the systems controlling action. If the checking of conditions were to be done in parallel, then two incompatible action-sequences could be triggered simultaneously. If a production is identified with an action-system, then the dominance property of the latter allows only one action-system/production to be operative, so that conditions could be checked in parallel without the problem of the production of incompatible actions.

If to model cognition one identifies production-systems that have a nonquantitative conceptual structure and action-systems that operate under a continuum of levels of activation, some method of mapping from the continuum on to discrete states is necessary. As pointed out above, the dominance property allows an identification to be made between the operative production and the dominant action-system. However, for the identification to hold a similar property is required for inputs, since on the production-system approach satisfaction of a condition is an all-or-none matter. Thus, of the inputs that could possibly be utilized by the operative production-system one would need to be much more strongly activated than the others. Therefore, the dominance property would have to operate between recognition units as well as between action-systems; in other words, at least within a category only one recognition unit would be able to be strongly activated.

3.3. Conscious Content and Dominant Action-System Operation

In the previous version of this theory conscious content was identified with the selector input to the dominant action-system. The selector input not only activated it and set its goal, but also had to be retained in memory so that it could act as a selector input at a later time, say, by setting the goal of another action-system if the first one attempted failed to reach its goal or by resetting the first goal if the task was interrupted.

These functions are not all taken over by a (strong) input to a dominant action-system in the present version. The reactivating function would result from difference goals having been set up continuing, if not achieved, to prime potential productions even if the action-system/production is no longer dominant. As these difference goals cannot be identified with the input that led to their being set up, it would be wrong to consider them just as (strong) inputs. The memory system that retains the details of the levels of control above that of the presently dominant action-system is not then a memory of inputs.

Yet, a probably different memory that contains a record of the conditions fulfilled and action-sequences undertaken would be useful if any of four possibilities are used when a goal is impossible or difficult to achieve: to try another action-system, to put it off until a more favorable time, to get another member of the culture to attain it (normally through speech), or, possibly, to alter the action-system. Empirically this would fit with the now-standard view in the study of episodic memory that one retains not just a passively coded representation of the stimulus, but a complex of the stimulus related to the orienting task (e.g., Hyde and Jenkins, 1973; Craik and Tulving, 1975).

One needs, though, to differentiate between information that needs to be stored, and that which does not. Information not previously available to the action-system, such as the color of the traffic light in the example give in Table I, would need to be stored. That already available, such as whether one is moving or stationary, would not. The former would correspond to focal awareness, but the phenomenological status of the latter would presumably be that of part of the "background of consciousness," to be discussed later.

Two types of perceptual input do, however, fit closely with the previous selector input concept: the activation of preprimed monitors, which switch dominance unexpectedly, and also speech input. Following Luria (1966), it seems most appropriate to view speech input as having the function of activating an action-system and setting its goal. This would seem compatible with procedural semantics approaches to language comprehension (e.g., Miller and Johnson-Laird, 1976). One consequence would be that one must be conscious of what someone says for it to direct the thought processes. In the output mode speech would be a means of attaining a difference goal. Using both modes together, through inner speech, is a powerful way of selecting appropriate action-sequences; it is necessarily a conscious process.

However, while the selector input concept needs to be partially replaced, the criteria for conscious correspondence can remain, namely, that certain processes have the common properties of assisting in the control of action, being retained in memory, and being capable of being spoken about. Strong inputs to the dominant action-systems have these properties. Weak inputs and unrelated strong inputs that excite no appropriate monitors do not. Moreover, strong inputs are organized by the nature of the perceptual system, and the specific requirements of the action-system both organize this input and limit its content.

Strong inputs to the dominant action-system remain the paradigm case for an information-processing correspondence for consciousness. Other aspects of dominant action-system operation may well also have the appropriate properties, the action-sequence aspect, for one. One knows (at some level) what one is doing and can conceptualize it given the limitations of vocabulary. Yet, further parts of action-system operation, control parts—why one is doing something—and the activation parts—related to, say awareness of effort—will be discussed later.

4.   Phenomenological Correspondences

4.1.   Percepts

In this section, the isomorphism introduced between consciousness and aspects of the operation of the dominant action-system will be used to provide an explanation of different states of mind and why there should be no conscious experience in certain situations. Where appropriate the explanation will be contrasted with those that can be derived from the short-term memory approach and from the tacit/ explicit knowledge approach.

When engaged in a particular task, one's perceptual experience is normally dominated by the task. So, when overtaking another car on a narrow road one is conscious of the other car, its size, the speed that it is going, the width and direction of the road, of potential obstacles, and so on. An explanation of perceptual experience in terms of strong inputs from the perceptual units to the dominant action-system, inputs that are specified by it, seems entirely appropriate.

Even in such situations one is, though, aware in some sense, of other aspects of the scene, of colors, for instance. Moreover, in reflective experience, much more typical of experiments on perception, the assumption that percepts are strong system-specific inputs to an action-system seems in conflict with much of the basic phenomenology of perception. Visual perception is of a spatially related set of objects having color, shape, size, and so on.

Action-systems specific to perception must exist as demonstrated by the existence of verbs such as "looking for," "listening for," and as other complex cognitive activity cannot be performed simultaneously with a demanding perceptual task. In perceptual experiments, therefore, it is plausible that action-systems mediating detecting, judging, recognizing exist. The act of recognition, for instance, is not just a matter of the activation of a recognition unit. The appropriate object has to be selected from all those in the scene and the appropriate output to effector systems programmed.

However, this still does not explain the richness of conscious perception. It will be argued that perceptual experience is in fact not dependent on the particular action-systems in operation, but can be characterized by the type of input the dominant action-system receives and the potential input available for immediately following action-system operation. What counts as a percept, then, is partially determined by context. Thus, if one is perceiving an apple, while at that instant the dimension of the apple that is acting as input to the dominant action-system may be its size, input to the same or another action-system is potentially available about its position, color, movement, apparent rottenness, and so on, and similar information is available about neighboring objects. Contrast, for instance, a percept with an image when all these potential changes of input are not available. This potential for providing immediate inputs to the dominant action-system is a characteristic of short-term memory systems too, as retrieval from such systems is much faster than from episodic memory (see Waugh, 1970). This property seems the reason why they have been such popular candidates for the contents of consciousness.

The property, however, seems to make the contents of STM like perceptual input processed in parallel correspond more with William James's "background of consciousness." Focal awareness, in either case, demands that an input be accepted by the dominant action-system.

The complementary problem to that of the richness of perceptual experience is its absence when indications of perceptual processing exist. The best-known such situation is perceptual defense (Dixon, 1971). The existence of such situations led Turvey (1974) to extend Polanyi's (1966) distinction between tacit and explicit identification to experimental studies of perception. Explicit identification for Turvey demands a further distinct operation in addition to tacit identification, the result of the passive "cascade" processing. He does not specify very clearly what this extra process consists of, but it depends on the matching of a "constructed" model with the trace of the passive processing. On the present theory, by contrast, perceptual processing does not lead to conscious awareness if it is not appropriate for the dominant action-system or if it is too weak.

Of the arguments presented by Turvey, some, such as the ability to discriminate a letter from a background of numbers before it is identified (e.g., Brand, 1971; Jonides and Gleitman, 1972) and the way that a letter can be more easily identified if part of a word (e.g., Wheeler, 1970; Reicher, 1969), can be simply explained as due to words, letters, and numbers being identified by neuropsychologically distinct recognition units (see Konorski, 1967; Shallice and Warrington, 1977a). They are therefore not relevant to the issue.

The strongest line of evidence put forward by Turvey (1974) and supported by Allport (1977) and Marcel and Patterson (1978) concerns work on the ability to "identify" visually presented words semantically in conditions where they are not "identified" graphemically, and analogous work in audition where nonperceived inputs bias perception of simultaneously occurring words (e.g., Lewis, 1970; MacKay, 1973). For instance, Marcel (1974) showed that a word that is pattern masked so as not to be perceptible, still has a strong priming effect on the speed of making a subsequent lexical decision—deciding whether a letter string is word—for a semantically related word. One is quicker at deciding that "bread" is a word if it is preceded by "butter," masked such that it is not seen, than if preceded by an unrelated word so masked. When discussing this and related findings, Marcel and Patterson (1978) argue that visual experience depends upon the preservation of a visual trace, which is obliterated by pattern masking; semantic processing, however, occurs normally, but it remains tacit as no visual trace remains for a successful match.

One problem with this theory is that successful matching with a visual trace cannot be essential for conscious perception. Subjects do make semantic errors when presented tachistoscopically with a number of unrelated words (Allport, 1977; Shallice and McGill, 1978); these are words related in meaning but not in visual form. Sometimes they even lack any visual form; one of our subjects responded with "a farmyard animal" to a stimulus containing the word "pork."

On the present model consciousness of a particular aspect of the stimulus necessitates strong activation of a unit at the appropriate level of the perceptual system. If an action-system that can utilize that level of perceptual input is dominant or becomes dominant, conscious preception will occur. "Disembodied" perception of meaning without visual form is very rare as strong activation at a late level and *not* at an earlier level is very rare. The presentation of a pattern mask, however, will end the activation in the units, which are responsible for visual whole-word pattern analysis, but word meaning units will already have received some activation, although normally insufficient for strong activation. Since these units are not strongly activated there can be no consciousness of word meaning, but nor will there be any inhibitory damping since no unit becomes dominant. So priming of related words can occur, the relatively low level of activation of the priming unit being compensated by the absence of inhibitory damping.

Since inhibition is presumed not to be present, one would also expect that disambiguation of stimuli should not occur. Thus, Marcel's finding that a masked homonym such as "palm" still primes the target lexical decision, i.e., "hand," even if preceded by its other context, i.e., "tree," can be explained. This effect does not occur when "palm" is unmasked, for then inhibitory disambiguation would occur. Moreover this absence of inhibition for subconscious stimuli would help to explain the different type of priming that occurs with such stimuli when compared with stimuli of which one is aware, their primary process quality (Dixon, 1971).

On the present view semantic errors are rare events occurring when graphemic and semantic units are activated at about borderline level; inhibitory effects do not occur as the "correct" semantic unit never becomes dominant but an associated semantic unit may receive sufficient activation that with chance prior "noise" activation enables dominance to be achieved by it. The weakness of the word form unit activation means that conscious suppression of the incorrectly dominant semantic unit would not occur. Semantic errors, indeed, occur just with this borderline sort of input (Shallice and McGill, 1978).

Although it has been argued that the evidence is if anything more compatible with the present approach to conscious perception than with the Turvey/Allport/Marcel one, the type of matching process suggested by them is clearly an important part of the operation of the perceptual systems. However, the experimental results that provide the strongest evidence for such processes also suggest that they have nothing to do with consciousness. Thus, Sokolov's (1963) finding that habituation of a stimulus depends on the construction of a "neuronal model" was best supported by the way one becomes aware of the failure of the input to match a neuronal model, as when one notices the clock stop. Similarly, there is much evidence that before an eye movement a model of the input to be expected after it is constructed, and that whether one perceives movement depends on whether the subsequent input differs from this reafferance copy (e.g., Gregory, 1958). This all occurs well below the level of consciousness, so any necessary relation between these construction and matching processes and conscious experience seems unlikely.

The view that conscious perception corresponds to strong input specified by an action-system has the problem of determining what action-system is operative. However, some process must intervene between activity in the perceptual system and a response. Moreover, analysis of virtually the simplest type of act—choice reaction time— provides evidence that this "translation" process between stimulus analysis and response involves a complex system, which can itself be primed. Thus, Duncan (1976) has shown that the transformation involved in the mapping from stimulus to response is subject to repetition and interference effects, independently of the particular stimuli and responses used, as one would expect if different transformations were mediated by different action-systems. If the process intervening between stimulus analysis and response organization in as simple a task as choice reaction time is that complex, the assumption that as complex a process intervenes between activation of units in the perceptual system and effecting a response in a perceptual experiment seems entirely reasonable. If one just reflects on one's perceptual experience then the process mediating reflection too is highly complex.

4.2. Thoughts

Much is known about the information-processing system involved in perception. Moreover, reasonable agreement between subjects on the phenomenological description of perceptual experience is often possible. Neither condition is met in the area of the higher thought process. For instance, even the Würzberg school which provided the most useful, relevant, phenomenological analysis of the thought process could obtain little agreement about the phenomenological classification of thought other than that states of awareness exist that are not acts of will, images, or percepts (see Humphrey, 1951).

This is hardly surprising as in this area the introspective act involves thought processes very similar to those being introspected about, so a problem of recursion arises. Thus, the higher thought processes are hardly the ideal area for establishing the appropriate isomorphism between the conceptual systems of information processing and phenomenology.

However, Würzberg-type phenomenology does offer both opportunities and problems for the type of correspondence being advanced here. Take the awareness of determination that Ach (1905) defined through "the individual knows directly, as a characteristic experience, whether the given psychic experience is proceeding in the sense of a previously established determination or not," in other words whether it is "willed." This would seem to depend on whether the dominant action-system in operation has been called in by a previously dominant higher-level system. In such cases information about what is to be done when the action-system achieves its goal must be available in the control memory. Some conscious correspondence would therefore be expected for this information-processing requirement, as mentioned earlier.

Nonwilled conscious states appear to be of two sorts. An orienting response is, in a sense, unwilled, but so in very different ways are free association and hypnagogic imagery. Why do such thoughts appear unwilled? It will be argued that they arise in situations where no single action-system has been dominant; in other words, where a number of action-systems are relatively weakly activated.

To make this more plausible, consider a type of problem patients with frontal lobe lesions find difficult, so-called cognitive estimation problems (Shallice and Evans, 1978) where the patient must use items of common knowledge in a rather unusual way. Typical problems include, What is the length of the spine? What is the largest object normally found in a house?, and How many camels are there in Holland? Frontal patients even with normal measured "intelligence" appear to be unable to produce a reasonable plan easily or to check their answer adequately. Yet, such processes are not normally ones of which one is aware.

Presented with the first problem, how does the method of analyzing "body minus head minus legs occur"? How after making a mistake in calculation and producing an answer of 4'6" does one realize that this is in fact close to the height of a person and so must be wrong? Introspection gives no guide.

Dominant action-system operation is cybernetically appropriate for a cognitive task, if a reasonable method is immediately available or can be obtained by a relatively routine procedure for working back from the goal. Yet, situations like the ones discussed above are ones where no obvious line of attack is available. In such a situation it would seem most valuable to be able to conduct many potential strategies simultaneously. For instance, it would be optimal in the case of the "spine" question for methods concerned with subdividing the spine or matching it to a roughly equivalent length could be assessed at the same time as the more complex method of embedding the length in a greater known length. Moreover, provided no action results without checking, the dangers of a number of action-systems operating simultaneously are removed.

It is therefore suggested that in such situations a number of action-systems can be weakly activated. Being weakly activated they each would work less efficiently and rapidly than if they were dominant. If a potential output is obtained that fits the "indefinite goal" (to use Greeno's (1976) term) then the action-system producing it becomes strongly activated. This is the analogue on the present theory to Neisser's (1963) assumption of the potentially multiple nature of the thought processes, which he supports by considering creativity, intuition, and primary process thinking in contrast to constrained, "logical," and secondary process thought.

Planning systems would therefore be required in addition to action-systems in order to maintain a group of weakly activated action-systems relatively free from other inhibitory effects. It would not need to control the critical action-systems' activation since none would be sufficiently strongly activated to be dominant. It is unclear whether the planning system also monitors the provisional outputs of the action-systems so as to allow them to become dominant only when provisional "success" is achieved, an application of Turvey's (1974) ideas in a different, less stimulus-constrained area, or whether the "successful" action-system becomes dominant through a process internal to itself; this could be analogous to Selz's (1913) view that a partially activated "thought complex"—for him the basic building block of knowledge—once partly activated tends to become completely so. The crucial point, though, is that this approach predicts that situations occur with no action-system dominant. One would therefore expect no conscious content at such times and their product to appear in consciousness "unwilled."

If one considers how action-systems are learned, this would suggest that the relation between input and consequences or, in Newall and Simon's (1972) terms, satisfaction of a "condition" and operation of an "action sequence" is not automatic, not an all-or-none process, but again has a "strength." If an action-system operates successfully, then the link between aim and action-system is made stronger and direct calling-in of the action-system without recourse to the planning system becomes more likely if the analogous stimulus conditions recur.

One of the functions of the planning system then appears to be that of enabling a number of simultaneously operating weakly activated action-systems to operate and possibly of monitoring their output. No action-system becomes dominant until provisional success is achieved. This complements the function suggested earlier that planning systems are needed to equalize the activation of two action-systems, which have to operate together in the dual task situation, when both are receiving sufficiently strong activation to become dominant. Neisser (1976) has indeed argued on the grounds of the results of such dual task experiments that conscious experience is a very unreliable guide to cognitive processing. He was led to this conclusion by the experiment of Spelke, Hirst, and Neisser (1976), in which subjects eventually learned to categorize auditorily presented words for meaning while reading as effectively and rapidly as they could without an additional task. This took many sessions of practice. In this sort of situation, the authors point out, introspective reports are very variable. Sometimes the subjects reported that they thought clearly about each word they heard and repeated it to themselves; at other times they were unaware even of writing to dictation (another possible secondary task) while reading. Similar conflict between introspections occurs in work by previous authors (e.g., Solomons and Stein, 1896; Downey and Anderson, 1915).

This situation is, however, most atypical. On the present theory frontal planning systems would be gradually learning to protect the activation of the action-system controlling the secondary task (e.g., word-categorization) at an increasingly high, although subdominant level from the inhibitory effects of the dominant system controlling reading. This is presumably a difficult planning task given "executive ignorance" of the details of the skills. A gradual increase in the activation of the action-system controlling semantic analysis of dictated words would fit with subjects' gradual increase in ability to analyze the dictated words semantically. This, presumably, though, would eventually result in the most atypical situation of two action-systems both being fairly strongly activated. This would lead to confused introspective reports, especially as the level of activation in each action-system would presumably fluctuate with "concentration," itself a property of frontal planning systems.

Monitoring the operation of multiple weakly activated action-systems when no clear heuristic is available and controlling mutually inhibitory interactions of two potentially strongly activated action-systems have been assigned to a special system, the planning system. Sloman (1977) has, in fact, argued from entirely theoretical considerations that humans must have complex planning abilities in addition to their well-learned cognitive skills. Indeed, the dissociation also seems to be neurologically valid (Luria, 1966; Shallice and Evans, 1977). The interrelation between such processes and action-systems is at present unclear. For instance, how far "aims" are mediated through routine working-back is not apparent. However, it seems likely that many planning system operations are fundamentally nonserial and would therefore not correspond to any conscious state. One may therefore be left with the paradox that consciousness, whose function is to ensure coherent control of action, does not correspond to the highest level of control, but to an intermediate level: action-systems. Clinically, this conclusion seems less paradoxical.

5. Further Problems

5.1. Other States of Mind

Even if the previous highly speculative analysis were accepted, five types of problem remain. Firstly, there is the problem of producing isomorphisms in information-processing terms for many other states of awareness, for instance, doubt or expectation. Secondly, there is the related problem of lack of awareness in situations such as guessing or those that precede understanding in language comprehension. Thirdly, what is the relation of the present model to abnormal function? Fourthly, there are conceptual questions about how effector systems, action-systems, and planning systems are to be distinguished. Finally, is the attempt to develop a unitary information-processing concept corresponding to consciousness useful, given, for instance, the objections implicit in Wittgenstein's (1953) analysis of the inherent ambiguities of mental terms?

The aim of the present paper has primarily been to argue for the isomorphism between aspects of the operation of dominant action-systems and conscious experience by arguing from a very limited number of types of experience and mainly from the difference between nonconscious and conscious states. However, the isomorphism should theoretically allow correspondences for all types of experience to be obtained. Some can be simply if trivially dealt with. An image would involve an input to the dominant action-system from the higher levels of the perceptual system, without the possibility characteristic of a perceptual experience that many different types of input are simultaneously available for potentially dominant action-systems. A memory, for instance, would correspond to an input to the dominant action-system from the episodic memory system. Yet, even this crude isomorphism presents problems. Why, for instance, is a subject not aware in free recall whether an item has been retrieved from auditory-verbal short-term memory or from episodic memory? Maybe because the sound and the meaning of a word are so closely linked that in retrieving one the other is automatically activated.

More interesting correspondences are, however, possible. The "tip-of-the-tongue" state (Brown and McNeill, 1966) would reflect a state of a memory system in which activation had risen, but no single unit was strongly activated. The compulsive nature of this state suggests that it produces a strong tendency for the memory look-up program to demand more activation, presumably from planning systems. In fact this tendency seems a more general one for partially attained items as in the tendency to attend to a face one half recognizes. Moreover, it appears related to the process assumed to operate following the achieving of an indefinite goal by one of a number of parallel acting action-systems.

Yet, the tip-of-the-tongue state is different from conscious states considered previously, for in a sense it has no specific content, only control/effort content. Even more complex is a state such as doubt. Maybe it is an abstraction based on the rapid succession of alternative action-systems, each being briefly dominant in an attempt to achieve some aim. However, such assumptions require complication of the original correspondence notion, to be discussed further later.

5.2. Lack of Conscious Content

More tractable are the problems concerned with lack of conscious correspondence for certain processes. For some, such as the lower levels of skills, the simple explanation is that they are not being carried out by the dominant action-system. In skill learning, a hierarchy of control systems is gradually constructed (Miller, Galanter, and Pribram, 1960) so it is natural that what one is conscious of will change. The way that guessing can be performed at above chance accuracy is also tractable. If consciousness depends upon a high-level of activation in the appropriate units, low levels of activation will still have the potential for influencing responses and giving above chance accuracy in responding.

A less obvious case is the lack of any awareness of the processes that mediate sentence comprehension. However, here, as with the developing of strategies for nonroutine problems, Turvey's type of approach seems more appropriate. For instance, on Winograd's (1972) simulation of language comprehension alternative semantic interpretations of the input are constructed in parallel. It would, therefore, seem reasonable to assume that in language comprehension only if a provisional construction fits most checks on its coherence does an action-system become strongly activated and conscious "understanding" occur. That the end product of the comprehension process can be described in programming terms has been extensively argued by Miller and Johnson-Laird (1976); thus, it should be analyzable in action-system terms. As with the other examples where the parallel action of submaximally activated action-systems is assumed, one is dealing with a situation where cognitive "output" (in this case, "understanding") is not closely dependent on the activation of just one precognitive unit (a recognition unit) but on that of a number of such units operating in no fixed relation. The situation differs considerably, say, from normal object recognition in this respect.

5.3.   The Relation to Abnormal Function

This problem is far too large to be discussed at all adequately here. In general, explanation of altered states of consciousness whether induced by dreams, drugs, psychiatric conditions, or unusual environments would seem to require conceptual systems (e.g., physiological and personality ones) in addition to the ones considered here. The model does, however, offer certain possibilities for correspondences with aspects of Freudian theory with which it has in common an unfashionable reliance on psycho-economics.

It would, for instance, be simple to add a strong recurrent inhibitory process to the activation of particular action-systems, memory engrams, or even recognition units that would prevent them from being activated above a certain level, given the assumption that inhibition is the more powerful at high levels of activation (see also Appendix). They could then never be able to have any representation in consciousness however strongly their inputs were activated; they would form part of the Freudian "unconscious."

Moreover, the contrasting properties of the primary and secondary processes could follow from the absence or presence of cortical inhibitory processes. For instance, it could be argued that in REM sleep cortical inhibitory processes are much weaker than in the waking state. Indeed, Evarts (1967) has suggested from a comparison of single cell activity in the waking and sleeping state that sleep does result in a reduction of the excitability of cortical inhibitory interneurons. Moreover, single cell activity in REM sleep is at least as strong as in the waking state so excitatory inputs must still be operative. If, indeed, a selective decrement does occur to inhibitory processes, strong activation should be occurring without dominant action-system control, which, it was argued earlier, are heavily dependent on inhibitory processes. Primary process principles such as condensation, compromise, the use of low-level associations (e.g., clang ones), and toleration of contradiction could then result.

5.4.   The Criteria for Distinguishing Subsystems

The model depends on the differentiation between three levels of control systems—effector systems, action-systems, and planning systems—but no operational criteria have been provided for distinguishing between them.

An internal criterion is available on the model for the differentiation between action and effector-systems. An action-system is capable of becoming dominant, an effector system is not. This is a potentially powerful criterion. For instance, all actions, describable by verbs that are used to express an intention, must be controlled by an action-system. Thus, one does not have a verb referring to an increase in the size of the pupil, but one does for active control of the sense organs such as "look" and "listen." Thus, the latter actions would be mediated by one or more action-systems but the former response would not. The division between action-systems and planning systems is even less clear-cut. At present the appropriate criterion would again appear to be the potentiality for dominance, but this would assume that planning systems are high-level systems that must always operate in parallel, a highly speculative assumption.

5.5.   The Usefulness of Relating Consciousness with Information-Processing Concepts

On the present approach the term "consciousness" exists because it corresponds to a process with widely different sorts of consequences. Something of which one is aware is an aspect of the system controlling ones thought or action; it has the possibility of being remembered, one can talk about it, and it can be utilized by later actions. These properties are not independent nor do they entirely map into each other. Certain mental states, particularly emotional or aesthetic ones, are not describable by many people. Others such as, for instance, those that occur under the effects of alcohol are not easily remembered. Moreover, certain stimuli that one does not experience may in fact enter memory, if the Pötzl phenomenon is not artifactual (see Dixon, 1971).

The problem, however, is not just that the criteria are "fuzzily" matched. Which aspect of the dominant action-system is retained or expressible is also unclear. The initial correspondence utilized the content input, but consideration of say, the tip-of-the-tongue state and the "awareness of determination" indicate that control aspects of action-system operation independent of any content input also have some (different) type of phenomonological correspondence. More complex still are intentions that, in some sense, correspond to an output of either a dominant higher-level action-system or of the planning system. It is possible that in one sense to be conscious of an intention it needs to be made explicit, say, by being made an input from the language or the perceptual systems (i.e., through inner speech or imagery respectively), or through actually priming an action-system that becomes briefly dominant even though it cannot at that instant be fulfilled. By contrast it could be argued that the formulation of an intention is such a major change in potential action-system dominance that at any future time it will have very similar attributes to actual content inputs that make action-systems dominant.

This paradox is related to Wittgenstein's (1953) comments: " 'For a moment I meant to. . .' That is, I had a particular feeling, an inner experience; and I remember it. And now remember *quite precisely*: Then the 'inner experience' of intending seems to vanish again. Instead one remembers thoughts, feelings, movements, and also connections with earlier situations. It is as if one had altered the adjustment of a microscope." One might argue that the ways by which the system "knows" about high-level action-system output are somewhat different from those that are used for inputs. However, it is also apparent that the length of time to which phenomenological concepts refer and their levels of abstraction vary. Moreover, it has already been argued that one needs to distinguish a percept and an image partially by their contexts, so this type of factor becomes relevant even for the most simple of experiences.

These qualifications suggest that the conceptual systems of information processing and phenomenology may not map onto each other completely. Indeed, they can be used to argue that a reductionist, as opposed to a correspondence approach to phenomenology, is in principle impossible. By analogy with the way that even perception of figure/ground can be critically dependent on meaning, so the form of direct experience would be dependent on culturally determined concepts. More positively, they entail that a more complete model for explaining consciousness must contain a model of the "knowing" process as well as of the "known" process. Such a recursive model, for this is what would be entailed, is beyond the scope of the present paper. However, the need for such a model does not mean that the "known" cannot be modeled for certain phenomena without much consideration of the "knowing" process; percepts and actions are of this type. Indeed, this is probably a useful stage in the achievement of the more complex goal. The identification of consciousness with parts of the operation of action-systems (a specific level of control), and more particularly, with aspects of their strongly activated operation, the dominance property, makes materially comprehensible why the term "consciousness" should be so vital a concept for describing ourselves, by explaining the conscious/unconscious distinction in information-processing terms.

Appendix

In Shallice (1972) the activation of a system of n action-systems was modeled by the operation of n differential equations that produce a positive feedback relation within an action-system and inhibitory interactions between them. The model would predict that, given sufficient input into at least one action-system and inhibitory effects being the more powerful at high levels of activation only, activation in one and only one system would rise increasingly rapidly to infinity and in all others drop increasingly rapidly to zero.

There need to be additional mechanisms that limit the feedback rise and fall respectively. Recurrent inhibitory effects (see Eccles, 1967) could limit the positive feedback rise. In addition, this could be mediated by external systems such as Kahneman's (1973) "effort system" acting directly on inhibitory interneurones (see also Walley and Weiden, 1973). To prevent the fall to a total lack of activation, different neurons within the action-system assembly might be differentially sensitive to inhibitory effects; those least sensitive could then still remain active when the remainder were silent. Modeling of the process by stochastic rather than continuous variable methods would also predict low levels of firing in a generally inhibited system if firing in all systems obeyed a Poisson process. Finally, frontal planning systems might help to maintain low-levels of activation.

References

Ach, N. *Über die Willenstätigheit und das Denken.* Göttingen: Vardenhoek, 1905.

Allport, D. A. On knowing the meaning of words we are unable to report; the effects of visual masking. In S. Dornic (Ed.) *Attention and performance.* Vol. 6. London: Academic Press, 1977.

Allport, D. A., Antonis, B., and Reynolds, P. On the division of attention: A disproof of the single-channel hypothesis. *Quarterly Journal of Experimental Psychology,* 1972, 24, 225-235.

Atkinson, R. C., and Shiffrin, R. M. The control of short-term memory. *Scientific American,* 1971, 224, 82-90.

Baddeley, A. D. *The psychology of memory.* London: Harper & Row, 1976.

Baddeley, A. D., and Hitch, G. Working memory. In G. Bower (Ed.) *Recent advances in learning and motivation.* Vol. 8. New York: Academic Press, 1974.

Baddeley, A. D., Scott, D., Drynan, R., and Smith, J. C. Short-term memory and the limited capacity hypothesis. *British Journal of Psychology,* 1969, 60, 51-55.

Bartz, W. H., and Salehi, M. Interference in short- and long-term memory. *Journal of Experimental Psychology,* 1970, 84, 380-382.

Bernstein, N. A. *The co-ordination and regulation of movements.* Oxford: Pergamon, 1967.

Brand, J. Classification without identification in visual search. *Quarterly Journal of Experimental Psychology,* 1971, 23, 178-186.

Broadbent, D. E. *Decision and stress.* New York: Academic Press, 1971.

Brown, R., and McNeill, D. The "tip of the tongue" phenomenon. *Journal of Verbal Learning and Verbal Behaviour,* 1966, 5, 325-337.

Bullock, T. H., and Horridge, G. A. *Structure and function in the nervous systems of invertebrates.* Vol 1. San Francisco: Freeman, 1965.

Cattell, J. McK. The time taken up by the cerebral operations. *Mind,* 1886, 11, 220-242, 377-392, and 524-538.

Craik, F. I. M., and Tulving, E. Depth of processing and the retention of words in episodic memory. *Journal of Experimental Psychology: General,* 1975, 104, 268-294.

Craik, F. I. M., and Watkins, M. J. The role of rehearsal in short-term memory. *Journal of Verbal Learning and Verbal Behaviour,* 1973, 12, 599-607.

De Groot, A. D. *Thought and choice in chess.* The Hague: Mouton, 1965.

Dixon, N. *Subliminal perception: the nature of a controversy.* Maidenhead: McGraw-Hill, 1971.

Downey, J. E., and Anderson, J. E. Automatic writing. *American Journal of Psychology,* 1915, 26, 161-195.

Duncan, J. "Association" and "decision" — S-R compatibility in choice reaction tasks. D. Phil. Thesis: Oxford University, 1976.

Easterbrook, J. A. The effect of emotion on cue utilization and the organisation of behaviour. *Psychological Review,* 1959, 66, 183-201.

Eccles, J. C. Postsynaptic inhibition in the central nervous system. In G. C. Quarton, T. Melnechuk, F. O. Schmitt (Eds.) *The neurosciences study program.* New York: Rockefeller University Press, 1967.

Egeth, H., Jonides, J., and Wall, S. Parallel processing of multielement displays. *Cognitive Psychology,* 1972, 3, 674-698.

Erdelyi, M. H. A new look at the New Look: Perceptual defense and vigilance. *Psychological Review*, 1974, *81*, 1-25.

Eriksen, C. W. and Johnson, H. J. Storage and decay characteristics of nonattended auditory stimuli. *Journal of Experimental Psychology*, 1964, *68*, 28-36.

Evarts, E. V. Unit activity in sleep and wakefulness. In G. C. Quarton, T. Melnechuk, F. O. Schmitt (Eds.), *The neurosciences study program*. New York: Rockefeller University Press, 1967.

Fehrer, E., and Raab, D. Reaction time to stimuli masked by metacontrast. *Journal of Experimental Psychology*, 1962, *63*, 143-147.

Garner, W. R. *The processing of information and structure*. New York: Wiley, 1974.

Gazzaniga, M. S., Bogen, J. E., and Sperry, R. W. Some functional effects of sectioning the cerebral commissures in man. *Proceedings of the National Academy of Science*, 1962, *48*, 1756-1759.

Gibbs, C. B. Servo-control systems in organisms and the transfer of skill. In D. Legge (Ed.), *Skills*. London: Penguin, 1970.

Greeno, J. G. Indefinite goals in well-structured problems. *Psychological Review*, 1976, *83*, 479-491.

Gregory, R. C. Eye movements and the stability of the visual world. *Nature*, 1958, *182*, 1214-1216.

Hamilton, P., Hockey, G. R. J., and Rejman, M. The place of the concept of activation in human information processing theory: an integrative approach. In S. Dornic (Ed.), *Attention and performance*. Vol. 6. London: Academic Press, 1977.

Hawkins, H. L. Parallel processing in complex visual discrimination. *Perception and Psychophysics*, 1969, *5*, 56-64.

Hebb, D. O. *The organization of behavior*. New York: Wiley, 1949.

Hillyard, S. A., and Picton, T. W. Event-related brain potentials and selective information-processing in man. In J. E. Desmedt (Ed.), *Cerebral evoked potentials in man*. Basel: Karger, 1977.

Hillyard, S. A., Hink, R. F., Schwent, V. L., and Picton, T. W. Electrical signs of selective attention in the human brain. *Science*, 1973, *182*, 177-180.

Hochberg, J. Attention, organisation and consciousness. In D. I. Mostofsky (Ed.), *Attention: Contemporary theory and analysis*. New York: Appleton-Century-Crofts, 1970.

Hockey, G. R. J. Effect of loud noise on attentional selectivity. *Quarterly Journal of Experimental Psychology*, 1970, *22*, 28-36.

Humphrey, C. *Thinking*. London: Methuen, 1951.

Humphrey, N. K. What the frog's eye tells the monkey's brain. *Brain, Behaviour and Evolution*, 1970, *3*, 324-337.

Humphrey, N. K., and Weiskrantz, L. Vision in monkeys after removal of the striate cortex. *Nature*, 1967, *215*, 595-597.

Hyde, T. S., and Jenkins, J. J. Recall for words as a function of semantic, graphic and syntactic orienting tasks. *Journal of Verbal Learning and Verbal Behaviour*, 1973, *12*, 471-480.

James, W. T. *Principles of psychology*, New York: Holt, 1890.

Jonides, J., and Gleitman, H. A conceptual category effect in visual search: "O" as letter or as digit. *Perception and Psychophysics*, 1972, *10*, 457-460.

Kahneman, D. *Attention and effort*. Englewood Cliffs, N. J.: Prentice-Hall, 1973.

Kinsbourne, M. Lateral interactions in the brain. In M. Kinsbourne and W. L. Smith (Eds.), *Hemispheric disconnection and cerebral function*. Springfield, Ill.: Charles C Thomas, 1974.

Kinsbourne, M. The mechanism of hemispheric control of the lateral gradient of attention. In P. M. A. Rabbitt and S. Dornic (Eds.), *Attention and performance*. Vol. 5. London: Academic Press, 1975.

Konorski, J. *Integrative activity of the brain*. Chicago: University of Chicago Press, 1967.

Laberge, D. Acquisition of automatic processing in perceptual and associative learning. In P. M. A. Rabbitt and S. Dornic (Eds.), *Attention and performance*. Vol. 5. London: Academic Press, 1975.

Lewis, J. L. Semantic processing of unattended messages under dichotic listening. *Journal of Experimental Psychology*, 1970, *85*, 225-228.

Lissauer, H. Ein Fall von Seelenblindheit nebst einem Beitrag zur Theorie derselben. *Archiv für Psychiatrie und Nervenkrankheiten*, 1890, *21*, 222-299.

Logue, V., Durward, M., Pratt, R. T. C., Piercy, M., and Nixon, W. L. B. The quality of survival after rupture of an anterior cerebral aneurysm. *British Journal of Psychiatry*, 1968, *114*, 137-160.

Luria, A. R. *Higher Cortical Functions in Man*. London: Tavistock, 1966.

MacKay, D. G. Spoonerisms: The structure of errors in the serial order of speech. *Neuropsychologia*, 1970, *8*, 323-350.

MacKay, D. G. Aspects of the theory of comprehension, memory and attention. *Quarterly Journal of Experimental Psychology*, 1973, *25*, 22-40.

Mandler, G. *Mind and Emotion*. New York: Wiley, 1975.

Marcel, A. J. Perception with and without awareness. Paper presented to the Experimental Psychology Society, Stirling, July, 1974.

Marcel, A. J., and Patterson, K. Word recognition: reciprocity in clinical and normal studies. In J. Requin (Ed.), *Attention and performance*. Vol. 7. Hillsdale, N. J.: Erlbaum, 1978.

Maruyama, M. The second cybernetics: deviation - amplifying mutual causal processes. *American Scientist*, 1963, *51*, 164-179.

Miller, G. A. *Psychology: the science of mental life*. New York: Harper & Row, 1962.

Miller, G.A., and Johnson-Laird, P. N. *Language and perception*. Cambridge: Cambridge University Press, 1976.

Miller, G. A., Galanter, E. H., and Pribram, K. *Plans and the structure of behaviour*. New York: Holt, Rinehart & Winston, 1960.

Milner, P. M. The cell assembly: mark II. *Psychological Review*, 1957, *64*, 242-252.

Milner, P. M. *Physiological psychology*. New York: Holt, Rinehart & Winston, 1970.

Murdock, B. B., Jr. Effects of a subsidiary task on short-term memory. *British Journal of Psychology*, 1965, *56*, 413-419.

Neisser, U. The multiplicity of thought. *British Journal of Psychology*, 1963, *54*, 1-14.

Neisser, U. *Cognition and reality*. San Francisco: Freeman, 1976.

Newall, A., and Simon, H. A. *Human problem solving*. Englewood Cliffs, N. J.: Prentice-Hall, 1972.

Newall, A., Shaw, J. C., and Simon, H. A. Elements of a theory of human problem-solving. *Psychological Review*, 1958, *65*, 151-166.

Pew, R. W. Human perceptual-motor performance. In I. B. H. Kantowitz (Ed.), *Human information-processing*. Hillsdale, N. J.: Erlbaum, 1974.

Polanyi, M. *The tacit dimension*. Garden City: Doubleday, 1966.

Posner, M. I. Psychobiology of attention. In M. Gazzaniga and C. Blakemore (Eds.), *Handbook of psychobiology*. New York: Academic Press, 1974.

Posner, M. I., and Klein, R. M. On the functions of consciousness. In S. Kornblum (Ed.), *Attention and performance*. Vol. 4. New York: Academic Press, 1973.

Posner, M. I., and Snyder, C. Facilitation and inhibition in the processing of signals. In P. M. A. Rabbitt and S. Dornic (Eds.), *Attention and performance*. Vol. 5. London Academic Press, 1975.

Posner, M. I., Nissen, M. J., Ogden, W. C., and Davidson, B. J. Attention to position in space. Paper presented to the Psychonomics Society, October, 1975.

Ratliff, F. *Mach bands*. San Francisco: Holden Day, 1965.

Reason, J. Absent minds. *New Society*, 4 November 1976.

Reicher, G. M. Perceptual recognition as a function of stimulus material. *Journal of Experimental Psychology*, 1969, *81*, 275–280.

Saffran, E. M., and Marin, O. S. M. Immediate memory for word lists and sentences in a patient with deficient auditory short-term memory. *Brain and Language*, 1975, *2*, 420–433.

Saraga, E., and Shallice, T. Parallel processing of the attributes of single stimuli. *Perception and Psychophysics*, 1973, *13*, 261–270.

Schneider, G. E. Two visual systems. *Science*, 1969, *163*, 895–902.

Selfridge, O. Pandemonium: A paradigm for learning. In *Mechanization of thought processes*. London, H. M. S. O., 1959.

Selz, O. *Über die Gesetze des geordneten Denkverlaufs*. Stuttgart: Speman, 1913.

Selz, O. *Zur Psychologie des produktiven Denkens und des Irrtums*. Bonn: Cohen, 1922.

Shaffer, L. H. Multiple attention in continuous verbal tasks. In P. M. A. Rabbitt and S. Dornic (Eds.), *Attention and performance*. Vol. 5. London: Academic Press, 1975.

Shallice, T. Dual functions of consciousness. *Psychological Review*, 1972, *79*, 383–393.

Shallice, T. On the contents of primary memory. In P. M. A. Rabbitt and S. Dornic (Eds.), *Attention and performance*. Vol. 5. London: Academic Press, 1975.

Shallice, T. Neuropsychological research and the fractionation of memory systems. In L.-G. Nilsson (Ed.) *Perspectives in memory research*. Hillsdale, N. J.: Erlbaum, in press.

Shallice, T., and Evans, M. E. The involvement of the frontal lobes in cognitive estimation. *Cortex*, 1978 (in press).

Shallice, T., and McGill, J. The origins of mixed errors. In J. Requin (Ed.), *Attention and performance*. Vol. 7. Hillsdale, N.J.: Erlbaum, 1978.

Shallice, T., and Warrington, E. K. Independent functioning of the verbal memory stores: a neuropsychological study. *Quarterly Journal of Experimental Psychology*, 1970, *22*, 261–273.

Shallice, T., and Warrington, E. K. The possible role of selective attention in acquired dyslexia. *Neuropsychologia*, 1977a, *15*, 31–42.

Shallice, T., and Warrington, E. K. Auditory-verbal short-term memory impairment and conduction aphasia. *Brain and Language*, 1977b, *4*, 479–491.

Sherrington, C. S. *The integrative action of the nervous system*. New Haven: Yale University Press, 1906.

Sloman, A. *The computer revolution in philosophy*. London: Harvester, 1977.

Smith, K. U., and Akelaitis, A. J. Studies on the corpus callosum. *Archives of Neurology and Psychiatry*, 1942, *47*, 519–543.

Sokolov, E. N. *Perception and the conditioned reflex*. London: Macmillan, 1963.

Solomons, L., and Stein, G. Normal motor automatism. *Psychological Review*, 1896, *3*, 492–512.

Spelke, E., Hirst, W., and Neisser, U. Skills of divided attention. *Cognition*, 1976, *4*, 215–230.

Sutherland, N. S. Intelligent picture processing. Proceedings of the conference on the evolution of the nervous system and behavior, Florida State University, 1973.

Treisman, A. M. Contextual cues in selective listening. *Quarterly Journal of Experimental Psychology*, 1960, *12*, 242–248.

Treisman, A. M., Sykes, M., and Gelade, G. Selective attention and stimulus integration. In S. Dornic (Ed.), *Attention and performance*. Vol. 6. London: Academic Press, 1977.

Trevarthen, C. B. Functional interactions between the cerebral hemispheres of the split-brain monkey. In G. C. Ettlinger (Ed.), *Functions of the corpus callosum*. London: Churchill, 1965.

Trevarthen, C. B. Two mechanisms of vision in primates. *Psychologische Forschung*, 1968, *31*, 299–337.

Trevarthen, C. B. Functional relations of disconnected hemispheres with the brainstem and with each other: monkey and man. In M. Kinsbourne and W. L. Smith (Eds.), *Hemispheric disconnection and cerebral function*. Springfield, Ill.: Charles C Thomas, 1974.

Turvey, M. T. Constructive theory, perceptual systems and tacit knowledge. In W. B. Weimer and D. S. Palermo (Eds.), *Cognition and the symbolic processes*. Hillsdale, N.J.: Erlbaum, 1974.

Turvey, M. T. Preliminaries to a theory of action with reference to vision. In R. Shaw and J. Bransford (Eds.), *Perceiving. acting and knowing: toward an ecological psychology*. Hillsdale, N.J.: Erlbaum, 1977.

Walley, R. E., and Weiden, T. D. Lateral inhibition and cognitive masking: a neuropsychological theory of attention. *Psychological Review*, 1973, *80*, 284–302.

Warrington, E. K. Constructional apraxia. In P. J. Vincken and G. W. Bruyn (Eds.), *Handbook of clinical neurology*. Vol. 4. Amsterdam: North Holland, 1969.

Warrington, E. K. The selective impairment of semantic memory. *Quarterly Journal of Experimental Psychology*, 1975, *27*, 635–658.

Warrington, E. K., and Taylor, A. M. The contribution of the right parietal lobe to object recognition. *Cortex*, 1973, *7*, 152–164.

Watt, H. J. Experimentelle Beiträge zu einer Theorie des Denkens. *Archiv für die Gesamte Psychologie*, 1905, *4*, 289–436.

Waugh, N. C. Retrieval time in short-term memory. *British Journal of Psychology*, 1970, *61*, 1–12.

Weiskrantz, L., Warrington, E. K., Sanders, M. D., and Marshall, J. Visual capacity in the hemianopic field following a restricted occipital ablation. *Brain*, 1974, *97*, 709–728.

Wheeler, D. D. Processes in word recognition. *Cognitive Psychology*, 1970, *1*, 59–85.

Winograd, T. *Understanding natural language*. Edinburgh: University Press, 1972.

Wittgenstein, L. *Philosophical investigations*. Oxford: Blackwell, 1953.

Woodworth, R. S., and Schlosberg, H. *Experimental Psychology*. New York: Holt, 1954.

6

Two Streams of Consciousness: A Typological Approach

Paul Bakan

> Since we all swerve rather more towards one side or the other, we naturally tend to understand everything in terms of our own type.
>
> —C. G. Jung

There is no doubt that the stream of consciousness is somehow related to the functioning of the brain. If, now, it is argued that man has not one brain, but two, a right and a left brain, then is it reasonable to speak of two streams of consciousness rather than one? And, further, can the two streams mediated by the two brains be qualitatively different from each other? And can it be that individual differences in consciousness are due to a bias favoring one or the other stream of consciousness? In this essay I propose to defend the proposition that affirmative answers are appropriate to these questions.

1. Duality of Mind and Brain in History

The history of man's reflections on the nature of his mind, soul, or consciousness is marked by references to duality. In the book of Genesis, referring to God's forming of animals and his forming of man, the word for "formed," *vayitzer*, has one *y* (or yod) when referring to animal formation (II, 19) and two *y*s, *vayyitzer*, for the

Paul Bakan • Department of Psychology, Simon Fraser University, Burnaby, British Columbia, Canada.

formation of man (II, 7). Biblical scholars have interpreted this to mean that man alone is endowed with two aspects, inclinations, or imaginings, a duality that distinguished him from the animals. Early interpretations of this duality are based on the greatest discontinuity in evolution, namely, the development of speech and reason (Isaiah and Sharfman, 1949). The Kabala, a collection of Jewish mystical writings, extracts from the Bible the notion that man has two souls and "one should not think that both of them are alike . . . one soul comes from . . . one side, the other . . . from the other side. Each of the two . . . takes its place in one of the brains . . . " (Rosenberg, 1973). The Zohar, one of the main books of the Kabala, distinguishes between two kinds of cognition, *hokmah*, or wisdom, associated with the right brain and operating through the principle of synthesis, and *binah*, or intelligence, associated with the left brain and operating through the principle of analysis (Schaya, 1971). This Jewish tradition takes the suggested duality of man from the Old Testament and from it derives two essentially different forms of consciousness, each mediated by a different side of the brain.

Duality is also central in other ancient systems of thought. Thus, the yin and yang of Chinese philosophy that represent the two basic forms of energy found in all things. Yin is passive, feminine, weak, and dark in contrast to yang, which is active, masculine, strong, and light. In Buddhist thinking a distinction is made between two forms of consciousness related to nostril laterality. When the right nostril is clear the right side of the body and the left hemisphere are predominant. The person is then ready for aggressive and assertive interactions such as are involved in reading, teaching of difficult sciences, and athletic sports. When the left nostril is clear, the left side of the body and the right hemisphere are predominant. This is a time for more passive and less assertive activities such as spiritual and musical activities (Rana, Ballentine, and Ajaya, 1976).

A relationship between the duality of consciousnesses and the duality of the brain is considered again in the nineteenth century by the British physician, A. L. Wigan in his book, *The Duality of the Mind* (Wigan, 1844). Having attended an autopsy where one cerebral hemisphere was absent in a patient who was functioning normally only a few days before his death, Wigan concluded that "it takes one hemisphere to have a mind"; and since the brain has two hemispheres it is normal to have two minds. In fact, Wigan argued "the two hemispheres of the brain are really . . . two distinct and entire organs . . . each as complete . . . and as fully perfect . . . for the purposes it is intended to perform, as are the two eyes." Wigan also concludes that each cerebrum (i.e., hemisphere) is a whole organ of thought; that two thought processes can occur simultaneously, one in each cerebrum; that each cerebrum is capable of a separate volition, often opposing that of the other cerebrum; that the incoherence of insane consciousness results from an alternating intermixture of two trains of thought; and that the superiority of a disciplined scholar lies in his power of habitually combining the attention of both brains to the same object. Wigan believed that this theory of dual consciousness, based on a dual brain, a theory with important implications for the psychology of cognition, psychopathology, and education would "form a great trunk of a railway to an important truth." In fact, his theory had minimal impact.

A more influential approach to the dual brain was based on Broca's discovery of a relationship between language and the left side of the brain. This turned attention to the left hemisphere and its functions. The great importance of language and the dominance of the right hand, also controlled by the left hemisphere, led to the conclusion that the left hemisphere was more important than the right. The left is therefore considered the dominant hemisphere. Zangwill (1961) not long ago characterized the generally accepted neurological view, namely, that there are no functional differences between the two hemispheres other than those conventionally related to handedness and speech.

It is against the background of this conventional (though fallacious) wisdom that the work of J. Hughlings Jackson assumes its importance. Jackson had discovered, independently of Broca, the relationship between speech and the left hemisphere. But he rejected the oversimplified notion of cerebral dominance that was to become popular. Jackson's view, much closer to contemporary understanding, was that the "leading" hemisphere for speech might not be the leading hemisphere for all functions, but that the so-called minor or right hemisphere might be the leading one for some functions. I have called this the dual-dominance model (Bakan, 1971). Jackson's conception of cerebral dominance leads to a search for those functions for which the left hemisphere is dominant and those functions for which the right hemisphere is dominant. Two years after Broca's announcement Jackson wrote: "If . . . the faculty of expression . . . resides in one hemisphere, there is no absurdity in raising the question as to whether perception—its corresponding opposite—may not reside in the other" (Jackson, 1958, p. 43).

Over the past two decades a body of research has appeared that tends to support the thinking of both Jackson and Wigan. The evidence supports the dual-dominance concept of Jackson in showing a difference in the psychological functions mediated by the right and left cerebral hemispheres, and it supports Wigan's speculation of two potentially independent minds, mediated by two hemispheres, each of which is sufficient for consciousness, personality, and thought. These insights have been based on a variety of techniques applied to both normal and brain-injured subjects. Perhaps the most dramatic results have come from the work with split-brain subjects. Myers and Sperry (1953) prepared a cat in such a way that the input to each eye went to the cerebral hemisphere on the same side, and the two hemispheres could not communicate with each other. A cat so prepared and with a blindfold over the left eye could learn to respond positively to a circle. With the blindfold over the right eye, there was no evidence that the cat had learned to respond to the circle because the right eye input had educated the right hemisphere, and without interhemispheric communication, the left hemisphere was not influenced by what the right hemisphere had learned.

A modified form of this surgery has been applied to humans for the treatment of severe epilepsy. The human split-brain is produced by surgically separating the right from the left hemisphere by cutting the commissures connecting them. Since the optic chiasma is left intact in the human (as it was not in the cat) the eye-brain connection is more complicated. Stimuli impinging on the nasal retina of the right eye and the temporal retina of the left eye, (i.e., stimuli from the right visual field) go to the left hemisphere, and stimuli from the left visual field go to the right hemisphere. Careful experimentation with split-brain patients has led to strong evidence in support of the theory that there are two minds or streams of consciousness in one head. This is clear in Sperry's (1968) summary of his investigations with the split-brain patients:

> Instead of the normally unified single stream of consciousness these patients behave in many ways as if they had two independent streams of conscious awareness, one in each hemisphere, each of which is cut off from and out of contact with the mental experiences of the other. . . . Each . . .seems to have its own separate and private sensations, its own perceptions, its own concepts, and its own impulses to act.

Though the differences between the hemispheres and the resulting differences in consciousness and behavior are real, the differences are often quite subtle. Sperry, in discussing his results with split-brain patients, points out the subtlety of left-right differences in cognitive style and then concludes that "even subtle differences become meaningful . . . when you see the same individual performing the same test tasks and reaching the same solutions in two different ways, using different strategies, much like two different people, depending on whether it is the left or the right hemisphere in use" (Sperry, 1976). Thus, the notion of two minds or two streams of consciousness as mediated by two brains in one head is confirmed. An idea suggested by ancient philosophy and religion, rejected when proposed by Wigan and Jackson, appears now to be an idea whose time has come.

2. Functional Asymmetry of the Cerebral Hemispheres

What is of the greatest interest in the findings about the duality of the brain is that the "mind" of the right brain appears to be qualitatively different in its basic mode of functioning from that of the left brain. It has been known since Broca that the left brain is verbal, and the right brain is nonverbal. Since then and especially in recent years, great advances have been made in spelling out the functional differences between the hemispheres. There is evidence of left hemisphere superiority in tasks involving grammatically organized word sequences, mathematics, analysis, logic, sequences over time, and motor coordination. Right hemisphere function seems dominant in tasks involving imagery, certain visual and constructive activities such as drawing, copying, assembling block designs, perception and manipulation of spatial relations of and between objects or configurations, and the simultaneous grasping of fragments or particulars as a meaningful whole. Various descriptions of the two modes of thought mediated by the two hemispheres have been suggested. The left hemisphere mode is described as symbolic, abstract, linear, rational, focal, conceptual, propositional, secondary process, digital, logical, active, and analytic. The right hemisphere mode is described as iconic, concrete, diffuse, perceptual, appositional, primary process, analogue, passive, and holistic (Dimond and Beaumont, 1974; Kinsbourne and Smith, 1974; Nebes, 1974). The two modes are antagonistic and complementary, suggesting that a unity and struggle of opposites is characteristic of mental functioning.

The stream of consciousness may, in the light of the findings of functional asymmetry of the hemispheres, be conceived of as two streams of consciousness or a river consisting of selections, combinations, or interactions of streams from the right and left hemispheres. It now becomes meaningful to ask questions that would not too long ago have appeared ridiculous. For example, does the nature of consciousness in an intact normal individual differ depending on which hemisphere is stimulated? Does it matter whether one takes his right or left hemisphere to the movies? This is exactly the question proposed by Dimond, Farrington, and Johnson (1976). Using a special contact lens they could project the contents of a film (without sound) to either the right or left hemisphere. They found that films shown to the right hemisphere were reported as more unpleasant and horrific than films shown to the left hemisphere. The two hemispheres of the intact human brain seem to possess a different emotional vision of the world. The authors suggest that the right hemisphere "adds its own emotional dimension . . . as more unpleasant and horrible and this aligns itself more with the characteristic perception of the depressive patient. . . ."

3. Hemispheric Differences and Individual Differences

If two different modes of thought are mediated respectively by the right and left cerebral hemispheres, then it becomes meaningful to ask whether individuals differ in the degree to which they rely on one or the other hemisphere in their overall psychological functioning. A bias toward greater reliance on one hemisphere, be it right or left, could significantly influence the quality of consciousness. Individual differences in the quality of consciousness, and the behavior based on the quality of consciousness, may be due to different biases toward use of one of the hemispheres. A bias toward the use of one hemisphere is called hemisphericity (Bogen, 1969). The typological approach to personality and cognition is largely characterized by dualistic typologies, e.g., extraversion-introversion, field dependent-field independent, impulsive-reflective. Can hemisphericity be at the root of dualistic typologies?

Francis Bacon (Critchley, 1966) noted a "radical distinction between different minds . . . that some minds are . . . apter to mark the differences of things, others to mark their resemblances." The "acute" mind can "fasten on the sublest distinctions"; the "discursive" mind "recognizes and puts together the finest and most general resemblances." Pavlov (1932, p. 275) writes:

> Life clearly reveals *two* groups of human beings; artists and thinkers. There is a striking difference between them. The first group, artists of all kinds— writers, musicians, painters, etc., perceive reality as a single whole . . . without breaking it up or decomposing it. The other group, the thinkers, on the contrary, dismember it, thereby, as it were, killing it and making of it a kind of temporary skeleton; only afterwards do they gradually . . . assemble its parts . . . but this . . . they are unable to fully accomplish . . . the combination in one and the same person of great artist and great thinker is an exceedingly rare phenomenon. In the overwhelming majority of cases they are represented by different individuals.

Heine, the German poet (Jung, 1976) observes *two* distinct human natures, inimically opposed, either like Plato, or like Aristotle—Plato, the mystic and visionary, and Aristotle, the practical and orderly. Plato, drawing ideas and symbols from the fathomless depths of the soul, and Aristotle, using ideas to produce fixed systems or dogmas. More recently Conant (1964) has distinguished between *two* types of people, each with a distinctive mode of thought, the empirical-inductive and the theoretical-deductive.

These dualistic typologies appear to have a distinct similarity to the antagonistic modes of thought and functioning that are character-istic of the two cerebral hemispheres. The minds apt at seeing differences, the acute mind of Bacon, those of Pavlov's thinkers who dismember reality, the mind of Heine's Aristotle, practical and orderly and the theoretical-deductive mind of Conant all line up with the left hemisphere. On the other hand, the discursive mind of Bacon, better at noting resemblances than differences, the mind of Pavlov's artist, perceiving reality in holistic terms, Heine's Platonic visionary mind and Conant's empirical-inductive mind, line up with the right hemi-sphere. This suggests that the types are what they are because they result from individual differences in preferred use of one or the other hemispheres. Hence the notion of hemisphericity has relevance for the consistent duality found in so many typological systems.

In this light it might be useful to examine one of the better worked-out typological systems, namely Witkin's field dependent-independent typology (Witkin, Dyk, Faterson, Goodenough, and Karp, 1962). Like other typological thinkers, Witkin conceives of his basic dichotomy as a reflection of the synthetic-analytic dimension. Subjects are placed into one or the other classification as a result of certain perceptual tests. Good performance on these tests is based on ability to break up a gestalt, to be analytic, or to differentiate the stimulus material. Subjects who do well on these tests are said to be field independent; those who do poorly, field dependent. When field dependent and field independent subjects are then compared it is found that they differ significantly on a wide variety of personality, cognitive, and physiological variables. The field dependent-independ-ent dimension is seen as the manifestation in perception of the more general construct of psychological differentiation. Our interest in this typology is based on the concept so similar to other dualistic typolo-gies, namely, the global-differentiated or analytic-synthetic dimen-sion. The dimension is similar to noting differences versus resem-blances (Bacon), decomposing reality versus perceiving it as a whole (Pavlov), and deductive versus inductive (Conant). Do the differences between field-dependent and independent subjects align themselves

with the characteristics of right- and left-hemisphere thinking? To the
extent that the right-hemisphere mode of thinking is more global and
the left-hemisphere mode is more differentiated (Nebes, 1974) this
seems to be the case. Field-dependent people not only are more global
in perceptual performance, but their body concept is less differentiated, their self-concept is less differentiated, and even their defense
mechanisms are more global, consisting of denial and repression in
contrast to isolation and intellectualization in field-independent individuals (Witkin *et al.* 1962).

In view of the importance of the left hemisphere for the mediation
of language, it is interesting to note that field-independent individuals, for example, have been shown to do better in tasks of verbal
fluency (De Fazio, 1973). Analytic ability, another important aspect of
left-hemisphere functioning, is also better in field-independent individuals. In a study by Ehri and Muzio (1974), for example, it was
found that field independence was associated with better solutions of
a problem requiring reasoning about the relative speeds of horses on a
merry-go-round. Sequential or linear thinking is characteristic of left-
hemisphere functioning. Berent (1976) has found that field-independent subjects did better than field-dependent subjects on a timed serial
subtraction task. Berent and his colleagues have also found that field-
dependent subjects did not do as well as field independents on a
copying task (writing), and on a verbal paired association task. It has
even been suggested that extreme field dependence is a symptom of
left-hemisphere dysfunction (Cohen, Berent, and Silverman, 1973;
Berent, 1974).

A most interesting demonstration of the relationship between
field-dependence and brain lateralization is found in a study by
Cohen, Berent, and Silverman (1973). They administered the rod and
frame test, a test of field dependence, before and after a single
electroconvulsive shock treatment (ECT) delivered either to the left or
right cerebral hemisphere of depressed patients. Subjects with left
ECT showed an increase in field dependence on the second test
whereas those with right ECT showed a decrease in field dependence
on the second test. There was no overlap in the distribution of before
shock—after shock change scores. This is strong evidence of an
association between field dependence and relative right-hemisphere
dominance, and between field independence and relative left-hemisphere dominance. Further evidence suggesting relationships between
field dependence and laterality is found in the work of Oltman,
Ehrlichman, and Cox (1976), and Pizzamiglio (1974).

Another example of a typology-hemispheric relationship is found
in the case of a lesser-known typology suggested by experiments on

the classical conditioning of eyeblinks. Differences in the form of conditioned eyeblinks has led to the classification of subjects as either C- or V-form responders. The V-form response is a relatively rapid, more complete eyelid closure of longer duration and earlier onset than the C-form response. There is hardly any information on how Cs and Vs differ in tasks outside of the conditioned eyeblink situation. However, Hellige (1975) has recently shown that the conditioning performance of Cs was more influenced by the semantic attributes of the stimuli when they were presented directly to the left hemisphere (right visual field) than when they were presented to the right hemisphere (left visual field). In the case of the Vs there was no difference between the right and left hemisphere with respect to semantic processing; i.e., the functions of the hemispheres appear less differentiated. A similar finding of less hemisphere differentiation has been shown in the performance of field-dependent subjects for a face-perception task, with field-independent subjects showing greater lateralization of face perception to the right hemisphere (Oltman *et al.*, 1976). These differences between types of subjects, whether they are called field independent and dependent or Cs and Vs (or names associated with other typologies), suggest that qualitatively different kinds of processing are related to cerebral hemispheric organization, and that individuals differ in the extent to which each hemisphere is engaged for a given task.

4.   Eye Movements, Hemisphericity, and Individual Differences

The first explicitly hemispheric typology was developed by Bakan (1969), and is based on a bias toward the use of either the right or left hemisphere in an individual's cognitive, and affective functioning. The direction of the bias is inferred from the lateral direction of certain conjugate lateral eye movements (CLEM), and leads to the classification of individuals as right- or left-hemisphere people.

Teitlebaum (1954) observed that during mental concentration a person moves his eyes conjugately in the horizontal direction; the nature of the movement being characteristic for a given individual. He felt that the function of these eye movements was to break contact with the external environment, go out of focus, and thus reduce external stimulation incompatible with the internal reflective behavior of thought or concentration. Day (1964) also noted a lateral movement of the eyes associated with thought. He observed that if, when facing a subject, he asked a question requiring thought or reflection, the subject would turn his eyes to the right or left upon beginning to reflect upon an answer. Day made a number of important observations, namely, that the direction of the eye movement, right or left, was reasonably consistent for individuals, that about half of the population moved their eyes to the right and about half to the left, and perhaps most important, that there were differences between the right movers and the left movers in various aspects of their cognitive, personality, and physiological functioning (Day, 1964, 1967a, 1967b). Bakan (1969, 1971) traced the relationship between conjugate lateral eye movements and the cerebral hemispheres, and provided Day's eye movement typology with a hemispheric basis. Essentially, the relationship between the lateral direction of eye movements and the brain is contralateral; i.e., right-hemisphere activation produces left-eye movements and left-hemisphere activation produces right-eye movements. These findings date from the work of Fritsch and Hitzig (1870), confirmed by Ferrier (1876), showing that upon stimulation of the frontal eye area of one hemisphere in the monkey, there was a turning of the eyes to the opposite side. Mott and Schaefer (1890) showed that with equal simultaneous bilateral stimulation of points that when unilaterally stimulated produced conjugate lateral deviation, the result was straight-ahead fixation with no lateral deviation. It appears then that the eyes move in the direction opposite to the hemisphere receiving the greater excitation. This relationship is essentially the same for humans (Penfield and Boldrey, 1973; Bender, 1964).

The contralateral relationship between the right cerebral hemisphere (or left) and left (or right) conjugate lateral eye movements leads to the following model. Conjugate lateral eye movements are symptomatic of easier excitation of activity in the hemisphere contralateral to the direction of eye movement. Individuals who tend to move their eyes to the right as they begin to reflect on a question are individuals whose central nervous system is organized in such a way as to facilitate left hemisphere activity either by lower latency, lower threshold, or greater strength of excitation. For left movers the reverse is the case. Thus, right eye movers are "left brained" and left eye movers are "right brained." It is proposed that since each hemisphere serves a primary mediating function for certain cognitive and emotional "styles," persons in whom the right hemisphere is the more dominant, in the sense of ease of excitation, i.e., left movers, will have the type of consciousness reflecting greater representation of the "style" of right-hemisphere functioning. Persons in whom the left hemisphere is the more dominant, the right movers, will have a type of consciousness reflecting greater representation of the "style" of left-hemisphere functioning. These different types of consciousness imply differences in cognition and personality as well.

In the light of this model it is important to look at some of the differences between the left-brained right movers and the right-brained left movers. The initial clinical observations of Day will be considered first. According to Day, right and left movers differ in their attentional mechanisms. The left mover, he says, has a more passive mode of attending while the right mover attends in a more active manner. Consonant with this difference along the active-passive dimension, the left mover prefers attending in the auditory mode whereas the right mover shows a preference for visual and haptic attention (Day, 1967a). The left mover is more attentive to subjective, internal, visceral experience, whereas the right mover shows a more externalized distribution of attention. Day believes that right and left movers differ in their experience of anxiety. The left mover describes anxiety as having a definite internal locus and a physiological arousal pattern similar to that of an auditory startle pattern. Visual experience of the left mover is said to emphasize hyperactivity of the upper viscera with increased heart and breathing rate. The large postural muscles tend to be flaccid, but facial expressiveness and mobility appear increased. Anxiety is described by the left mover as tensional and jittery. For the right mover anxiety is described as having an external locus, a panicky "fear in search of an object" quality. Large muscles appear tense while facial muscles show less tone and the face is less expressive. There is more lower visceral activity with slowing and strengthening of heart and breathing rate. Often there is an increase in armpit perspiration. Another area of difference between right and left movers mentioned by Day is language usage. The language of the left mover is more feeling oriented whereas that of the right mover is more action oriented. The left mover might say "I feel hungry," but his right-mover counterpart says "I have to get something to eat." The left mover is also said to use more adjectives, whereas the right mover uses more verbs.

Other differences between right and left movers mentioned by Day are greater amplitude and lower frequency EEG for left movers, a tendency for right movers to marry left movers and vice versa, a tendency for right and left movers to be susceptible to different diseases, and a tendency for right and left movers to benefit from different kinds of psychotherapy. This is an extensive and provocative list of differences between right and left movers, but the differences are based largely on clinical impressions and need further confirmation.

Duke (1968) confirmed the intrasubject consistency in lateral direction of eye movements, showing that individuals average about 86% of movements in the same direction. Bakan and Strayer (1973) have shown that this consistency of direction holds up over time. Duke also found that the direction of the eye movements was unrelated to eye dominance.

Since the work of Day there has developed a growing literature on the correlates of CLEM direction. Bakan and Shotland (1969) found that right movers perform significantly better on the Stroop color-word interference test, a finding recently confirmed by DeWitt and Averill (1976). In this test the subject has to resist the interfering effect of color words, while naming the ink color of the printed word; thus, he responds "yellow" upon seeing the word "red" printed in yellow ink. The task requires that the subject break up the stimulus into its word component, and its color component. The superiority in this task is common to both right movers and field-independent subjects (Bloomberg, 1969; Hochman, 1971) suggesting an overlap between these two typologies, as suggested earlier. The right-mover (and hence left-hemisphere) superiority is consistent with the more analytic nature of the left hemisphere. The performance of the right mover is thus analogous to that of the left hemisphere.

Bakan and Shotland (1969) also found that the reading speed of right movers was greater than that of left movers. This finding was confirmed and extended in a study by Ogle (1972). This is in line with the relationship between right CLEM, the left hemisphere, and language skills.

On the basis of a similarity between Day's description of the left mover and Hilgard's description of the good hypnotic subject (Hilgard, 1965), Bakan studied the relationship between CLEM direction and hypnotizability. Day described the left mover as a person with a tendency to focus attention on subjective experience, and Hilgard described the good hypnotic subject as "one who has rich subjective experiences." Bakan found that left movers scored significantly higher than right movers on a scale of hypnotic susceptibility (Bakan, 1969). Similar relationships between CLEM direction and hypnotizability have been found in other studies (Morgan, McDonald, and Mac-Donald, 1971; Gur and Gur, 1974; DeWitt and Averill, 1976). Sherrod's (1972) finding of a greater tendency of left movers to respond to a persuasive message is consistent with these findings. These results suggest a greater left-mover aptitude for hypnosis and, in line with the theoretical model proposed, a greater right-hemisphere involvement in hypnosis.

The amount of EEG alpha produced in the resting state has been found to correlate with hypnotizability (London, Hart, and Leibovitz, 1968; Nowlis and Rhead, 1968). Since both high alpha and a preponderance of left CLEM are associated with hypnosis, Bakan and Svorad (1969) predicted a relationship between CLEM laterality and EEG alpha. They found that left movers produce more resting EEG alpha than right movers, paralleling the results with high and low hypnotizable subjects. This result found support in the work of Strayer (1970). The greater amount of EEG alpha in left movers is also consistent with Day's finding of higher amplitude and lower-frequency EEG activity in left movers (Day, 1967a). There is also evidence of a relationship between CLEM laterality and EEG alpha increase produced with bio feedback (Strayer, 1970; Selzer, 1974). The association of EEG alpha with left CLEM is of special interest in view of the fact that more alpha is usually recorded over the right hemisphere (Liske, Hughes, and Stowe, 1967). This further supports the hypothesis that those with a preponderance of left CLEM are right brained.

The association of left CLEM with hypnosis suggests the possibility that other altered states of consciousness might be more common in left movers. If daydreaming is considered in this category, then the work of Meskin and Singer (1974) supports this hypothesis. They found that left movers were significantly more inner attentive in that they had more vivid and frequent daydreaming activity than right movers (Singer, 1974). There have been no systematic comparisons between right and left movers with respect to night dreaming or REM sleep. However, in a preliminary study I have found a tendency for left-mover males to sleep longer. Since long sleepers usually have more REM sleep, it may be that left movers dream more. Bakan (1975, 1976) has suggested a close relationship between REM sleep and activation of the right hemisphere.

Other findings reported by Bakan (1969) that suggest a different style of consciousness for right and left movers are the right movers' relatively superior performance on the mathematics score of the Scholastic Aptitude Test (SAT), and their preference for mathematics/science majors in university. In an unpublished study Bakan found a tendency for left movers to describe themselves as musical and religious on an adjective checklist. Weiten and Etaugh (1973) confirmed the difference between right and left movers found on the SAT and the preference of right movers for mathematics/science studies. They also report right-mover superiority on a concept-identification task requiring verbal and analytic skills, greater theoretical and economic interests for right movers in contrast to greater aesthetic and social interests for left movers, and better performance for left movers on an inverted alphabet printing task involving perceptual-spatial ability. Weiten and Etaugh conclude that this pattern of differences between right and left movers is "internally consistent with . . . Bakan's findings and theory regarding the relationship between lateral eye movements and cerebral dominance."

The experience of anxiety is an important component of the stream of consciousness. There is evidence to suggest that there are differences between right and left movers in the experience of anxiety. As mentioned earlier, Day reported differences especially obvious in pathologically anxious individuals (Day, 1968). The anxiety of the left mover he described as "tensional-jittery" with definite internal locus and adrenergic upper-visceral activity. Right-mover activity, he described in terms of a sinking, immobilizing fear in search of an object quality with definite external locus and cholinergic lower-visceral activity. Bliss (1971) studied subjective reports of anxiety symptoms in left and right movers, and though he was unable to confirm Day's description, he did find evidence for differences between left and right movers on a dimension of inner versus outer reactivity, especially for male subjects. Left-mover anxiety appears to center in the alimentary canal and suggest parasympathetic reactivity. Thus, left movers are more likely to report upset stomach, biting fingernails, diarrhea, need to urinate, need to defecate, and drinking of alcohol. The anxiety pattern of the right mover centers on the body surface and motor functions, somewhat suggestive of sympathetic reactivity. Right movers report cold hands and feet, perspiration, muscle tics and twitches, muscle tension in jaw and biting down, and incoherent speech.

Gerdes and Kinsbourne (1974) classified subjects under the stress of oral surgery in terms of subject's reports of anxiety cues as being inside or outside the body. They found that "internals" were more often left movers and "externals" were more often right movers. They also found that left mover had a higher pulse-rate elevation prior to surgery though they were more likely to underestimate cardiac arousal in subjective reports. In contrast the right movers tended to overestimate cardiac arousal. Other evidences on differences in cardiac responsivity comes from a study of Ogle (1972). He found that during the Stroop color-word interference task, a task described as stressful, left movers showed a significantly greater cardiac acceleration than did right movers. On a speeded information-processing task, requiring verbal comprehension, right movers showed substantial heart-rate deceleration while left movers showed a slight heart-rate acceleration. Though the findings to date are not conclusive, there is enough evidence available to suggest that right and left movers experience a difference in the quality of anxiety.

Creativity is another area that has attracted interest in the light of the CLEM typology. There is a strong tradition in the creativity literature associating the initial state of the creative process with primary process, regressive thinking, divergent thinking, and nonverbal thinking in contrast to logical, linear, analytic, verbal, and convergent thought (Barron, 1969). These descriptions of creative thinking are suggestive of the right-hemisphere mode of thought. It has in fact been suggested that hemispheric dynamics are intimately related to the creative process (Bogen and Bogen, 1969; Harnad, 1973). Harnad considers that the right hemisphere, not restrained (as is the left) by categorical boundaries, subserves the free interplay of engrams . . . out of which felicitous new combinations can emerge. This has led to the hypothesis that left movers or right-brained people may be more creative. Harnad (1972) found that among the professors of mathematics at Princeton University, the left movers used more imagery, were more artistically inclined, and were rated by students as more creative than the right movers. In another group of subjects Harnad found that left movers achieved higher scores on the Remote Associates Test (RAT), said to be a measure of creativity (Mednick, 1962). Jean (1975) confirmed these results. On the other hand, Smith (1972) found no difference between right and left movers on the RAT, but he found that the group of bidirectionals (those with a mixture of right and left CLEM) did better than either right or left movers on the RAT. He suggests, as do Bogen and Bogen (1969), that creativity arises from the optimal balance of both hemispheres. A relationship between creative thought and schizophrenic thought has often been noted and both kinds of thought have been associated with the right hemisphere (Bakan, 1976). It is likely that the difference between normal creative and schizophrenic individuals is due to the presence of left-hemisphere criticality operating on the products of the right hemisphere in "normal" creative thought but not in schizophrenia. The left hemisphere interacts with right-hemisphere mentation by attaching to it names, identification, categorization, classification, analysis, and explanation, thus transforming it to a reality context and making of it a socially acceptable creative product. The description of creativity as "regression in the service of the ego" may be translated into hemispheric terms as "right hemisphere mentation in the service of the left hemisphere." Hines and Martindale (1974) claim to have improved performance on the RAT by forcing the eyes to turn left while engaging in the task. They do this with goggles that can block stimuli from either the right or left visual field, thus producing a simulated right or left looker. Though many problems remain to be solved with respect to the relationship between creativity and the CLEM typology, the evidence available certainly suggests that this promises to be a fruitful area of research.

The differences in performance and consciousness considered so far do not exhaust the differences found between right and left movers. This section will briefly summarize some of the other differences obtained. If different individuals are differentially reliant on the two halves of the brain, and by inference different forms of consciousness, then this should have considerable educational implications (Bogen, 1975; Day, 1970). Hartnett (1976) reports that when students are given a choice between a "deductive" and an "inductive" approach to the study of a second language, the right movers show a preference for the inductive approach. Furthermore, the right movers tend to do better with the inductive approach. This kind of finding may have important implications for the very important problem of matching particular teaching methods to "types" of students. Perhaps, in the teaching of reading, the left mover would benefit more from the "look-say" approach and the right mover from the phonetic approach. Better results in the teaching of reading as well as other skills might result from matching the teaching method to the hemisphericity of the student. Gur, Gur, and Marshalek (1975) find a difference between right and left movers in classroom-seating preference, with right movers preferring to sit on the left and left movers on the right. The effect of this may be to activate the preferred hemisphere while attending to a lecturer. They also report a tendency for classroom-seating choice to be dependent on the subject matter (arts or science) for some subjects.

Another area of interest for comparison of right and left movers is that of psychodynamics. Differences in the experience of anxiety have already been considered. The greater susceptibility of the left mover to hypnosis suggests a difference in psychodynamics. Interestingly, when the hypnotic induction instructions are translated into language more congruent with left-hemisphere function, there is an increase in the hypnotic susceptibility of right movers (Gur and Reyher, 1973). Gur and Gur (1975) have reported differences between right and left movers in the kinds of defense mechanisms used. The preferred defense mechanisms of right movers are projection and outward turning of aggression. Left movers are more likely to use denial, repression, and reaction formation and are more likely to report psychosomatic symptomatology. There are some similarities between the defense-mechanism pattern of the left mover and the field-dependent subject (Witkin et al., 1962). The finding of a relationship between right CLEM and obesity may have a bearing on the psychodynamics of obesity (Rodin and Singer, 1976).

To the extent that heterosexual interest is related to psychodynamics, a set of studies relating CLEM direction, heterosexual interest, and body attention patterns is of great interest. In their experiment on hypnotizability Gur and Reyher (1973) found that when male subjects had a choice of a male or female experimenter the left movers showed a distinct preference for the female experimenter, whereas right movers showed no such preference. In another context, Fischer (1966) observed that males who tend to be more aware of the left side of their body are more spontaneous, uninhibited, and involved in heterosexual relationships. These two findings are linked by the finding of Hines, Martindale, and Schulze (1974) that left movers are more aware of the left side of the body. Thus, a hemisphericity favoring the right hemisphere produces not only a dominance of left CLEM but also a greater attentiveness to the left side of the body. Perhaps the greater spontaneity and lack of inhibition manifested in easier heterosexual relationships is due to a right hemisphericity. Gur (1972) has suggested that the male left movers of her study were "more in tune with their feelings showing a higher tendency to act in terms of the emotional arousal caused by the female E," in contrast to the right movers, who "tend to repress the emotions involved." This line of reasoning is in keeping with reports of greater "emotionality" in right-hemisphere functioning (Schwartz, Davidson, and Maes, 1975). The relationship between CLEM direction and personality and psychodynamics has also been considered by Etaugh (1972), Etaugh and Rose (1973), Weiten and Etaugh (1973), Libby and Yaklevich (1973), Ashton and Dwyer (1975), Barnet (1974), Fischer (1971), and Crouch (1976).

Not only is hemisphericity as elicited by the eye-movement technique important by virtue of showing differences between right and left movers in cognition, emotion, and consciousness, but it may also serve as a moderating variable in determining the results when other techniques are used to investigate aspects of laterality. Consider, for example, the dichotic listening technique, a promising technique for, among other things, the establishment of hemispheric speech dominance. When different verbal material is simultaneously presented to each ear, the material presented to the right ear is usually more often reported than the material presented to the left ear (Kimura, 1967). This right-ear advantage is related to a left-brain advantage for processing verbal material. Goldstein (1974), in an interesting variation of the dichotic listening situation, had subjects wear prisms that displaced the visual environment 13° to the right, or left, or not at all. As a result the normal right-ear advantage was increased when the subjects had the visual field displaced to the right, thus causing their eyes to move to the right and increasing left hemisphere activity. With the visual field displaced to the left, the normal right ear advantage for verbal material was decreased, since this produced a leftward movement of the eyes and increased right-hemisphere activation.

Nielsen and Sorensen (1976) hypothesized that the right and left mover should show differences with respect to the right-ear advantage for verbal input in dichotic listening. The left mover, they argued, is like the subject with the left displacing prism even when he doesn't wear the prism because he has a built-in bias for relatively greater right-hemisphere activation. They found, as predicted, that the right-ear advantage was more pronounced in the right-mover group than in the left-mover group. For the right movers alone there was a significant right-ear superiority, but for the left movers no significant ear superiority could be found. It thus seems that results with the dichotic listening paradigm are mediated by CLEM direction. It would not be surprising to find that CLEM direction exerts a moderating influence in other experimental and clinical situations.

5. Some Problems, Methodological and Otherwise

In the interest of ease of exposition, a simple form of the argument about types of consciousness, types of people and the cerebral hemispheres has been presented. Now that the argument has been presented it is time to consider some of the problems and complicating considerations.

First, since a cerebral laterality model is involved, it is reasonable to consider the influence of handedness on the model based on CLEM direction. There is no clear evidence that CLEM direction is related in any simple way to handedness. A simple relationship is ruled out by the fact that right-handers are a clear majority, whereas the split between right and left movers is close to an even split. Most studies in the CLEM literature eliminate the left-handed individuals. Where left-handers have been included (Kinsbourne, 1972) there is evidence of an interaction between handedness and hemispheric factors associated with eye movements. The reason for such interactions is not clear. However, it is known that in other matters related to aspects of laterality, e.g., dichotic listening, the behavior of left-handers can be described as less lateralized. It has been suggested (Bakan, Dibb, and Reed, 1973; Bakan, 1975) that left-handedness is a result of perinatal cerebral insult to the left hemisphere. The effect of such insult might be a compensatory reorganization of interhemispheric relationships. As a result, the behavioral correlates of being either a right mover or a left mover may not be the same for right-handed, left-handed, and ambidexterous subjects. There is a clear need for experimental work to trace out the possible interactions between handedness and hemisphericity.

Differences between the sexes in the hemispheric organization of the brain pose another problém for the hemispheric typology proposed here. There is now a considerable literature (Bakan and Putnam, 1974; Hannay and Malone, 1976; McGlone and Kertesz, 1973; Ray, Morell, and Frediani, 1976) suggesting that the female brain is less functionally lateralized than the male brain. Duke (1968) has reported that females are more likely to have a mixed CLEM pattern, i.e, more females than males are neither right nor left movers, but are inconsistent or bidirectional in CLEM direction. This has been confirmed in my laboratory. Studies of the correlates of CLEM laterality should analyze results for sexes separately in order to get a better understanding of the sex by hemisphericity interaction.

Another relatively unexplored though potentially important subject variable is the bidirectional pattern of CLEM. There is a minority of individuals who are unreliable within a session in CLEM direction. They will sometimes move their eyes right and sometimes left. Most experiments on CLEM eliminate these subjects from analysis. There is some indication, however, that these bidirectional individuals may turn out to be of considerable interest. Smith (1972), in a study of the relationship between CLEM direction and creativity, found that the bidirectional subjects achieved the highest scores on one of the tests of creativity, the Remote Associates Test.

There is evidence that the direction of CLEM can be influenced by the content of the question used to elicit the eye movement (Galin and Ornstein, 1974; Kinsbourne, 1972; Kocel, Galin, Ornstein, and Merrin, 1972; Weiten and Etaugh, 1974a, 1974b) though this finding has not always been confirmed (Ehrlichman, Weiner, and Baker, 1974). Questions that require left-hemisphere processing are reported to increase the probability of right-eye movements, and questions requiring right-hemisphere processing increase the probability of left-eye movements. This effect of question type appears weak when compared with the tendency for a given subject to be a right or left mover (Bakan, Coupland, Glackman, and Putnam, 1974). The matter of question content is further complicated by the finding that question content has an effect on eye movements when the experimenter is behind the subject as he asks the question, but not when he is face to face with the subject (Gur, Gur, and Harris, 1975). The matter is still further complicated by reports of some individual differences in eye movements in the up-down dimension (Galin and Ornstein, 1974, Libby and Yaklevich, 1973; Kinsbourne, 1972) and a relationship between question type and up-down eye movements (Kinsbourne, 1972, Ehrlichman *et al.*, 1974). There is no apparent hemispheric explanation for up-down effects.

A question of great interest with respect to the CLEM typology is the question of the origins of CLEM laterality. At the present time there is no evidence bearing on the genetic or environmental determination of CLEM direction. However, it has been found that as early as three years of age the direction of conjugate lateral eye movements is already consistent (Weigl, 1970). Studies of familial tendencies and twin studies are likely to throw light on this problem.

6. Beyond the Hemispheres

The arguments presented thus far dwell on the right and left hemispheres. But it would be more accurate to consider instead a right- and left-hemisphere *system*. Each of these systems includes biochemical, autonomic, hormonal, and subcortical functions. Lateral asymmetries in function have been shown at the level of the thalamus (Ojemann, 1974; Vilkki and Laitinen, 1974). This suggests subcortical asymmetry as well. In view of the functional differences between the anterior and posterior parts of the hypothalamus (Gellhorn and Loofbourrow, 1963), I suggest that the anterior hypothalamus has better functional relationships with the right hemisphere, and the posterior hypothalamus has better functional relationships with the left hemisphere. The parasympathetic and sympathetic systems may also be functionally associated with the right and left hemisphere systems respectively (Bakan, 1971; Bakan, 1975, 1976). The physiological systems mediating REM and NREM sleep have been associated with the right-and left-hemisphere systems respectively (Bakan, 1975; Bakan, 1976). Even hormonal systems related to orgasm and the menstrual cycle may be associated differentially with the right- and left-hemisphere systems (Bakan, 1976; Cohen, Rosen, and Goldstein, 1976). Perhaps other dual physiological systems, e.g., adrenergic/cholinergic, will be shown to be differentially associated with the right- and left-hemispheric systems. Further investigations of subcortical, autonomic, and biochemical asymmetries related to the right- and left-hemisphere systems will be important in further understanding the implications of the hemispheric typology model suggested here.

7. Summary and Conclusions

Almost every major religious and philosophical system has postulated a basic duality in the nature of man. This duality gives rise to a number of typological systems in which the particular combination of the two basic components determines types of people. One of the significant ways in which these types differ is in the nature of their conscious experience. In prescientific writings it was suggested that the basic duality in man has an anatomical basis in the two functionally asymmetric hemispheres of the brain. Neurological discoveries of the nineteenth century demonstrated clearly the functional asymmetry of the hemispheres. More recent work using a variety of techniques has confirmed the fact that the human brain consists of two cerebral hemispheres that mediate different cognitive and affective functions and that function in a qualitatively different manner.

This paper suggests that the existence of two qualitatively different kinds of thought or consciousness, mediated by the two hemispheres, constitutes an anatomical foundation of a typology of individual differences. This is based on the concept of hemisphericity, that is, the tendency to greater reliance on either the right or the left hemisphere in the overall psychological functioning of the individual. Hemisphericity of individuals can thus be either right or left. It is argued that hemisphericity can be determined by observing the direction of an individual's conjugate lateral eye movements (CLEM) upon the initiation of reflection in response to a question. Right-eye movements are associated with left hemisphericity and left-eye movements are associated with right hemisphericity. The literature dealing with differences between right and left movers in a wide variety of psychological areas is reviewed. Analogies between this hemispheric typology and other typological systems are suggested.

It should be emphasized that in dealing with two types, "there can never be a pure type in the sense that it possesses only one mechanism with the complete atrophy of the other" (Jung, 1976). As Dr. Jekyll said, "I saw that of the two natures that contended in the field of my consciousness, even if I could be rightly said to be either, it was only because I was radically both."

References

Ashton, V. L., and Dwyer, J. H. The left: lateral eye movements and ideology. *Perceptual and Motor Skills*, 1975, 41, 248-250.

Bakan, P. Hypnotizability, laterality of eye movement and functional brain asymmetry. *Perceptual and Motor Skills*, 1969, *28*, 927–932.

Bakan, P. The eyes have it. *Psychology Today*, 1971, *4*, 64–67 and 96.

Bakan, P. Are left handers brain damaged? *New Scientist* 1975a, July 24, 200–202.

Bakan, P. Dreaming, REM sleep and the right hemisphere. Second Intl. Cong. Sleep Research, Edinburgh, 1975. Abstract in Chase, M. H., Stern, W. C., Walter, P. L. (Eds.) *Sleep Research* 4, Brain Information Service/Brain Research Institute, UCLA, Los Angeles, 1975b, p. 23.

Bakan, P. The right brain is the dreamer. *Psychology Today*, 1976, *10*, 66–68.

Bakan, P., and Putnam, W. Right-left discrimination and brain lateralization: Sex differences. *Archives of Neurology*, 1974, *30*, 334–335.

Bakan, P., and Shotland, L. Lateral eye movement, reading speech, and visual attention. *Psychonomic Science*, 1969, *15*, 93–94.

Bakan, P., and Strayer, F. F. On reliability of conjugate lateral eye movements. *Perceptual and Motor Skills*, 1973, *36*, 429–430.

Bakan, P., and Svorad, D. Resting EEG alpha asymmetry of reflective lateral eye movements. *Nature* 1969, *223*, 975–976.

Bakan, P., Dibb, G., and Reed, P. Handedness and birth stress. *Neuropsychologia*, 1973, *11*, 363–366.

Bakan, P., Coupland, S., Glackman, W., and Putnam, W. H. Direction of lateral eye movements: Individual differences and cognitive content effects. Paper to Canadian Psychological Assn., 1974, Windsor.

Barnet, M. Some personality correlates of the conjugate lateral eye movement. *Journal of Personality Assessment*, 1974, *38*, 223–225.

Barron, Frank. *Creativity and personal freedom*. Princeton, N.J.: D. Van Nostrand, 1968.

Bender, M. *The oculomotor system*. New York, N.Y.: Hoeber, 1964.

Berent, S. Field-dependence and performance on a writing task. *Perceptual and Motor Skills*, 1974, *38*, 651–658.

Berent, S. Rod-and-frame performance and calculating ability: A replication. *Perception and Motor Skills*, 1976, *43*, 562.

Bliss, A. R. *Conjugate lateral eye movement and subjective reports of anxiety symptoms*. M. A. thesis, Michigan State University, 1971.

Bloomberg, M. Differences between field independent and field dependent persons on the Stroop Color-Word test. *Journal of Clinical Psychology*, 1969, *24*, 45.

Bogen, J. E. The other side of the brain II: An appositional mind. *Bulletin of the Los Angeles Neurological Societies*, 1969, *34*, 135–162.

Bogen, J. E. The other side of the brain VII: Some educational aspects of hemispheric specialization *UCLA Educator*, 1975, *17*, 24–32.

Bogen, J. E., and Bogen, G. M. The other side of the brain III. The Corpus callosum and creativity. *Bulletin of the Los Angeles Neurological Societies*, 1969, *34*, 191–220.

Cohen, B. D., Berent, S., and Silverman, A. J. Field-dependence and lateralization of function in the human brain. *Archives of General Psychiatry*, 1973, *28*, 165–167.

Cohen, H. D., Rosen, R. C., and Goldstein, L. Electroencephalographic changes during human sexual orgasm. *Archives of Sexual Behavior*, 1976, *5*, 189–199.

Conant, J. B. *Two modes of thought*. New York, N.Y. Trident, 1964.

Critchley, M. *The parietal lobes*, New York, N.Y.: Hafner, 1966.

Crouch, W. Dominant direction of conjugate lateral eye movements and responsiveness to facial and verbal cues. *Perceptual and Motor Skills*, 1976, *42*, 167–174.

Day, M. E. An eye-movement phenomenon related to attention, thought and anxiety. *Perceptual and Motor Skills*, 1964, *19*, 443–446.

Day, M. E. An eye-movement indicator of individual differences in the physiological organization of attentional processes and anxiety. *Journal of Psychology*, 1967a, *66*, 51–62.

Day, M. E. An eye movement indicator type and level of anxiety: Some clinical observations. *Journal of Clinical Psychology*, 1967b, *23*, 438–444.

Day, M. E. Attention, anxiety and psychotherapy. *Psychotherapy: Theory, Research and Practice*, 1968, *5*, 146–149.

Day, M. E. Don't teach until you see the direction of their eye movements. *Journal of Special Education*, 1970, *4*, 233–239.

De Fazio, V. J. Field articulation differences in language abilities. *Journal of Personality and Social Psychology*, 1973, *25*, 351–356.

DeWitt, G. W., and Averill, J. R. Lateral eye movements, hypnotic susceptibility and field independence-dependence. *Perceptual and Motor Skills*, 1976, *43*, 1179–1184.

Dimond, S. *The double brain*. Edinburgh: Churchill Livingstone, 1972.

Dimond, S. J. and Beaumont, J. G. (Eds.) *Hemisphere function in the human brain*. New York: Halstead Press, 1974.

Dimond, S. J., Farrington, L., and Johnson, P. Differing emotional response from right and left hemispheres. *Nature*, 1976, *261*, 690–692.

Duke, J. B. Lateral eye-movement behavior. *Journal of General Psychology*, 1968, *78*, 189–195.

Ehri, L. C., and Muzio, I. M. Cognitive style and reasoning about speed. *Journal of Educational Psychology*, 1974, *66*, 569–571.

Ehrlichman, H., Weiner, S. L., and Baker, A. H. Effects of verbal and spatial questions on initial gaze shifts. *Neuropsychologia*, 1974, *12*, 265–277.

Etaugh, C. F. Personality correlates of lateral eye movement and handedness. *Perceptual and Motor Skills*, 1972, *34*, 751–754.

Etaugh, C., and Rose, M. Lateral eye movement: Elusive personality correlates and moderate stability estimates. *Perceptual and Motor Skills*, 1973, *37*, 211–217.

Ferrier, D. *The functions of the brain*. New York, N.Y.: G. P. Putnam, 1876.

Fischer, K. L. *Lateral eye-movement as related to marital selection and adjustment*. M. A. thesis, Michigan State University, 1971.

Fischer, S. Body attention patterns and personality defenses. *Psychological Monographs*, 1966, *80*, No. 9 (Whole No. 67).

Fritsch, G., and Hitzig, E. Über die elektrische Erregbarkeit des Grosshirns. *Arch. Anat. Physiol. Wiss. Med.* 1870, *37*, 300–332.

Galin, D., and Ornstein, A. Individual differences in cognitive style I. Reflective eye movements. *Neuropsychologia*, 1974, *12*, 367–376.

Gellhorn, E., and Loofburrow, G. N. *Emotions and emotional disorders: A neurophysiological study*. New York, N.Y.: Hoeber, 1963.

Gerdes, E. P., and Kinsbourne, M. Lateral eye movements and state anxiety. *Catalog of Selected Documents in Psychology*, 1974, *4*, 118–119.

Goldstein, L. Sideways look at dichotic listening. *Journal of the Acoustical Society of America*, 1974, *55*, 110.

Gur, R. E. *The effect of different hypnotic induction styles on hypnotic susceptibility of right-movers, left-movers and bidirectionals*. M. A. thesis, Michigan State University, 1972.

Gur, R. E. Conjugate lateral eye movements as an index of hemispheric activation. *Journal of Personality and Social Psychology*, 1975, *31*, 751–757.

Gur, R. C., and Gur, R. E. Handedness, sex, and eyedness as moderating variables in the relation between hypnotic susceptibility and functional brain asymmetry. *Journal of Abnormal Psychology*, 1974, *83*, 635–643.

Gur, R. E., and Gur, R. C. Defense mechanisms, psychosomatic symptomatology and conjugate lateral eye movements. *Journal of Consulting and Clinical Psychology*, 1975, *43*, 416–420.

Gur, R. E., and Reyher, J. The relationship between style of hypnotic induction and direction of lateral eye movement. *Journal of Abnormal Psychology*, 1973, *82*, 499–505.

Gur, R. E., Gur, R. C., and Marshalek, B. Classroom seating and functional brain asymmetry. *Journal of Educational Psychology*, 1975a, *67*, 151–153.

Gur, R. E., Gur, R. C., and Harris, L. J. Hemispheric activation as measured by the subjects' conjugate lateral eye movements, is influenced by experimenter location. *Neuropsychologia*, 1975b, *13*, 35–44.

Hannay, H. J., and Malone, D. R. Visual field effects and short term memory for verbal material. *Neuropsychologia*, 1976, *14*, 203–209.

Harnad, S. R. Creativity, lateral saccades and the nondominant hemisphere. *Perceptual and Motor Skills*, 1972, *34*, 653–654.

Harnad, S. R. Interhemispheric division of labour. Paper presented at Transformations of Consciousness Conference, 1973, Montreal.

Hartnett, Doyle D. The relation of cognitive style and hemispheric preference to deductive and inductive second language learning. Brain Information Service Conference on Human Brain Function BIS Conf. Rep. #42, 1976, p. 41.

Hellige, J. B. Hemispheric processing differences revealed by differential conditioning and reaction time performance. *Journal of Experimental Psychology*, General, 1975, *104*, 309–326.

Hilgard, E. *Hypnotic susceptibility*, New York, N.Y.: Harcourt Brace Jovanovich, 1965.

Hines, D., and Martindale, C. Induced lateral eye movements and intellectual performance. *Perceptual and Motor Skills*, 1974, *39*, 153–154.

Hines, D., Martindale, C., and Schulze, S. Lateral body sensitivity and lateral eye-movements. *Perceptual and Motor Skills*, 1974, *38*, 1293–1294.

Hochman, S. H. Field independence and Stroop Color-Word performance. *Perceptual and Motor Skills*, 1971, *33*, 782.

Isaiah, A., and Sharfman, B. *The Pentateuch and Rashis commentary*. Brooklyn, N.Y.: SS and R. Publ. Co., 1949.

Jackson, J. H. *Selected writings of John Hughlings Jackson*, J. Taylor (Ed.). New York, N.Y.: Basic Books, 1958.

Jean, P. Eye movements and creativity, 1971 (unpublished) paper, Simon Fraser University.

Jung, C. G. *Psychological types*. Princeton, N.J.: Princeton University Press, 1976.

Kimura, D. Left-right differences in the perception of melodies. *Quarterly Journal of Experimental Psychology*, 1964, *16*, 355–358.

Kimura, D. Functional asymmetry of the brain in dichotic listening. *Cortex*, 1967, *3*, 163–178.

Kinsbourne, M. Eye and head turning indicates cerebral lateralization. *Science*, 1972, *176*, 539–541.

Kinsbourne, M. Direction of gaze and distribution of cerebral thought processes. *Neuropsychologia*, 1974, *12*, 279–281.

Kinsbourne, M., and Smith, W. L. (Eds.) *Hemispheric disconnection and cerebral function*. Springfield, Ill.: Charles C Thomas, 1974.

Kocel, K., Galin, D., Ornstein, R., and Merrin, E. L. Lateral eye movement and cognitive mode. *Psychonomic Science* 1972, *27*, 223–224.

Libby, W. L., and Yaklevich, D. Personality determinants of eye contact and direction of gaze aversion. *Journal of Personality and Social Psychology*, 1973, *27*, 197–206.

Liske, E., Hughes, H., and Stowe, D. Cross correlation of human alpha activity: normative data. *EEG and Clinical Neurophysiology* 1967, *22*, 429–436.

London, P., Hart, J., and Leibovitz, M. EEG alpha rhythms and susceptibility to hypnosis. *Nature*, 1968, *219*, 71–72.

McGlone, J., and Kertesz, A. Sex differences in cerebral processing of visuo-spatial tasks. *Cortex*, 1973, *9*, 313–320.

Mednick, S. The associative basis of the creative process. *Psychological Review*, 1962, *69*, 221–232.

Meskin, B., and Singer, J. Daydreaming, reflective thought and lateral eye movements. *Journal of Personality and Social Psychology*, 1974, *30*, 64–71.

Morgan, A. H., McDonald, P. J., and MacDonald, H. Differences in bilateral alpha activity as a function of experimental task with a note on lateral eye movements and hypnotizability. *Neuropsychologia*, 1971, *9*, 459–469.

Mott, F. W., and Schaefer, E. A. On associated eye movements produced by cortical faradization of the monkey's brain, *Brain*, 1890, *13*, 165–173.

Myers, R. E., and Sperry, R. W. Interocular transfer of a visual form discrimination habit in cats after section of the optic chiasma and corpus callosum. *Anatomical Record*, 1953, *115*, 351–352.

Nebes, R. D. Hemispheric specialization in commissurotomized man. *Psychological Bulletin*, 1974, *81*, 1–14.

Nielsen, H., and Sorensen, J. H. Hemispheric dominance, dichotic listening and lateral eye movement behaviour. *Scandinavian Journal of Psychology*, 1976, *17*, 129–132.

Nowlis, D., and Rhead, J. C. Relation of eyes closed resting EEG alpha activity to hypnotic susceptibility. *Perceptual and Motor Skills*, 1968, *27*, 1047–1050.

Ogle, W. T. Lateral eye movements: their relationship to reading speed, cardiac responsivity, and ability to process speeded information in the visual and auditory modes. Ph.D. dissertation, 1972, Washington University. *Dissertation Abstracts International* 1972, *33*, (3-B) 1293.

Ojemann, G. A. Mental arithmetic during human thalamic stimulation, *Neuropsychologia*, 1974, *12*, 1–10.

Oltman, P. K., Ehrlichman, H., and Cox, P. W. Visual asymmetry in the perception of faces and field independence. Educational Testing Service Research Bulletin 76-13, 1976 (unpublished).

Pavlov, I. P. Essay on the physiological concept of the symptomatology of hysteria (1932) in *Psychopathology and psychiatry: Selected works*, Moscow: Foreign Lang. Publ. House, 255–281.

Penfield, W., and Boldrey, E. Somatic motor and sensory representation in cerebral cortex of man as studies by electrical stimulation. *Brain*, 1937, *60*, 389–443.

Pizzamiglio, L. Handedness, ear preference and field dependence. *Perceptual and Motor Skills*, 1974, *38*, 700–702.

Rana, S., Ballentine, R., and Ajaya, S. (Weinstock, A.) *Yoga and psychotherapy*. Glenview, Ill.: Himalayan Institute, 1976.

Ray, W. J., Morell, M., and Frediani, A. W. Sex differences and lateral specialization of hemispheric functioning. *Neuropsychologia*, 1976, *14*, 391–394.

Rodin, J., and Singer, J. L. Eye-shift, thought, and obesity. *Journal of Personality*, 1976, *44*, 594–610.

Rosenberg, R. A. (Transl.) *The anatomy of God.* New York, N.Y.: Ktav Publ., 1973.

Schaya, L. *The universal meaning of the Kabbalah.* Baltimore, Md.: Penguin, 1971.

Schwartz, G. E., Davidson, R. J., and Maes, F. Right hemisphere lateralization for emotion in the human brain: Interactions with cognition. *Science*, 1975, *190*, 286–288.

Selzer, F. A. Auto-regulation of EEG alpha wave production as a function of the direction of conjugate lateral eye movements. *Dissertation Abstracts International,* 1974, *34,* (12-B) 6250.

Sherrod, D. Lateral eye movements and reaction to persuasion. *Perceptual and Motor Skills,* 1972, *35,* 355-358.

Singer, J. L. Daydreaming and the stream of thought. *American Scientist,* 1974, *62,* 417-425.

Smith, J. *Lateral reflective eye movements and creativity.* M. A. thesis, Michigan State University, 1972.

Sperry, R. W. Hemisphere deconnection and unity in conscious awareness. *American Psychologist,* 1968, *23,* 723-733.

Sperry, R. W. Changing concepts of consciousness and free will. *Perspectives in Biology and Medicine,* 1976, *20,* 9-19.

Strayer, F. F. *Lateral eye movements as an index of alpha enhancement with auditory feedback.* M. A. thesis, 1970, Simon Fraser University.

Teitelbaum, H. A. Spontaneous rhythmic ocular movements: their possible relationship to mental activity. *Neurology,* 1954, *4,* 350-354.

Vilkki, J., and Laitinen, L. V. Differential effects of left and right vertrolateral thalomotomy on receptive and expressive verbal performances and face matching. *Neuropsychologia,* 1974, *12,* 11-19.

Weigl, Doris. *Lateral eye movements: a development study.* 1970, M. A. thesis, Michigan State University.

Weiten, W., and Etaugh, C. F. Lateral eye movement as related to verbal and perceptual-motor skills and values. *Perceptual* and Motor Skills, 1973, *36,* 423-428.

Weiten, W., and Etaugh, C. Lateral eye-movement as a function of cognitive mode, question sequence, and sex of subject. *Perceptual and Motor Skills,* 1974a, *38,* 439-444.

Weiten, W., and Etaugh, C. Lateral eye-movement as related to mathematical and musical problem solving. *Perceptual and Motor Skills,* 1974b, *39,* 481-482.

Wigan, A. L. *The duality of the mind.* London: Longman, Brown, Green, and Longmans, 1844.

Witkin, H. A., Dyk, R. B., Faterson, H. F., Goodenough, D. R., and Karp, S. A. *Psychological differentiation.* New York, N.Y.: John Wiley, 1962.

Zangwill, O. L. Asymmetry of cerebral hemisphere function. In Garland, H. (Ed.), *Scientific aspects of neurology,* Edinburgh: E. and S. Livingston, 1961, 51-62.

PART III

Experimental Approaches to Studying the Stream of Consciousness

7

Experimental Studies of Daydreaming and the Stream of Thought

Jerome L. Singer

1. From Introspection to Experimentation

Perhaps symbolic of some deep irony in the history of psychology, the death of William James in 1910 coincided with the dramatic emergence of behaviorism in American psychology and with the turn from sensitive introspection toward a kind of mindless but well-documented motor responsiveness that characterized behaviorism. The young psychologists who emerged during the next half-century, establishing their bastions and rat-laboratories in Indiana, Iowa, and dozens of the land-grant universities scattered over the face of America, had no patience with the quiet speculations about the self and consciousness of William James. Indeed, led by Watson, they mocked the dry efforts of Titchner and his students to separate out sensation, perception, and imagery in consciousness by introspecting about the degree of "purpleness" of a light. American psychologists wanted *facts*, hard data, and precise methodologies that could lead to replicable experiments.

It is sometimes fun to speculate on where psychology might be today if the great energy of that vigorous generation of empiricists of that middle period of the century had focused on generating experiments about human thought, emotion, and social experience rather than upon elaborating the response capacities of the Norwegian white

Jerome L. Singer • Department of Psychology, Yale University, New Haven, Connecticut.

rat, to whom Tolman dedicated his great book on purposive behavior. We can never know whether the half-century of behaviorism represented a massive detour from the major thrust of psychology or simply a necessary evolution in the field. We have reached a point today, however, where many of the questions and issues raised by the introspective orientation of nineteenth-century psychologists, or of the psychoanalysts from Freud through Rapaport, are now increasingly susceptible to study through some more direct form of experimentation or systematic empirical data collection.

Introspection continues to deserve respect because it can engender valuable hypotheses. Indeed, self-examination can often suggest that the reported implication of a particular experiment or even the results of such an experiment may actually not be as broadly generalizable as might have been thought (Singer, 1966). And, of course, philosophical and theoretical analyses of the implications of methods for the types of problems studied and possible outcomes remain a necessary feature that moves psychology beyond the level of simple collections of unrelated facts.

The important thrust of the period since 1960 in psychology has been the emergence of the cognitive movement, and of a whole series of methodological developments that make it possible for us to study with some degree of precision and replicability processes hitherto believed to be private and indeed ruled "out of court" by Watson. In the chapter that follows, I shall try to review a particular research program built around the study of imagination, daydreaming, and related facets of the stream of thought that has attempted to translate many of our most private experiences into forms susceptible to systematic research. Other chapters in this volume will make clear in even more detailed fashion how what once seemed an impossibly ephemeral subject, the human flow of thought, can eventually emerge as a topic susceptible to systematic scientific inquiry. The evolution of a research program on daydreaming and the stream of thought has been described in detail elsewhere (Singer, 1966, Singer, 1974, Singer, 1975a, b). In the present chapter the emphasis will be upon pointing up some of the specific studies and their relationships to a point of view concerning the nature of ongoing thought.

Table I presents a grouping of many of the studies carried out as part of this research program. It includes a number of studies that were either directly a part of my own research activities with a variety of collaborators, especially John Antrobus, and also a number of studies carried out as masters or doctoral dissertations under my supervision. Studies have been included in the table, which while done completely independently, made use of specific methods devel-

TABLE 1. Experimental Studies of Daydreaming and the Stream of Thought

I. *Individual differences:* Normative studies and personality correlates
Large sample interview and questionnaire studies
  a. Background factors, e.g., age, sex, sociocultural groups
  b. Patterns of content and norms
  c. Psychometric Questionnaire Construction
  1. Singer and McCraven (1960)
  2. Singer and Schonbar (1961)
  3. Singer and Antrobus (1972)
  4. Wagman (1968); Wooten (1973) Oakland (1968)

Personality correlates
  1. Relation to dreams, anxiety, creativity, self-awareness, hostility
  2. Identification with parents (Singer and Schonbar (1961); Singer and Rowe (1962); Wagman (1967); Rabinowitz (1975)

Factor analytic studies (Normal Ss)
  1. Singer and Antrobus (1963, 1972)
  2. Starker (1973
  3. Isaacs (1974)
  4. Segal and Singer (1976) study (Kentucky Fantasy Project)
    a. College students N = 1,000 (drug and alcohol users and nonusers)
    b. "Reasons" for use (Segal, Huba and Singer, 1977) study
    c. Cross-year and group study of daydreaming and personality (Huba, Segal and Singer, 1977)
    d. Discriminant function study: Prediction of drug and alcohol use (Segal, Huba and Singer, 1976; Segal, 1974)
  5. Giambra—daydreaming across life span (aged) (Giambra 1974, 1977a)
  6. Taylor (1975)

Studies of psychopathology
  1. Starker and Singer (1975a,b) hospitalized psychiatric patients
  2. Streissguth, Wagner and Sarason (1977)
  3. Giambra and Traynor (1977) depression
  4. Beit-Hallahmi (1971) prisoners
  5. Starker and Hasenfeld (1976) sleep disturbance

Behavioral correlates of daydream questionnaire responses
  1. Meskin-Singer (1974) eye-shift
  2. Fusella (1972) perky phenomenon imagery
  3. Starker (1973, 1974) dream recall; dream content and daydreams
  4. Schultz (1976) depressed patients and type of daydreaming
  5. Isaacs (1975) language analysis of verbalization and daydreaming
  6. Antrobus, Coleman and Singer (1967) stimulus-independent thought during signal detection
  7. Feldstein (1972) REM deprivation
  8. Pope (1977) ongoing thought sequences
  9. Starker and Hasenfeld (1976) daydreaming and sleep disturbance

Sexual daydreams
  1. Coital fantasies in women (Hariton and Singer, 1974)
  2. Masturbation fantasies in freshman (Campagna, 1976)
  3. Primal scene fantasies (Hoyt, 1977)
  4. Adult males (Giambra and Martin, 1977)
  5. College women's sexual fantasies (Davidson, 1975)

II. *Cognitive Studies Stream of thought and priorities for internal vs. external processing* (Stimulus-independent thought)
  1. Varied internal activity and vigilance (Antrobus and Singer, 1964)
  2. Payoff studies (increasing and decreasing S.I.T.) (Antrobus, Singer and Greenberg, 1966)

TABLE 1. *(Continued)*

3. Auditory vs. visual imagery and internal vs. external processing (Antrobus, Singer, Goldstein and Fortgang, 1970)
4. Parallel vs. sequential processing (Antrobus *et al.*, 1970)
5. Parameters of S.I.T. (relation to information load demands; reaction time and search time) (Ritter, 1974)
6. Antrobus (1968)
7. Fein and Antrobus (1977)
8. Filler and Giambra (1973)
9. Drucker (1967)
10. Wheeler (1969) time experience

Naturalistic ongoing thought
1. Pope (1977) shifts in ongoing thought; laboratory setting
2. Hurlburt (1976) stream of thought in daily activity
3. McDonald (1977) daily stream of thought and pattern of daydreaming
4. Csikszentmihalyi (1974, 1975)
5. Giambra (1977)
6. Kripke and Sonnenschein (1973)

III. *Ocular motility and physiological correlates of daydreaming and imaginative processes: eye movement, alpha and heart rate*
1. Antrobus and Singer (1964)
2. Antrobus and Singer (1968)
3. Singer and Antrobus (1965)
4. Singer, Greenberg and Antrobus (1971) optokinetic nystagmus, OKN
5. Kahn (unpublished) replication of OKN study
6. Rosenberg (1977) study of OKN, type of mentation and direction of eye-shift (brain lateralization)
7. Meskin and Singer (1974) eye-shift and fantasy in face-to-face interview
8. Rodin and Singer (1977) obes-

ity, fantasy eye-shift, and processing information
9. Marks (1972) imagery and eye movement
10. Klinger, Gregoire and Barta (1973) physiological correlates of imagining and concentrating
11. Ruth and Giambra (1974)
12. Kripke and Sonnenschein (1973) daydreaming, eye movement, and alpha
13. Ehrlichman and Wiener (1977a,b) Weiner and Ehrlichman (1976)

IV. *Affect and stress studies of daydreaming (theoretical model–Tomkins: affect & cognition*
1. Singer and Rowe (1964) anxiety and aggression
2. Rowe (1964) heart rate and stress
3. Pytkowicz, Wagner, and Sarason (1964)
4. Wheeler (1969) time estimation and positive fantasies
5. Singer, Auster and Antrobus (unpublished) toleration of silence and daydreaming
6. Paton (1972) aggressive and neutral fantasy following anger arousal
7. Biblow (1973) aggressive and benign TV-viewing after frustration in children differing in imagination
8. Hariton (1972, 1976) coital fantasies and affect
9. Campagna (1976) sex fantasy and sexual arousal
10. Zachary (1978) positive and negative affect arousal, task completion and the stream of thought
11. Vanderbeck and Antrobus (1977) in preparation
12. See also various M. Horowitz studies, e.g., Horowitz and

TABLE 1. *(Continued)*

Becker (1971); Becker and Horowitz (1973)

V. *Make-believe play and fantasy in childhood* (for literature reviews see Singer and Singer, 1976; Singer, 1977)
   1. Singer (1961) interview and waiting behavior
   2. Singer and Singer (1973, 1974, 1977a) nursery school observation studies of ongoing play
   3. Pulaski (1973) toy structure and fantasy
   4. Franklin (1976) block play and modeling
   5. Freyberg (1973) training for fantásy play in disadvantaged kindergarten children
   6. Biblow (1977) affect and aggression studies in early school age
   7. Singer and Streiner (1966) sighted-blind children
   8. D. Singer and Lenahan (1971) daydreams of deaf children
   9. Gottlieb (1974) modeling imaginative behavior at two age levels
   10. Tucker (1975) reality in recall and fantasy
   11. Griffing (1974) social class variations in make-believe play
   12. Gershowitz (1974) make-believe in play therapy
   13. Dennis (1976) family patterns and imaginative play
   14. Schmukler (1977) mother–child interaction and make-believe play
   15. Fein (1975) pretend play in the first two years
   16. Gould (1972) psychodynamics of make-believe games
   17. Bach (1973)

VI. *Applied research on daydreaming and imagination*
   1. *Projective-techniques and Rorschach inkblot-measurement of imagination* (see reviews of research literature by Singer, 1968; Singer and Brown (1977))
   2. Training in make-believe, e.g.,
      1. Smilansky (1967)
      2. Feitelson (1972)
      3. Freyberg (1972)
      4. Marshall and Hahn (1967)
      5. Saltz and Johnson (1974)
      6. Nahme-Huang, Singer, Singer and Wheaton (1977) imaginative training of disturbed hospitalized children
   3. *TV and fantasy play*
      1. Singer (1971; 1978) review
      2. Singer and Singer (1976a,b) Mister Rogers studies
      3. Singer and Singer, (1976) parent consultation
      4. Singer, Tower, Singer and Biggs (1977) Mister Rogers and Sesame Street comparison
      5. (See also studies by Stein and Friedrich, 1972; 1974, etc.)
   4. *Daydreaming and imagery methods in psychotherapy*
      1. Singer (1974) review and theory
      2. Frank (1976) role playing and daydreaming training
      3. Schultz (1976) modifying depressive affect in hospitalized patients
      4. Singer and Pope (1978) collection of studies of varied uses of imagination in psychotherapy

VII. *References*
Singer, J. L. *The child's world of make-believe.* New York: Academic Press, 1973.
Singer, J. L. *Imagery and daydream methods in psychotherapy and behavior modification.* New York: Academic Press, 1974.
Singer, J. L. Daydreaming and the stream of thought. *American Scientist*, 1974.

TABLE 1. *(Continued)*

Singer, J. L. Navigating the stream of consciousness: Research in daydreaming and related inner experience. *American Psychologist*, 1975.

Singer, J. L. Imaginative play and pretending in early childhood. In Davids, A. (Ed.) *Child personality and psychopathology*. Wiley, 1976.

Singer, J. L. *The inner world of daydreaming*. New York: Harper & Row, 1975.

Singer, J. L. Singer, D. G. *Partners in play: A step by step guide to imaginative play in pre-schoolers*. New York: Harper & Row, 1977.

Singer, J. L. & Pope, K. (Eds.) *The power of human imagination*. New York: Plenum, 1978.

oped in our laboratory or employed some of the instruments developed for evaluating predispositional characteristics to imagination, such as the Singer-Antrobus Imaginal Processes Inventory (IPI). References to the work of a number of key investigators who have contributed to research in this area, e.g., Klinger, Giambra, Horowitz, Csikszentmihalyi are also listed in the table but no attempt is made to provide an inclusive bibliography in this rapidly growing field.

Some comment is necessary to help the reader comprehend the complex table. The group of studies to the left of the table represent various attempts to establish baseline or normative information on the frequency, patterning, and structural properties of daydreaming and related imaginal processes. Since so much information until recently on private processes, such as recurring fantasies or other features of the stream of thought, had depended upon individual introspective reports or case reports of clinical patients, it seemed desirable to accumulate in some reasonably organized fashion information on the range and frequency of private experiences such as daydreaming. This whole group of studies makes use of questionnaires, occasionally supplemented by interview procedures of a systematic type, and relies heavily on the developments in psychometrics in psychology to establish through techniques, such as factor analysis, the recurrent patternings of private experience. Thus, the studies in that column are largely cross-sectional samplings of private, anonymous respondents, generally based on large samples and primarily on normal individuals. In some instances, an attempt has been made to validate the self-reports that are essentially retrospective that characterize questionnaire responses, by studying the same subjects in other more experimentally controlled situations. In such cases we have a blending of several columns with research on cognitive aspects of behavior or on laboratory studies also being carried out with subjects whose responses to the questionnaires are available.

The second major grouping of studies involves more circum-scribed researches in the main, with a view toward understanding the relationship between the occurrence of private thoughts and other self-generated responses in relation to the broader, cognitive function-ing of the individual. Here we are dealing with essentially laboratory studies under, in many cases, rather artificial circumstances with the vigilance or signal-detection experiment serving as the methodological instrumentality for the study.

The next column of the table continues essentially the general issue of the relation of the stream of thought to cognitive functioning, but focuses also upon specific concomitant physiological properties of the organism, such as the relation of eye movement to ongoing thought, or some of the relationships of other bodily processes such as heartrate to fantasy and daydreams.

The next column lists a group of studies that, using experimental formats, have attempted to examine the interrelationships between specific or general affective patterns and emotional arousal to particu-lar patterns of fantasy or daydreaming, and also to test hypotheses about interrelationships of drive, emotion, and cognitive content. Further columns of the table list a whole series of studies that have attempted to examine the emergence of daydreaming and the stream of thought from the spontaneous play and imaginative games of childhood. Finally, the extreme right column lists some of the applied studies or practical approaches that have developed from the overall research program. The present chapter, however, will not stress the research with children, which is extensively reviewed elsewhere (Singer, 1975b; Singer and Singer, 1976a; Singer, 1977), or the various applied studies (Singer, 1974; Pope and Singer, 1978a).

2. Projective Techniques and the Study of Imagination

One of the exciting developments in psychology during the period of the late 1930s through about 1960 was the emergence of the projective methods, especially instruments such as the Rorschach inkblot method and the Thematic Apperception Test (TAT). These instruments provided reasonably quantifiable data that seemed to be tapping basic ongoing or recurring imaginative products of individu-als and offered an opportunity for linking private thought, both their structural properties and their specific contents or relationships to major motivational trends to other forms of overt behavior or to the course of treatment processes in clinical work. I have summarized some of the research uses of these instruments elsewhere (Singer, 1968) and will not deal with this issue further at this point. The general use made of these tools has been to study what might be called the structural properties of personality, issues of control, or defense primarily through relationships to the inkblots and to focus on issues of the content of conflict, or the major motivational trends of the individual through the analysis of stories told to the ambiguous pictures of the Thematic Apperception Test.

An especially intriguing aspect of the Rorschach psychodiagnostic method has been the examination of the Human Movement-response (M) to the inkblots, or of the relationship of "movement-determined" percepts to "color-determined" percepts. Rorschach ingeniously noticed that individuals who associated more frequent images of human beings in motion to the inkblots also were inclined to be, on the one hand, somewhat controlled or inhibited in motor activity and, on the other, to be much given to imagination and to attention to their own fantasies and ongoing thoughts. For a time it appeared that the use of this M score from the Rorschach might open the way to exploration of individuals who had well-developed capacities for using their imaginative resources or who in general preferred to rely on such resources rather than engaging in impulsive direct action.

An extensive and on the whole reasonably consistent literature has grown up around the study of the behavioral correlates of the Rorschach M-response and also of the relationship between movement to color as a measure of introversion-extroversion (Singer and Brown, 1977). In general, the data of a large number of studies suggest that individuals who show a relative frequency of M-responses in response to Rorschach inkblots or an introversive Experience-type (when the movement-to-color ratio of response determinants in the test is taken into account) are also likely to be individuals who show evidence of considerable imaginativeness as measured by other instruments or observational approaches. The M-response correlates with the degree to which an individual tells original and complex stories to ambiguous pictures, introducing characters, settings, and times not immediately represented in the scene before him. M-response tendency also is positively correlated with the frequency of reported daydreaming as measured by questionnaire responses, and also with the relative frequency of recall of night dreams. The other aspect of Rorschach's proposed linkage, movement to inhibited or controlled motor activity, has also been fairly extensively supported. High M-responders tend to be slower to react in a variety of situations, they tend to be less likely to behave impulsively in various experimental situations or in daily life, and they are less likely to engage in antisocial or aggressive behaviors.

While the network of interrelations between the inkblot score and a variety of behaviors is indeed important and impressive, the psychometric limitations of the Rorschach method restrict the conclusions we can draw from such data with respect to the nature of imagination and the stream of consciousness. There simply have been no extensive studies of the relationship of producing human movement-responses to inkblots and other aspects of the thought process in a more refined fashion. In other words, we have very little clear notion as to what it means to give human movement-responses to inkblots and whether the same process is at work when we have individuals report in other forms the patterns of ongoing thought. For example, in seeing "two clowns playing patti-cake" on Card II of the Rorschach inkblots, is a person indicating a tendency also to see "movements in the mind's eye"? No careful studies have been carried out of the process of giving such responses to the inkblots and of the variations in such responses that might be obtained by different kinds of presentations of ambiguous stimuli or by different kinds of stimulus conditions established either for the subject or in the environment. While it is helpful to know that people who see more M-responses on the blots also respond to questionnaires by saying that they have many daydreams, the direct linkages have yet to be established. There seems little question that Rorschach was on to something terribly important, but essential basic analytic and parametric work remains to be carried out before we are to understand why this somewhat trivial-seeming business of seeing people in action on inkblots does indeed have such an impressive network of behavioral correlates.

3. Questionnaire and Interview Studies: Normative Bases and Personality Correlates of Daydreaming and Imaginal Processes

At some point it becomes necessary simply to ask people about the pattern of ongoing thought they experience, the recurrent daydreams or related sequences of imagery that they have noticed in themselves. The projective test movement developed in part because it was assumed that people would not respond to direct questions about private experiences, or would perhaps not be able to answer even if they cooperated because they lacked either verbal labeling capacities or were subject to the operation of defense mechanisms because of anxiety over disclosing significant conflicts or seemingly regressive trends in their personalities. While no doubt such considerations do exist, it has seemed increasingly clear that people will answer rather reliably and, within limits, veridically, questions about their frequency or types of daydreaming. An extensive series of questionnaire studies have been carried out with normal individuals to establish patternings of daydreaming and related inner processes. The first effort was largely to obtain indications of how often people daydreamed, whether daydreaming was indeed a normal reaction, and what circumstances led to its emergence in consciousness. Eventually the studies became increasingly sophisticated from a psychometric standpoint. That is, a series of subscales were developed (Singer and Antrobus, 1963, 1972) that permitted more extensive examination of intercorrelations between different types of daydreaming and related thought processes and also examination of these patterns in relation to other kinds of personality variables.

Briefly, a large number of studies indicate that most people report being aware of at least some daydreaming every day, and that their daydreams vary considerably from obvious wishful or "castles in Spain" thoughts to elaborate and complex visions of frightening or guilty encounters. Cultural differences in frequency and patterning of daydreaming as reported on these questionnaires also emerge (Singer and McCraven, 1961, 1962). A series of factor-analytic studies indicates that at least for the scales of the Imaginal Processes Inventory the data yield at least three major factors that characterize ongoing thought, a Positive-Vivid daydreaming style, a Guilty-Dysphoric daydreaming style, and a Mindwandering-Distractible pattern that is generally characterized by fleeting thoughts and an inability to focus on extended fantasy (Singer and Antrobus, 1963;, 1971; Starker, 1973; Isaacs, 1975; Segal and Singer, 1976; Huba, Segal, and Singer 1977; Giambra, 1974a, 1976). Giambra (1977a,b) also found evidence not only for similar factor patterns as have been reported in these studies but also tracked these across an extensive age range and in addition, checked the test-retest reliability of daydreaming reports in response to this set of scales and found them to be surprisingly high.

We are left, however, with the question as to whether self-reports to these highly structured questionnaires of the type employed can be truly reflective of persisting behavior patterns in other situations. This is not easy to demonstrate. There are, however, indications from a series of studies that individuals who report a good deal of daydreaming, particularly of a positive kind, to the questionnaires are also likely to report a good many task-irrelevant thoughts occurring to them while they are engaged in a laboratory experiment involving the detection of signals (Antrobus, Coleman, and Singer 1967), are more likely to report that their images are vivid or to actually experience the blocking of external signals when they are engaged in imaging (Fusella, 1972), are more likely to show a left-shifting of their eyes during reflective thought, presumably indicating greater activation of the right side of the brain—usually associated with image-production (Meskin and Singer, 1974), and are also more likely to report certain kinds of positive content in their recalled nocturnal dreams (see chap. 10 by Starker). Isaacs, in a very careful and extensive analysis of the language usage of subjects who reported on their thoughts during signal-detection tasks under controlled conditions, found that subjects high on the Positive-Vivid daydreaming scale of the IPI also were more likely to show stimulus-independent mentation occurring during the task. Their language usage also made more reference to analogies and phrases of a "this is like that" nature, reflecting a more metaphoric or elaboration-oriented turn of mind. Rodin and Singer (1977) found that overweight subjects reported less visual content in their daydreams than did normal-weight subjects. These differences between the weight groups were also reflected in the fact that the overweights were inclined to shut their eyes when presented with a reflective question that involved some need to engage in imagery (presumably in order to shut out the impact of the external cues). The overweight participants also were more inclined to be right-eye shifters during reflective thought, that is, emphasizing verbal rather than imagery forms of thinking. Differences in the effects of REM deprivation and in relationship between stimulus-independent thought in a laboratory setting and questionnaire responses of daydreaming were also found by Feldstein (1972). A series of studies by Segal and Singer, 1976 (see also Segal, Huba, and Singer, in preparation) have also indicated systematic differences in resort to drugs and alcohol by subjects who differ in their patterns of daydreaming style. In general, the trend of that data (based on more than 1,000 college students at Yale University and Murray State University in Kentucky) indicates that drug users, and particularly those who resort to halluco-genics or heroin and cocaine, tend to be rather externally oriented individuals, seeking external sensations and experiences and not much given to developing or elaborating inner fantasy. Drinking patterns seem somewhat more related to the Guilty-Dysphoric style of daydreaming. Presumably, for some individuals whose predominant ongoing inner experience has a negative, hostile, or self-recriminatory tone, drink seems to obliterate self-awareness and thought more effectively.

The use of questionnaires, also checked by systematic interview of smaller subsamples, has proven to be helpful in examining special ways in which daydreaming is reflected in daily life. Hariton and Singer (1974) explored the use by a group of suburban married women of a variety of fantasies while actually engaged in sexual intercourse with their husbands. Indications were in general that daydreaming frequency of a more general kind was likely to be linked to resort to daydreaming during sex itself. Specific differences in styles of daydream during the coital act and the relationship of such thoughts to relative satisfaction and dissatisfaction in the marriage was also explored.

Campagna (1975) made use of the IPI as part of a study of masturbatory fantasies in college freshmen. His results generally did not indicate much relationship between the more general daydreaming patterns and the specific form that masturbatory fantasy took, although there was some tendency for those subjects who showed high scores on the Positive-Vivid daydreaming factor to be inclined to have more storylike and fanciful masturbation fantasies, e.g., "I am a sultan who has a harem available at my every whim."

Hoyt (1977) made an ingenious use of questionnaire interview and guided imagery methods to study the so-called primal scene fantasy, the experience of observing one's parents engaged in intercourse. His data in general indicate a much higher frequency of not only such fantasies but of actual observation of such incidents in a group of normal young adults than might have been suspected from the clinical literature, which places a heavy and indeed somewhat negative emphasis on the implications of such experiences.

While it has often been believed that psychotic individuals, particularly schizophrenics, are likely to show excessive fantasizing, most of the evidence available from Rorschach reports (Singer and Brown, 1977) and from questionnaire studies seems to contradict this expectation. If anything, comparative studies of normal and disturbed individuals, while indicating some specialized patterns of fantasy for the psychotics, do not indicate any greater frequency or indeed do not indicate that the overall nature of daydreaming is at the heart of the psychotic process (Starker and Singer, 1975a, b; Giambra and Traynor, 1974; Schultz, 1976; Streissguth, Wagner, and Eschler, 1969).

In general, the questionnaire studies of daydreaming point up the fact that there is a tremendous amount of ongoing thought that people can report a great range of elaborate and complex fantasies that are detectable in average individuals, and that the thought-world, while perhaps ultimately relevant to certain specific behavior patterns, is far more varied and complex than might have been assumed. Thus, while fantasies such as those of aggression or violence (Rabinowitz, 1975,

Beit-Hallahmi, 1971) may occur and prove to be associated with other indications of attitudes about violence and aggression, there is no necessary relationship to actual overt aggressive behavior. Klinger (1971) had examined some of the possible relationships between fantasy (particularly as evaluated through projective methods) and the likelihood of the occurrence of overt behavior particularly aggressive in nature. The general indications are that if a strong monotopical aggressive fantasy recurs in individuals' productions, then there is likely to be some correlation with overt behavior. If, on the other hand, the fantasy is a part of a broader range of fantasy and is not dominant, or if there are indications of qualifications of the fantasy, e.g., awareness of the risks of overt execution or defenses against the expression of the fantasy, then translation of the fantasy into overt behavior is contraindicated. The data from our questionnaires, while less precisely related by current research to direct action does, on the whole, suggest that we entertain far more possibilities at the imaginal level than we could ever possibly execute in overt action, and that the report of fantasies by an individual must be taken only within the framework of the more general fantasy pattern presented rather than as a suggestion that direct action along these lines is likely to follow.

In summary, the increasing body of data from questionnaires suggest that we can begin to explore and mark out some of the major dimensions of private experience through self-report techniques of this kind. We need considerable more research relating the patterning of daydreaming and imaginal processes to other kinds of overt behavioral situations or other forms of attitudinal expression. We need much better evidence of the personality correlates of different day-dreaming styles than has emerged as yet. The questionnaires available are lengthy and cumbersome, and their vocabularies are geared for reasonably literate adolescent and adult groups. Although some un-published studies under my direction have indicated that working-class subjects, both Black and white, from a Florida community showed essentially the same patterns of daydreaming as had been reported by middle-class samples, and also that early adolescents showed comparable factor patterns, we have little data from very young age groups and very little from a great range of working-class samples in the society. There are almost no data available on daydream-ing patterns from subjects in other countries. Clearly, much yet remains to be done in this sphere.

With the increased interest in imagery as a general human phenomenon and with the studies relating absorption and concentra-tion to hypnotizability, it may well be that we should explore more extensively recurring daydreaming patterns as represented in the IPI with measures such as the Tellegan absorption scale or the measures developed by Theodore X. Barber and his colleagues for creative imagining as an alternative to formal hypnotic induction.

4. Cognition and Stimulus-Independent Mentation

Beginning in 1960, John Antrobus and I developed a series of experiments designed to determine if we could in some way tap into ongoing thought. Our intention in effect was to capture the daydream or fantasy as it occurred, or come as close to doing so as possible. The model grew out of the vigilance and signal-detection studies developed in World War II to study how individuals could adjust to tasks that required considerable attention but under monotonous conditions or environments of minimal complexity and stimulation.

In this model the subject in effect has different degrees of demand made upon him or her for processing externally derived information under conditions of reasonably high motivation. Since the amount of external stimulation can be controlled, it remains to be determined by the study to what extent individuals will shift their attention from processing external cues in order to earn money by accurate signal detections, toward the processing of material that is generated by the presumably ongoing activity of their own brain. (See Klinger, chap. 8 for a discussion of different definitions on an operational basis for describing private experience in an experimental setting.) Our attempt was to determine whether we could ascertain the conditions under which individuals, even with high motivation for external signal-processing, would still show evidence that they were carrying on task-irrelevant thought or, in the term we have been using more recently, stimulus-independent mentation (SIM).

Thus, the formulation was somewhat to the effect that if while detecting signals an individual was interrupted periodically, say, every fifteen seconds, and questioned about whether any stimulus-independent thoughts occurred, a "yes" response would be scored as SIM. By establishing in advance a common definition between subject and experimenter as to what constituted such task-irrelevant thought, one could have at least some reasonable assurance that reports were more or less in keeping with the operational definition established. Thus, a thought that went something like the following, "Is that tone louder than the one before it? It sounded like it was," would be considered stimulus-dependent or task-relevant and would elicit a "no" response even though it was indeed a thought. A response such as "I've got to remember about picking up the car keys for my

Saturday night date" would, of course, be scored as stimulus-independent mentation. A thought about the experimenter in the next room, "Are they trying to drive me crazy?," even though in some degree generated by the circumstances in which the subject found himself, was nevertheless scored as SIM because it was not directly relevant to the processing of the signal that was defined for the subject as his or her main task.

By keeping the subjects in booths for a fairly lengthy time and obtaining reports of the occurrence of stimulus-independent thought, after 15" of signal detection it was possible to build up rather extensive information on the frequency of occurrence of SIM, their relationship to the speed of signal presentation, the complexity of the task, and to other characteristics of the subject's psychological situation. Indeed, as Antrobus (1968) showed, it was possible to generate a fairly precise mathematical function of the relationship of stimulus-independent thought to the information load confronted by the subject in the course of ongoing processing.

By using periodic inquiries for content as well as for presence or absence of SIM, it was also possible to examine the range and type of content available and to score this material along dimensions similar to those also used for night-dream research, e.g., vividness of imagery, modality of imagery, degree of personal content versus impersonal content, future or past references, etc. The alternative method of establishing content was to make use of continuous free association by the subject during a vigilance task (Antrobus and Singer, 1964).

In the latter study, it was possible to show that while subjects spoke continuously in a varied and undirected fashion (with white noise piped into their ears so they could not hear their own verbalization), they were more likely to maintain arousal during a lengthy session in a darkened booth detecting visual signals. In contrast, counting from one to nine repetitively during the same situation led to actual sleep, sleepiness, and, indeed, irritability and gross discomfort. The arousal effects of continuous free association were to some degree at the cost of accuracy, for when arousal was maintained artificially by periodically piping marching band music into the subject's ears, the accuracy rate of the counting condition was significantly greater than for the free-association condition. In other words, responding to one's inner experiences provides to some extent a varied internal environment that maintains moderate arousal under conditions of a fairly routine or boring task. This is at the cost, however, of some inaccuracies. If external situations are sufficiently arousing, then a restricted internal focus of attention, as in the counting task, may actually lead to more accurate response to the environment. In a sense, then, daydreaming may be one way we maintain interest and arousal in boring or redundant situations with the likelihood that because the situations are so redundant we will not miss too much of what happens. The situation is analogous in many ways to that of driving on a well-known, relatively untraveled highway. Clearly, under conditions of driving in heavy traffic in a midtown area, daydreaming would be less functional than concentration almost completely on the physical environment. Experimental research with driving simulators to test out some of these implications remains to be done, however.

A number of generalizations have emerged out of the signal-detection experiments. It was possible to indicate that stimulus-independent thought could be reduced significantly if the amount of reward paid subjects or the complexity of the task was systematically increased. As a matter of fact, although significant reductions did occur, it turned out to be difficult to reduce reports of stimulus-independent thought to zero unless signals came at such irregular intervals that subjects could not apparently learn to pace themselves. While this would suggest that the general pattern of dealing with stimulus-independent thought involves a sequential style, there has been evidence in a study by Antrobus, Singer, Goldstein, and Fortgang (1970) that, under certain circumstances, it is possible to demonstrate parallel processing, that is, reports of stimulus-independent thought occurring even as the subject was accurately processing signals. (See chap. 5 by Shallice for a discussion at a more general level of the issue of sequential versus parallel processing in the organization of perceptual material).

When new, potentially personally relevant information is presented to the subjects just prior to a signal detection "watch," there is a greater likelihood of an increase in stimulus-independent mentation. Despite such increases in stimulus-independent thought, however, errors may not necessarily increase for some time. It is as if in many instances for tasks of this kind subjects are not using their full channel capacity for processing private as well as external cues. The model of examining how newly presented information, usually of a more emotional nature, becomes incorporated into the ongoing stream of thought, has been adapted for a series of studies by Horowitz and various collaborators to which we will refer shortly.

The signal-detection method for tapping in on ongoing thought presents some elegant opportunities for measuring more precisely what the odds are that any task-irrelevant mentation will take place at all. Fein and Antrobus (1977) were able to demonstrate that even though a trial of signal detections was increased from, say, one minute to two minutes (with signals coming every second, this would mean from perhaps 60 to 120 detections required of the subject), the relative frequency of reports of stimulus-independent mentation was capable of being described by a Poisson distribution once the subject made an *initial* report of an SIM. In other words, while there might be as long as an 8" period of "no" reports of SIM in a given trial of one or two minutes of signal presentation, once the subject reported a positive occurrence of stimulus-independent thought, the frequency of such reports was describable by a Poisson distribution rather than by a binomial distribution.

A procedure such as this provides some opportunity for us to see before us exactly what inherent capacities there are for processing private as well as public material, and the extent to which there may actually be inherent brain rhythms that play a role in the pattern of either sequential shifting that can occur, or in the emergence of parallel processing as well. It has also been possible to show by systematically examining content of reports in relation to whether or not the signal being presented was either visual or auditory that essentially the visual system is implicated in the production of visual SIM while the auditory system is more implicated in the production of sounds in the "mind's ear." In effect, this study lent further support to increasing evidence that privately generated phenomena do relate fairly closely to the basic imagery modalities implicated in the perceptual process as well as in the thought process (Antrobus *et al.*, 1970).

The signal-detection model also permits the study of some degree of individual differences. Antrobus *et al.*, (1967) were able to show that subjects, already by self-report predisposed to be imaginative, were more likely as time went on to report more stimulus-independent thought than subjects who reported on a questionnaire that they were little given to daydreaming. The differences between the two groups increased over time and indeed so also did the number of errors. Initially, the high daydreamers reported a considerable amount of stimulus-independent thought without differing in the level of errors from the low daydreamers. As time went on, however, there was suggestion that they seemed to be preferring to respond to stimulus-independent mentation and their error-rate increased significantly compared with the relatively stable rate of errors for the subjects who showed relatively little stimulus-independent mentation.

The cognitive processing model has a great many other implications that have not been examined fully. In addition to individual differences and to studies of the very process or relationship of information load from the external environment to self-generated material, we can also look at the task of processing in relation to the kind of priorities the individual may set more generally for processing in life situations, whether to stress internally generated material or externally generated signals, and we can also look at the role of private material in generating specific emotional reactions. Thus, the same signal detection task has been used in several studies to which we will refer below for establishing the implications of positive and negative affect.

Of course, these studies have on the whole been somewhat artificial. They take place in a darkened booth, subjects wear earphones that present white noise into their ears to prevent external sounds from interfering with the specific auditory signals, movement is at a minimum to reduce kinesthetic feedback, etc. More recently, there has been increasing interest in studying situations that come closer to ordinary daily settings (see chapters by Klinger, Pope, and Kripke and Sonnenschein) by having subjects report on the degree to which they are paying attention to certain external cues or carrying on some externally generated task when they are suddenly interrupted (for example, by an electronic beeper). Hurlburt (1976) pioneered in such a method and a similar technique has, of course, been employed even more elaborately by Klinger (see chap. 8).

McDonald (1976), in a study directed by this author, used Hurlburt's random signal generator with a dozen subjects. She was able to show that more than 40% of the time when they were interrupted over a two-day period by random signals from the generator they carried with them, they reported being engaged in stimulus-independent mentation. Csikszentmihalyi (see chap. 12) has pointed out that when individuals are not engaged in a challenging but feasible task that absorbs tremendous attention and thus leads to the "flow experience," there is a likelihood that they will either become extremely irritable or engage in autotelic behaviors, chewing gum, smoking, listening to music, drumming their fingers, or daydreaming. His data suggest that daydreaming may be one of the more functional of such activities, for when individuals were required systematically to reduce the frequency of such activities during the course of a few days time, the subjects who suffered most were those who had to give up the daydreaming activity, while those who suffered the least were those who gave up the activities of a nonmental nature, such as eating, drug use, smoking (Csikszentmihalyi, 1974, 1976).

In effect, then, the increasing body of results from comparisons of cognitive processing and attention to private thoughts or fantasy suggest that a great deal more private activity takes place than had probably ever been realized. Most people simply do not recall a great deal of such processing because they have moved on rapidly to new externally generated materials or to new thoughts. Systematic interruption under controlled conditions makes it clear that people are indeed processing a great deal of material from their long-term memory systems. Much of the material, of course, is not quite as fanciful or bizarre as some people are inclined to think appropriate for use of a term like "daydreaming." Nevertheless, a surprising amount of the material does involve wishful or fanciful explorations of the future. Indeed, it seems likely that one overriding purpose (see chapter by Rychlak for discussion of this issue) of the nature of ongoing thought may be that it involves an adaptive preparation for future action, drawing upon what Klinger has termed the many "current concerns," or the many bits of "unfinished business" or "intentions," to use the terminology of Kurt Lewin. But even beyond this long-range planning implication of attention to private thought or long-term memory-derived material, there may be an inherent stimulating function of such material, an alternative to the drowsiness or negative affect occasioned by redundant or otherwise boring environments. We have already mentioned the possible arousal value of moderate degrees of continued private free association. Wheeler (1969) found that subjects in a signal-detection task who reported that they were having a good deal of stimulus-independent mentation were much more likely to underestimate the amount of time they had actually spent in the booth engaging in the boring task. That is, time filled by response to their own ongoing thoughts led them to experience the absolute time that had passed as going by more rapidly.

5. Eye Movements and Daydreaming

Growing out of the emphasis on daydreaming or stimulus-independent thought as an alternative stimulus field to which one can assign different priorities for responding relative to the demands made by the external environment, it has seemed reasonable to explore how we shift our attention from the environment to private processes in the ordinary waking state. One consequence of this interest has been to study some of the physiological concomitants of ongoing thought and also in particular to examine how the eyes, which are our major source of information on the environment, may play a role in this shift of attention.

The early studies on night-dreaming had brought to the fore by the late 1950s the important association between reports of cycles of rapid eye movement and concomitant reports of dreaming. While initially such reports suggested that the eye movements might be "looking" responses, comparable to the saccads of normal visual exploration in the waking state, the major body of evidence now contradicts this assumption. Indeed, our own pilot studies of ongoing thought and daydreaming during the waking state, when electrocular-grams were being registered, suggested that if a subject is to respond to his or her own thoughts through fantasy, the likelihood is that the eyes will become fixed. There seems to be a necessity on the part of individuals to reduce the complexity and novelty of material presented by the environment in order, in effect, to "look with the mind's eye." If, indeed, the visual system is implicated in a good deal of daydream-ing, then one might be overburdening his channel capacity by looking around actively in a room while at the same time trying to process private material.

In a number of studies (Antrobus, Antrobus, and Singer 1964; Singer and Antrobus, 1965; Antrobus and Singer, 1968; Antrobus *et al.*, 1970) we have been able to demonstrate that for the most part engaging in extended private thought in the waking state is associated with a minimum of ocular movement. The results of these studies indicate that while subjects may show systematic eye movements when they are visualizing very specific events, such as a man jumping up and down on a trampoline or imagining themselves watching a tennis match, in most instances, allowing a fantasy to develop fully in a private form leads to a fixation of the eye. Very likely the eyes by fixating on a particular stimulus in the environment may either go out of focus, blurring the image and reducing its input, or there may be the brief period of satiation of ocular activity (retinal fading) that has been extensively studied in the perceptual situation itself.

These studies also indicated that extended daydreaming was associated not only with limited eye movement but also with a relatively stable heart rate and also to some degree with the occurrence of the alpha rhythm. If anything, it was in the attempt to abolish an ongoing thought, to suppress an unpleasant fantasy or image, in which one observed considerable eye movement, an increase in heart rate, or other evidence of motor responsivity.

Evidence of reduced eye movement in association with imagining or daydreaming has also been reported by Klinger Gregoire, and Barta, 1973, and by Marks (1972) who found clear evidence that persons who were rated as good visualizers made fewer eye move-ments while "looking at" self-generated images, and they made it clear that scanning movements were not intrinsic to the process at all.

An ambitious attempt to pin down more precisely what happens to the eyes when one is processing daydream-like material was developed by Singer, Greenberg, and Antrobus (1971). In this case subjects were presented with a film of a moving band of stripes that would ordinarily generate the optokinetic-nystagmus reflex (OKN). Under various conditions these individuals either engaged in mental arithmetic tasks or were encouraged to generate daydream-like material. The results indicated that when subjects were following the daydreaming instructions there was a reduction in the characteristic tracking motion despite the fact that the "pull" of the stripes would be expected to be very great. When subjects were forced to focus on the fixation point, 6' in front of them, by the use of special lenses they wore, it became more difficult for them, especially the male subjects in the study, to reduce the eye-tracking and to engage in private imaginative thought. There was a negative correlation between amount of eye movement in the study and the degree to which the subjects reported that their attention was turned "inward," toward private mentation. These results were replicated in an unpublished study by Kahn under the author's direction.

There were some confusing results in this experiment, however. There were indications that engaging in mental arithmetic led to an increase in eye movement. Since the direction of eye movement was not taken into account in the study or in the earlier research mentioned, one could not evaluate the possibility that eye-shifts might reflect the degree of involvement of the left or right hemisphere in the processing of the task.

Since the work of Sperry, Gazzaniga, and others began to appear on the implications of the split-brain experiment (see chapter 6 by Bakan), it seemed desirable to consider not only a cognitive blocking model of the type emphasized so far in explaining the fixation of eye movements during daydreaming, but also to look at the possibility that the direction of eye movements might be related to the kind of material being processed. A study by Meskin and Singer (1974) set up a number of alternative models for consideration in understanding what would happen to an individual who was engaging in reflective thought while in a face-to-face interview. Eye movements were photographed on video tape during an interview. In general, the emphasis of the study was on examining whether a subject in a face-to-face situation might have more difficulty processing imaginative material because of the likelihood that the human face confronting him was so complex and motivationally significant a stimulus (Tomkins, 1962, 1963) that an eye shift would be necessary so that the individual could focus on some neutral or less meaningful part of the room. It was also considered likely that shifting might be a function of the personality style of the individual so that persons given to producing more visually oriented or imagery-related material as habitual response pattern might shift their eyes more to the left, while those individuals more prone to thinking in logical-verbal sequential terms might be more likely to shift their eyes to the right.

In general, the results indicated support for both models with indications that when no interviewer was present, and questions were simply asked by a loudspeaker, there was much less eye-shifting, but that if someone was present the shifting was related to the individual style and to the type of report presented by the subject. Thus, reports that involved verbal clichés were more likely to be associated with right-shifting tendencies, and reports that were more associated with vivid imagery were more likely to be associated with left-shifting tendencies. In addition, persons who reported themselves on the IPI as high in daydreaming were more likely to be left-shifters in the experiment.

This study was followed up by an even more elaborate experiment of Rodin and Singer (1977) in which the personality style brought to the situation by the subject as represented by the degree of over-weight or normalcy of weight, the degree of field-dependence or field-independence, or the daydreaming style were among the variables, as well as the type of processing demanded of the subject: minimum reflection questions, reflective questions involving verbal-analytic material, or reflective questions involving visual or spatial imagery. Finally, the situation of the room was also set up so that in some cases there was not only one interviewer facing the subject but also a confederate seated either to the left or to the right of the subject, and therefore there was variation in the likelihood that the subject, when shifting eyes from the face of the experimenter, might encounter still another face. Results were quite complicated, but in general indicated that overweight subjects tended indeed to be right-shifters, tended to close their eyes in order to process private material (despite the rules of the study, which required them to keep eyes open), and also that imagery and visual-spatial material led more likely to left-shifting of the eyes while more verbal material led more likely to right-shifting of the eyes. The role of the face of another person was also of importance, so that individuals in general tended to shift away from having to confront the face of someone. This was especially true for the obese people and those who were in addition more likely to be field-dependent. That is, such individuals seemed to lack a capacity for blotting out external stimulus and generating extensive private material without having literally to "rest their eyes" on some blank wall or fairly neutral stimulus.

Quite recently Rosenberg (1977) combined the research on the Optokinetic-Nystagmus Reflex with the work on the direction of eye movement to study patterns of processing of different kinds of cognitive material, and also to look at daydreaming in this context. Her results are quite complex but also indicate support for the notion that when subjects are in effect attending to privately generated daydream-like material, their eyes tend to show reduction in movement and, in effect, some degree of blotting out of external stimulation. There are also clear indications of a leftward-shifting of the eyes associated with the production of visual imagery and dayream-like material, and right-shifting more likely associated with verbal, analytic content. Rosenberg's study was especially elegant because it included not only a range of content but also took into account the direction of movement of the stripes producing the Nystagmus effect. In this study in some conditions stripes moved from left to right across the visual field, and at other times from right to left.

It is not easy to draw simple conclusions from the work in this area. It is likely that to some extent we learn to blot out external stimulation while engaged in elaborate private mentation by either allowing our eyes to go out of focus, or by shifting our eyes in the direction of a blank stimulus. To the extent that either habitually or because of the specific nature of the content processed, we are dealing with visual images or more global types of material, our eyes may shift systematically to the left, indicating greater activation of the right hemisphere. The stream of consciousness is probably a complex mixture of verbal interior monologues and commentaries and visual images of recalled conversations or melodies. Eye movements ought to be by and large moving back and forth in both directions much of the time. It is possible that certain individuals clearly show predominance of one or the other direction because their main pattern of thought takes either a more global or visually differentiated form or because they are much more inclined to think in words and carefully drawn-out phrases than in pictures or in sounds. Confronted with complex visual stimulation in the environment such as another's face, many people shift toward neutral stimuli in the area or confirmed daydreamers may learn simply to let their eyes go out of focus without a shift of gaze.

In general, then, the examination of eye movement and perhaps (where telemetry can also be used) of EEG patterns in more natural-occurring situations involving different degrees of attention to external cues or private thought would seem to be a worthwhile area for exploration (see chapter by Kripke and Sonnenschein). It is obvious that our thinking behavior is at least to some extent reflected in body postures, facial attitudes, and apparently, so far, particularly in ocular activity. It remains to be seen whether some of the methods developed and described briefly here can be elaborated in further studies of more extended periods of ongoing thought.

6. Daydreaming and the Emotions

While the emphasis so far in this chapter has been on daydreams as part of the overall cognitive processing orientation of the organism, much of the interest in the phenomenon of daydreaming and also on the more general topic of the stream of thought has related to the implications of these experiences for the emotional state of the individual. Freud originally proposed that daydreaming represented an attempted solution of a deprivation state or underlying conflict in the individual, and the fantasy that emerged into consciousness might well represent a compromise between a frustrated wish and the demands of social adaptation or moral restrictions of the society. Much of the literature on the psychological importance of fantasy activity has stressed its role as a partial reduction of aroused drive energy. This position, while initially attractive and suggestive of important broader implications (Singer, 1955), nevertheless fails to account for many important and complex aspects of the thinking process. Clearly, fantasies can serve to be drive-arousing as well as drive-reducing, and indeed the notion that vicarious fantasies as expressed in movies or in television would reduce aggressive trends clearly has been disproven by an extensive series of researches (Singer, 1971).

A number of experiments have been carried out that have attempted to examine the relationship between the arousal of a strong emotion, such as anger, and the subsequent effects of daydreaming or engaging in some type of fantasy following such arousal. The pioneering work of Feshbach (1955) seemed to suggest some support for a drive-reduction model of fantasy. But subsequent studies using more direct daydreaming activities (Pytkowicz, Wagner, and Sarason, 1967; Singer and Rowe, 1962; Paton, 1972; and Biblow, 1973) have all suggested that a broader model is needed. For example, it seems increasingly clear that we are dealing not so much with the arousal of drives when we anger people, but specifically with the arousal of differentiated emotions, in keeping with Tomkins' cognitive-affective theory (Tomkins, 1962, 1963).

This theory emphasizes that we are born with a differentiated series of emotions that are themselves aroused in part by the cognitive demands imposed on the organism. For example, sudden complex information presented will startle an individual or produce the emotions of fear or terror. Information that is presented at a moderate rate and is more easily assimilable will arouse the more positive affect of interest and surprise, which lead to exploratory behaviors. Information that has been surprising or novel, but is assimilated into established cognitive schema, will lead to the experience of joy or a smiling response. Thus, if we walk past a stranger and then suddenly become aware of a facial resemblance to an old friend, we may be curious and interested, and then when indeed it turns out to be the old friend, we respond with a smile and a strongly positive affective state. Information and situations that are difficult to comprehend and assimilate and that persist over long periods of time are likely to evoke the affect of anger. A persisting loud noise that we cannot reduce or the awareness of an obstacle to our progress that we cannot change through any intervention on our own (being stuck in the middle of the street during a construction tie-up while driving to an important appointment) will arouse anger. A situation of less urgency and complexity may simply lead, if it persists over time, to the affect of sadness or to a depressed mood.

To the extent that our own thoughts may themselves have important implications in occasionally surprising us or in involving novelty, or in reminding us of persisting frustrations, these thoughts themselves may be able to generate specific affective states. The evidence for a differentiated emotional system is increasing (Izard, 1977). The research data from studies carried out in relation to ongoing thought in daydreaming seem in general to accord more with this position. Thus, Paton (1971) found that subjects who were aroused to anger and who were then given opportunities to fantasize about relatively benign materials showed a reduction in subsequent anger. Those exposed to violent materials after being angered and encouraged to fantasize did not show the theoretical reduction that might be expected by a catharsis theory, but, if anything, were inclined toward an increase in anger if their fantasies were aggressive, or toward a reduction in anger if the fantasies they produced were more benign. Biblow (1973) obtained generally similar results with children and Bach (1974) has reported similar findings with adults.

Fantasy and daydreaming, particularly of a positive kind, has been shown to be associated with experience of time as passing rapidly (Wheeler, 1969) and also in an unpublished study by Singer, Antrobus, and Auster, with the ability to tolerate long periods of silence in a solitary chamber. The Hariton and Singer (1974) study of women's sexual fantasies suggested that for many women an elaborate and complex sexual fantasy was actually emotionally arousing and helped generate and maintain excitement during intercourse. This fantasy was not necessarily a reflection of a withdrawal of interest and involvement with the husband. Indeed, it was much more likely a long-standing, well-established private stimulus that the women had developed from adolescence as a means of sustaining and increasing sexual arousal. And they simply continued the practice in their marital relationships.

Campagna (1975) in an experiment on sexually arousing fantasy found that when young men were initially sexually aroused by reading pornographic material, they were able to sustain or increase their level of arousal primarily by recalling their own recurring sexual daydreams, rather than by reading additional pornographic material. Arousal was reduced in their case when they read sexually irrelevant material. In general, Campagna's results suggest that private fantasies continue to have a strongly arousing impact, more effective than externally generated pornographic material after a certain point.

Vanderbeck and Antrobus in an unpublished study used the signal-detection experiment to study how thoughts themselves might increase or reduce specific emotions. They studied subjects who were initially in elated moods or in depressed states. By giving them tasks that made heavy demands on them for processing external information and thus reducing the levels of stimulus-independent thought, these investigators were able to demonstrate reduction either in the elated mood or in the depressed mood of the subject. In other words, preventing the subjects from continuing to attend to their own fantasies and mood-related mentation actually could modify the moods of the subjects. In a sense, then, this study, if confirmed by further research, points up again the powerful stimulus value of *attention to ongoing thought* and its capacity for arousing particular affective reactions. Indeed, Schultz (1976) in an important study with practical implications was able to demonstrate that encouraging severely depressed hospitalized men to engage either in daydreams of self-esteem enhancement or daydreams of a positive nature, such as nature scenes or other relaxing situations, made a difference in reducing their degree of depressive affect, making them more able to laugh at jokes or to show more positive responses. A control condition, in which depressives simply were allowed to free associate mentally more or less in the same manner they had been doing did not produce a comparable reduction in depression. Among other things this study suggests that helping individuals generate particular types of imagery may be able to direct the pattern of emotional response into specific directions.

A series of studies by Horowitz and various collaborators (Horowitz and Becker, 1971; Horowitz, Becker, and Moskowitz, 1971) have been examining the ways in which different emotional experiences eventually lead to the recurrence of particular thoughts in the ongoing thought stream. Horowitz's group has been using the signal detection format with individuals who have previously been exposed to particular kinds of emotional information. The studies demonstrate that there is a relative increase in spontaneously occurring thought ("unbidden imagery") associated with the particular affective state or particular information produced.

Zachary (1978) in a recent as yet unpublished study attempted to examine more extensively some of the implications of Horowitz's work in relation to cognitive-affective theory. Zachary raised the question as to whether ambiguity or incompletion of a situation might in itself account for the recurrence of the event in the ongoing thought stream, or whether the recurrence of such a situation was primarily a function of the particular type of affective arousal. He showed different kinds of films to groups of subjects prior to their engaging in tasks in which stimulus-independent mentation reports were then required. Zachary found that for tasks of moderate or low arousal, the recurrence of material in the ongoing thought stream depended on ambiguity or incompletion. When, however, the material itself was extremely arousing (as in the case of viewing an anatomical dissection or watching a couple making love), the nature of the affect, positive or negative, was less significant than the level of arousal.

In general, the model of establishing systematic input of different degrees of emotional import and taking into account positive and negative emotion, or looking indeed at very specific emotion, such as anger, disgust, curiosity and interest, or joy would be a valuable new direction for exploring the extent to which our ongoing thought reflects special types of affective experiences to which we've been exposed, or is simply a function of the relative importance of unfinished business that we confront in our lives. The relative effectiveness of the research done by Horowitz and his group and by Zachary indicates that we have essentially a methodology that should permit ultimately more extensive tests of some of the notions of current concerns or unfinished business that have been stressed by Klinger and myself or by Breger, Hunter, and Lane (1971) on how material becomes a part of the recurring thought stream.

As indicated above, a major phase of the overall research program deals with studies of ongoing play behavior in children. Here, we have been examining the nature particularly of imaginative or make-believe games where children introduce characters, settings, and situations not immediately given in their physical environment. We have been using process recording of spontaneous play behaviors in day-care centers and nursery schools, and most recently have been examining the way in which television-viewing by the children, something that already is taking up almost three hours a day for preschoolers, works its way into the consciousness of the child and into play behavior. As yet, however, we lack the longitudinal data to help us understand whether children who show a good deal of imaginative play in preschool and elementary school years turn out in adolescence to also report a good deal of daydreaming and response to internal processes. While there are suggestions from the literature to support such a belief (Singer, 1975a, Singer and Singer, 1976), the evidence based on any long-term follow-ups are simply not available.

7. Toward a Cognitive-Affective Theory of Daydreaming and the Stream of Thought

A series of papers have recently begun to elaborate the possibilities of describing the characteristics of the stream of thought in relation to more general theories of cognition, emotion and personality (Singer, 1977; Pope and Singer, 1977, 1978b). Reflecting in general the experiences of this extended research program and the accumulating research of others in this area, the position taken essentially proposes that we begin with a notion of the brain as continuously active. That is, the vast amount of material to which we are exposed is at least to some extent stored by the brain not in a "place" but through continuous representation. Thus, we are exposed almost continuously not only to a complex of stimulation from the external environment, but to a potential elaborate stimulus-field provided by the actual workings of our brain. We must learn initially to attend primarily to external stimulation, and indeed it might be argued that our sensory experience and general inclination is in effect "wired up" to respond to external cues.

Indeed, the affect system, an inborn differentiated system of emotions, may be itself closely related to the information-processing demands that environmental stimuli make upon us, and the relative positive or negative occurrence of such affects insures that we will attend to novelty and complexity and also experience joy when we can make a match between such novelty and already established schema (Tomkins, 1962). Once, however, we have begun to develop some reasonably established sets of schema, we begin the process of developing expectations or plans with well-learned subroutines that will make movement through the environment smoother for us without the necessity for constantly screening each new stimulus or being alert to each external experience. The establishment of plans or anticipatory images also means that we will respond with interest if there are mild discrepancies between our projected expectations and what we perceive, and explore further. If there are gross discrepancies we may respond with startle or fear or distress, and concomitant flight or avoidance responses. If the material presented to us is extremely redundant, we will seek other stimulation, as the sensory-deprivation research has suggested, or we will turn our attention toward the ongoing internal stimulus source.

Since there is probably a certain randomness involved in ongoing thought, particularly when confronted under low levels of arousal, we may find ourselves reacting to our own thoughts and fantasies with much of the same affects that we do to the external environment. That is, we can become surprised by odd juxtapositions of associations or memories, we can become upset when particular images or thoughts (such as the face of a dead loved one) recur in consciousness with the consequence that we become distressed or show the weeping response, even though, to an outsider, there is no visible basis for our reaction.

Some people gradually learn to develop a set of plans or expectations about their inner experience as well. For many, inner experience is an annoyance, a sign of inattentiveness or wishy-washiness, or it may reflect a potential sinful attitude. Such persons may plunge actively into overt activities that demand constant externally oriented attention. Or, they may adopt certain compulsive mannerisms that will involve them in attention to tiny details or into routinized experiences such as repetitions of certain prayers, counting activities of various kinds, attention to tiny details around the household, etc. For others, presumably those who show high scores on our dimensions of daydreaming, there may be particular plans for systematically attending to ongoing thought, and also using such thought in a more active way to produce further images and explorations. In the case of those subjects who would score high on the scales of the Positive-Vivid daydreaming factor, one might expect such persons in many cases to find inner experience a welcome alternative to the routine aspect of day-to-day life. Indeed, such individuals may also prove on some instances to be more creative and to be able to use this resource for artistic or literary purposes or to simply liven up the quality of their conversations and social interaction by the extensive recourse to their own ongoing inner processes. Others may have developed a set of expectations that inner life is essentially formed around recrimination and self-negation, and may be constantly playing out negative and distressing fantasies in this regard (Giambra and Traynor, 1977; Rabinowitz, 1975).

There may be particular characteristics of the stream of thought that lead to heightened attention of inner experience. Certain images, perhaps even randomly presented, may in themselves have higher likelihood of attracting one's attention. Some of these may do so because, of course, they touch on powerful unfinished business or important current concerns; the recollection that an important business appointment is set up for later that day may flash into one's mind while one is in the midst of a tennis match and lead to a missed shot. Sometimes simply the inherent properties of certain associational materials may themselves demand attention, as in the case of repetitive rhymes or lyrics or melodies that are especially catchy. We've all had the experience of a tune like "Hello, Dolly!" going around and around in one's head for sometimes days at a time. Or, occasionally an odd phrase we read someplace will attract our attention and then we find it recurring, not because of its inherent sense, but because of its sheer oddness. A demure young lady, for example, overheard the phrase, "Shape up or ship out," and was intrigued by its sound. She found herself for several years suddenly recalling the phrase and then finding it difficult to stop repeating the oddly symmetrical sound in her mind.

While there may indeed be a certain randomness, in effect the working of the machinery of the body, underlying ongoing thought from an adaptive standpoint one can still recognize the possibility that the continuous regurgitation of material presents us particularly with the likelihood that those major issues in our life or unfinished businesses that need attention will indeed come back before us. In the case of issues that we cannot cope with at all, their recurrence may, of course, produce extreme distress. On the other hand, being forced to face these impossibilities could also impel us toward constructive action that, while not relieving the original difficulty, might at least lead us to some alternative situation. Even seemingly playful or unrealistic fantasies of the "castles-in-Spain" variety may reflect some preparatory or planning behaviors, a movement in a new direction, a beginning recognition of a desire for a more varied or colorful turn in one's life.

In a very profound sense, then, the function of the stream of consciousness may well be to provide us with a major system for looking to the future, planning and sequencing our behavior, and preventing us from avoiding some of the important issues of human experience. All of us may seek to suppress conscious thoughts about the dangers of nuclear war, for example, but it is likely that if we sample the continuous thought of individuals who have been in any way exposed to the implication of atomic bombing, reflections of this danger will be found threading through such samples of day and night dreams. We may learn to ignore thinking about such things by shifting attention rapidly to something else, by taking a drink, by turning on the television, and so on. But somewhere along the line the thought will recur and we may have at some point to take some more meaningful action in relation to this thought. Such action might simply mean to vote for or against a particular candidate or particular bill, or it might impel even more active participation by a small number of individuals. Nevertheless, in a certain sense these recurrent thoughts do in a strange way force us to confront realities that we actually seek to avoid by plunging into the seeming reality of the hustle and bustle of daily life.

Playful or wishful fantasies, fantasies of being the first explorer of a far-off galaxy, or of winning the love of a famous beauty, or of being detected as the heir of Howard Hughes all may at first seem trivial and dubious adaptive significance. On the other hand, recurrences of such fantasies may be the basis for clues as to action one might take to at least move some steps toward the accomplishment of a certain number of ambitions. Or, they might suggest humorous stories or humorous material to develop if one is of a literary turn of mind. Or, they might reflect also very profound and deep-seated desires that need to be explored more fully with professional help, as psychoanalysts well recognize. At the very least such positive fantasies provide a source of alternative stimulation in circumstances that are inherently redundant or boring and that simply allow one to pass the time pleasantly, and to avoid the anxiety and strain of endless waiting. Indeed, to the extent that there may be subtle neurochemical consequences of particular types and patterns of thought (Pribram, 1977; Elkes, 1977), one might consider that positive fantasies could actually yield a variety of constructive neurochemical and psychophysiological reactions that would operate against stress-related diseases. Increasing evidence that certain types of guided fantasy, humor (Cousins, 1976), and other forms of positive imagery may be beneficial in dealing with both psychological and physical distress (Singer, 1974, 1978) ought to yield increasing attention to ways in which we can all learn not only to welcome the availability of the thought stream, but indeed to plunge more readily into it in an approach of active exploration.

References

Antrobus, J. S. Information theory and stimulus-independent thought. *British Journal of Psychology*, 1968, *59*, 423–430.

Antrobus, J. S., and Singer, J. L. Visual signal detection as a function of sequential task variability of simultaneous speech. *Journal of Experimental Psychology*, 1964, *68*, 603–610.

Antrobus, J. S., Antrobus, J. S., and Singer, J. L. Eye movements accompanying daydreaming, visual imagery, and thought suppression. *Journal of Abnormal and Social Psychology*, 1964, *69*, 244–252.

Antrobus, J. S., Coleman, R., and Singer, J. L. Signal detection performance by subjects differing in predisposition to daydreaming. *Journal of Consulting Psychology*, 1967, *31*, 487–491.

Antrobus, J. S., Singer, J. L., and Greenberg, S. Studies in the stream of consciousness: Experimental enhancement and suppression of spontaneous cognitive processes. *Perceptual and Motor Skills*, 1966, *23*, 399–417.

Antrobus, J. S., Singer, J. L., Goldstein, S., and Fortgang, M. Mindwandering and cognitive structure. *Transactions of the New York Academy of Science*, 1970, *32*(2), 242–252.

Bach, S. Notes on some imaginary companions. *Psychoanalytic Study of the Child*, 1971, *26*, 159–171.

Becker, S., Horowitz, M., and Campbell, L. Cognitive response to stress: Effects of changes in demand and sex. *Journal of Abnormal Psychology*, 1973, *82*, 519–522.

Beit-Hallahmi, B. Sexual and aggressive fantasies in violent and nonviolent prison inmates. *Journal of Personality Assessment*, 1971, *35*, 326–330.

Biblow, E. Imaginative play and the control of aggressive behavior. Chapter in J. L. Singer, *The child's world of make-believe: Experimental studies of imaginative play*. New York: Academic Press, 1973.

Breger, L., Hunter, I., and Lane, R. W. *The effect of stress on dreams*. New York: International Universities Press, 1971.

Campagna, A. Masturbation fantasies in male college freshmen. Unpublished doctoral dissertation, Yale University, 1975.

Cousins, N. Anatomy of an illness. *New England Journal of Medicine*, 1976, *295*, 1458–1463.

Csikszentmihalyi, M. *Flow: Studies of enjoyment*. Public Health Service Grant, Ro1, HM22883-02 Report. University of Chicago, 1974.

Csikszentmihalyi, M. *Beyond boredom and anxiety*. San Francisco: Jossey-Bass, 1976.

Davidson, A. D. The relationship of reported sexual day-dreaming to sexual attitude, sexual knowledge, and reported sexual experience in college women. Unpublished doctoral dissertation, University of Cincinnati, 1975

Dennis, L. B. Individual and familial correlates of children's fantasy play. Unpublished doctoral dissertation, University of Florida, 1976.

Drucker, E. Studies of the role of temporal uncertainty in the deployment of attention. Unpublished doctoral dissertation, City University of New York, 1969.

Elkes, J. Subjective and objective observation in psychiatry: A note toward discussion. In N. Zinberg (Ed.), *Alternate states of consciousness*. New York: Free Press, 1977.

Erlichmann, H., and Weiner, M. S. Dimensions of EEG activity during covert mental activity. Submitted to *Psychophysiology*.

Erlichmann, H., and Weiner, M. S. EEG asymmetry during spontaneous mental activity. Submitted to *Psychophysiology*.

Fein, G. A transformational analysis of pretending. *Developmental Psychology*, 1975, *11*, 291–296.

Fein, G. G., and Antrobus, J. S. Daydreaming: A Poisson process. *Cognitive Psychology*, 1977

Feitelson, D. Developing imaginative play in pre-school children as a possible approach to fostering creativity. *Early Child Development and Care*, 1972, *1*, 181–195.

Feldstein, S. REM deprivation: The effects on inkblot perception and fantasy processes. Unpublished doctoral dissertation, City University of New York, 1972.

Feshbach, S. The drive-reducing function of fantasy behavior. *Journal of Abnormal and Social Psychology*, 1955, *50*, 3–11.

Filler, M. S., and Giambra, L. M. Daydreaming as a function of cueing and task difficulty. *Perceptual and Motor Skills*, 1973, *37*, 503–509.

Frank, S. Fantasy and internalized role-taking. Unpublished doctoral dissertation, Yale University, 1976.

Frank, S. Just imagine how I feel: How to improve empathy through training in imagination. In J. L. Singer and K. S. Pope (Eds.), *The power of human imagination*. New York: Plenum, 1978.

Franklin, D. Block play modeling and its relationship to imaginativeness, impulsivity-reflection and internal-external control. Unpublished predissertation research, Yale University, 1976.

Freyberg, J. Experimental enhancement of imaginative play of kindergarten children in a poverty area school. Unpublished doctoral dissertation, City University of New York, 1970. (See also Chapter in J. L. Singer, *The child's world of make-believe*. New York: Academic Press, 1973.)

Fusella, V. Blocking of an external signal through self-projected imagery: The role of inner acceptance, personality style, and categories of imagery. Unpublished doctoral dissertation, City University of New York, 1972.

Gershowitz, M. Fantasy behaviors of clinic-referred children in play encounters with college undergraduates. Unpublished doctoral dissertation, Michigan State University, 1974.

Giambra, L. M. Daydreaming across the life span: Late adolescent to senior citizen. *International Journal of Aging and Human Development*, 1974, *5*, 115–140. (a)

Giambra, L. M. The working world of Walter Mitty: Daydreams: The backburner of the mind. *Psychology Today*, 1974, *8*, 66–68. (b)

Giambra, L. M. Adult male daydreaming across the life span: A replication, further analyses, and tentative norms based upon retrospective reports. *International Journal of Aging and Human Development*, in press, 1977. (a)

Giambra, L. M. Daydreaming about the past: The time setting of spontaneous thought intrusions. *The Gerontologist*, 1977, *17*(a), 35–38. (b)

Giambra, L. M. A factor analytic study of daydreaming, imaginal process, and temperament: A replication on an adult male life-span sample. *Journal of Gerontology*, 1977, *32*, 675–680. (c)

Giambra, L. M. Independent dimensions of depression: A factor analysis of three self-report depression measures. *Journal of Clinical Psychology*, in press, 1977. (d)

Giambra, L. M. Longitudinal changes in adult male daydreaming: A single item analysis. Unpublished manuscript, 1977. (e)

Giambra, L. M. Sex differences in daydreaming and related mental activity from the late teens to the early nineties. *International Journal of Aging and Human Development*, in press, 1977. (f)

Giambra, L. M., and Martin, C. E. Sexual daydreams and quantitative aspects of sexual activity: Some relations for males across adulthood. *Archives of Sexual Behavior*, in press, 1977.

Giambra, L. M., and Traynor, T. D. Depression and daydreaming: An analysis based on self-ratings. *Journal of Clinical Psychology*, in press, 1977.

Gottlieb, S. Modeling effects upon fantasy. In J. L. Singer (Ed.), *The child's world of make-believe*. New York: Academic Press, 1973.

Gould, R. *Child studies through fantasy*. New York: Quadrangle Books, 1972.

Griffing, P. Sociodramatic play among young Black children. *Theory into Practice*, 1974, 13(4), 257–265.

Hariton, E. B. Women's fantasies during sexual intercourse with their husbands: A normative study with tests of personality. Unpublished doctoral dissertation, CUNY, 1972.

Hariton, E. B., and Singer, J. L. Women's fantasies during sexual intercourse: Normative and theoretical implications. *Journal of Consulting and Clinical Pyschology*, 1974, 42, 313–322.

Horowitz, M., and Becker, S. Cognitive response to stress and experimental demand. *Journal of Abnormal Psychology*, 1971, 78, 86–92.

Horowitz, M., Becker, S., and Moskowitz, M. Intrusive and repetitive thought after stress: A replication study. *Psychological Reports*, 1971, 29, 763–767.

Hoyt, M. The primal scene: A study of fantasy and perception regarding parental sexuality. Unpublished doctoral dissertation, Yale University, 1977.

Huba, G. J., Segal, B., and Singer, J. L. The consistency of daydreaming styles across samples of college male and female drug and alcohol users. *Journal of Abnormal Psychology*, 1977, 86, 99–102.

Hurlburt, R. Self-observation and self-control. Unpublished doctoral dissertation, University of South Dakota, 1976.

Isaacs, D. Cognitive styles in daydreaming. Unpublished doctoral dissertation, City University of New York, 1975.

Izard, C. *Human emotions*. New York: Plenum, 1977.

Klinger, E. *Structure and functions of fantasy*. New York: Wiley-Interscience, 1971.

Klinger, E., Gregoire, K. C., and Barta, S. G. Physiological correlates of mental activity: Eye movements, Alpha, and heart rate during imagining, suppression, concentration, search and choice. *Psychophysiology*, 1973, 10, 471–477.

Kripke, D. F., and Sonnenschein, D. A 90-minute daydream cycle. Paper presented at the meeting of the Association for the Psychophysiological Study of Sleep, San Diego, 1973.

Marks, D. F. Individual differences in the vividness of visual imagery and their effect on function. In P. Sheehan (Ed.), *The function and nature of imagery*. New York: Academic Press, 1972.

Marshall, H., and Hahn, S. C. Experimental modification of dramatic play. *Journal of Personality and Social Psychology*, 1967, 5(1), 119–122.

McDonald, C. Random sampling of cognitions: A field study of daydreaming. Unpublished master's dissertation, Department of Psychology, Yale University, 1976.

Meskin, B. B., and Singer, J. L. Daydreaming, reflective thought, and laterality of eye movements. *Journal of Personality and Social Psychology*, 1974, 30, 64–71.

Nahme-Huang, L., Singer, D. G., Singer, J. L., and Wheaton, A. Imaginative play and perceptual motor intervention methods with emotionally-disturbed, hospitalized children: An evaluation study. *Journal of Orthopsychiatry*, 1977, 47, 238–249.

Oakland, J. A. Note on the social-desirability response set in Singer's Daydreaming Questionnaire. *Psychological Reports*, 1968, 22, 689–690.

Paton, R. Fantasy content, daydreaming frequency and the reduction of aggression. Unpublished doctoral dissertation, City University of New York, 1972.

Pope, K. S. The flow of consciousness. Unpublished doctoral dissertation, Yale University, 1977.

Pope, K. S., and Singer, J. L. Some dimensions of the stream of consciousness: Towards a model of on-going thought. In G. Schwartz and D. Shapiro (Eds.), *Consciousness and self-regulation*. New York: Plenum, 1977.

Pope, K. S., and Singer, J. L. Determinants of the stream of consciousness. In J. Davidson, R. Davidson, and G. Schwartz (Eds.), *Human consciousness and its transformations*. New York: Plenum, 1978a.

Pope, K. S., and Singer, J. L. (Eds.). *The stream of consciousness*. New York: Plenum, 1978b.

Pribram, K. H. Some observations on the organization of studies of mind, brain and behavior. In N. Zinberg (Ed.), *Alternate states of consciousness*. New York: Free Press, 1977.

Pulaski, M. A. Toys and imaginative play. In J. L. Singer, *The child's world of make-believe*. New York: Academic Press, 1973.

Pytkowicz, A. R., Wagner, N., and Sarason, I. An experimental study of the reduction of hostility through fantasy. *Journal of Personality and Social Psychology*, 1967, *5*, 295–303.

Rabinowitz, A. Hostility measurement and its relationship to fantasy capacity. *Journal of Personality Assessment*, 1975, *39*, 50–54.

Ritter, G. W. Production of stimulus independent thought as a function of task priority, signal predictability, and rate of signal presentation. *Dissertation Abstracts International*, 1974, *34*, 5230.

Rodin, J., and Singer, J. L. Eyeshift, thought, and obesity. *Journal of Personality*, 1977, *44*, 594–610.

Rosenberg, B. Mental activity and environmental responsiveness: Optokinetic nystagmus during mental tasks associated with the left and right cerebral hemispheres. Unpublished doctoral dissertation, Yale University, 1977.

Rowe, R. R. The effect of daydreaming under stress. Unpublished doctoral dissertation, Teachers College, Columbia University, 1963.

Ruth, J. S., and Giambra, L. M. Eye movements as a function of attention and rate of change of thought content. *Psychophysiology*, 1974, *37*, 475–480.

Saltz, E., and Johnson, J. Training for thematic-fantasy play in culturally disadvantaged children: Preliminary results. *Journal of Educational Psychology*, 1974, *66*, 623–630.

Schultz, K. D. Fantasy stimulation in depression: Direct intervention and correlational studies. Unpublished doctoral dissertation, Yale University, 1976.

Segal, B. Imagery as a predictor of potential drug users. *Journal of Alcohol and Drug Education*, 1974, *19*, 24–28.

Segal, B., Huba, G., and Singer, J. L. *Daydreaming, drugs and drinking: A study of college youth in the '70's*. Hillsdale, N.J.: Erlbaum, in preparation.

Segal, B., and Singer, J. L. Daydreaming, drug and alcohol use in college students: A factor analytic study. *Addictive Behaviors*, 1976, *1*, 227–235.

Singer, D. G., and Lenahan, M. L. Imagination content in dreams of deaf children. *American Annals of the Deaf*, 1976, *121*, 44–48.

Singer, D. G., Tower, R., Singer, J. L., and Biggs, A. Differential effects of TV programming on preschoolers' comprehension and subsequent play behavior: Sesame Street versus Mister Rogers. Paper presented at the meeting of the American Psychological Association, San Francisco, August 1977.

Singer J. L. Delayed gratification and ego-development: Implications for clinical and experimental research. *Journal of Consulting Psychology*, 1955, *19*, 259–266.

Singer, J. L. Imagination and waiting ability in young children. *Journal of Personality*, 1961, *29*, 396–413.

Singer, J. L. Daydreaming and planful thought: A note on Professor Stark's conceptual framework. *Perceptual and Motor Skills*, 1966, *23*, 113–114.

Singer, J. L. The importance of daydreaming. *Psychology Today*, 1968, *1*, 18–26.

Singer, J. L. The influence of violence portrayed in television or motion pictures upon overt aggressive behavior. In J. L. Singer (Ed.), *The control of aggression and violence*. New York: Academic Press, 1971.

Singer, J. L. Daydreaming and the stream of thought. *American Scientist*, *1974, 62*, 417–425. Reprinted in I. Janis (Ed.), *Current trends in psychology*. New York: Kaufman, 1977, 244–252.

Singer, J. L. Navigating the stream of consciousness: Research in daydreaming and related inner experience. *American Psychologist*, 1975, *30*, 727–738. (a)

Singer, J. L. *The inner world of daydreaming*. New York: Harper and Row, 1975. (b)

Singer, J. L. The constructive potential of imagery and fantasy processes. In E. Witenberg (Ed.), *Recent developments in interpersonal psychoanalysis*. New York: Gardner Press, 1978.

Singer, J. L., and Antrobus, J. S. A factor-analytic study of daydreaming and conceptually-related cognitive and personality variables. *Perceptual and Motor Skills, Monograph Supplement* 3-V17, 1963.

Singer, J. L., and Antrobus, J. S. Eye movements during fantasies: Imagining and suppressing fantasies. *Archives of General Psychiatry*, 1965, *12*, 71–76.

Singer, J. L., and Antrobus, J. S. Daydreaming, imaginal processes, and personality: A normative study. In P. Sheehan (Ed.), *The function and nature of imagery*. New York: Academic Press, 1972.

Singer, J. L., and Brown, S. L. The experience-type: Some behavioral correlates and theoretical implications. In M. A. Rickers-Orsiankina (Ed.), *Rorschach Psychology*. Huntington, New York: Krieger, 1977, 325–374.

Singer, J. L., Greenberg, S., and Antrobus, J. S. Looking with the mind's eye: Experimental studies of ocular motility during daydreaming and mental arithmetic. *Transactions of the New York Academy of Sciences*, 1971, *33*, 694–709.

Singer, J. L., and McCraven, V. Some characteristics of adult daydreaming. *Journal of Psychology*, 1961, *51*, 151–164.

Singer, J. L., and McCraven, V. Patterns of daydreaming in American subcultural groups. *International Journal of Social Psychiatry*, 1962, *8*, 272–282.

Singer, J. L., and Rowe, R. R. An experimental study of some relationships between daydreaming and anxiety. *Journal of Consulting Psychology*, 1962, 26,446–454.

Singer, J. L., and Schonbar, R. Correlates of daydreaming: A dimension of self-awareness. *Journal of Consulting Psychology*, 1961, *25*, 1–17.

Singer, J. L., and Singer, D. G. A member of the family. *Yale Alumni Magazine*, 1975, *38*, 10–15. Reprinted as: Television, a member of the family. *Elementary School Principal*, 1977.

Singer, J. L., and Singer, D. G. Imaginative play and pretending in early childhood: Some experimental approaches. In A. Davids (Ed.), *Child personality and psychopathology: Current topics* (Vol. 3). New York: Wiley-Interscience, 1976. (a)

Singer, J. L., and Singer, D. G. Can TV stimulate imaginative play? *Journal of Communications*, 1976, *26*, 74–80. (b)

Singer, J. L., and Singer, D. G. *Creativity and imaginative play in the* pre-school child. New York: Parents Magazine Films, 1977. (Film strip series.)

Singer, J. L., and Streiner, B. F. Imaginative content in the dreams and fantasy play of blind and sighted children. *Perceptual and Motor Skills*, 1966, *22*, 475-482.

Smilansky, S. *The effects of sociodramatic play on disadvantaged preschool children.* New York: Wiley, 1968.

Starker, S. Aspects of inner experience: Autokinesis, daydreaming, dream recall and cognitive style. *Perceptual and Motor Skills*, 1973, *36*(2), 663-673.

Starker, S. Two modes of visual imagery. *Perceptual and Motor Skills*, 1974, *38*, 649-650.

Starker, S., and Hasenfeld, R. Daydream styles and sleep disturbance. *Journal of Nervous and Mental Disease*, 1976, *163*, 391-400.

Starker, S., and Singer, J. L. Daydreaming and symptom patterns of psychiatric patients: A factor analytic study. *Journal of Abnormal Psychology*, 1975, *84*, 567-570. (a)

Starker, S., and Singer, J. L. Daydream patterns and self-awareness in psychiatric patients. *Journal of Nervous and Mental Disease*, 1975, *161*, 313-317. (b)

Stein, A. H., and Friedrich, L. K. Television content and young children's behavior. In J. P. Murray, E. A. Rubinstein, and G. A. Comstock (Eds.), *Television and social behavior* (Vol. 2): *Television and social learning.* Washington, D. C.: Government Printing Office, 1972, 202-317.

Stein, A. H., and Friedrich, L. K. The effects of television content on young children. In A. D. Pick (Ed.), *Minnesota Symposium on Child Psychology* (Vol. 9). Minneapolis: University of Minnesota Press, 1975.

Streissguth, A. P., Wagner, N., and Weschler, J. D. Effects of sex, illness and hospitalization on daydreaming. *Journal of Consulting and Clinical Psychology*, 1969, *33*, 218-225.

Taylor, P. L. Adolescent daydreaming: Instrument development, sex differences, and relationships to demographic variables, IQ, school achievement, and behavior. Unpublished doctoral dissertation, New York University, 1975.

Tomkins, S. S. *Affect, imagery, consciousness* (Vol. I & II). New York: Springer, 1962, 1963.

Wagman, M. Relationship of sensitization-repression dimension to daydream behavior types. *Perceptual and Motor Skills*, 1967, *24*, 1251-1254 (a)

Wagman, M. Sex differences in types of daydreams. *Journal of Personality and Social Psychology*, 1967, *7*, 329-332. (b)

Weiner, S. L., and Erlichmann, H. Ocular motility and cognitive process. *Cognition*, 1976, *4*, 31-43.

Wheeler, J. Fantasy, affect, and the perception of time. Unpublished doctoral dissertation, City University of New York, 1969.

Wooten, A. J. The relationship of daydreams to cultural role prescriptions and some comparisons of two methods of assessing daydreams and sexrole stereotypes. *Dissertation Abstracts International*, 1973, *34*, 1765-1766.

Zachary, R. Cognitive and affective determinants of ongoing thought. Unpublished doctoral dissertation, Yale University, 1978.

8

Modes of Normal Conscious Flow

Eric Klinger

When we speak of consciousness we are referring to the sum total of events in awareness. The term by no means exhausts the realm of things psychological, but it does encompass all of an individual's direct experience. When we speak of the flow of consciousness we are referring to the changes that take place in consciousness over time. The events of consciousness are, of course, extremely complex and varied. They embrace images in every sensory modality and in every degree of vividness, realism, and believability, including inner dialogue, hallucinations, reveries, and dreamlike sequences; and they also embrace qualities that are at the same time less figured and more pervasive than these—the affects. This chapter focuses on a broad class of these conscious contents. They do not contain the imagery of current perceptual activity but they contain imaginal qualities that one can describe in terms of forms, colors, sounds, words, smells, tastes, temperatures, and the like. I shall refer to this class as "thought." This chapter brings together ideas and data regarding ways to observe thought, the dimensions and forms of thought, and the factors that determine the content of thought as it changes from one moment to the next.

Eric Klinger • Division of the Social Sciences, University of Minnesota, Morris, Minnesota. The research was supported by Grant No. 1-RO1-MH 24884 from the National Institute of Mental Health. Essential pilot studies not reported here were made possible by grants-in-aid from the University of Minnesota Graduate School.

1. Methods for Observing Thought

1.1. General Considerations

Empirical science proceeds on the basis of observation. Scientists must do a good deal more than observe, but the current accepted truths of a science rest on a body of observations, and these must be the products of commonly accepted observational methods. Observational methods have been subject to more controversy in the study of consciousness than in most areas of scientific investigation, to the point that for some decades the conventional wisdom in psychology itself ruled out the possibility that appropriate methods could ever be devised. However, as behaviorist dogma has loosened its grip, psychologists interested in inner experience have in fact devised a number of methods for producing quantitative or quantifiable data. Since the strengths and limitations of these methods condition the body of results we shall unfold in this chapter, this section presents an overview of how observations of thought are currently being performed.

1.1.1. The Nature of Observation in the Science of Inner Experience.
Observations of inner experience have long been regarded as in some important respects different from other kinds of scientific observation, but views of how they differ have changed. At one time, psychologists took pride in the belief that their science was the only one in direct contact with its subject matter, unlike other sciences whose experience of their subject matter was filtered through the distorting lenses of physical sensation. Following a long period in which introspective methods were denied the status of scientific observation altogether, the increasing acceptance of experiential reports is accompanied by recognition that reporting one's own inner experiences is a form of observation subject to the limitations that are necessarily imposed by the usual human processes of attention, selection, categorization, memory, and communication (e.g., Natsoulas, 1970). There is also another limitation: Whatever event one introspective observer can experience can never be experienced by any other observer. Therefore, no observation as such can ever be verified by a second observer. All that can be recorded and communicated is a greatly abbreviated, more or less distorted account, one not subject to psychometric assessments of reliability or validity.

How severely does this special limitation handicap observation of inner experience? Not very severely, I believe. The relevant question is not of handicap but of what special burdens this feature of introspective observation places on an investigator to validate the observations. The burden does not seem appreciably different from that placed on most sciences in practice. Whereas astronomy requires that observations be validated by direct confirmations of newly observed phenomena, it is a rare comparative psychologist whose observations are confirmed by another comparative psychologist observing the selfsame event, and a rare chemist whose titrations are checked by a colleague on the selfsame substances. Indeed, with computerization of scientific observation, often no human observes more than a computer printout of numerical data. The psychologist of inner experience cannot use measures of observer agreement to help develop self-observational methods as easily as the comparative psychologist or the chemist can, but the principle they use is the same. No comparative psychologist knows what is going on in the inner experience of his or her colleague. He or she can only assess whether, when observing under the same conditions, two observers come out with similar accounts. That is, the real criterion even here is replicability not traceable to artifact. Thus, in observations of inner experience as in such other procedures, the validating process resides in ruling out artifacts, in replications, and, ultimately, in the usefulness of data or theory for making possible other forms of prediction and perhaps control.

1.1.2. The Problem of Memory. One problem faced by any observer is retaining information long enough to record it accurately. The decay and dynamic changes that vitiate and distort memories with time and with interference from newer information are too well known to warrant documenting here. However, one method of observing inner experience, thinking out loud, makes little use of memory. We shall see that other observational methods provide useful information despite some time lag between experience and report; but although time lags before reporting need not be fatal, clearly the sooner the report takes place the better.

1.1.3. Description versus Generalization. People generally provide more reliable information when they are asked to describe particular events than when they are asked to form generalizations about heterogeneous multiple events. Thus, for instance, personality ratings are more reliable when raters describe particular acts than when they describe a person's enduring attributes (Fiske, in press). It seems reasonable to conclude that reports of inner experience are likely to be most reliable when observers are asked to describe or rate well-specified attributes or particular, momentary conscious events rather than enduring characteristics of their inner experience.

1.2. Standard Methods and Their Limitations

There are roughly five classes of procedures currently in use for obtaining systematic reports of inner experience. First, there are questionnaires to be filled out by participants retrospectively. Second, participants may be asked to think out loud, reporting the verbal elements in their consciousness as they occur. Third, participants may be asked to engage in some task or to go about their everyday living, during which they are interrupted periodically and asked to describe the inner events they recall occurring just before the interruption. Fourth, in a consciousness-sampling procedure like the foregoing, they may be asked not to describe their inner experience narratively but to rate it on particular, previously agreed-upon scales. Fifth, people can be asked to report particular kinds of events each time they occur during some time period, using a simple reporting device whose use can be automatized.

All five kinds of methods have produced some interesting data. Since four of them were used to obtain results to be reported below, and since other results obtained with them bear on the discussion of the new data, the five kinds of methods are reviewed briefly in this section.

1.2.1. Questionnaires. Questionnaires to study inner experience have been used at least since Galton (1883) devised one to assess the qualities of people's imagery. One early such questionnaire is still in use (Betts QMI: Betts, 1909) and has been joined by others (e.g., the Gordon Test of Visual Imagery Control: Gordon, 1949) and the Richardson VVQ (Richardson, 1977). The most commonly used general questionnaire is the Singer-Antrobus Imaginal Processes Inventory (IPI) of 400 self-descriptions ("I can be aroused and excited by a daydream"; "I daydream about what I would like to see happen in the future"; etc.) for each of which the respondent indicates how true or characteristic the statement is of him or her. The IPI has succeeded in producing a number of interesting results. For instance, it has shown that daydreaming patterns can be described by an assortment of independent factors, such as absorption in daydreaming, unpleasant daydreams, and mindwandering/distractibility (Singer and Antrobus, 1963; Isaacs, 1975); that self-reports of daydreaming continue through the whole adult lifespan, with a slight decline in the oldest years and a shift away from sexual and heroic daydreams (Giambra, 1974); and that depressed individuals daydream more than others but are more bored with their daydreams (Traynor, 1974). The daydreaming and mindwandering factors of the IPI have been shown to predict some aspects of the thoughts reported by subjects in a thought-sampling format using 30-second reporting intervals during a laboratory signal-detection task (Isaacs, 1975).

1.2.2. Thinking Out Loud. The first means of finding out what is going through a person's mind is to have him or her think out loud. Investigators interested in problem solving have used the method systematically at least since the 1940s (Bloom and Broder, 1950; DeGroot, 1965) and more recently it has been used to study spontaneous thought of other kinds as well (Klinger, 1971, 1974; Pope, 1977). The method requires the participant to speak continuously as he or she is thinking, rather than to give periodic synopses of thought between reports. If the participant can do that—not all can—the reports provide the information not only about the gross moment-to-moment thematic content of thought but also about the sequence in which it occurred.

The method has a number of disadvantages. First, it necessarily puts people into a situation that is unnatural to most. Many subjects, however, seem able to overcome this problem. Second, the subject can express only a small fraction of what is going on inside, since giving voice to more than the main verbal stream would cause the subject's report to interfere with the natural flow of thought. Third, there is evidence that thinking out loud leads subjects to spend more time on each content theme: Pope (1977) found thinking-out-loud subjects shifted their thoughts to new topics about every 30 sec, on the average, whereas subjects who were not thinking out loud indicated shifts with a key every 5 or 6 sec, on the average. The latter figure is very likely closer to normal durations of thought segments, since under thought-sampling conditions the trained participants in our research (see below) estimated the length of their thought segments at means of 8.8 sec (standard deviation of 9.0 sec) in a laboratory situation (listening with moderate attention to a tape-recording) and 14.5 sec (standard deviation of 21.8 sec) in a sample of everyday normal out-of-the-laboratory situations, with a median of 5 sec under both conditions.

1.2.3. Thought-Sampling (Descriptive). A second on-the-spot method for determining thought content is thought-sampling, where an experimenter stops people in the middle of whatever they happened to be doing and requests narrative descriptions of what had been going on in their consciousness just before the interruption. Thought-sampling has the advantage that the subject can try to reconstruct whatever was going on just before the interruption, however complex. Nevertheless, subjects must rely on memory for their reports, and since it is sometimes hard to recapture the order in which thoughts occurred, some of the sequential fine grain is lost.

Thought-sampling has the additional virtue that it is a highly flexible procedure and relatively unobtrusive. It is actually a specialized application of time-sampling procedures, which have a long history of use in the social sciences. Time-sampling procedures were described in industrial settings to study patterns of work as early as 1935 (Tippett, 1935), and they have been used frequently since then. There has been an upsurge of their use academically and, increasingly, by psychologists in recent years. Aserinsky and Kleitman (1953) initiated an enormous outpouring of research using EEG-contingent, nonrandom dream-sampling. Lorents (1971) applied them to study the working patterns of university business school faculty. Others have used them to study "ecological" patterns of activity and mood in normal everyday living (e.g., Csikszentmihalyi, Larson, and Prescott, 1977). Finally, they have been used to study patterns of inner experience in laboratory settings (Foulkes and Fleisher, 1975; Klinger, Barta, Mahoney, et al. 1976) and in everyday living (Hurlburt, 1976; Prescott, Csikszentmihalyi, and Graef, unpublished; Prescott and Haertel, unpublished; see also below).

How severe a handicap is reliance on fading memory traces in thought-sampling? In our research, participants are asked to report the thoughts that had occurred immediately before the interruption. They generally report two to three segments of thought and their median estimate of how long individual segments last is 5 sec. This is well within most investigators' estimates of the span of short-term memory, but it is hard to apply the literature on short-term memory in any simple way. If one were to calculate time lapse not from the occurrence of an isolated bit of imagery but from the end of an integrated thought segment, then, of course, the time lapse between event and reporting is nearly zero. Furthermore, short-term memory is thought to be affected at least as much by interference from interpolated events as by time-related decay (Cermak, 1972), but in the thought-sampling situation, what shall we count as interference? Later parts of the same brief thought segment? Probably not. External stimuli to which participants were paying little attention? Unlikely. Thus, fading of short-term memory is probably not a major source of concern in our procedure.

A more serious problem is that short-term memory is already a severely stripped-down encoding of the original event. Much more of it is retained in "immediate" memory (or "iconic" or "echoic" memory), but immediate memory probably vanishes within a few hundred milliseconds—long enough, possibly, for use in the earliest part of a thought report, but disappearing quickly in the very process of reporting. Therefore, thought-reporting that proposes to tap immediate memory must be made as efficient as possible, which probably requires that participants know in advance what variables they are to report on, and that they use a reporting system more efficient than narrative report. Similarly, thought-reporting that relies on short-term memory probably requires that participants know in advance what kinds of events they are to encode for storage beyond the span of immediate memory.

1.2.4. Thought-Sampling (Using Ratings). Besides being too cumbersome to exploit immediate memory fully, narrative reporting of thought content introduces some further procedural problems. Narrative reports are likely to take rather idiosyncratic forms, which makes them hard to compare across individuals. Participants may not recognize or attend to the aspects of their inner experience that are of greatest interest to the investigator. The reports are often couched in words that are ambiguous and hard to quantify. In order to avoid these difficulties, investigators may ask subjects to rate their inner experience instead of or in addition to providing a narrative description. For instance, Antrobus, Singer, and Greenberg (1966) asked people to indicate the presence or absence of thoughts about something other than the immediate situation during the foregoing 15 sec. In our research we supplement subjects' narrative descriptions of their thoughts with ratings of their imagery on a series of rating scales (see below).

To rate one's inner experience may seem to pose a rather difficult task. However, there are indications that the task at least feels manageable to ordinary experimental participants. We ask our participants to rate the confidence with which they make some of their experiential ratings. The three confidence levels are "very confident," "moderately confident," and "not at all confident." When rating the duration of their latest thought segment, for instance, our participants rate themselves as "very confident" of their estimate 64% of the time and as "moderately confident" 35%. When they rate the directedness of their thoughts, the percentages are 75% "very confident" and 22% "moderately confident." The raters themselves, then, are hardly overwhelmed by the task.

1.2.5. Event Recording. People can be asked to indicate whenever a certain kind of event occurs in their consciousness. For instance, behavior therapists may ask obsessive clients to record on a chart each time they have a certain disturbing kind of thought. Pope (1977) asked experimental subjects to move a key whenever their thoughts shifted to a new topic. We have trained subjects in a dichotic listening experiment to tell us with a toggle switch whenever their attention shifts from the stimuli being piped into one ear to those piped into the other ear (Klinger *et al.*, 1976).

2. Summary of Method in a Minnesota Thought-Sampling Study

In discussing the variety of methods in use for studying inner experience, we have already noted a number of interesting results: average durations of normal thought, dimensions of daydreaming questionnaire reports, and the confidence with which participants rate their own inner experience. This chapter will shortly turn to a more direct, systematic look at findings on the major dimensions of thought, on the qualities of normal moment-to-moment thought, and on the factors that determine the themes that a particular thought segment is about. Since many of the findings to be reported emerged from our thought-sampling studies at the University of Minnesota, Morris, it will be well first to describe briefly the methods we used to obtain them.

2.1. Student Participants

College students were recruited for an intensive, longitudinal study of motivation, inner experience, and life situations that would involve each participant for periods of up to 9 months. Their names were selected randomly from registration lists. Of 106 people contacted, 60% volunteered, of whom 5% later withdrew and 37% were not used. Thus, our data are representative of a large proportion of UMM college students. There were no sex differences in volunteer rates. We report here on results from 20 Caucasian students (19% of those contacted), 12 male and 8 female, in the case of experimental thought-sampling sessions, and on a subset of 12 students in the case of thought-sampling outside the laboratory. They were paid at prevailing student wages for an average of about five hours a week each.

2.2. Procedure

Participants were first screened to ascertain commitment to the substantial time demands of the research and to rule out gross hearing defects. They were subsequently trained in an eight-step individual program to become aware of their inner experience, to estimate the duration of short time intervals, to use a toggle switch to indicate which sound track of a dichotic tape recording they were listening to, to distinguish thoughts that occurred after the onset of a tone from those that came before, to divide the stream of thought into thematically homogeneous segments, to identify and signal transitions between segments, and to report their thoughts orally with the use of a

Thought-Sampling Questionnaire. They took a battery of personality and imagery tests and a specially designed 500-item Goals Checklist.

The main experimental procedures began with an intensive structured interview and continued every few weeks with reinterviews. Each reinterview was followed within one or two days by an individual experimental thought-sampling session. The participant listened through earphones dichotically to two simultaneous 15-min prose narratives. At each session, the tape-recorded dichotic narratives were interrupted 12 times after varying intervals by a tone that signaled the participant to start describing his or her latest thought content, as well as the last portions of the prose passages recalled. Throughout the playing of the tape, participants indicated continuously to which track they were attending. We report here on 936 thought samples obtained in 78 such sessions from 20 participants.

Interspersed with the experimental sessions, participants engaged in out-of-the-laboratory thought sampling. On each out-of-the-lab occasion participants received a random alarm device (a "beeper") that emitted a soft tone at random intervals with a mean of about 40 min. They were instructed to carry the beeper in their normal activities for 24 hr while awake, although they were permitted to interrupt use under circumstances in which it would prove embarrassing. At each tone, participants filled out a written version of the Thought-Sampling Questionnaire answer form. We report here on 285 thought samples gathered on 24 thought-sampling days by 12 participants.

2.3. Dependent Variables

During experimental sessions, participants used the toggle switch to indicate continuously which narrative he or she was attending to. In addition, using the format of the Thought-Sampling Questionnaire, participants responded to each signal tone with open-ended reports of their inner experiences just before each tone and of the latest taped passages they could recall. The analyses of these measures of attention, thought content, and recall are described in a later section. The Thought-Sampling Questionnaire (modified from a dream-sampling questionnaire by Allan Rechtschaffen) yielded participants' ratings of their inner experiences on the following additional variables: (1) estimated duration of the latest thought segment, (2) estimated duration of the previous segment, (3) vagueness versus specificity of the imagery, (4) amount of directed thought, (5) amount of undirected (respondent) thought, (6) amount of detail in the imagery, (7) number of things that seemed to be going on simultaneously, (8) visualness of the imagery, (9) auditoriness of the imagery, (10) intentness of listening to the stimulus tape, (11) amount recalled from the latest few seconds of the tape, by participants' self-estimates, (12) degree to which the imagery felt controllable, (13) participants' degree of trust in the accuracy of their memory of the latest experience, (14) familiarity versus unfamiliarity or bizarreness of the latest experience, and (15) the time in the participant's life associated with the experience. For out-of-the-laboratory thought-sampling the questions were either identical or parallel. Thus, intentness of listening and recall of the tape became attentiveness to and recall of environmental events. Variable 14, Familiarity, was divided into two new variables, Usualness and Distortedness, which had been confounded in the in-lab thought reports. (The correlation between Usualness and Distortedness was $-.52$.)

The response-limited Thought-Sampling Questionnaire items are answered by choosing from among three to seven response alternatives, each labeled. For instance, in rating Specificity/Vagueness, participants could choose from among "involved in specific thought," "aware of vague content," "aware of vague content but can't verbalize it," and "nothing—mind was blank." In rating amount of directed thought, they could choose from the five categories of "all," "mainly," "some," "a little," and "no" directed thought. Clearly, there is little basis here for assuming equal intervals between adjacent response alternatives. Therefore, although product-moment correlation coefficients are reported here for convenience, it is understood that the relationships among these variables are seen best, though much less efficiently, in contingency tables.

3. Qualities of Thought and Imagery

Since thought is such a complex phenomenon, it is not surprising that there are numerous ways to classify and to characterize it. Many variables have in fact been suggested, although few of them have come under systematic investigation. Some characterize chiefly the imagery taken more or less statically—properties such as visualness, controllability, and so forth—and others characterize relationships within the stream, such as transformations over time, responsivity to cues, organization of segments, and so on. Section 3.1 considers primarily the latter kind of dimension, whereas section 3.2 presents data regarding both. Note that section 3 does not consider affective or thematic content dimensions of consciousness.

3.1. Dimensions or Classes of Thought

Most writers and investigators of thought have explicitly or implicitly assumed a two-class division of thought or perhaps a single continuous dimension. It has gone by many names. The presently most widely used name for the dimension is "directedness," the nether end of which is generally regarded as corresponding to "daydreaming" or "fantasy." With increasing attention to thought as a phenomenon, however, it has become plainer that the various characteristics attributed to it cannot be taken as just semantic differences or differences in emphasis. For instance, about the time that Singer (1966) was operationalizing daydreaming as "stimulus-independent" thought, I was operationalizing its presumed equivalent, "fantasy," as "respondent" thought (Klinger, 1971). As we shall see, however, it is quite possible for thought to be stimulus-independent and operant or stimulus-bound and respondent. Furthermore, most of the thought that could be classified as either respondent or stimulus-independent is rather humdrum. "Fantasy," it appears, need not be fanciful. Going still further, it appears that both directed and undirected thought may be more or less subject to certain kinds of dreamlike errors or "fusions." Finally, there appears to be a dimension of ego relationships to one's imagery that cuts across the others.

The upshot of these considerations is that we must complicate our taxonomy of thought. This section describes five presumed dimensions and some data that bear on them.

3.1.1. Operant versus Respondent Thought. The division of thought into "operant" and "respondent" classes has many precursors: active versus passive reason (Aristotle; Windelband 1901/1958), secondary versus primary process thinking (Freud, 1900/1961), thought with or without "designe" (Hobbes, 1651/1958), conscious versus foreconscious or affective thought (Varendonck, 1921), R-thinking versus A-thinking (McKellar, 1957), realistic versus impulsive thinking (Hilgard, 1962), and directed versus autistic thinking (Berlyne, 1965). There are no doubt others. The underlying distinction seemed to accord with Skinner's (1935) distinction between operant and respondent behavior, labels that I then for various theoretical reasons (Klinger, 1971) adopted to characterize thoughts. In very general terms, operant thinking appears to differ from respondent thinking in that it is accompanied by a sense of volition, is checked against feedback concerning its effects, is evaluated according to its effectiveness in advancing particular goals, and is protected from drift and distraction by the thinker's deliberately controlling his or her attention.

Regarding the last two of these distinguishing characteristics of operant thinking, we now have some data (Klinger, 1974). The participants in this study were asked to think out loud under four kinds of conditions: while they were solving a manual puzzle, solving a logic problem, letting their minds wander, and reclining with eyes closed. Content analysis of the thinking-out-loud protocols revealed significantly more utterances that indicated the participant was evaluating the effectiveness of previous thought segments or controlling the direction of attention in the first two conditions—the task conditions—than in the last two. Attention-control utterances tended to occur at points where the participant had apparently bogged down during problem solving (46%), after a mindwandering episode during a task condition (32%), and after successfully completing a problem-solving step, while trying to figure out what to do next (16%). In other words, participants seemed to need to steer their attention deliberately when the smooth flow of their integrated activity had been terminated or had wandered from the task.

One tempting inference from this finding is that during integrated operant segments the flow of mental activity has a great deal in common with mental flow during respondent activity. That is, apart from certain elements such as attention control, the determinants of operant mentation are the same as those that govern respondent thought, and that the nature of the imaginal stream is similar, too.

Our Minnesota thought-sampling results provide a partial test of this inference, since they enable us to relate the participants' ratings of how directed their thoughts were with the other rating variables of the Thought-Sampling Questionnaire (Table I). If we now consider only relationships that are consistently significant for both in-lab and out-of-the-lab results, with correlation coefficients of at least .20, we find four kinds of differences between mostly operant (directed) and mostly respondent (undirected) thought.

First, directed thoughts were more often specific and less often vague: 95% of the time completely directed out-of-the-lab thoughts were rated specific as compared with 41% of the completely respondent thoughts, and the relationship is linear for intermediate values. For in-lab thoughts the corresponding percentages are 79 and 42.

Second, participants tended to be slightly more attentive to external cues during directed thought (or thought more directedly while attending to external cues) outside the laboratory. A weak trend in the same direction in-lab was almost outweighed by the fact that, of the completely directed thoughts people had while the tape was running, 47% occurred while they were not listening at all. There were few completely directed thoughts in these sessions (only 4% of the

TABLE I. Correlations among Thought-Sampling Questionnaire Variables: Pooled within Participants

Variable	DuL	DuP	Sp	Dir	Und	Sim	Det	Vis	Aud	Att	Rec	Con	Tr	Fam	Str
Duration, latest thought		20[a]	06	17	-18	-04	18	13	21	07	15	16	12	-07	-05
Duration, previous thought	22		10	11	-08	-09	08	07	22	03	12	03	05	-08	-02
Specificity	04	-04		35	-28	-21	44	16	21	14	26	27	43	16	-14
Directedness	06	02	25		-80	-19	18	11	10	23	26	42	23	23	-09
Undirectedness	-05	00	-14	-83		29	-16	-06	-10	-17	-24	-35	-19	-17	-06
Simultaneous thoughts	03	00	-05	-05	06		01	07	-04	00	01	-02	-07	-08	05
Detailedness	14	-00	43	07	-03	01		59	38	11	24	17	48	03	00
Visualness	02	-04	27	-08	11	06	59		24	03	10	10	24	-07	01
Auditoriness	12	10	10	-05	04	05	19	11		19	21	17	21	04	-11
Attentive to cues	-01	-01	-04	07	-07	-02	-08	-03	06		69	49	17	26	-16
Recall of cues (subjective)	08	01	-01	02	03	-01	01	01	10	62		47	40	24	-11
Controllability	04	-05	16	30	-24	-03	16	10	01	09	13		28	36	-28
Trust in memory of thought	10	01	27	12	-10	04	25	22	05	04	08	18		12	-09
Familiar/usual	-02	-07	15	01	-00	-09	03	01	-04	-09	-11	10	06		-52
Strangeness															

[a] Coefficients above the diagonal are for 285 out-of-the-lab thought samples, those below the diagonal are for 936 in-lab thought samples. Missing data reduced some individual cell Ns to as low as 276 and 889, respectively. Before pooling the data across participants, the ratings were converted to standard scores within each participant in order to eliminate biasing effects of individual differences. Assuming independent observations, correlations are significant at $p < .05$ with values of $r = .12$ above the diagonal and of $r = .06$ below.

total), and most of these were evidently inconsistent enough with the taped passages that subjects shut the tape out. A similar pattern occurred with respect to the participants' sense of having remembered the external cues, with which the attentiveness ratings were highly correlated.

Third, participants had a significantly greater sense of being able to control their directed thoughts than their respondent ones. In the laboratory sessions, 53% of the thoughts that felt completely uncontrollable were rated as completely respondent, as compared to only 5% of the completely controllable thoughts. Outside the laboratory, the percentages were 70 and 1. Looking at it from another viewpoint, 68% of the completely directed in-lab thoughts felt moderately or completely controllable, as compared with only 36% of the completely undirected thoughts. The corresponding out-of-the-lab percentages are 91% and 38%. These figures, then, establish a moderate degree of relatedness between the fact of a thought being directed and the sense that it is controllable. However, it is nevertheless noteworthy that more than a third of the completely undirected thoughts nevertheless felt *at least moderately* controllable. Evidently, experimental participants distinguish between these two variables.

Fourth, there is a very weak linear tendency for participants to place greater trust in memories of directed than of undirected thoughts.

Of at least equal interest to these differences between operant and respondent thought is the lack of difference in other important respects. Thus, there are no consistent or appreciable differences in duration of the thought segments, the number of different things going on in the thoughts, the amount of detail in the imagery, the degree to which the images were visual or auditory, the familiarity versus strangeness of the imagery, or the time of the participant's life associated with the thoughts. In some important attributes of their imagery, then, operant and respondent thought segments are very similar.

3.1.2. Stimulus-Independent (Task-Irrelevant) versus Stimulus-Bound (Task-Related) Thought. One of the traditional features of daydreaming is that it takes one's attention away from whatever else one may be doing. Therefore, one way of operationalizing it, in a way that would make it easy for experimental partipants to judge when they were daydreaming, is to define it as any mental activity not related to the task situation at hand. This was done in a series of studies (e.g., Antrobus, Singer, and Greenberg, 1966) that produced some interesting findings: at least a minimum amount of stimulus-independent thought seems to occur under almost any conditions, judging from self-reports of experimental participants, but is greatly reduced when the stimuli to which participants are asked to attend are closely spaced, when participants must perform mental operations on their perceptions, and when the money incentives for accurately reporting stimuli are large. Isaacs (1975) has shown that people who score high on a daydreaming factor of the Imaginal Processes Inventory report more stimulus-independent thought in a signal-detection task than do people who score low.

Nevertheless, it would be surprising if task-irrelevant thoughts were always respondent or if stimulus-bound thoughts were always operant. We may hypothesize, then, that operantness and stimulus-boundedness are correlated variables but that they are far from identical. Our Minnesota thought-sampling study shows that this is indeed the case. For each of our out-of-the-laboratory thought samples, participants had noted what they were doing and where they were at the time of the signal tone. Content analysts compared these descriptions with the reported thought content and placed the thought samples into one of three categories: clearly setting-related, clearly unrelated to the setting, and questionable. For 285 analyzable thought samples from 12 participants on 24 occasions, 69% of the thoughts were related to the participants' setting at the time, 21% were clearly not, and only 10% were hard to place in one or the other category. Taking just the setting-related thoughts—which we assume correspond to task-related or stimulus-bound thoughts—only 26% were rated by participants as exclusively operant and 65% were rated as wholly or mainly operant. In fact, 27% of them were rated as wholly or mainly respondent. Conversely, only 25% of the setting-unrelated thoughts were rated as wholly or mainly respondent, as compared with 37% that were rated as wholly or mainly operant. Another 42% of the setting-unrelated thoughts were rated as having "some" operant thought. We shall examine the distributions of these kinds of thought more closely in a later section. The main point for now is that although stimulus-independence and operantness are correlated ($r = .18$, $p <$ .01), they are far from interchangeable variables. To provide an idea of the thoughts distinguished by these variables, Table II lists some examples.

Apart from operantness, stimulus-boundedness was related to little else in our data. There were barely significant tendencies for setting-related thoughts to be rated more usual and less distorted than setting-unrelated thoughts, but there were no significant relationships with durations of thought segments, specificity/vagueness, number of things going on at a time, amount of detail, visualness, auditoriness, attentiveness to external cues, sense of having recalled external cues, controllability of the images, trust in the accuracy of memory for the thoughts, or the time of the participant's life associated with the thought.

3.1.3. Fanciful versus Realistic Thought.

Most thought, judging from our thought samples, is quite unfanciful. Yet, obviously people do produce highly fanciful ideas. They may do this in dramatic daydreams—that is, when their thought can be regarded as both respondent and unrelated to the immediate setting. However, fanciful thought can also be task-relevant and operant, as when people think up improbable solutions to problems in brainstorming sessions. We have seen in our data that whether thoughts are operant or related to the person's immediate situation has little to do with whether they are rated usual or distorted. We may therefore conclude that being operant or setting-related is functionally if not statistically independent of being fanciful.

Fancifulness as a dimension of thought has received little systematic attention. In fact, I am unaware of any attempt to define such a dimension to the exclusion of others. What I mean by "fanciful"

TABLE II. Thought Samples to Illustrate Different Combinations of Setting-Relatedness and Operantness

Type of thought	Setting and activity	Thought content
Setting-related		
Operant	1. In barn feeding cows.	1. What happened to the truck and where it was.
	2. Living room doing homework.	2. Thinking how you would say a Spanish expression in English.
Respondent	1. Driving a car and watching a friend in another car.	1. Vague, just watching. Light should change, [friend] didn't make it through—just barely.
	2. At a restaurant, seeing her own checkbook.	2. Thinking about balancing my checking account.
Not setting-related		
Operant	1. In bedroom doing Spanish homework.	1. Trying to think of the name of this one boy who died about 4 years ago.
	2. Lying on bed, resting.	2. Whether or not I should hustle [girl] and whether or not I want to.
Respondent	1. In snack parlor reviewing a script.	1. Worrying about my dad in the hospital and being glad it wasn't my mother.
	2. Upstairs changing clothes.	2. Thinking of going to Texas, lying in the sun. Going swimming. Being with [friend].

thought encompasses imaginings that are unrealistic for the thinker—imaginings of events that have a very low likelihood of occurring or of succeeding from the standpoint of the thinker. To put it another way, we could apply the word "realism" to plausible extrapolations from the thinker's present life situation and the word "fancy" to events that the thinker could enact or experience in actuality only by violating important social role expectations or current versions of natural laws. Within this definition, fancifulness is very much a function of the thinker's own perceptions of his or her world and of current social context. For instance, in 1953 it would have been fanciful for a professional man to imagine himself wearing shoulder-length hair, but by 1973 it was quite realistic. The thoroughly fanciful science fiction of the 1930s that put humans on the moon had become realistic by the 1960s. Sexual escapades that are fanciful in some people's daydreams are often being enacted by their neighbors. In this framework, paranoid delusions would have to be considered unfanciful (though possibly degenerate—see below)—a kind of pseudofantasy. Much research on the training of creative thinking appears to be getting at a fancifulness dimension in a problem-solving context, but it warrants broader and more direct consideration in its own right.

    3.1.4. Well-Integrated versus Fused or Degenerated Thought. Ordinary waking thought more often than not has about it a certain quality of intactness that sets it off from dreamlike thought: Particular thoughts tend to have a coherent quality, things that are separate topics retain their separateness, and images of different things retain their individual character; whereas dream images often flow without respect to beginnings or endings, shift gears drastically in the middle, interweave different concerns with one another, and offer images that seem to be the fused representatives of different basic ideas or forms. These differences can be related to a general theory of response organization (Klinger, 1971) and within such a framework I have labeled this dimension "degenerateness" of thought sequences.

    The important point for present purposes is that this dimension is once again functionally independent of those previously considered. Degeneration of this kind occurs during operant thought in schizophrenia, during severe sleep deprivation (e.g., Morris, Williams, and Lubin, 1960), during certain kinds of drug states, and during sleepiness (Mintz, 1948). It occurs as well, of course, during respondent thought. Instances could be cited from both stimulus-bound and stimulus-independent thought, involving content either fanciful or not.

    Thought that is at least moderately degenerate occurs quite frequently in psychologically normal participants. Our Minnesota thought sampling data show that outside the laboratory participants rated 21% of their thoughts as somewhat strange or distorted and 1% as very strange or distorted. There was little relationship to operantness or setting-relatedness. Foulkes and Fleisher (1975) thought-sampled waking participants after instructing them to relax and inviting them to close their eyes. Of these participants' thought samples, fully 39% were either hallucinatory (14%) or regressive (isolated, fragmented, distorted, bizarre, etc.: 19%) or both (6%). Since Foulkes and Fleisher call an image "hallucinatory" if the participant was unaware at the time the image occurred that it was only an image, their hallucinatory variable accords with my fifth dimension (below) rather than to degenerateness. However, their "regressiveness" variable corresponds fairly closely to degenerateness. From this standpoint, the similarity between their 25% incidence of regressive features and our 22% incidence of strange and distorted features is striking.

3.1.5. Relation of "Ego" to Imagery. Watkins (1976) draws a sharp distinction between "daydreams" and "waking dreams." In daydreams, the "ego" remains essentially intact, identifying itself with the imaginal activity as it unfolds and responding to it(self) with evaluation and "advice." In waking dreams, on the other hand, the ego becomes receptive to and observant of the imaginal stream, exercising little influence but maintaining an observational posture, one that continues to discern ego from image and image from reality. The distinction between daydreams and waking dreams is not simply a matter of respondentness, since both absorbing daydreams and the stream of imagery Watkins calls waking dreams can be respondent. Nor is the distinction simply one of stimulus-boundedness, fancifulness, or degenerateness. It appears to constitute a potentially separate dimension of inner experience about which we know very little.

3.2. Qualities of Thought and Imagery

Our Minnesota thought-sampling data provide a first look at the momentary qualities of thought and imagery, at least as participants described them within a few seconds of having experienced the thought. Some major features of normal thought are presented in Table III, both for thoughts sampled randomly during ordinary daily activities and for thoughts sampled while participants listened to tape-recorded literary passages in the laboratory.

The results from the out-of-the-lab condition are undoubtedly the more representative, and they yield some interesting findings. Most of our participants' thoughts were quite specific rather than vague, about

TABLE III. Qualities of Thought and Imagery Stated in Percentages of Self-Ratings of Thought Samples by 6 Men and 6 Women

Quality	In-lab (N = 936 thoughts) %	Out-of-lab (N = 285 thoughts) %	Significance level of difference[a]
Specific (vs. vague)	60	70	$p < .02$
Directed (all or mainly)	36	56	$p < .02$
Undirected (all or mainly)	43	27	$p < .01$
Detailed (greatly or moderately)	66	48	n.s.
Number of things at one time (more than one)	46	61	n.s.
Visual (very or moderately)	61	64	n.s.
Auditory (very or moderately)	20	38	n.s.
Attentiveness to external cues (great or fair amount)	32	66	$p < .02$
Recall for external cues (at least moderate)	21	77	$p < .005$
Controllability (complete or moderate)	56	77	n.s.
Trust in memory of thought (complete or moderate)	89	91	n.s.
Familiarity (similar to normal daily experience)	87	—	—
Usualness (at least fair)	—	96	—
Strangeness/distortedness (very or somewhat)	—	22	—
Time of life (present)	50	75	$p < .05$
(past)	17	5	$p < .01$
(future)	5	6	n.s.
(no special time)	28	14	n.s.

[a] Because of time and within-participant dependencies in these data, significance testing used two-tailed t-tests for correlated data on the mean ratings by the 12 participants whose thoughts were sampled both in and outside the laboratory. With 11 d.f., these are highly conservative tests.

half of the thoughts were at least moderately detailed, about three fourths of them were focused on the present and felt at least moderately controllable, and more than half of them seemed to have more than one thing going on at a time. In nearly all cases their content could be considered as at least fairly usual for the everyday life of the participant, but more than a fifth of them seemed somewhat or very strange or distorted. Almost two thirds were moderately or very visual, compared with only 38% that were mainly or moderately auditory. In fact, no participant produced a mean visual rating over all the person's thoughts that was greater than his or her mean auditory rating, and in only one case were the mean ratings equal. Thoughts were rated more operant than respondent 56% of the time, less operant than respondent 26% of the time, and equally operant and respondent 18% of the time. Participants reported at least some respondent activity in 79% of their thoughts. The participants were at least fairly attentive to external cues on two thirds of the thought-sampling occasions. Finally, they felt at least moderate confidence that their memories of their thoughts were accurate 91% of the time.

The distributions of thought qualities in the laboratory sessions were similar to those outside on a number of important variables. Thoughts were about equally visual and only slightly less auditory and specific, and participants expressed an approximately equal amount of trust in their memories. However, there were also a number of impressive differences. Participants were far less attentive to the tape-recorded cues than to their out-of-the-lab stimulus situations, and they rated their thoughts far less operant, more respondent, less controllable, more detailed, more often focused on a single thing, and more often focused on the past or on no special time period than they rated their out-of-the-lab thoughts. In the laboratory sessions, thoughts were rated more operant than respondent only 37% of the time, less operant 45%, and equally operant and respondent 18%. In the laboratory sessions, participants reported at least some respondent activity in 93% of their thoughts.

Some of the differences between the laboratory and outside thought ratings can probably be accounted for by the instructions. Participants in the laboratory had been instructed to listen to the tape recordings with only moderate attention in order to encourage them to engage in substantial thought even while remaining accessible to the influence of experimental stimuli. Thus, they could be expected to be less attentive to cues than in a more task-oriented situation. Some of the other differences, such as in operantness, may be attributable to this less task-oriented atmosphere. However, the laboratory sessions exerted other special influences as well. For instance, the intervals between thought-sampling periods ranged from 60 to 90 sec—unusually short periods of time for thought to start flowing and become organized. Then, too, the literary cues in the laboratory sessions may well have cued off unusually self-concerned, introspective trains of thought. The particular dependencies can only be teased out with further research, but in the meantime we can at least conclude that such thought qualities as operantness, controllability, and time focus can be changed significantly with the kinds of experimental variables used in these studies.

The relationships among the variables of the Thought-Sampling Questionnaire are presented in Tables I and IV. Those in Table I are in the form of within-participant correlations, pooled over participants, in order to eliminate biasing effects of participants' different means and variances. They thus do not reflect individual differences. The relationships involving the Directedness variables have already been discussed above. A number of the remaining relationships are worth noting. First, the estimated duration of a participant's latest thought is related only very slightly ($r = .20$ outside the lab, $.22$ in the lab) to the estimated duration of his or her previous thought. Evidently, estimation biases account for a small proportion of the within-subjects variance. Second, the specificity of a thought is moderately well related to the amount of detail reported ($r = .44, .43$) and to the participant's trust in the accuracy of the memory for the thought ($r = .43, .27$), and specificity is somewhat related to the visualness of the imagery ($r = .16, .27$) and to the participant's sense of having control over the imagery ($r = .27, .16$). Third, the degree of detail in the imagery is closely related to the visualness of the imagery ($r = .59$) and to a much smaller extent to its auditoriness ($r = .38, .19$); and detail contributes to the participant's trust in the accuracy of the memory ($r = .48, .25$). Fourth, the visualness of the imagery is weakly but nevertheless positively related to its auditoriness ($r = .24, .11$). This confirms again, though in a new way, that the two modalities are not mutually antagonistic in normal thought but seem if anything to reflect a common factor of imaginal vividness. They are also weakly associated with trust in the accuracy of the memory for the thought, but this relationship is eliminated when degree of detail is partialed out, whereas the relationship of detailedness with trust in the accuracy of memory remains robust when, say, visualness is partialed out. Fifth, outside the laboratory images are more likely to seem controllable when the person feels attentive to ($r = .49$) and able to recall ($r = .47$) the external cues operating at the time of the thought sample. Under these conditions a person is somewhat more likely to trust his or her memory for the thought and to find the imagery more like everyday experiences. Evidently stimulus-bound, realistic thought feels more controllable and recallable than stimulus-independent, fanciful thought.

The relationships reported in Table IV are in the form of correlations among individual participants' mean ratings on each variable. These are therefore the between-participants individual differences that were removed from Table I. With only 20 participants, or 12, the results must obviously be regarded as quite tentative, but some of them are sufficiently striking to warrant comment.

First, some of the relationships that were found within participants appear again in between-participant correlations. Thus, people

TABLE IV. Correlations among Responsivity and Thought-

Variable	Response to concern cues					
	Rec	Time	End	W&Th	Them	Word
Response to concern cues						
Recall of cues	—	—	—	—	—	—
Time listened	52	—	—	—	—	—
Listened to end	36	60	—	—	—	—
Thoughts related						
Words and theme	70	54	43	—	—	—
Theme	24	25	22	49	—	—
Words	43	11	04	48	40	—
Thought sample Q. ratings						
Duration latest thought	03	−41	−05	08	11	21
Duration prev. thought	−02	−52	−11	09	18	24
Specificity	10	01	38	17	11	18
Directedness	13	−05	04	09	15	35
Undirectedness	−02	11	06	02	02	−23
Simultaneous thoughts	44	33	30	22	27	28
Detailedness	19	29	53	31	32	02
Visualness	−31	15	18	−12	20	−04
Auditoriness	19	32	48	15	30	−04
Attentive to cues	38	46	23	43	21	−04
Recall of cues	49	48	51	60	38	−02
Controllability	08	17	42	12	36	21
Trust in memory	03	−22	07	18	35	24
Familiarity	09	02	02	00	00	−02

[a] Coefficients above the diagonal are for mean ratings of 12 participants outside the laboratory, those below for 20 participants in the laboratory. Coefficients on the diagonal represent correlations

who reported their imagery to be more detailed also reported it to be more visual ($r = .52$ outside the lab, .72 inside), trusted their memories of their thoughts more ($r = .66$, .47), and switched attention less from one taped channel to another (for instance, $r = .53$ with "stay on passage" variable, explained below). They also felt a greater sense of control over their images ($r = .57$, .49). This cluster of attributes is essentially uncorrelated with operantness/respondentness, even though imaginal controllability is highly correlated with operantness ($r = .72$, .68). Individuals' mean ratings of detailedness are also correlated with their Betts QMI Vividness of Imagery scores ($r = .52$); no other imagery variable was.

Second, there were some interesting relationships among the modality of the participant's imagery, the modality of stimulation, and the number of things that the participant reported going on in his or her head at a time. Overall, participants reported their thought imagery to be slightly *less* auditory in the laboratory sessions, where

Sampling Questionnaire Variables: Individual Differences

			Thought-sampling questionnaire rating variables										
DuL	DuP	Sp	Dir	Und	Sim	Det	Vis	Aud	Att	Rec	Con	Tr	Fam
—	—	—	—	—	—	—	—	—	—	—	—	—	—
—	—	—	—	—	—	—	—	—	—	—	—	—	—
—	—	—	—	—	—	—	—	—	—	—	—	—	—
—	—	—	—	—	—	—	—	—	—	—	—	—	—
—	—	—	—	—	—	—	—	—	—	—	—	—	—
—	—	—	—	—	—	—	—	—	—	—	—	—	—
79	85[a]	23	54	−26	05	04	00	−45	−17	16	41	37	−44
89	50	20	33	00	03	16	19	−33	−18	−04	36	28	−21
36	26	77	57	−29	−12	08	57	28	48	13	50	13	21
39	39	51	71	−75	−09	−02	40	19	38	40	72	32	11
−28	−26	−42	−95	48	10	19	−05	−11	−31	−38	−51	−37	−03
−30	−17	07	31	−23	83	77	37	−20	60	73	39	57	−03
09	07	77	25	−14	35	67	52	−34	46	58	57	66	19
−03	−06	45	06	−03	19	72	54	53	71	37	65	14	30
−03	−12	24	24	−17	55	52	31	01	41	−12	−02	−57	29
−34	−30	−15	−36	39	17	24	00	06	−05	72	62	39	37
−18	−21	03	−14	19	47	37	01	32	64	45	75	75	−03
21	14	63	68	−60	15	49	29	27	01	10	68	72	11
58	50	69	42	−29	−15	47	20	14	−05	00	46	−14	10
−19	−09	35	−01	−06	−10	29	45	00	−26	−27	13	10	63

between 12 participants' mean ratings outside with their mean ratings inside the laboratory. Correlations are significant at $p < .05$ with $r = .47$ below the diagonal, $r = .63$ otherwise.

the main source of stimulation was auditory, than outside. There was no such difference in visual imagery. This suggests that at the very least the modality of an external stimulus does not systematically cast thought imagery into the same modality, and it raises the possibility of a suppression effect. Moreover, highly auditory imagers, but not visual ones, thought about more different things at a time in the laboratory ($r = .55$) but not outside ($r = -.20$). This could not simply signify that people are able to accommodate more information through a favored modality, since our participants were inconsistent in this regard: Participants' mean auditory ratings in the laboratory were correlated .007 with their mean ratings outside! (Correlations of in-lab with out-of-the-lab means on most other Thought-Sampling Questionnaire variables were much higher, as shown in Table IV.) The result might, however, signify that people who match their imaginal modality to the modality of the input process more simultaneous information.

Third, people who switch their attention more from channel to channel of the tape recording feel less well able to control their thoughts. This seems particularly true ($r = -.52$) of people who frequently switch from "center" (that is, from listening to neither channel or both channels) to passages containing material relevant to their current concerns (see below).

Fourth, perhaps unsurprisingly, people who stayed longer with particular taped passages reported more detailed imagery ($r = .53$) and recalled more of those passages ($r = .51$). They also reported more auditory imagery ($r = .48$) but not more visual imagery ($r = .18$). These relationships suggest a number of alternative hypotheses. Does the modality of external stimulation affect the modality of the thought imagery going on at the time? (Perhaps, but then how do we account for less average auditory imagery in the laboratory than outside?) Do people remain more attentive to external cues that are presented in the individual's stronger imaginal modality? Do people with more de-tailed or more auditory imagery attend longer to external stimuli of whatever modality?

Fifth, there do seem to be clear individual differences in estimated duration of thought segments. The mean estimated duration of a participant's most recent thought segment is correlated at $r = .85$ and .89 with the mean estimated duration of the next-to-the-latest seg-ments. Note that these measures were not substantially related within participants. We might infer that these correlations tap merely system-atic errors of estimation, although the mean estimated durations of thoughts are also correlated in the laboratory with the degree of trust individuals place in the accuracy of their memories of the thoughts ($r = .58$ and .50 for latest and next-to-latest thoughts, respectively.) Since duration estimates are not related to mean amounts of detail reported, we are not dealing here with a global confound of amount of information experienced. It thus remains possible that these figures represent at least in part real differences among individuals in dura-tions of thought segments.

4. Determinants of Thematic Thought Content and Content Change

4.1. Motivational Concepts and Current Concerns

Psychologists have long assumed that people's moment-to-mo-ment thoughts are determined jointly by motivational factors and by ambient or internal cues. The challenge is to specify the motivational factors, the properties of the effective cues, and the nature of the interactions between cues and motivation that ultimately determine thought. Although these questions have been investigated systematically for decades, research has tended to focus rather narrowly on a few concepts and a few methods. Most of the attention has gone to motivational variables rather than to stimulus ones. The concepts most used have been "drive" (or psychoanalytic instinct concepts) and "need" or "motive." The instrument has most typically been some variant of thematic apperception—the "picture-story" techniques. Investigations such as these have left us a rich legacy of data which, unfortunately, seem to indicate that none of the above-mentioned concepts or instruments is well suited to our task. Thematic appreceptive techniques are an extremely oblique way to get at moment-to-moment thought. Drive states are unnecessary to energize goal-related thought in humans or goal-directed acts in animals. "Need" or "motive" is a poorly defined construct, as it has most commonly been used, except as an inference from thematic apperceptive stories or as a psychometrically defined trait. Its most promising definition has been as the effective incentive value a certain class of objects or events has for a particular individual (Atkinson and Birch, 1970; Heckhausen, 1967, 1977). However, the class of objects or events is typically defined more broadly than is optimal for predicting moment-to-moment thought. The arguments and evidence to support these assertions have been detailed elsewhere (Klinger, 1971, 1975, 1977).

How then shall we explain motivational effects on thought? The motivational construct that best seemed to fit the evidence as of 1970— evidence largely from thematic apperceptive studies but also from studies of play and dreams—was the new construct of "current concern." A current concern is defined as the state of an organism between the time it becomes committed to pursuing a goal and the time it either gains the goal or abandons the pursuit. By this definition there is a separate current concern corresponding to each such goal. Thus, an individual is typically in the grip of multiple current concerns: to get home to dinner tonight, to beat a particular friend at tennis this weekend, to finish writing a particular article, and so on. "Current concern" is not a mentalistic construct: A current concern can be said to persist (within its definitional limits) regardless of what may be going on in the person's consciousness. Nevertheless, people tend to think about things connected with their current concerns.

4.2. The Induction Principle

Motivational constructs—even current concern—are insufficient to predict moment-to-moment thought. A great variety of thoughts typically pass through consciousness between the beginning and end of any particular current concern, and even taking into consideration the variety of an individual's simultaneous concerns the construct of current concern cannot by itself enable one to predict the timing or sequence of particular thoughts. However, a good deal of previous evidence has suggested that being in a state of current concern about some goal sensitizes one to notice, perceive, and have thoughts about cues related to the goal one is concerned about (Klinger, 1975, 1977). This suggests, then, a general principle: At any given moment, the next thematic content of thought is induced by the combination of a current concern and a cue related to that concern. The "cue" is construed as either a cognitively meaningful stimulus in the external environment or a symbolic event in the stream of the individual's own consciousness. This "induction principle" is still very general, in that it says nothing about the properties of current concerns that make them more or less influential in sensitizing people to cues, about the specific properties of a cue that make a person see it as concern-related, or about the properties of concern-related cues that affect their potency in influencing thought. Nevertheless, this principle is a starting point, and our Minnesota thought-sampling studies were designed to test it.

4.3. Current Concerns, Cues, and the Content of Thought: Some Evidence

It will be recalled that participants in the Minnesota thought-sampling study listened dichotically to tape-recorded narrations and that each such session was preceded by an interview. The chief purpose of the interviews was to assess each participant's current concerns. For each session the investigators chose four of these concerns and then chose four other goals ("nonconcerns"), roughly matched with those of the participant in category width, commonness, emotional grippingness, and social desirability, but that were not—so far as we could ascertain—goals of the particular participant on that day.* Each of the

---

* Decisions on the identity of a participant's current concerns were made consensually by two content analysts working primarily from interviews. Their reliability was checked by asking each content analyst to submit an independently compiled list of descriptions of each participant's concerns and having judges decide how many members of one list corresponded to a member on another list. When both lists came from the same participant at the same point in time, agreement was 80%. Since some disagreements are attributable to different degrees of conservatism, it is of interest that 90% of the members of the shorter list in a pair had a corresponding concern on the other list. When the two lists came from different participants, agreement was 21%.

participant's four current concerns was thus paired with a "nonconcern." Two fifteen-minute literary passages were chosen from the same literary work to be tape-recorded for the subsequent experimental session. On each pair of such narratives 12 synchronous "embedding sites" were identified at varying intervals. At each embedding site the texts of the pair of narrative passages were modified so that they would be obliquely related to one of the individual participant's current concerns on one narrative and to the paired nonconcern on the other narrative. Which narrative of the pair received the concern-related modification was varied randomly from embedding site to embedding site. Working in this way, cues for each concern-nonconcern pair were embedded three times on each pair of literary narratives, a different modification each time. When these pairs of literary narratives were tape-recorded, then, they contained 12 places in which the participant would hear cues related obliquely to one of his or her current concerns through one ear and at the same time cues related to the paired nonconcern through the other ear. The text modifications at each embedding site spanned 25 sec. Ten sec after the end of an embedding site, the participant heard a signal tone, the tape stopped, and the participant proceeded to report his or her latest thoughts and to rate them in accordance with the Thought-Sampling Questionnaire already described. Participants also reported their recollections of the most recent taped passages, and, with the toggle switch, reported continuously between thought samples to which channel of the tape recording they were listening. (The procedure is described in greater detail by Klinger et al., 1976.)

The results are summarized in Table V. Participants attended somewhat more closely to the concern-related than to the nonconcern-related embedded passages, and they recalled and had thoughts associated with the concern-related passages about twice as often as the other passages.

In the case of attention, participants switched toward concern-related passages sooner, spent more time listening to them, and were more inclined to remain listening to them for the entire length of the passage. The data therefore suggest that "preattentive processes" (Broadbent, 1977; Neisser, 1967) are sensitive to concern-related cues.

Concern-relatedness of passages affected recall significantly more strongly than it affected attention ($p < .01$ for the difference between recall and attention).* The passages participants recalled had attracted

---

* The rating of whether parts of a passage had been recalled was made without reference to participants' self-estimates of recall. Agreement between pairs of content analysts working independently on whether a passage had been recalled was 97%.

TABLE V. Attention to, Recall of, and Thought Associated with Concern-Related and Nonconcern-Related Embedded Passages[a]

Dependent variable	Type of embedded passage		Significance of differences	Percent of variance accounted for [b]	
	Concern	Nonconcern		All variance	Excluding subject differences
Attention (number per session)					
Shifts toward passage	3.28	2.82	$p < .01$	0.72	2.92
First shift to passage	1.59	1.25	$p < .05$	1.98	3.65
Passages attended from start to end	1.99	1.47	$p < .025$	1.08	2.14
Attention (mean sec)					
Latency of first shift from nonattention	6.30	7.58	$p < .005$	5.52	12.19
Time spent listening/ session	74.56	58.90	$p < .0005$	5.03	7.62
Recall					
Number of passages recalled per session	2.78	1.38	$p < .0001$	11.77	17.06
Passages per session related to thoughts	3.73	1.95	$p < .0001$	8.39	18.59

[a] The differences were tested by directional t-tests for correlated data, with each session's mean difference between Concern and Nonconcern conditions taken as the unit of analysis, adjusted to compensate for differing numbers of sessions per participant. The data are based on 68 sessions from 20 participants, but because a Behrens-Fisher problem renders the correct degrees of freedom arguable, they are tested here with the most conservative number, 19 d.f. (15 d.f. in the case of Latency). Six other sessions, run during or after two participants expressed suspicions that material had been embedded to relate to them individually, are excluded, but they revealed a substantially similar pattern.

[b] Percentage of variance accounted for was estimated from a subsample of 17 subjects (14 in the case of Latency), with the unit of analysis being each participant's mean over all sessions, using an analysis of variance format. The right-hand column excludes variance associated with the main effect of subject differences in overall responsiveness to cues.

no more attention shifts than other passages, but participants had spent more time listening to them ($p < .05$) and more often listened to the whole embedded passages ($p = .003$). This suggests that recall constitutes a second-round processing step admission to which is more stringent, involving a clearer confirmation of concern-relatedness, than the cruder, less discriminating preattentive processes.

About a third of the embedded passage pairs were reflected in participants' immediately subsequent thought content. Participants recalled most of the passages they thought about, and they thought about a majority of the passages they recalled. Since participants probably forgot some thoughts that occurred early in the embedded passages and were probably cut off by the signal tone before they could think some thoughts about the passages that they might otherwise have thought, the relation between recall of cue passages and thought associated with them is understated in these data. Thus, retaining information and working it over explicitly in thought seem closely related processing steps, and both are highly selective in favor of material related to current concerns.

Moreover, the effects of concern-relatedness on recall cannot be attributed simply to rehearsal in thought, since of the passages not reflected in thought the concern-related ones were recalled much more often than the nonconcern-related ones ($p < .001$); and, likewise, concern-related passages that had not been recalled were reflected in thought much more often than unrecalled nonconcern-related passages ($p < .01$). Thus, even though recall and thought-processing are closely related in a statistical sense, both reflect the effects of concern-related cues independently and neither seems to be prerequisite for the other, at least insofar as we can measure recall and thought with the methods of this investigation.

The fact that participants failed to respond to some concern-related embedded passages and sometimes responded to nonconcern-related passages might seem damaging to the theory. However, the concern-related passage cues were after all competing with participants' own internal cues, which would sometimes prevail; and what we regarded as nonconcern-related cues could be expected to be sometimes concern-related, in that our procedures for determining that a participant did not have a certain concern were undoubtedly not perfect and in that the particular cues we devised would sometimes have unexpected associations to concerns other than those we thought we were working with. Thus, the results can be regarded as providing strong support for the theory.

Two other kinds of questions need to be resolved. One question is whether our judgments that thoughts were associated with cues really reflected cue effects on thoughts. The procedure for rating association here cannot be at fault, since it was a satisfactorily reliable blind rating system in which a judge rated the similarity in language or thematic content of each thought sample to the two embedded passages that just preceded it. However, if it is true that people think about matters related to their current concerns, would we not expect to find the kind of relationship we found just because both the concern-related cues and the thought samples reflected a participant's current concerns? To examine this possibility, we performed an analysis that compares the thoughts with (a) embedded passages that had just preceded them and (b) embedded passages, written for other current concerns, that occurred later in the same session. If the previously reported association of thoughts with cues was an artifact of their both simply reflecting a participant's current concerns, then thoughts ought to be equally well related both to passages preceding the thoughts and to passages following them. In fact, however, only 4% of the passages following thoughts were judged related to the thoughts, as compared with 23% of the passages that had just preceded the thoughts ($p <$ .001 for the difference). The embedded cues were indeed responsible for the effects on thought, thus confirming the cue side of the Induction Principle.

Another kind of question has to do with the several kinds of artifacts and biases that may have crept into the procedures. For instance, did we unwittingly select more plausible concerns for the "concern" than for the "nonconcern" stimuli? Did our cue embedders unwittingly write the concern-related cues more dramatically? Are the concern-related cues such that they would grab just about anyone's attention and thought processes? Analyses have ruled out each of these possibilities. Blind ratings of the written cues revealed no differences between concern-related and nonconcern-related passages in the extent to which they blended into their narrative contexts, were written in a noticeable writing style, or seemed intuitively more memorable. Judges who were given the same descriptions of concerns and nonconcerns used by the embedded-passage writers were unable to distinguish which member of a concern-nonconcern pair was the "real" concern of a college student. Finally, eight participants went through thought-sampling sessions with taped narratives that had been prepared for other participants of the same sex. The previously reported effects of cues on thought did not occur. In fact, the concern-nonconcern × condition (own tape versus other participant's tape) interaction was statistically significant for similarity of thought to cues ($p < .01$) with only seven degrees of freedom. (Other variables produced less highly significant interactions or fell short of significance with this number of degrees of freedom, but the trends were plainly as expected.) It is apparent that the cue effects on thought are not only specific to the particular cues but also to the particular participants for whom the cues were designed.

It should be noted that the effects of concern-related cues on mental activity cannot be attributed to effects of drives or of central excitatory states. Most of the concerns cannot readily be associated with discrete, physiologically based drives. There was no reason to suspect that our participants were in elevated drive states during the experimental sessions with respect to any of the goals that had been identified in interviews performed one to two days earlier. Finally, very few of the incentives about which our participants were thought to be concerned could be construed to be present during the experimental sessions, and the sessions provided no opportunity for the participant to advance toward the goals of his or her current concerns. Thus, neither drive arousal nor drive induction can satisfactorily explain these results.

Table IV reveals some interesting individual differences in responses to concern-related passages. First of all, people seem to differ in responsiveness in general, in that people whose thoughts were couched in more of the language used in the concern-related cues also produced more thoughts related to the cues in thematic content, even when there was no similarity in language. Second, people who spent more time listening to concern-related passages reported themselves to have listened more intently ($r = .46$), felt they remembered more of the tape ($r = .48$), reported shorter thought segments ($r = -.41, -.52$), and produced more "A" matches, indicating greater similarity between thoughts and passages in both language and thematic content ($r = .54$). Third, people who typically switched their attention to concern-related passages after longer latencies had more associations in their thoughts that reflected the language but not the thematic content of the passages ($r = .59$), had more directed thought ($r = .48$), rated themselves as having recalled less of the passages ($r = -.44$) and in fact recalled fewer ($r = -.43$), and trusted their memories for their thoughts more ($r = .54$).

5. Summary

This chapter considers some special requirements for observing inner experience, methods currently in use, five dimensions in the flow of thought, some characteristics of everyday normal thinking, and the combinations of motivational and stimulus factors that govern changes in the content of thought from one moment to the next. On most of these issues, the chapter provides evidence from a thought-sampling investigation of moment-to-moment inner experience. The evidence supports the following main conclusions: (1) The five dimensions of thought—operant (directed) versus respondent, stimulus-independent versus stimulus-bound, fancifulness, degenerateness, and relation of ego to imagery—are functionally separable even though they may be statistically related. (2) The median thought segment lasts about five seconds, although the mean duration may be two to three times longer. (3) Most thought in college student participants is specific, detailed, predominantly visual, unfanciful, controllable, present tense, related to the immediate situation, and recallable within a few seconds with at least moderate confidence. About a fifth of thought segments are at least somewhat strange and distorted. (4) Thought is more often predominantly operant than predominantly respondent, but most thought segments involve at least some respondent activity. (5) Operant thought differs from respondent thought at least in including periodic evaluations of how useful the thought train is for advancing toward a goal and in periodic attempts to control the direction of attention, and operant thought feels on the average, but not always, more controllable; but in other observed respects operant and respondent thought display similar properties. (6) Current concerns dispose people to attend to, retain, and reflect in their thoughts cues related to the current concern; and at any given moment thought content is induced by concern-related cues. The chapter also considers evidence on relationships among the various attributes of thought and on individual differences in thought qualities.

ACKNOWLEDGMENTS

The development of the ideas and methods of the research reported in this chapter, as well as the carrying out of the investigation, have involved so many people so intensely that it is hard to say where authorship ought to leave off and footnote credit begin. Steven G. Barta has been associated with this research since before the inception of the phases reported here, and Thomas W. Mahoney joined before the present methods had been developed. Both have been continuously and integrally involved in the creative as well as administrative functions of this program. In addition, the following people made clearly definable conceptual and methodological contributions to the research: Roxanne M. Anderson, Rachel Froiland Quenemoen, Deborah A. Smith, and Susan Stumm. We thank the following for extensive technical and observational contributions: John F. Andrews, Jane M. Delage, Paul F. Heyl, Mary K. Martin, Madeline E. Maxeiner, Anthony M. Palmer, George A. Peterson, and Stephen C. Peterson. Wei-Ching Chang provided valuable statistical consultation. We thank the following for their general assistance: Cheryl L. Barta, Mary L. Browen, Daniel W. Carlin, Charles E. Cornillie, David Farmer, Bayne E. Holley, Sandra R. Johnson, Katherine Miksche, Linda M. Powers, Kathleen Reiman, Gail Rixen, Gloria J. Rixen, Yvonne Storck, and Charlotte Syverson. Finally, I am indebted to Steven G. Barta, Karla M. Klinger, and Madeline E. Maxeiner for helpful comments on a preliminary draft of this chapter.

References

Antrobus, J. S., Singer, J. L., and Greenberg, S. Studies in the stream of consciousness: Experimental enhancement and suppression of spontaneous cognitive processes. *Perceptual and Motor Skills*, 1966, *23*, 399-417.

Aserinsky, E., and Kleitman, N. Regularly occurring periods of eye mobility and concomitant phenomena during sleep. *Science*, 1953, *118*, 273-274.

Atkinson, J. W., and Birch, D. *The dynamics of action*. New York, N.Y.: Wiley, 1970.

Berlyne, D. E. *Structure and direction in thinking*. New York, N.Y.: Wiley, 1965.

Betts, G. H. *The distribution and functions of mental imagery*. New York, N.Y.: Columbia University Teachers College, 1909.

Bloom, B. S., and Broder, L. J. *Problem-solving processes of college students: an exploratory investigation*. Chicago: University of Chicago Press, 1950.

Broadbent, D. E. The hidden preattentive processes. *American Psychologist*, 1977, *32*, 109-118.

Cermak, L. S. *Human memory: Research and theory*. New York, N.Y.: Ronald, 1972.

Csikszentmihalyi, M., Larson, R., and Prescott, S. The ecology of adolescent activity and experience. *Journal of Youth and Adolescence*, 1977, *6*, 281-294.

DeGroot, A. *Thought and choice in chess*. The Hague: Mouton, 1965.

Fiske, D. W. *Observables and judgments: Their utilities in personality and behavioral science*. San Francisco: Jossey-Bass, in press.

Foulkes, D., and Fleisher, S. Mental activity in relaxed wakefulness. *Journal of Abnormal Psychology*, 1975, *84*, 66-75.

Freud, S. *The interpretation of dreams* (J. Strachey, Ed. and trans.). New York, N.Y.: Wiley, 1961. (Originally published, 1900.)

Galton, F. *Inquiries into human faculty*. New York: Macmillan, 1883.

Giambra, L. Daydreaming across the lifespan: Late adolescent to senior citizen. *International Journal of Aging and Human Development*, 1974, *5*, 115-140.

Gordon, R. An investigation into some of the factors that favour the formation of stereotyped images. *British Journal of Psychology*, 1949, *39*, 156-167.

Heckhausen, H. [*The anatomy of achievement motivation*] (K. F. Butler, R. C. Birney, and D. C. McClelland, trans.). New York, N.Y.: Academic Press, 1967.

Heckhausen, H. Achievement motivation and its constructs: A cognitive model. *Motivation and Emotion*, 1977, *1*, 283-329.

Hilgard, E. R. Impulsive versus realistic thinking: An examination of the distinction between primary and secondary processes in thought. *Psychological Bulletin*, 1962, *59*, 477-489.

Hobbes, T. *Leviathan*. Indianapolis: Bobbs-Merrill, 1958. (Originally published, 1651.)

Hurlburt, R. T. Self-observation and self-control. Unpublished Ph. D. dissertation, University of South Dakota, 1976.

Isaacs, I. Self reports of daydreaming and mindwandering: A construct validation. Unpublished Ph.D. dissertation, City University of New York, 1975.

Klinger, E. *Structure and functions of fantasy*. New York, N.Y.: Wiley, 1971.

Klinger, E. Utterances to evaluate steps and control attention distinguish operant from respondent thought while thinking out loud. *Bulletin of the Psychonomic Society*, 1974, *4*, 44-45.

Klinger, E. Consequences of commitment to and disengagement from incentives. *Psychological Review*, 1975, *82*, 1-25.

Klinger, E. *Meaning and void: Inner experience and the incentives in people's lives*. Minneapolis: University of Minnesota Press, 1977.

Klinger, E., Barta, S. G., Mahoney, T. W., et al. Motivation, mood, and mental events:

Patterns and implications for adaptive processes. In G. Serban (Ed.), *Psychopathology of human adaptation*. New York, N.Y.: Plenum, 1976. Pp. 95-112.

Lorents, A. C. Faculty activity analysis and planning models in higher education. Unpublished Ph. D. dissertation, University of Minnesota, 1971.

McKellar, P. *Imagination and thinking*. New York, N.Y.: Basic Books, 1957.

Mintz, A. Schizophrenic speech and sleepy speech. *Journal of Abnormal and Social Psychology*, 1948, *43*, 548-549.

Morris, G. O., Williams, H. L., and Lubin, A. Misperception and disorientation during sleep deprivation. *Archives of General Psychiatry*, 1960, *2*, 247-254.

Natsoulas, T. Concerning introspective knowledge. *Psychological Bulletin*, 1970, *73*, 89-111.

Neisser, U. *Cognitive psychology*. New York, N.Y.: Appleton-Century-Crofts, 1967.

Pope, K. S. The stream of consciousness. Unpublished Ph. D. dissertation, Yale University, 1977.

Prescott, S., and Haertel, E. An ecology of the home: The experiential sampling approach. Unpublished manuscript, 1976.

Prescott, S., Csikszentmihalyi, M., and Graef, R. Environmental effects on cognitive and affective states: The experiential time sampling approach. Unpublished manuscript, 1976.

Richardson, A. Verbalizer-visualizer: A cognitive style dimension. *Journal of Mental Imagery*, 1977, *1*, 109-125.

Singer, J. L. *Daydreaming: An introduction to the experimental study of inner experience*. New York, N.Y.: Random House, 1966.

Singer, J. L., and Antrobus, J. S. A factor-analytic study of daydreaming and conceptually-related cognitive and personality variables. *Perceptual and Motor Skills*, 1963, *17*, 187-209.

Skinner, B. F. Two types of conditioned reflex and pseudo type. *Journal of General Psychology*, 1935, *12*, 66-77.

Tippett, L. H. C. A snap reading method of making time studies of machines and operatives in factory surveys. *Journal of the British Textile Institute Transactions*, 1935, *26*, 51-55.

Traynor, T. D. Patterns of daydreaming and their relationships to depressive affect. Unpublished masters thesis, Miami University, 1974.

Varendonck, J. *The psychology of daydreams*. New York, N.Y.: Macmillan, 1921.

Watkins, M. M. *Waking dreams*. New York, N.Y.: Gordon and Breach, 1976.

Windelband, W. [*A history of philosophy*.] (J.H. Tufts, trans.) New York, N.Y.: Harper & Row, 1958. (Originally published, 1901.)

9

How Gender, Solitude, and Posture Influence the Stream of Consciousness

Kenneth S. Pope

1. Introduction

What sources contribute to our knowledge of normal, ongoing consciousness? The fine arts present numerous representations of what William James (1890/1950) termed "the stream of thought." James Joyce, Marcel Proust, Virginia Woolf, Joseph Heller, Sergei Eisenstein, and Alain Resnais are but a few who have portrayed the ever-changing constellation of memories, sense-data, anticipations, fantasies, rational thoughts, and images that constitute our moment-to-moment awareness as we go about our lives.

The sciences—particularly American psychology—have been more reluctant to address this phenomenon. Only in the last decade or two has normal, everyday, ongoing consciousness emerged as a legitimate area for scientific study.

Retrospection furnishes most of the scientific evidence influencing current ideas about the stream of consciousness. Formats for providing these retrospective data have included questionnaires (Singer and Antrobus, 1963, 1971; Singer, 1966; Beit-Hallahmi, 1972), daily or weekly diaries (Csikszentmihalyi, 1974; Frank, 1978), and interviews (Csikszentmihalyi, 1974; Hariton and Singer, 1974) about what people remember of their habitual patterns of awareness.

Alternatively, a "thinking-aloud" procedure—asking people engaged in ordinary activities (e.g., chess playing, idle reverie, riddle

Kenneth S. Pope • Brentwood Veterans Administration Hospital, Los Angeles, California.

solving) to verbalize their thoughts as they occur—emerged as a method not so dependent on the reporter's memory and therefore better able to capture moment-to-moment sequences of consciousness (Antrobus and Singer, 1964; Bertini, Lewis, and Witkin, 1964; De-Groot, 1965; Klinger, 1971, 1974).

The present study began as an attempt to use the "thinking-aloud" procedure to explore the following possible influences on the flow of consciousness.

1.1. Posture

Several studies have demonstrated the effect of posture on thought processes. Kroth (1970) found that people who were reclining rather than sitting could free associate with greater freedom, spontaneity, and general effectiveness. Morgan and Bakan (1965) reported that people in a sensory deprivation situation experienced much more vivid imagery while reclining than while sitting. Berdach and Bakan (1967) found, in a memory study, that earlier and more memories occurred when people were in a reclining rather than a sitting position. Segal and Glickman (1967) reported that people were much less likely to recognize an external signal (in an experiment on the Perky effect: the tendency to confuse internal images with external stimulation) while lying than while sitting. In the present study, people charted the flow of consciousness while lying, while sitting, and while walking.

1.2. Solitude

Laboratory studies by Antrobus, Singer, and Greenberg (1966) and Drucker (1969) and interview studies by Csikszentmihalyi (1974) have indicated that people in a relatively simple, barren environment offering little stimulation are more likely to daydream or think about matters not directly related to the immediate situation. In the present study, some people reported the flow of consciousness while alone in a room with simple furnishings that offered little stimulation. For other reporters, the room was made "less barren" by having an experimenter present in the room. My decision to add another person to enrich the environment was based in part on the work of Tomkins (1962–1963) and Izard (1971) establishing the human figure, particularly the face, as an extremely salient, informative stimulus. The possibility that people would alter their reports because the experimenter was listening led to the creation of two "enriched" environments. In one condition, the experimenter simply sat in the room, not overtly attending to the person giving the report, but clearly able to hear whatever was being said; in the other condition, the experimenter was present in the room, but unable to hear the reporter.

1.3. Sex

Though a literature search failed to uncover evidence that males differ significantly from females in the ongoing stream of thought, an equal number of each sex were included to explore possible differences.

In addition to these three possible influences, certain predispositions, habits, and characteristics also might relate to the flow of consciousness. Recent studies suggest that mood is related to ongoing thought processes, but the findings are contradictory. Rychlak (1973) and Blatt (1974), for example, present findings to suggest that a negative mood is associated with increased thoughts about the present situation whereas Naranjo (1973) holds that positive mood is associated with increased thoughts about the present situation.

Likewise, general tendencies to daydream rather than to think about the present environment, as measured by the Imaginal Processes Inventory (Singer and Antrobus, 1970), were assumed to have a relationship to the flow of consciousness as recorded in this study.

In addition to mood and daydreaming habits, a number of other predispositions or characteristics—tendency to seek exciting experiences; field independence (the tendency to differentiate or to distinguish a figure from its background); marijuana, alcohol, and other drug usage—could be assumed to bear a relationship to the stream of thought, though no formal attempt was made to specify what those relationships might be. Measures of these characteristics were therefore included in the study.

To address the issues raised thus far, Experiment I was designed. Each person reported aloud the flow of consciousness, indicating (by saying the word "shift") where substantial shifts or changes occurred in the content, focus, tone, or direction of the stream of thought. Further experiments addressed two additional issues raised by investigations conducted prior to the formal experiments.

During the preliminary work, participants occasionally remarked that they were unsure of just where to say "shift" and that at times they forgot to note a shift as it occurred. Experiment II used copies of the transcripts from Experiment I, with the shifts omitted. A pair of raters determined where the shifts occurred. It was thus possible to assess the reliability of two raters in determining shifts, and to assess the relationship of these rater-given shifts with the subject-given shifts.

Other comments by the pilot subjects raised questions about the "thinking-aloud" procedure as a method for tapping the flow of consciousness. Many participants expressed the difficulty of putting their thoughts into words and doing so quickly enough so that they neither slowed down their thoughts nor left our parts of a description because they were in a hurry or because they could not find the right words. The writers of "stream of consciousness" mentioned earlier also had to deal with this problem. Wyndham Lewis describes Joyce's solution in *Ulysses*:

> Joyce had to pretend that we were really surprising the private thoughts of a real and average human creature, Mr. Bloom. But the fact is that Mr. Bloom was abnormally *wordy*. He *thought in words*, not images, for our benefit, in a fashion as unreal, from the point of view of the strictest naturalist dogma, as a Hamlet soliloquy. (Lewis, 1926, pp. 413–414)

Therefore, in Experiment III, people conveyed information about their flow of consciousness, not by thinking aloud, but with a simple key-press device.

The three experiments represent three methods of charting the flow of consciousness. In order to compare the results of each method, this study focuses on three aspects of the stream of thought that seem appropriate to the material produced by all three methods:

1. Number of shifts: During each period of reporting, how many times does the stream of thought shift (undergo a substantial change in content, focus, tone, or direction)?

2. Number of "Present" segments: During the reporting period, how many thought segments (the thought occurring between two adjacent shifts) are focused primarily on the present situation or environment? During a given period of time, how often do our thoughts turn to that which is currently and physically present?

3. Cumulative duration of "Present" thought segments: During each five-minute reporting period how much time is spent with consciousness primarily focused on the present situation or environ-ment? In other words, what is the total time of all "Present" segments during a given reporting period?

Examining these aspects of the flow of consciousness for each method of reporting, this study attempts to answer questions within several major areas of concern. (In the following paragraphs, a specific prediction is denoted by a letter in parentheses.) The first major area embraces possible influences on the flow of consciousness: Do pos-ture, solitude, or gender affect the flow of consciousness? The studies mentioned previously suggested that thought processes not directly concerned with the immediate environment—memories, vivid imagery, free association, decreased ability to recognize external signals—occurred more frequently while lying than while sitting. The present study hypothesized a continuum of postures from lying (associated with less interaction with the present environment) to walking (associated with greater interaction), with sitting probably near the middle. It was predicted, then, (a) that people would think more often about the present situation (have a greater number of "Present" thought segments) and (b) spend more time with consciousness focused upon the present situation (have a longer cumulative duration of "Present" thought segments) while walking than while lying down, with the sitting period probably falling somewhere in between. Lying down seems to offer some freedom from the opportunities or demands to monitor the constantly changing environment. For this reason, it was predicted (c) that lying down would encourage less frequent interruption of thought segments (fewer shifts during the reporting period) than walking, with sitting again falling somewhere in between in terms of number of shifts.

The assumption that the presence of another person (an experimenter) would make the present environment much more salient led to the prediction (d) that a person reporting while alone would produce fewer thoughts focused on the present environment and (e) would spend less time with consciousness focused on the present situation. (f) No sex differences were predicted.

A second major area concerns the ability to determine reliably where shifts occur and to classify thought segments reliably as either "Present" or "Absent." Three main questions were addressed. First, what is the interjudge agreement between two independent readers of the "thinking-aloud" transcripts in determining where shifts occur? Second, to what degree do the shifts identified by the readers correspond to the shifts noted by the subjects themselves? And third, what is the interjudge reliability between pairs of readers in independently classifying thought segments as "Present" or "Absent"?

A third major area of concern focuses on potential differences among the methods of reporting. Does the nonverbal (key-press) method of charting the flow of consciousness produce material significantly different from that of either of the two "thinking-aloud" methods in regard to the three selected aspects (number of shifts, number of "Present" segments, and cumulative duration of "Present" segments)? It was predicted (g) that shifts would occur more frequently in the key-press method partly because the translation of consciousness into words (in the "thinking-aloud" methods) may slow down the report and cause each segment to occupy more time than it normally does in our private, unspoken flow of consciousness.

A fourth major area concerns possible relationships of certain predispositions, habits, and characteristics to the flow of consciousness. Of these possible relationships, only one led to a specific prediction: (h) People indicating frequent daydreaming on the Imaginal Processes Inventory would tend to spend less time with consciousness focused on the present environment.

2. Method

2.1. Subjects

Ninety undergraduates participated as subjects in return for either $2.50 per hr or credit toward the introductory psychology course requirement. Each subject attended an individual session lasting 1 hr; some subjects attended an additional session also lasting 1 hr.

2.2. Experimenters

Two experimenters were undergraduates (a junior English major and a sophomore psychology major) participating out of interest in the area of study and to gain experience in psychological investigation. Both were blind to the hypotheses. The third experimenter was aware of the hypotheses. All three experimenters were males.

Each experimenter saw 30 subjects (15 males; 15 females). A weekly sign-up sheet posted on the psychology department undergraduate bulletin board listed chronologically the available times of the experimenters. Subjects signed up at their own convenience for any available time slot.

A prearranged list determined under which conditions each subject would render his or her report.

2.3. General Procedure and Overview

Each subject was assigned to one of five main groups: He or she reported the stream of consciousness either verbally (under one of three conditions) or nonverbally (under one of two conditions). All subjects gave these reports during three 5-min periods: (a) while lying down on the cot provided in the room; (b) while sitting down; and (c) while walking freely around the room. A prearranged (to minimize order effects) list determined under which conditions each subject would render his or her report.

When the subject arrived, the experimenter introduced himself, invited the subject to sit down, and assigned a number to serve as the subject's "name" throughout the experiment. The experimenter then invited the subject to read over the following introduction:

> This study is concerned with what and how people think. During several periods you will simply be asked to describe your stream of consciousness, to indicate what is going through your mind. The following ground rules apply to every aspect of the study.
>
> (1) Measures have been taken to insure your privacy and to guarantee confidentiality concerning your participation in this study. To be specific:
>
> > (a) you were assigned a number which will be the only identifying mark on all of the data-gathering items in this study;
> >
> > (b) there is no "key" or master-list linking your name to your subject number or to any of the data-gathering materials.
>
> (2) When asked to report on your thoughts, please convey whatever information you can on your stream of consciousness at that moment. Your report might include (*but is not limited to*) descriptions of: images, ideas, memories, feelings, fantasies, plans, sensations, observations, daydreams, objects which catch your attention, efforts to solve a problem. There are no restrictions, qualifications, conventions, or expectations: simply report on whatever is going through your mind (whatever you are conscious of or aware of). If you have any questions, please ask.

Throughout the experiment, except during periods of reporting, the experimenter made clear that he would answer any questions fully and truthfully. Subjects agreed to delay questions about specific experimental hypotheses until after the experiment.

The experimenter then gave the subject an informed consent form, which stressed: (1) the subject could withdraw at any time; (2) that the investigator would be glad to answer any questions; and (3) that the study involved no deception, that no "tricks," misdirections, or "surprises" would be played on any subject. No one withdrew from the study.

The experimenter provided precise instructions about how and under what condition the subject would report the stream of consciousness. These instructions are discussed in the following sections on the three separate experiments. The subject practiced for a few minutes to make sure she or he understood the procedure and equipment. A brief instruction sheet preceded and introduced each of the three reporting periods (lying, sitting, and walking).

At the conclusion of the reporting periods, subjects filled out a brief Differential Emotions Scale (Izard, 1971). Afterward, the experimenter either informally discussed the experiment with the subject (for the 36 participants in Experiment III), or scheduled a second appointment for further data collection and informal discussion of the study (for the 54 participants in Experiments I and II). Limitations in size of the subject pool and money available to pay subjects for additional hours precluded scheduling a second session for all subjects involved in the study.

2.4. Experiment I: Subject-Shift Material

2.4.1. Procedure. Each subject reported her or his stream of consciousness during three consecutive 5 minute periods by "thinking aloud" into a portable cassette recorder. As part of the report, the subject said "shift" to indicate substantial changes in the focus, content, tone, organization, or direction of conscious experience.

Each subject reported under only one of three conditions. In the "Alone" condition, the subject was alone during the three reporting periods. In the "Dyad" condition, the experimenter was present in the same room during the reporting periods, but was wearing head-phones over which radio music was being played to prevent him from hearing the subject's voice. Each subject tried on these headphones to verify that they did indeed shut out all room sounds. During the informal discussion at the end of the experiment, none of the subjects said that he or she suspected any deception. In the "Listen" condition, the experimenter was present in the same room and made it clear that he would be able to hear the subject's voice.

Because the conditions were balanced for sex of subject, the experiment forms a 3 × 3 × 2 design having three different postures (the three reporting periods: lying, sitting, walking), three conditions (alone, dyad, listen), and both male and female subjects. Each of the three experimenters worked with an equal number of male and female subjects balanced across conditions. Fifty-four subjects participated in this experiment.

2.4.2. Data Preparation. The tape recordings were transcribed. The word "shift" was omitted from the final typed copies. A timekee-per read these copies while listening to the tape recordings. Using a stopwatch, he marked the "shifts" onto the transcripts and recorded the duration of each thought segment (defined as the amount of time elapsed between each two adjacent "shifts"). Finally, two judges independently classified each thought segment as either "Present" (primarily focused on the subject's immediate situation or present environment) or "Absent" (focused on or concerned with something not in the immediate situation or environment, as, for instance, something in the past or future but not currently present, something elsewhere than in the experimental room, or something imaginary). Because these two judges were unable to reconvene, disputed segments were decided by a third judge.

The typist, timekeeper, and judges were blind to the hypotheses of the study and to the reporting period, condition, experimenter, or subject's gender for all transcripts (unless, of course, the subject mentioned this information in the report, which happened in slightly less than 20% of the transcripts). None had any previous interest or experience in studies of this nature.

2.4.3. Predispositions of the Subjects. Immediately after the final reporting period, subjects completed the Differential Emotions Scale, which assesses ten discrete positive and negative emotions (Izard, 1971). Subjects were then asked to return for a second appointment that was scheduled between one and two weeks later. At the second appointment, subjects completed the Embedded Figures Test (Witkin, Oltman, Raskin, and Karp, 1971); the Experience-Seeking subtest of Zuckerman's (1971) Sensation-Seeking Scale; three subtests (daydreaming frequency, positive reactions in daydreaming, and visual imagery in daydreams) of the Imaginal Processes Inventory (Singer and Antrobus, 1970); and a brief questionnaire on alcohol, marijuana, and other drug usage.

2.5. Experiment II: Rater-Shift Material

2.5.1. Data Base. Copies of the original transcripts from Experiment I, with shifts omitted, served as a data base for Experiment II.

2.5.2. Data Preparation. Two judges independently divided each transcript into thought segments by putting in "shifts," using the same criterion (a substantial change in the focus, content, tone, organization, or direction) as that employed by the subjects themselves in Experiment I. Disagreements were resolved later through discussion between the judges.

A timekeeper then listened to the tapes and recorded the duration of each segment (amount of time elapsed between adjacent "shifts"). Finally, the two judges independently classified each thought segment as either "Present" or "Absent," using the same criteria as in Experiment I. Disagreements were resolved through discussion between the judges. The timekeeper and judges (different from those of Experiment I were blind to the reporting period (lying, sitting, walking), condition (alone, dyad, listen), experimenter, or subject's gender for each transcript unless the subject conveyed that information while "thinking aloud." The author served as timekeeper and as one of the judges and was, of course, aware of the hypotheses being tested. The other judge had no previous interest or experience in studies of this kind and was blind to the hypotheses.

2.6. Experiment III: Key-Press Material

Each subject charted his or her stream of consciousness during three consecutive five-minute periods using a small portable key-press device. This box, held or carried in the subject's hand, presented two keys labeled "Present" and "Absent." The subject pressed (and held down) the "Present" key whenever her or his consciousness was focused on or concerned with something immediately present. He or she pressed the "Absent" key during those moments when his or her consciousness was focused on or concerned with something not in the immediate situation or environment. The subject indicated shifts in the stream of consciousness (a substantial change of focus, content, tone, organization, or direction) by briefly releasing whichever key was currently pressed and then immediately re-pressing the same key or switching to the other, whichever was appropriate.

Each subject participated under only one of two conditions, identical with the "Alone" and "Dyad" conditions of Experiments I and II. The "Listen" condition of Experiments I and II was omitted here because the subject gave no oral report to which the experimenter might listen directly.

Because the conditions were balanced for sex of subject, the experiment assumes a 3 × 2 × 2 design having three different postures (the three reporting periods: lying, sitting, walking), two conditions (alone and dyad), and both male and female subjects. Each of the three experimenters worked with an equal number of male and female subjects balanced across conditions. Thirty-six subjects participated in Experiment III.

2.6.1. Data Preparation. A polygraph, connected to the key-press box by a 15-foot cord, recorded the key-presses on spools of moving paper. A colleague measured the segments (distance between shifts or brief releases of the keys) on the resulting spools. He then prepared a record of the length of each segment and whether it was "Present" or "Absent." The colleague was blind to the hypotheses of the experiment, and had no previous experience in the area and had no descriptive information about the subject whose record he was preparing.

3. Analyses

The experiments constitute three possible methods to obtain material representing the flow of consciousness:

1. "Subject-shift": The subject verbalizes the flow of consciousness and indicates the shifts.

2. "Rater-shift": The subject verbalizes the flow of consciousness and independent raters identify the shifts.

3. "Key-press": The subject nonverbally charts the flow of consciousness and indicates the shifts.

For the material generated by each of these methods, three dependent variables were selected to represent characteristics of the stream of consciousness:

1. The number of shifts within a 5-minute period of reporting.

2. The number of thought segments for each period of reporting that were judged to be focused on the present situation or environment (i.e., the number of "Present" thought segments).

3. The cumulative duration of time spent with consciousness primarily focused on the present situation or environment during a 5-minute reporting period (i.e., the sum of the durations of "Present" thought segments).

In order to address the four major areas of concern described in the Introduction, four major sets of analyses were performed.

3.1. The Major Sets of Analyses

1. To identify which factors seem to influence the selected characteristics of the flow of consciousness, analyses of variance were performed separately on the data produced by all three methods of reporting (subject-shift, rater-shift, and key-press). Possible influences that were included as independent variables were conditions, sex of subject, and posture (a repeated measure). Where results indicated differences among means, the Newman-Keuls procedure (Winer, 1962, pp. 309–312) was used to evaluate the significance of differences.

Although the order in which each subject would give the three reports (lying, sitting, and walking) was arranged so that any possible order effects would be equally distributed across every condition, subject, sex, and posture, a preliminary analysis of variance was performed to assess order effects for each method of reporting. In these preliminary tests, order of report (first period of reporting, second period of reporting, and third period of reporting, regardless of the posture assumed during each period) was the only independent variable.

2. The second set of analyses focuses on the ability to determine reliably where shifts occur and to classify thought segments reliably as either "Present" or "Absent." The agreement of the two raters in determining where shifts occurred in the transcripts and in classifying thought segments as either "Present" or "Absent" was evaluated using the *kappa* statistic (Cohen, 1960) and the revised, standard error due to Fleiss, Cohen, and Everitt (1969). The same measure of agreement was used along with an analysis of variance to compare the shifts noted by the subjects themselves with the shifts determined by the raters.

3. To determine whether the verbal and nonverbal methods of reporting themselves produce differential effects on the selected characteristics (number of shifts, number of "Present" segments, and cumulative duration of the "Present" segments) of the flow of consciousness, separate analyses of variance were computed comparing key-press with subject-shift and comparing key-press with rater-shift.

4. In order to determine if certain predispositions were associated with variations in the flow of consciousness, the correlations were computed between each of the selected characteristics (number of shifts, number of "Present" segments, and cumulative duration of Present-centered Thought) obtained from the subject-shift material and each of the following variables described earlier: positive affect, negative affect, field dependence (EFT), frequency of daydreaming (IPI), positive reactions in daydreaming (IPI), visual imagery in daydreams (IPI), experience-seeking score (Zuckermann's Sensation-Seeking Scale), frequency of marijuana smoking, average alcohol consumption, and frequency of use of other drugs.

4. Results

4.1. The Thinking-Aloud Transcripts

The transcripts of the verbal reports were marvelously varied; no summary description is adequate. The appendix presents three transcripts in their entirety, chosen at random. Here are a few examples of thought segments judged to be "Present" (primarily focused on the present situation):

> It's not in here.
> There's a hair sticking in my pants.

My throat hurts.
I need new shoes.
Noticing the instructor's watch and thinking about my own watch.
Thinking about my button on my sleeve, I've been sort of fooling with and
slightly hurt my finger.
This floor is stone.

Here are some segments judged to be "Absent":

I can sort of see myself in a room writing papers but I'm not thinking about
it much.
I just had an image of a you know a sixty-year-old businessman walking
you know back and forth in his office, sweating about some business deal
that's going to be made, reading a tickertape.
I'm thinking about sex. I heard on the radio once that a young person's
mind has a sexual thought every one or two minutes.
I had a car accident over Christmas vacation.
Walking on the Riviera, the boardwalk, the uh, all the people, the cook, a
twenty-two-year-old cook.
Thinking about (name) and (name) who were at the party and how (first
person's) father is dying.
On the road outside Davenport Photo, a man at Caraphano's telling me
that clip-ons will not work.

4.2. General Characteristics of the Flow of Consciousness

Table I presents the mean, standard deviation, and range of each
of the selected characteristics (number of shifts, number of "Present"
thought segments, and cumulative duration of "Present" thought
segments) of the flow of consciousness for the subject-shift, rater-shift,
and key-press methods of reporting. Though the number of shifts
seems to vary with the method of reporting, the data indicate that,
within this experimental situation, about 35–55% of the thought
segments were focused on the present situation and that about 30–
40% of the time was spent with consciousness primarily focused on
the "here and now." It is important to note, however, that the
standard deviations are quite large. Some periods had no "Present"
segments, while others had no "Absent" segments. Clearly, and not
surprisingly, the flow of consciousness is subject to great individual
differences, even when measured within the constraints of a laboratory situation.

The correlations between any two selected characteristics range
from −0.07 to 0.90. Correlations between each pair of characteristics of
the flow of consciousness for each method of reporting are available in
Pope (1977).

TABLE I. Mean ($\bar{X}$), Standard Deviation (SD), and Range for Selected
Characteristics of Subject-Shift, Rater-Shift, and Key-Press Five-Minute
Reporting Periods

Selected characteristic	$\bar{X}$	SD^a	Minimum	Maximum	Range
Subject-shift (3 reporting periods for each of 54 subjects)					
Number of shifts	10.2	5.7	1	40	39
Number of "present" segments	3.7	3.4	0	25	25
Cumulative duration of "present" segments (in sec)	105.7	74.8	0	300	300
Rater-shift (3 reporting periods for each of 54 subjects)					
Number of shifts	12.1	6.1	1	40	39
Number of "present" segments	6.4	7.2	0	29	29
Cumulative duration of "present" segments (in sec)	87.2	63.6	0	300	300
Key-press (3 reporting periods for each of 36 subjects)					
Number of shifts	55.5	30.0	6	132	126
Number of "present" segments	29.7	18.8	2	107	105
Cumulative duration of "present" segments (in sec)	126.3	42.0	7	261	254

[a] The standard deviations are based on between-subject variation only.

4.3. Order Effects

Whether it was the subject's first, second, or third time to report did not seem to affect the reports themselves. The analyses of variance comparing reports given during the three periods (regardless of the posture assumed during a particular period) showed no significant differences for the subject-shift (see Table II), rater-shift (see Table III), or key-press (see Table IV) material.

4.4. The Main Effects of Posture

The mean number of shifts, number of "Present" segments, and cumulative duration of "Present" segments for the different postures within each method of reporting (see Table V) fall into a fairly consistent pattern. The means for the walking period always exceed those for the lying period. The means for the sitting period fall in between these two extremes, with two exceptions: the number of shifts obtained by the subject-shift method and the number of

TABLE II. Analyses of Variance of Number of Shifts, Number of "Present" Segments, and Cumulative Duration for Order (First, Second, and Third Periods of Reporting) for Subject-Shift Material

Variable	Source	df	MS	F
Number of shifts	Within Ss			
	Order	2	4.06	0.29
	Error	106	14.23	
Number of "present"	Within Ss			
segments	Order	2	8.62	1.32
	Error	106	6.55	
Cumulative duration	Within Ss			
	Order	2	2038.28	0.39
	Error	106	5241.19	

"Present" segments obtained by the rater-shift method. The analyses of variance, discussed in more detail in the following paragraphs, revealed a significant main effect of posture in eight of the nine tests. The subsequent Newman-Keuls analyses on these eight cases showed that the mean for the walking posture always differed significantly from that for lying. The other differences between postures are not as significant. (Throughout this study, the Newman-Keuls test is applied only in cases where the overall F test is significant.)

The analyses of variance for the subject-shift material (see Table VI) indicated that posture exerts significant effects on both the number of "Present" segments and the cumulative duration of "Present" thought segments. The Newman-Keuls procedure applied to the number of "Present" segments shows the walking period to be significantly different from both the sitting ($q = 5.56$, $r = 2$, $df = 96$, $p < .01$) and the lying ($q = 5.86$, $r = 3$, $df = 96$, $p < .01$) periods.

TABLE III. Analyses of Variance of Number of Shifts, Number of "Present" Segments, and Cumulative Duration for Order (First, Second, and Third Periods of Reporting) for Rater-Shift Material

Variable	Source	df	MS	F
Number of shifts	Within Ss			
	Order	2	48.23	2.31
	Error	106	20.87	
Number of "present"	Within Ss			
segments	Order	2	15.24	1.08
	Error	106	14.13	
Cumulative duration	Within Ss			
	Order	2	7210.94	2.47
	Error	106	2914.77	

TABLE IV. Analyses of Variance of Number of Shifts, Number of "Present" Segments, and Cumulative Duration for Order (First, Second, and Third Periods of Reporting) for Key-Press Materials

Variable	Source	df	MS	F
Number of shifts	Within Ss			
	Order	2	217.03	1.07
	Error	70	202.94	
Number of "Present"	Within Ss			
segments	Order	2	5.58	.04
	Error	70	125.00	
Cumulative duration	Within Ss			
	Order	2	640.41	.38
	Error	70	1689.93	

Applied to the cumulative duration of "present" segments, the Newman Keuls procedure again shows the walking period to be significantly different from both the sitting ($q = 12.22$, $r = 2$, $df = 96$, $p < .01$) and the lying ($q = 14.35$, $r = 3$, $df = 96$, $p < .01$) reporting periods.

For the rater-shift material, all three characteristics of the flow of consciousness were significantly affected by posture (see Table VII). The walking period had a significantly greater number of shifts than both the sitting ($q = 5.17$, $r = 2$, $df = 96$, $p < .01$) and the lying ($q = 5.35$, $r = 3$, $df = 96$, $p < .01$) periods. The mean number of "Present" segments was greater for the walking period than for either the sitting

TABLE V. Mean Number of Shifts, Number of "Present" Segments, and Cumulative Duration of "Present" Segments for Postures of Each Reporting Method

Method	n	Posture		
		Lying	Sitting	Walking
Mean number of shifts				
Subject-shift	54	9.9	9.6	10.9
Rater-shift	54	11.0	11.0	14.1
Key-press	36	51.6	56.9	58.0
Mean number of "present" segments				
Subject-shift	54	3.0	3.1	4.9
Rater-shift	54	4.5	4.5	8.1
Key-press	36	24.9	28.2	36.1
Cumulative duration of "present" segments				
Subject-shift	54	85.8	93.5	137.6
Rater-shift	54	69.8	73.5	118.2
Key-press	36	108.1	120.3	150.5

TABLE VI. Analyses of Variance of Number of Shifts, Number of "Present" Segments, and Cumulative Duration for Condition, Sex, and Posture of Subject-Shift Material

Source	df	MS	F
Number of shifts			
Between Ss			
Condition (C)	2	305.40	3.44[a]
Sex (S)	1	28.54	0.32
C × S	2	88.17	0.99
Error	48	88.85	
Within Ss			
Posture (P)	2	25.17	1.79
P × C	4	18.74	1.33
P × S	2	10.23	.73
P × C × S	4	4.30	.31
Error	96	14.09	
Number of "present" segments			
Between Ss			
Condition (C)	2	92.60	2.74
Sex (S)	1	18.67	0.55
C × S	2	24.15	0.71
Error	48	33.84	
Within Ss			
Posture (P)	2	58.15	10.26[b]
P × C	4	9.39	1.66
P × S	2	.30	0.05
P × C × S	4	3.14	0.55
Error	96	5.67	
Cumulative duration of "present" segments			
Between Ss			
Condition (C)	2	16963.91	0.96
Sex (S)	1	468.50	0.03
C × S	2	3080.44	0.17
Error	48	17698.32	
Within Ss			
Posture (P)	2	42244.75	8.98[b]
P × C	4	2354.81	0.50
P × S	2	847.53	0.18
P × C × S	4	3104.75	0.66
Error	96	4703.83	

[a] $p < 0.05$
[b] $p < 0.001$

($q = 8.43$, $r = 2$, $df = 96$, $p < .01$) or the lying ($q = 8.43$, $r = 3$, $df = 96$, $p < .01$) periods. Likewise, the cumulative duration of "Present" segments was longer during the walking period than during the sitting ($q = 6.75$, $r = 2$, $df = 96$, $p < .01$) or the lying ($q = 7.31$, $r = 3$, $df = 96$, $p < .01$) periods.

TABLE VII. Analyses of Variance of Number of Shifts,
Number of "Present" Segments, and Cumulative Duration for
Condition, Sex, and Posture of Rater-Shift Material

Source	df	MS	F
	Number of shifts		
Between Ss			
Condition (C)	2	345.45	3.17
Sex (S)	1	7.69	0.07
C × S	2	17.98	0.17
Error	48	108.86	
Within Ss			
Posture (P)	2	172.28	9.48[b]
P × C	4	44.50	2.45
P × S	2	11.71	0.64
P × C × S	4	5.16	0.28
Error	96	18.16	
	Number of "present" segments		
Between Ss			
Condition (C)	2	200.02	3.32[a]
Sex (S)	1	.03	0.00
C × S	2	29.75	0.49
Error	48	60.25	
Within Ss			
Posture (P)	2	231.13	23.50[b]
P × C	4	21.90	2.23
P × S	2	1.01	0.10
P × C × S	4	7.98	0.81
Error	96	9.84	
	Cumulative duration of "present" segments		
Between Ss			
Condition (C)	2	13761.41	1.09
Sex (S)	1	206.69	0.02
C × S	2	4100.53	0.32
Error	48	12638.51	
Within Ss			
Posture (P)	2	39184.81	16.54[b]
P × C	4	1817.88	0.77
P × S	2	64.34	0.03
P × C × S	4	2553.67	1.08
Error	96	2368.75	

[a] $p < .05$
[b] $p < .001$

Posture affected each of the characteristics of the flow of consciousness as measured by the key-press method (see Table VIII). In
general, subjects reported fewer shifts in the lying period than in the
walking ($q = 3.55$, $r = 3$, $df = 64$, $p < .05$) or in the sitting ($q = 2.94$, $r = 2$, $df = 64$, $p < .05$) periods. The mean number of "Present" shifts is

TABLE VIII. Analyses of Variance of Number of Shifts,
Number of "Present" Segments, and Cumulative Duration for
Condition, Sex, and Posture of Key-Press Material

Source	df	MS	F
Number of shifts			
Between Ss			
Condition (C)	1	4357.36	2.11
Sex (S)	1	2186.97	1.06
C × S	1	15648.02	7.59[b]
Error	32	2061.13	
Within Ss			
Posture (P)	2	421.95	3.60[a]
P × C	2	6.23	0.05
P × S	2	93.36	0.80
P × C × S	2	49.23	0.42
Error	64	117.16	
Number of "present" segments			
Between Ss			
Condition (C)	1	3840.13	4.78[a]
Sex (S)	1	1281.32	1.60
C × S	1	6256.28	7.78[b]
Error	32	858.02	
Within Ss			
Posture (P)	2	1179.69	12.80[c]
P × C	2	13.90	0.15
P × S	2	220.75	2.39
P × C × S	2	16.69	0.18
Error	64	92.18	
Cumulative duration of "present" segments			
Between Ss			
Condition (C)	1	27074.94	6.15[a]
Sex (S)	1	960.00	0.22
C × S	1	16625.75	3.78
Error	32	4400.23	
Within Ss			
Posture (P)	2	17137.06	15.77[c]
P × C	2	945.74	0.87
P × S	2	880.12	0.81
P × C × S	2	6055.03	5.57[b]
Error	64	1086.56	

[a] $p < .05$
[b] $p < .01$
[c] $p < .001$

greater in the walking period than in the sitting ($q = 6.75, r = 2, df =$ 96, $p = <.01$) or the walking ($q = 7.31, r = 3, df = 96, p < .01$) periods.

Posture affected each of the characteristics of the flow of consciousness as measured by the key-press method (see Table VIII). In general, subjects reported more shifts in the walking period than in the sitting ($q = 4.49$, $r = 2$, $df = 64$, $p < .01$) or in the lying ($q = 9.28$, $r = 3$, $df = 64$, $p < .01$) periods. The sitting period, moreover, has significantly more shifts than the lying period ($q = 7.68$, $r = 2$, $df = 64$, $p < .01$). The mean number of "Present" shifts is greater in the walking period than in the sitting ($q = 4.94$, $r = 2$, $df = 64$, $p < .01$) or the lying ($q = 7.00$, $r = 3$, $df = 64$, $p < .01$) periods. People spent significantly more time (cumulative duration) with thoughts focused on the present situation while walking than while sitting ($q = 5.50$, $r = 2$, $df = 64$, $p < .01$) or lying ($q = 7.72$, $r = 3$, $df = 64$, $p < .01$).

In summary, as the person becomes more vertical and more active, the frequency of shifts, the number of "Present" thought segments, and the time spent with consciousness focused on the present situation all tend to increase. The results of the Newman-Keuls tests indicate that the means for the walking reports are significantly larger than those of the lying reports and, in a majority of cases, are significantly larger than those of the sitting reports.

4.5. The Main Effects of Condition

As Table IX shows, the means for the dyad and listen conditions within each method of report are larger than those for the alone conditions. In only four of nine test, however, did condition exert a significant main effect (see Tables VI, VII, and VIII).

For the subject-shift material, condition influenced the number of

TABLE IX. Mean Number of Shifts, Number of
"Present" Segments, and Cumulative Duration of
"Present" Segments for Conditions of Each Reporting
Method

Method	n	Condition		
		Alone	Dyad	Listen
Mean number of shifts				
Subject-shift	54	8.0	12.7	9.7
Rater-shift	54	9.2	13.8	13.3
Key-press	36	49.2	61.9	—
Mean number of "present" segments				
Subject-shift	54	2.4	5.1	3.6
Rater-shift	54	3.5	6.8	6.8
Key-press	36	23.8	35.7	—
Cumulative duration of "present" segments				
Subject-shift	54	86.1	120.6	110.3
Rater-shift	54	68.8	96.2	96.6
Key-press	36	110.5	142.1	—

shifts (see Table VI). The Newman-Keuls test indicated that the mean number of shifts was significantly larger in the dyad condition than in the alone condition ($q = 3.66$, $r = 3$, $df = 48$, $p < .05$), while the mean number of shifts in the listen condition was not significantly different from the other two conditions.

Condition influenced the number of "Present" segments in the rater-shift material (see Table VII). The dyad and listen conditions had the same mean number of "Present" segments, which was significantly larger than that of the alone condition ($q = 3.13$, $r = 2$, $df = 48$, $p < .05$).

The analyses of variance for the key-press data (which lacks a listen condition) indicate that condition affects both the number of "Present" thought segments and the cumulative duration of "Present" thought segments (see Table VIII). Persons in the dyad condition had more "Present" thought segments and spent a greater amount of time with consciousness focused on the present situation than subjects in the alone condition.

In summary, the tests suggest that the dyad condition, and perhaps also the listen condition, may produce a greater number of shifts, a greater number of "Present" thought segments, and a greater cumulative duration of "Present" thought segments than the alone condition.

4.6. The Main Effects of Sex

There were no significant main effects attributable to sex (see Tables VI, VII, and VIII).

4.7. A Two-Way Interaction: Condition × Sex

The analyses of variance on the key-press produced two two-way interactions between condition and sex (see Table VIII). For males, the mean number of shifts in the dyad condition (78) far outnumbers that for the alone condition (42). For females, however, the mean for the dyad condition (45) is slightly less than that for the alone condition (57).

Regarding the number of "Present" segments, the mean for males in the dyad condition (47) again far exceeded the mean for males in the alone condition (20). For females, however, there were slightly fewer "Present" segments in the dyad condition (25) than in the alone condition (28).

In summary, the tendency discussed earlier for the dyad condition to produce more shifts and a greater number of "Present" segments seems much more characteristic of males than females.

4.8. A Three-Way Interaction: Posture × Condition × Sex

The key-press data contain a three-way interaction among posture, condition, and sex (see Table VIII). The cumulative duration of "Present" segments for females in the alone condition increases in small increments from the lying (109) to the sitting (118) to the walking (133) posture. For females in the dyad condition, it increases in larger increments from lying (91) to sitting (125) to walking (164). For males in the dyad condition, however, the cumulative duration increases in very small steps from lying (151) to sitting (159) to walking (163). And for males in the alone condition, the cumulative duration, which has a mean of 82 in the lying period, dips slightly to 79 in the sitting period and then makes a huge jump to 142 in the walking period of report.

The mean and standard deviations for each cell (posture × condition × sex) of each characteristic of the flow of consciousness for all three methods of report are available in Pope (1977).

4.9. Agreement between Two Raters

In the rater-shift experiment, two raters independently divided each transcript into thought segments by putting in "shifts." A problem arose in the attempt to use *kappa* to evaluate the interrater agreement. *Kappa* is computed not only from the number of instances where both raters indicated a shift and where one rater indicated a shift and the other did not, but also from the number of instances where both raters did not indicate a shift. It is necessary, then, to determine the number of opportunities or instances where it is possible for a shift to occur. A very liberal estimation might be that a shift could occur between any two adjacent words in a transcript. Use of such a liberal estimation seems, however, spuriously to inflate *kappa*. It is more likely that the words are grouped according to some unknown factor, which I will call "size of the syntactic unit," and that shifts can only occur between these groups. My efforts to find or devise such a factor appropriate to the transcripts were unsuccessful. Breaking down the transcripts into small grammatical units, for instance, was unworkable because many sections of the reports of the flow of consciousness were ungrammatical. In order to obtain some sense of the interrater agreement, several *kappas* were computed with the "size of the syntactic unit" (in number of words) successively equal to one, two, three on up to fifteen. If the size of the syntactic unit is assumed to be somewhere between one and fifteen, the inter-rater agreement is quite strong (*kappa* falling somewhere between .935 and .955, $p < .01$).

The resultant shifts divided the transcripts into a fixed number of thought segments (segments defined as the thought occurring be-tween two adjacent shifts). These segments were then judged to be either "Present" or "Absent." The interrater agreement, using *kappa* and the revised, corrected standard error is $k = .95$ ($p < .001$).

The thought segments of the subject-shift transcripts were like-wise classified as either "Present" or "Absent." Interrater agreement is $k = .83$ ($p < .001$).

4.10. Agreement between Subjects and Raters

Raters indicated more shifts than the subjects ($F = 5.94$, $df = 1,53$, $p < .008$). Subjects and raters agreed less than did the two raters as to where the shifts occurred. In the absence of a known "size of syntactic unit," a number of *kappas* were computed. *Kappa* varied from .57 (for a syntactic unit size of 15 words) to .68 (for a syntactic unit size of one word) with $p < .001$.

4.11. Comparison of Key-Press and Thinking-Aloud Methods

The analyses of variance comparing key-press with subject-shift and those comparing key-press with rater-shift indicated clear differ-ences between the nonverbal and "thinking-aloud" methods of report. When key-press was compared with subject-shift, there was a signifi-cant effect of method of report on the number of shifts ($F = 83.88$, $df = 1,70$, $p < .001$), on the number of "Present" segments ($F = 66.21$, $df = 1,70$, $p < .001$), but not on the cumulative duration of "Present" segments ($F = 2.79$, $df = 1,70$, $p < .01$).

When key-press was compared with rater-shift, method of report-ing exerted a significant effect on number of shifts ($F = 79.76$, $df = 1,70$, $p < .001$) on number of "Present" segments ($F = 47.30$, $df = 1,70$, $p < .001$), and on cumulative duration of "Present" thought segments ($F = 13.08$, $df = 1,70$, $p < .001$).

Reexamining the means of Table I, we find that shifting occurs about five times more often with the key-press method than with either of the verbal methods. In an average key-press period, shifts were reported every five or six seconds. During subject-shift or rater-shift periods, however, a shift occurred on the average of every 25 or 30 seconds. Similarly, the frequency and cumulative duration of

"Present" thoughts were greater during key-press periods than during the verbal report periods.

4.11.1. Predispositions Associated with the Flow of Consciousness. Table X presents the correlations between each of the selected characteristics (number of shifts, number of "Present" segments, and cumulative duration of "Present" segments) for the subject-shift material and each of the personality or behavioral predispositions. The correlations are generally quite low. Though the correlations between field dependency (EFT) and number of "Present" segments (negative) and between experience-seeking and cumulative duration of "Present" segments (positive) are both statistically significant, the positive correlations between negative affect and both number of "Present" segments and cumulative duration of "Present" segments more strongly indicate a genuine (nonchance) relationship. This finding suggests that negative mood may be associated with more frequent or more persistent thoughts about the present situation.

5. Discussion

The results suggest that, even under conditions of fairly rigorous experimental control, it is possible to obtain rich and varied samples of ongoing thought, that these samples can be reliably categorized, and that they vary systematically in relation to specificable conditions. The flow of consciousness seems predominantly oriented toward long-

TABLE X. Correlations between Personality or Behavioral Predisposition Measures and the Number of Shifts, Number of "Present" Segments, and Cumulative Duration of "Present" Segments for Subject-Shift Material

	Number of shifts	Number of "present" segments	Cumulative duration
Negative affect	0.13	0.40^b	0.30^a
Positive affect	0.03	0.05	0.10
Field dependence	−0.26	$−0.28^a$	−0.21
Daydreaming frequency	−0.18	−0.02	0.07
Positive reactions in daydreaming	0.13	0.09	0.01
Visual imagery in daydreaming	0.19	0.03	−0.12
Experience-seeking	−0.14	0.07	0.28^a
Frequency of marijuana use	−0.16	−0.08	0.02
Frequency of alcohol consumption	−0.20	−0.11	0.09
Frequency of use of other drugs	0.07	0.20	0.11

$^a\ p < .05, df = 1.52$
$^b\ p < .01, df = 1.52$

term memory and future fantasy: On the average, only about a third of the time was spent with consciousness primarily focused on the "here and now." Physical movement or the presence of others, however, led both to greater discontinuity (more shifts of thought) and also to more focusing on the immediate situation.

Posture clearly influenced the flow of consciousness, as predicted. Posture effects emerged significant in eight of the nine analyses with considerable evidence that there were more shifts, more thoughts concerned with the present, and more time spent with thoughts focused on the present when subjects were walking than when they were reclining. Sitting showed an intermediate effect. These results agree with those of Kroth (1970), Morgan and Bakan (1965), Berdach and Bakan (1967), and Segal and Glickman (1967) and suggest that physical posture or relative mobility might be related to the pattern of ongoing thought. Possibly, a more active physical posture (walking or sitting up) might lead to greater stimulus input from the environment and generate more intrusions into a private thought sequence. Thus, some aspect of the environment will catch the attention, trigger off an association to private material, but before the private association is fully elaborated or leads into a chain of related private associations, another aspect of the environment attracts the attention and consciousness is once again pulled into the "here and now." The pattern is illustrated by the following brief excerpt, characteristic of many of the reports given while walking.

> For some reason, I'm thinking of my grandmother, but I don't think that has to do with the news reporter. These walls are very peculiar. Like I said, they remind me of a squash court, although they don't have the little black marks all over them. I guess that's because I just started taking lessons, which would be a good reason. I wonder what these pipes are for. . . The paintings, well, they're very eye-catching. . . I guess I don't like abstract art, which is too bad because I like to appreciate everything that I can, when it comes to, well, anything art, uhm, people, whatever. This floor is dirty . . . also on the floor is a burnt-out ashtray with a dead cigarette in it, dead cigarette, uhm . . . dead cigarette, that's a nice expression. I already got it. Whenever I get the chance I'd like to light one and get out of here. I'm not sure it makes sense to call a cigarette that's burnt out dead because it almost looks like a corpse, but it looks like what I would almost imagine a corpse to be . . . all white and burnt out . . . which reminds me of a med student I went to Florida with and all the stories he told me about working on cadavers. I wonder what that piece of wood on the floor is for, it's got two nails sticking out of one end. It reminds me of . . . oh, there's another one; of um, when my grandmother was building things and had to be careful not to walk on the planks because I'd get nails stuck in my boot.

A lying posture, however, appears to minimize the variety and importance of the environment. We do not need to scan the environment repeatedly to keep from bumping into things. Since we do not move around, our visual perspective does not change much. We may soon tire of staring at the ceiling and, perhaps closing our eyes, allow material from long-term memory or future fantasies to follow their course, uninterrupted by thoughts of the present environment. The following excerpt is characteristic of many reports given while lying down.

> I'd forgotten what it was like to talk in that voice. Poor (name #1), that girl. I wonder what she's going to do for a living next year. I wonder what I'm . . . I'm lucky, I guess. You know I've got no roommates but oh, poor thing, nobody wants to room with her. I mean a freshman, I mean a sophomore getting a single, its just impossible. I've never seen a young girl who so many people know. I mean like everybody at (school name) knew her. Even that girl at (place name) (name #2), I mean there are a lot of (school name) people, but everybody knew (name #2), too. I mean it's incredible. Word really gets around. I wonder what that (name #3)'s doing today. I wonder if he's still here. I don't see what he sees in (name #2). I mean, boy, of course, I'm beginning to think he's a little strange, too. (name #4), I wonder what (state)'s like. It must be a lot warmer down there than it is up here. My mom was telling me not to bring back my winter clothes. I mean, "Why don't you leave some of those sweaters home? Surely you won't need them." I mean Dad was right. He said it was going to be winter for another month or so up there and I could surely use them. And he was right, boy. I've never been so cold. I mean I feel colder today than I've ever been during most, most of this winter except, except for (school). I wonder, I wonder what (school) is doing. I wonder what (name #5) is doing at (school) is doing. I wonder what (name #5) is doing at (school), speaking in voice. I wonder if speaking in voices includes ESP. I wonder like if she could understand my thoughts if I, if I tried to communicate something to her, if she'd really feel it since she's so in tune with God, well, so in tune with what He's saying. I wonder if she'd get in tune with what I was saying or if that would be unreligious because the world doesn't say that.

Like lying, being alone seems to involve fewer shifts and less preoccupation with the present environment, as predicted. The effect of this social variable (presence of another person) was less clear-cut, however. The major impact on shifts and on emphasizing present-oriented thought came from the mere presence of another person; the effect of whether or not he or she (the experimenter) could hear thought content, for example, was less striking. These results are consistent with the studies of Antrobus, Singer, and Greenberg (1966), Drucker (1969), and Csikszentmihalyi (1974) indicating that people in relatively simple, barren environments are more likely to daydream or think about matters not directly related to the immediate situation. If one assumes that the addition of another human to the environment makes it more complex and stimulating, then it is logical that another's presence can set the stage for more "Present" thoughts. It may also be the case, however, when an individual's interior monologue unrolls in the presence of another person—and indeed may actually be overheard—that this leads to some distortion and censorship of the reports, avoidance of extended fantasy or recollection of material that could be too revealing. The following subject, in the presence of an experimenter unable to hear him, becomes preoccupied with the present situation, but also with the reception of his report.

> Maybe this won't take very long. What'er you listening to on that radio? Hmmmm. All right. Gotta ask him what his name is. As long as I have this microphone in my hand, let me tell you a joke. I'll wait until the next time to tell you the joke. It's gonna be a good one. I'm tired of walking around. I wanna sit down. I'll lean up against the wall. He's listening to something.

Tendencies to censor or "play to the audience," however, may not be the sole cause of the alone/other-person differences, as suggested by the significant differences found between reports made alone and reports made in the presence of another person by the nonverbal, key-press method (in which content was never available to a person other than the subject).

There was no prediction of a main effect for sex and none occurred. There were, however, unpredicted two- and three-way interactions involving the sex of the subject. In the two significant sex condition interaction effects, the tendency discussed above to have greater discontinuity of thought and more focusing on the immediate situation when another person is present seems much more character-istic of males than of females. In the three-way (sex × condition × posture) interaction, the tendency to have an increase in present-centered thoughts in the presence of another person is more powerful for males than for females, even to the point of eliminating posture effects: When a male subject is reporting in the presence of another male, reclining fails to decrease significantly the amount of concentra-tion on the present (in all three postures, the percentage of time spent focusing on the immediate situation is very high, slightly above 50%). It seems appropriate to offer two speculative interpretations for these unpredicted effects. The first concerns social role-expectations for males and females. It may be that sensitivity to private experience (indulgence in long-term memories and fantasies of the future) is more socially acceptable for females than for males. When another person is present, therefore, a male subject may inhibit his tendency to pull away from present-centered thoughts. Even while lying down, a male subject may become preoccupied with aspects of the present environ-ment in order to defend against "letting down his guard." Another interpretation focuses on the sex of the experimenters: All were male.

Perhaps a person of the same sex is a more complex or salient addition to the environment than a person of the opposite sex. This perplexing finding does suggest a future experiment in which the sex of the experimenter is varied as a factor along with sex of subject.

There was excellent agreement between raters in classifying thought segments as "Present" or "Absent" and good agreement in determining where shifts occurred in the transcripts. There was not such consistent agreement, however, between the raters and the subjects regarding where shifts occurred. Raters tended to identify more shifts. Subjects might not have noted as many shifts as the raters simply because it is easy to forget to do so while engaged in verbalizing the flow of consciousness. As mentioned in the introduction, many of the pilot subjects commented on the difficulty of remembering to note each shift as it occurred. If this is an influential factor, giving each subject more practice and training may minimize the problem in future research. It is also possible, however, that many of the discrepancies are attributable to genuine differences of opinion as to where the shifts occur. The subject's consciousness may group extremely diverse or eclectic elements by personal, unique, and unarticulated connections: The flow of consciousness through these grouped elements may involve no shift in terms of the psychological reality of the subject but may seem like an obvious shift to a rater. Future research might pursue this idea as follows. Subjects could rate transcripts of their own reports, and could then identify any shifts that they forgot to note during the report. They could also comment on shifts noted by nonsubject raters that did not and still do not seem like shifts to the subject.

There was a clear difference between the nonverbal (key-press) and "thinking aloud" methods in regard to the selected characteristics of the flow of consciousness. As predicted, shifts occurred much more frequently in the key-press method. The translation of the flow of consciousness into words may be a relatively difficult and time-consuming task: The subject must pick out the correct words to convey the thoughts while keeping pace with the often chaotic rush of ongoing awarness. Moreover, brief thought-fragments—and especially momentary but vivid images—may take only seconds to occur but quite some time to describe.

Subjects using the nonverbal method of report also showed greater frequency and cumulative duration of present-centered thought segments than those giving verbal reports. A speculative interpretation of these results might revolve around the generally pejorative overtones associated with daydreaming and other nonpresent-centered forms of thought (see Singer, 1966). Subjects might be reluctant to identify themselves explicitly as having relatively few present-centered thoughts. While "thinking aloud," the subject is unaware of the "Present"/"Absent" classification that will later be applied to the thought segments. The key-press method itself, however, draws attention to this distinction (the two keys are labeled "Present" and "Absent"). It is, moreover, the subject who does the classification in the process of reporting. The "Absent" key may be less socially desirable for many subjects.

The prediction that subjects who reported frequent daydreaming on the Imaginal Processes Inventory would tend to spend less time with consciousness focused on the present environment was not confirmed. It is possible that habitual tendencies to daydream did not have time to emerge sufficiently within the constraints of this study or were suppressed by other influences (posture; solitude), but this is speculation.

It is interesting, however, that of the various self-report measures of predispositions and characteristics, only mood seemed to show a genuine relationship to the characteristics of the flow of consciousness; when thoughts about the present environment predominate in consciousness, they tend to be associated with more unpleasant emotions. This finding is consistent with the research of Rychlak (1973) and Blatt (1974), who found an inherent connection between present-centered thought and negative affect. An alternative explanation of the data in the present study is suggested by the fact that some subjects found the experimental room extremely aversive.

> I don't like this room.
> I just noticed the floor I'm walking on. It reminds me of a floor in a bathroom.
> It reminds me of . . . a hospital room.
> This room does look like a torture chamber.
> Oh, its cold in here. The bricks in the wall remind me of the Birdman of Alcatraz and the light's in my eye, a prison, and I want to go back to my room and put some music on.

If the experimental room was a depressing environment—and it apparently was—it may be that the experimental environment simply depressed anyone who happened to spend much time thinking about it. A future experiment, more successful in creating a warm, comfortable, pleasant experimental room, might test this idea.

In conclusion, several findings seem most significant. First, that the flow of consciousness is indeed rich and varied, but can be reliably categorized and seems to vary systematically in relation to specifiable conditions. Ongoing thought seems to be, on one hand, far more mobile and shifting in sequences than the output from formal studies of problem solving or associative learning would lead us to believe (Humphrey, 1951; Berlyne, 1965; Paivio, 1971; Bourne, Eckstrand, and Dominowsky, 1971). On the other hand, the flow of consciousness does not seem so idiosyncratic as to place it beyond the province of scientific research. Second, the method of report exerts an important effect, at least in terms of the characteristics of the flow of consciousness examined in this study. The key-press method sacrificed the richness of verbal accounts, but seemed better suited to keeping pace with the flow of consciousness. And, third, insofar as the findings of this study are characteristic of normal, "everyday" thinking, people seem to spend a great deal of time in fantasy and long-term memory.

6. Appendix: Three Transcripts

The following pages contain complete transcripts for three subjects picked at random.

6.1. Transcript A

6.1.1. Period 1. O.K. I'm looking at that piece of wood down there in the corner. I'm thinking that this is a really, very interesting stream of consciousness. I'm looking at my coat now. I got it from uhm Hadassah. And there's this great Jewish lady there that was uh, oh, I'm thinking about this tie that I had. Oh, now I'm thinking of a tie of my grandfather's. I'm thinking about the day that my grandfather died. I was at junior high school and (name) walked into the office. I was in the office and I was crying and I didn't really care if he, if he cared that I was crying uhm. I walked outside. I remember walking down by the football field. It was a long, curvy driveway sort of and I remember looking over through my tears at them playing football. Now I'm thinking about my coach in uh junior high school. He was (name) and he used to beat up all of, all of these, these kids uhm, but he liked me. And I'm still thinking of (name). I'm thinking of his big nose and bald head. Now I'm thinking of this pillow and it reminds me of something but I can't tell what is is. I'm looking at the sack on the wall. I'm looking at my coat again. I'm looking at this piece of cellophane on the floor. It's from a cigarette package. Uhm, I'm thinking of (name) and our pollution club in junior high school. I was vice president and she was president. Uhm, I'm thinking about the cigarette package again and I'm thinking that I'm smoking too many cigarettes. I should quit because I'm worried that I'm going to wind up just like my father because my father smokes, chain smokes cigarettes all the time. I'm concerned that I smoke too much dope which really isn't that much but because my father is an alcoholic I don't want to turn out like him. Uhm, last time I was home, my mother found some of my dope. It was a very bad scene. Uh, I'm looking at this plaid sort of uh, chaise lounge. I'm thinking of my old house on (street number) where I grew up that had a screened-in porch and we, I don't know if we had a chaise lounge on it or not, but it was the chaise lounge that made me think of our screen porch. I'm thinking of Daisy who was our dog. Oh, she died when she was about 12 years old. I always used to think Daisy was, I used to tell people that Daisy was older than 12 years old or however old she was when she died, I'm not really sure, because I always wanted it to seem like I had uh, that my dog was older than anybody else's. Uhm, I remember, I think it was (name), she was a girl in the neighborhood and I remember her running up and telling me that she had seen Daisy and another dog, uhm, having sexual intercourse. Uhm, now I'm looking at this light switch again and I'm thinking that uhm I'm trying to make an image in it and I can see that those two screws on the side are eyes and the light switch itself is a nose. I'm looking at the doorknob. I'm looking at this tape and I'm thinking that the carbon on it looks like a poster. Now, which, well, I'm thinking of the poster of *Pal Joey*. I was in *Pal Joey*. Uhm, there were a lot of gay people in the show. I don't want to think about that anymore. I'm looking at the light switch again, the light socket. It seems, it seems that whenever I don't want to think about something I look at a light socket. I'm looking at the floor now. I'm looking at the tile, uhm. I notice part of it is a phallic symbol. I'm looking at a piece of aluminum on the floor but actually I'm thinking why do I wa . . .

6.1.2. Period 2. O.K. I'm looking at this uh, o.k. I'm just thinking about laying here. I'm feeling ah my feet, uhm I can feel it where it's on top of the, the end of the chaise lounge and it, it reminds me of when I'm smoking, well smoking dope and I get these incredible rushes of sensitivity and I, I feel like I'm gaining these insights that, that I hadn't had before. And now I'm wondering why I'm so concerned with dope. Now I'm thinking of my sister and brother-in-law and uh, they smoke dope. Now I'm thinking about the time my sister was talking about (name), her husband (name) is getting really screwed up because he was using speed and all sorts of other drugs. Now I'm thinking of that (name) went to Princeton University. Now I'm thinking of (name) in high school. Uhm, I'm thinking that I never really, well I'm thinking, I was going to say that I'm thinking that I've never really liked (name). Uhm, now I'm thinking that I just can't tell if I do or not. I like him. It was good to see him. I feel uncomfortable around him. I don't really know why. Uhm, now I'm thinking of this picture or painting or something in their living room, uhm I don't even know what it is. Now I'm thinking of a Tiffany lamp and I'm, now I'm thinking of my mother. My mother got this, uh, she really liked Tiffany lamps and she ordered a couple through Lee Wards and uhm, they turned out to be really crappy, plastic lamps, but she liked them anyway. I'm thinking of the possible implications of that thought and I'm thinking that uh, well, I'm thinking that my mother doesn't have good taste, or some good taste or something, that uh, I'm thinking how much I love my mother. I'm thinking of my Aunt (name). Uhm, this is my great-aunt, my mother's aunt, and it's only because of her that I'm going to school because my par-, my father lost his job and uhm this, that was the only way that I could come to school and she gave me like three thousand dollars and uh, I haven't taken a job this year and I'm feeling sort of guilty because I haven't been working in school. I worked last summer my ass off. I worked two jobs, uhm. I'm thinking of how uhm callous I acted at home. I'm thinking uhm that I wasn't as sympathetic as I should have been. I'm thinking of the letter that I wrote last week to my mother which, oh, which, which I said something like uhm I'm sorry that I can't be there but all I can offer you is my love, which was something that I had never written before, and it was sort of a shock to myself that she got it but it felt really good when I got a letter from her the next week. Uhm, I'm thinking that in this letter she told, she told me that if I wanted to write to her about Dad's drinking problem that I should write to her at the hospital and she gave me an address. I'm thinking of my sister who's making more money than my mother. I'm wondering about the possible implications of this whole money preoccupation. I've always thought of myself as idealistic about money and I always told people that that was the reason I lost money all the time. Uhm, was because I was, I had no concern for it and I think that's true. Ah, money . . . money . . . I'm thinking of George Washington whose face is on the dollar bill and I'm thinking about George Washington cutting down the cherry tree. I'm thinking about lying and I'm trying to remember the last time that I lied . . .

6.1.3. Period 3. O.K. I'm sitting here and I'm looking at the green splotch on the floor over there, but I find it pretty uninteresting. Now I'm looking at two dots on the etching, how they look like eyes. Now I'm thinking of my father uh redecorating our uhm, of the same house on (street) where I grew up, redecorating the basement, redoing it. Uhm, we had, we had this sort of maple pa- paneling and I was really proud of my father for doing that. I'm thinking of times when I was proud of my father and I'm thinking of the latest time which was when he was saying that he was becoming more and more, uh, getting more and more into socialism, which shocked the shit out of me. Uhm, he was always, he was a banker. I'm thinking of (name), uhm I met (name), we were, I bought some socialist literature at school, uhm and I, I was thinking about (name's) wife and they wanted me to go down to New York and I remember talking to my friends about uh going down to New York and how socialist chicks fuck the best and her name was not (name), but uh, a really strange name. But now I'm thinking of (name) and I'm trying not to think of (name) because I know that (name) is a, (name) said that he was a bisexual and he's been coming into my room lately and I just don't want uhm and well, I'm not going to say that I don't want to talk about this uhm. I'm thinking of (name's) curly red hair and I'm thinking of (name) coming into my room at night and I'm thinking of the fire alarm. I'm thinking of (name) who lives next door and he smokes too many cigarettes and I was bumming too many cigarettes off of him lately and now (name), because (name) has been bumming a lot cigarettes off me lately. I'm remembering (name) when uh the guy was here with the socialist literature, (name), he came up to my room and (name) was there and he was, (name) came into the room and or later (name) said that uh none of it looked very interesting. (Name) who was sitting on the floor uhm like he was really getting into it what (name) was saying. Now I'm thinking of his wife again and uhm I can't, I was just wondering, I opened my eyes, and I was wondering why I was shutting my eyes, and I got them shut again and I'm wondering why I'm going to open them. Now I'm looking at the poster over there and I'm thinking that the bottom right corner looks like a little fat man with a red face and a bright green jacket sort of and he's going, he looks like a big fat golfer. Now I'm thinking about this big fat alumni dinner that we sang at, it was the (name). The (name). I'm thinking of uhm oh I have this uhn, oh I had this competition with this guy and he's, he's like the established beer drinker in the group. In fact it was (name), he's the topic for my psych paper. I was thinking of psychology. Now I'm thinking of Dr. (name). I'm thinking that I don't really think he's uh pretty shitty lecturer. I'm thinking of whether I'm here for actual learning because or if I'm here for grades. I'm remembering that when I came here first I, I was very sure that I could have worked just as hard as I wanted without grades. Uhm, I'm thinking about the A that I got on my English paper. I'm thinking of the B- over a C+ which I got on my Ethics paper and I was really upset, I was really distraught about it. Also, it was the same day was that the midterm for the class and I was sure I was going, completely fuck it up. And I took the test and I don't know if I did or not. I'm thinking of (name), my roommate, uhm the reason I'm thinking of him is because uhm, oh I told him that I was distraught. I'm thinking of the beginning of the year when he told me that he had already gone through two identity crises. Uhm, I'm wondering why my hand or . . .

6.2. Transcript B

6.2.1. Period 1. There's an uh, incredibly nuisance, incredible nuisance of the weight on my shoulder. Uh, I once had one of these as a child, which I broke. There was a sticker on it, a yellow submarine, blue meany sticker over the speaker that was uh covering a dent that been uh inflicted upon the uh wire grill over the speaker, uh, by me. My brother had one that was uh better than mine. He uh, they're both Christmas presents. Mine was given to me before he was got, before he got his, so to compensate for the lateness of, of his gift, it was better than mine. Of course, it's always been my opinion that it's better to have a good tape recorder late than a bad tape recorder early. But of course I don't uh. It's come to my attention that there might be snakes underneath the uh sofa or the couch, the cot here. I have my backpack on, my pitch helmet on, my khaki shirt and pants, but I'm not one of those jungle hunters who kill helpless animals such as the giraffes hiding behind the, the board over here on the wall. I am friendly jungle hunter who takes pictures of the animals. Of course, at uh cocktail parties, when my friends ask me what I do for a living, I tell them I shoot animals in Africa. You can imagine the consternation that this causes. You can also imagine the, the good laugh we have over it when I explain that I mean I shoot them with a camera and not with a gun. This resembles in many ways, as a matter of fact, a story I read in third grade, which uh as it happened did not cause me to laugh very much at all, but people in the story, uh, and their lives have since modeled my reactions, did laugh very much. This was before I received the tape recorder. This was before I knew about tape recorders, as a matter of fact. There's a movie; it's a short subject uh showing at the Surf Cinema in Lynn, Massachusetts. I don't remember what the main feature was, but it was about a man who went around shooting animals, with a gun and then in the last frame of the movie, the gun turned into a camera miraculously, in his hands. It was a terrible movie. I saw two kids, two kids were uh were arrested outside Phelps Gate today. I saw them taken out of the gate, the building there with handcuffs in their hands. They were undoubtedly waiting in a room similar to this before their escort took them away in a police car.

They probably did not have a tape recorder, but they did have handcuffs. When I was a kid, I, I wanted handcuffs at one time. That time never, that, that was of course a case of buying for myself, not a Christmas-type acquisition. There are snakes climbing the wall. There are long, straight white ones with . . .

6.2.2. Period 2. My bed was occupied about an hour ago like this cot is now. I was sleeping there, oblivious to the rigors of modern psychology which were about to descend upon me. There's a cross in this room near the ceiling. It is a, consisting of uh four snakes, you will recall. It might possibly be a transatlantic cable. Uh, there's an egg cutter, a hard-boiled egg slicer, cutter in the corner uh next to the cross. The cross of course uh was if the English uh, the stories I've been reading by a religious author. Uh, my back, my upper back which is pressed tightly against the plastic uh, the nylon of this cot . . . and this is certainly a cheap and shoddy cot to conduct a psychological test in. I'm sure that Freud would uh, insisted on much better equipment. (clears throat) There's a uh, a sun on the wall in the painting on the left but I know that someone in the, I assume that someone in the, one of the testers put that up on the wall and I'm not going to be connived into saying there's a sun on the wall just because uh some psychology tester has put one up there for me to notice. The floor, however, the floor is very clean, unlike my floor. Uh . . . humm . . . (long silence) there . . . the . . . I'm reminded of how sleepy I am . . . Salem, Salem, Massachusetts, uh, this bit of cons- this thought was inspired by the un ceiling which is of course very visible when you're lying down on a cot uh, especially such a cot as this one. Oh, I've slept in many cots such as this and they're all, all alike.

6.2.3. Period 3. The first three knocks were the best of all, I think. The first, the first three knocks of the first section were uh pretty good. The second set of three knocks was very weak, especially the first knock. These last three were the best, very similar to the beginning of Beethoven's Fifth Symphony, but not that similar. I think, although, it's more similar to Beethoven's Third Symphony. Ah, I think again not, not that similar at all, really. It's hard to draw, hard to draw many parallels . . . Tile floor, our floor in the bathroom where I live, . . . which looks like a movie, I don't know why, *Fantastic Voyage* occurs to me. Looks more like Mexico. Socks, shoes, blue jeans, pillow, thread, white thread, white and blue thread, white walls, tires, 1950, California, Allen Ginsburg, beards, hair, black hair, red hair, Lucille Ball, television, Bob Hope, nose, lustful Nathaniel West, H. L. Smith, half-dollars, six dollars and fifty cents, uh, George Washington, Abraham Lincoln, and Abraham Lincoln's birthday,

Valentine's Day, candy, cookies, sugar, white sugar, red sugar, brown sugar, white opium, white heroin, brown heroin, *Time* magazine, *Newsweek* magazine, *Life* magazine, Death magazine, in-between magazine, uh, television, uhm, radio, red socks, blue ones, ball games, popcorn, hot dogs, mustard, yellow, uh John Lennon, uh, glasses, lots of glasses, Elton John, uh borrowed Bob Hope, nose, uhm, ignorance, uhm, my math teacher in seventh grade, eggs, meat, uhm pie, uh the circumference of the circle, white-wall tires, red lights, white lights, blinkers, brakes, uhm eggs break, cakes rise, eggs scramble, uhm, summer camp, my grandmother's presents sent in the mail, grandmother's postcards sent in the mail, uhm mail, uhm Mailer, Norman Mailer and uh Knights in armor in a, and uh dragons, dragons and fish, fish and the aquariums and uhm Bruce in Boston and uh Watertown and water and scotch, scotch with water, with ice, with uh, with soda, with soda on the side, uh wine, (unclear) beer, uh vomit, nausea, headaches, uhm aspirin, No-Doze, Tums, uh Tums, little metal cases with railroad pictures on them and uh, uh the trains into clouds of smoke and dust and the painting in the Fogg Art Museum and fog also, and uhm California and uhm California and hum P. G. Wilthouse in G's and Little Orphan Annie and jeepers, creeper and uh peepers and creepers mostly, snakes and uhm.

6.3. Transcript C

6.3.1. Period 1. I'm sitting here thinking that I have to be thinking . . . I'm singing a song in my head, that new Ringo Starr song that I heard on the radio. It must have been the last thing that I heard when I went out of the house. It's funny I haven't been thinking about it all morning, I just, it just came to me. My mind feels like it's racing. I have so many things that I plan that I have to do for the rest of the day. Let's see, if I get out of here at three, I'm supposed to run errands. I have to go downtown. Have to stop at the student employment office. No thought. . . Preoccupied with the work that I have to do, (unclear) next week I have so many things that I've overextended myself, to think that I'm going to soccer practice for the first time, I have rehearsals that I have to go to, once every day and then I have a double rehearsal for another show every day, I have two exams. And yet I signed up to do these experiments and I'm sitting here and I feel like. I'm worried about wasting time. I wonder if I'll see my friend (name) this evening. He's been gone for three weeks. He went to (place). But I have so much work to do. Damn, there are so many things that I want to do. The sun's out and it's so pretty and it's so springy and I can't stand the fact that I have to sit and read . . . no thoughts. That stupid song keeps coming back in my mind. It's hot in here. It was freezing this morning . . . know, see, I'm not really thinking, I'm thinking, but I don't, I'm not realizing what I'm thinking in order to speak what I'm thinking. It's just in my head. My fingernail's filthy. And my mind's going along thinking about how my fingernail's and I wish I had a nail file so I could clean them. And then I was thinking to myself, you know, I'm supposed to be thinking, now wait a minute, let's say something. Not even realizing that if that's what I was thinking, then that's what I'm supposed to be recording . . . I should clean my fingernails. Thinking personal body things. There's hair sticking in my pants. My socks are too short. I ate too much at lunch. . . Where is my mind? I feel like it's at a standstill, only because I'm supposed to be saying something. This isn't very helpful. . . I wish I could . . . I think so much during the day when I'm thinking that I'm not supposed to be thinking that I can't concentrate on what I'm supposed to be concentrating on. Lucky I didn't go to class today. Yet, if I sat there I would have looked out the window thinking about the work that I'm supposed to be doing, thinking about how I'm not going to get it done and how I'd like to go dancing this weekend if there was a dance. And yet now when I'm sitting here and don't have to do anything but just think cause I love to think, I'm not thinking. I wonder if he can hear everything I'm saying through the door, cause I can hear the doors open and close and I can hear people's footsteps. I should have my hair cut. I'm getting bored with it. And when springtime comes, anyway, I get all these wonderful plans about how I'm going to start turning new leaves all over the place. I decided to make this a physical activity semester, so with the soccer and taking gymnastics at the gym and rehearsing for all different things, I've sort of pushed my work into the back. And so now with (unclear) I decided I'm going to diet and have my hair cut. I hear footsteps out there. I wonder if that's the experimenter . . . I also shouldn't be chewing gum. I decided I was going to give that up. That's a part of my new leaf.

6.3.2. Period 2. Oh, this is much better. I wish I could just go home and go to sleep. I just stayed up the whole night two nights ago trying to study for an exam. I wish I could just relax now that it was all over and now I have to turn around and face two more next week. My leg is uncomfortable. I feel like I'm in the army on one of these cots. I have an image of the barracks on Gomer Pyle, or one of those prison, prison wards where all the prisoners have to lie down and take a nap. I was just thinking of the $2.50 for each one of these sessions, cause next week, next Friday I'm having a dinner for five friends of mine, a big, a fun dinner. But I always get so worried about it, I walk around thinking about what time I'm going to have to put the roast in so that it will all be ready when everyone comes in, then at the same time later, once the roast has been in, I'm going to have to start the potatoes. And here it's not for a week yet and I can do all that thinking an hour beforehand. After all, I keep planning time schedules. I can still hear that song in my head. My mind keeps wandering back to (name). He's got a female kind of friend that works downtown and I wonder if he's gone to visit, to say hello since he just came back. I wish I could go to California. I'd love it there, but I'll be graduating next December and I'm taking off for Hawaii. I'd love to live for just an isolated amount of time, no pressure just knowing you were working, feeding yourself, going out of the house when you wanted, coming back when you wanted, no deadlines to meet. My father's been out of work for a year and a half. He's waiting on a possible position on the West Coast. I wonder if he's heard anything. My mother lives in (place) and she called last night, and I was supposed to call back and I didn't. I wonder if she's called. Oh, I have to get the parent's confidential statement to her, and take care of my financial aid business. Such nice bright-colored pictures on the walls, the bright yellows. Thinking of going dancing this weekend but I have too much work. Can't wait for the prom, that'll have top priority. No thoughts. . . After this, I guess I'll go to the library and meet my friend and take a break for an hour with her talking about things. I'm going to live in Hawaii with her; she's from Hawaii. See, I'm not letting my thoughts come, I'm reporting. I'm feeling like I have to back up what I'm saying for background information. The stitches on this cots reminds me I have to get my sewing done. . .

6.3.3. Period 3. Despite how confidential this is all going to be, there is nothing to stop anybody from as soon as I finish taking it in and listening to it and of course you can pinpoint it to me. I wonder how valid all this could be. It's too bad you can never, no one can ever let you know what they're thinking, the way they're thinking in any stream of consciousness or otherwise. I wish I could say the things that I think I want said, but when it comes right down to saying them, I can't say them anyway, even to people. I guess my mind's stuck on (name) for the moment. I spend too much time analyzing that and spending too much time looking forward to things. I can't wait for the summer term. It's, it's an exciting thought but I don't think I'm thinking seriously or reasonably. I'm not thinking of 95-degree weather and that I'm going to be sweltering in here. But it's something new and it'll help me get out in December. That's what's keeping me going, knowing that I'm going to end up somehwere in Hawaii. I like theater. It just reminded me speaking of Hawaii. I mean ultimately what I would love to do is be in New York, trying in one way or another in live theater to make my living through it, but (name) and I keep planning how when we get to Hawaii just don't do anything that's going to lead to anything. Maybe I'll go central casting for *Hawaii Five-O*. No, but I'd rather be in California. Any time there's a day like today, I can't imagine why anybody would choose to stay on the East Coast anywhere from October to February or March. If Yale wasn't here, I mean, I'm glad I'm at Yale, I wouldn't want to be anywhere else only because of, the only other reason that I would want to go anywhere is the climate. If this could be moved to California, that would be ideal. But it's enough, I don't have to worry. I mean this is four years. I'm not losing anything. I'm not missing out. Everything will be there when I get out and I'll just go do what I want to then. I wonder if (name's) paper is finished. . . No thoughts. I wonder what time (name's) having people over for dinner. She probably bought a dessert, leave me something to pick on. Oh, but I shouldn't. Damn. And tomorrow I have to go to work. I sure hope I don't eat all day. . . No thoughts. I feel melancholy all of a sudden. But that's silly, it's so sunny out. I'm just thinking about everything that has to get done and worrying is it going to get done or it, and wishing I could just go sit with (name). No thoughts. I feel guilty I didn't go to class today. And I didn't go yesterday because I was so tired. Oh damn it, I didn't go dancing. I didn't call my mother. I didn't call my father. I wish we could go out and visit this friend's in (place).

ACKNOWLEDGMENTS

The investigations reported here were part of the author's doctoral work done at Yale University. I wish to thank the Griswold Fund for the Humanities for their generous grant enabling me to study the stream of consciousness as it appears in the arts, sciences, psychotherapeutic context, and our everyday experiences. I also wish to thank a number of very special people—Jerome Singer, Irvin Child, Louis Heifetz, Leland Wilkinson, Joshua Auerbach, Domenic Cicchetti, Barbara Classon, Penny and Ed Trickett, Jeff Pusar, Mark Farb, Eileen Boyle, Jerry Levine, Ed Horahan, Dan Koffsky, Tim Singer, Barry Cook, and Jesse Geller—without whose warm support, sensitive understanding, deep caring, and good humor this work never would have been completed.

References

Antrobus, J. S., and Singer, J. L. Visual signal detection as a function of sequential variability of simultaneous speech. *Journal of Experimental Psychology,* 1964, *68,* 603–610.

Antrobus, J. S., Singer, J. L., and Greenberg, S. Studies in the stream of consciousness. *Perceptual and Motor Skills,* 1966, *23,* 399–417.

Beit-Hallahmi, B. Developing the prison fantasy questionnaire (PFQ) *Journal of Clinical Psychology,* 1972, *28,* 551–554.

Berdach, E., and Bakan, P. Body position and free recall of early memories. *Psychotherapy: Therapy, Research and Practice,* 1967, *4,* 101–102.

Berlyne, D. E. *Structure and direction in thinking.* New York: John Wiley, 1965.

Bertini, M., Lewis, H. B., and Witkin, H. A. Some preliminary observations with an experimental procedure for the study of hynagogic and related phenomena. *Archivo di Psicologia Neurologia e Psichiatria,* 1964, *6,* 493–534.

Blatt, S. J. Levels of object representation in anaclitic and introjective depression. *Psychoanalytic Study of the Child,* 1974, *29,* 107–157.

Bourne, L. E., Eckstrand, B. R., and Dominowsky, R. L. *The psychology of thinking.* Englewood Cliffs, N.J.: Prentice-Hall, 1971.

Cohen, J. A. coefficient of agreement for nominal scales. *Educational and Psychological Measurement,* 1960, *20,* 37–46.

Csikszentmihalyi, M. *Flow: Studies of enjoyment.* P. H. S. Grant Report N. 401 HM 22883-02, 1974.

DeGroot, A. *Thought and choice in chess.* The Hague: Mouton, 1965.

Drucker, E. Studies of the role of temporal uncertainty in the deployment of attention. City University of New York, unpublished doctoral dissertation, 1969.

Fleiss, J. L., Cohen, J., and Everitt, B. S. Large sample standard errors of kappa and weighted kappa. *Psychological Bulletin,* 1969, *72,* 323–327.

Frank, S. Just imagine how I feel: A comparison of behavioral and imaginative techniques in the facilitation of role-taking skills. J. L. Singer and K. S. Pope (Eds.) *The Power of Human Imagination: New Techniques of Psychotherapy.* New York: Plenum Press, 1978.

Hariton, E. B., and Singer, J. L. Women's fantasies during sexual intercourse: Normative and theoretical implications. *Journal of Consulting and Clinical Psychology,* 1974, *42,* 313–322.

Humphrey, G. *Thinking.* London: Methuen, 1951.

Izard, C. *The face of emotion.* New York: Appleton-Century-Crofts, 1971.

James, W. *The principles of psychology.* Vol. 1. New York: Dover, [1890] 1950.

Klinger, E. *Structure and functions of fantasy.* New York: Wiley-Interscience, 1971.

Klinger, E. Utterances to evaluate steps and control attention distinguish operant from respondent thought while thinking out loud. *Bulletin of the Psychonomic Society,* 1974, *4,* 44–45.

Kroth, J. A. The analytic couch and response to free association. *Psychotherapy: Therapy, Research, and Practice,* 1970, *7,* 206–208.

Lewis, W. *The art of being ruled.* New York: Harper, 1926.

Morgan, R., and Bakan, P. Sensory deprivation hallucinations and other sleep behavior as a function of position, method of report, and anxiety. *Perceptual and Motor Skills,* 1965, *20,* 19–25.

Naranjo, C. Present-centeredness in Gestalt therapy. In R. E. Ornstein (Ed.), *The nature of human consciousness.* San Francisco: Freeman and Company, 1973.

Paivio, A. *Imagery and verbal processes.* New York: Holt, 1971.

Pope, K. S. The flow of consciousness. Yale University doctoral dissertation, 1977.

Rychlak, J. F. Time orientation in the positive and negative free phantasies of mildly abnormal vs. normal high school males. *Journal of Consulting and Clinical Psychology,* 1973, *41,* 175–180.

Segal, S. J., and Glickman, M. Relaxation and the Perky effect: The influence of body position and judgments of imagery. *American Journal of Psychology,* 1967, *60,* 257–262.

Singer, J. L. *Daydreaming.* New York: Random House, 1966.

Singer, J. L., and Antrobus, J. S. A factor analytic study of daydreaming and conceptually-related cognitive and personality variables. *Perceptual and Motor Skills,* Monograph Supplement 3, Vol. 17, 1963.

Singer, J. L., and Antrobus, J. S. Dimensions of daydreaming: A factor analysis of imaginal processes and personality scales. NIMH Progress Report, 1970.

Tomkins, S. *Affect, imagery, and consciousness.* Vols. I and II. New York: Springer, 1962–1963.

Winer, B. J. *Statistical principles in experimental design.* New York: McGraw-Hill, 1962.

Witkin, H. A., Oltman, P. K., Raskin, E., and Karp, S. A. A manual for the embedded figures test. Palto Alto, California: Consulting Psychologists Press, 1971.

Zuckerman, M. Dimensions of sensation-seeking. *Journal of Consulting and Clinical Psycholgoy,* 1971, *36,* 45–52.

10

Dreams and Waking Fantasy

Steven Starker

Attempts to investigate the relation of the nocturnal dream to other types of fantasy have been more intriguing than conclusive. Early studies compared morning-after dream reports of individuals with their Thematic Apperception Test (TAT) stories and observed significant thematic resemblance between them (Sarason, 1944; Gordon, 1953; Shulman, 1955). More recent studies employing the sleep laboratory technique of dream collection, however, indicated negligible or inconsistent relations between dreams and TAT stories regarding thematic content, and noted instead some stylistic and structural similarities (Eagle, 1964; Foulkes and Rechtschaffen, 1964; Ben-Horin, 1967; Cartwright, 1969). Reliance on the relatively structured, volitional TAT story as the sole sample of waking fantasy, moreover, has limited the applicability of these research efforts regarding broad questions about the nature of fantasy in waking and sleeping. Upon completing an extensive review of the relevant literature, Klinger (1971) concluded " . . . the degree of relationship in thematic content between dreams and fantasy is highly dependent on the kind of fantasy. Clearly there is a pronounced need for the study of samples of normal waking fantasy to compare with samples of dreams." He also noted that evidence to date suggests that stylistic and structural consistencies such as length of report, imaginativeness, and conceptual activity are more likely to be found across waking and sleeping fantasy than thematic consistencies.

Steven Starker • West Haven Veterans Administration Hospital; and Yale University, New Haven, Connecticut. Present Address: Psychology Service, Portland Veterans Hospital and Department of Medical Psychology, University of Oregon School of Medicine, Eugene, Oregon.

Advances in the experimental study of daydreaming have now made it possible to examine the relationship between patterns of spontaneous waking fantasy and characteristics of nocturnal dreams. The existence of three "styles" of daydreaming has been documented in several factor-analytic studies using the Imaginal Processes Inventory (Singer and Antrobus, 1963, 1972; Starker, 1973; Isaacs, 1975). A Guilty-Dysphoric factor describes a waking fantasy life dominated by guilts, fears, hostilities, ambitions, and conflicts. A Positive-Vivid factor, on the other hand, involves an ability to enjoy vivid imaginal experiences that are not conflictual. The Anxious-Distractible factor involves absorption in fantasy that is often intrusive, frightening, or bizarre, along with markedly poor attentional controls. These three factors are not independent, and most people display aspects of each, but tendencies toward predominance of one or another of them describe an individual's personal fantasy style.

The three studies described below explore the possibility of significant thematic and structural continuities that transcend the arousal continuum of consciousness to manifest themselves in seemingly disparate types of fantasy experiences. They are part of a broader research effort into diverse aspects of inner experience (e.g., illusion, imagery, hallucination, hypnosis, sleep, dreams and daydreams) that attempts further to integrate our growing knowledge of the subjective (Starker and Goodenough, 1970; Starker, 1972, 1973, 1974a, b, c; Starker and Singer, 1975a, b; Starker and Starker, 1976; Starker and Hasenfeld, 1976; Brett and Starker, 1977).

1. Experimental Studies of Dreaming and Daydreaming

1.1. Study 1

1.1.1. Method. Fifty-five male college students were administered the Imaginal Processes Inventory. Composite scores were computed using those subscales known to be closely linked with the different daydream styles. For the Positive-Vivid style the relevant scales were those of Absorption in Daydreaming, Daydream Frequency, and Positive Reactions in Daydreams. The Guilty-Dysphoric style involved scales of Guilt in Daydreams, Fear of Failure in Daydreams, and Hallucinatory Vividness of Daydreams. For the Anxious-Distractible style the scales of Distractibility, Mind-wandering, and Boredom were employed. Composite scores indicated the degree to which a particular subject could be said to display a particular daydream pattern.

All students kept a dream diary at home for 14 nights, recording dreams in detail immediately upon awakening. In order to take an economical "first look" at this large pool of dream data, dreams of the three highest scoring subjects in each daydream category were chosen to represent that category for the data analysis. The three subjects scoring highest on Positive-Vivid daydreaming scales reported a total of 34 dreams, those scoring highest on Guilty-Dysphoric scales reported 32 dreams, and 27 dreams were turned in by subjects scoring highest on the Anxious-Distractible scales. The statistical design was a one-way ANOVA on the three daydream categories, with the individual dreams being treated as "subjects." This is not an optimal statistical approach, but it permitted rapid entré into a large body of data in order to determine whether more detailed analysis was warranted.

The nine selected dream diaries were broken up into 93 individual dreams and randomly ordered for rating by two judges "blind" as to the daydream scores. Mean ratings on each dream were employed for the statistical analysis. Variables rated were: length (in idea units), emotionality, bizarreness, and affective polarity.

1.1.2. Results. The ANOVA disclosed significant differences among the three daydream categories on all four dream variables. Most profound were the differences in bizarreness ($F = 14.6, p < .001$), length ($F = 12.5, p < .001$), and affective polarity ($F = 10.0, p < .001$). Results on the degree of emotionality expressed were less striking but still significant ($F = 4.6, p < .05$). Breakdown of the significant findings by Tukey's method of multiple comparison revealed that Anxious-Distractible daydreamers had the most bizarre dreams while Positive-Vivid daydreamers had the least bizarre. The Anxious-Distractible group also had the most emotional dreams and reported the most idea units. The Positive-Vivid group displayed the most positive affective tone in their dreams. A look at some of the actual dreams of the extreme Positive-Vivid daydreaming group helps to illustrate these results:

> I'm working at my job at Korvettes thinking about the girl dressed in brown from the party. I'm thinking to myself that she also had her eye on me, wanted to see me again, and thus went to the trouble to find out about me. She learns where I work and decides that she has to go shopping. I spot her from my counter, leave my department, and take an illegal break. We get to know each other better and I ask her for a date for next Saturday's concert. We went and had a great time. Then I pictured us months later still enjoying ourselves.
> I found myself winning the state lottery after many previous futile attempts. My dream covered the way that I spent the prize money—buying two new cars, going on a worldwide trip with my two very close friends (I found that in each city that I went to I was able to meet a girl whose company I enjoyed), buying my own house with the best stereo-tape system already hooked up to every corner of the house, and setting up my

own United Nations for peace which succeeded in ending all conflict throughout the world.

Some interesting differences were also observed among the three daydream groups in the frequency of nightmares. Nightmares were defined as only those highly anxious dreams from which subjects reported being awakened due to dream content. Using this strict criterion, no nightmares were found among the dreams of the Positive-Vivid group, two (6.25%) were reported by Guilty-Dysphoric daydreamers, and six (22.22%) were reported by the Anxious-Distractible group ($\chi^2 = 30.0, p < .001$).

Finding in this preliminary study such apparent continuity of fantasy style across dreams and daydreams made it clear that further work was warranted and suggested two directions. First, a more extensive study of the dream diaries was called for. Second, the intriguing finding regarding nightmare frequency and daydream style could be followed up by a study more specifically designed to investigate the relationship of sleep disturbance to daydream style.

1.2. Study 2

1.2.1. Method. Subjects were the same 55 college students; elimination of all reporting fewer than three dreams left 48 students and these reported a total of 420 dreams. Composite scores were again computed on the basis of relevant subscales of the IPI, yielding a score for each subject on each of the three styles. The composite scores on each style were ordered, and the upper third (16 subjects) of each ordered series was selected for study. Many people turned up in two categories, however, since none of these styles is "pure." It was decided, therefore, to compare daydream categories two at a time rather than attempting an ANOVA design with all three categories. With but two categories to deal with all subjects appearing in both could be eliminated, leaving a sizable pool of "pure" subjects, i.e., those who scored high on only one of the two daydream factors. Who was eliminated depended on which comparison was being made, so the subject pools involved in the three comparisons were appreciably different. After eliminating overlapping subjects the eight highest remaining persons in the two categories were compared as to nocturnal dream characteristics.

A judge "blind" to daydream scores and subject identity and trained in the scoring of dreams rated the randomly ordered individual dreams on a five-point scale for each of eleven categories. On the basis of the previous study it was clear that rating categories should include measures of length, emotionality, and bizarreness; other content categories were generated on the basis of theoretical considerations. The eleven categories selected were: length in idea units, positive affect, negative affect, aggression-hostility, sex, orality, frustration, gratification, fear-anxiety, affiliation, and bizarreness. Reliability of scoring in each of the categories was later checked by randomly selecting a subsample of dreams for rating by a second blind judge.

1.2.2. Results. Finding the reliability to be adequate, three comparisons were made:

Positive-Vivid vs. Guilty-Dysphoric. The single significant finding was of greater negative affect in the dreams of the Guilty-Dysphoric group ($p < .006$). It is noteworthy that this comparison did not involve groups that differed in dream length.

Guilty-Dysphoric vs. Anxious-Distractible. The Anxious-Distractible group reported dreams of greater length ($p < .04$) and considerably greater bizarreness ($p < .001$). The measure of fear-anxiety in dreams was elevated for this group as well, but not significantly so ($p < .10$).

Positive-Vivid vs. Anxious Distractible. The Anxious-Distractible group reported considerably longer ($p < .005$) dreams containing greater negative affect ($p < .002$), aggression ($p < .05$), fear ($p < .02$), and bizarreness ($p < .002$).

Finally, a Verimax factor-analytic solution of the data was performed on all 48 subjects using the method of principal components. Three factors accounted for 51.5% of the variance. Two of these were clearly "instrumental" factors contributed by the dream rating and daydreaming questionnaire methodologies. The third factor, however, involved both daydreams and nocturnal dreams. Dream characteristics loading highest were positive affect, gratification, affiliation, and sex, all clearly agreeable dream experiences. These are followed by high *negative* loadings on Fear of Failure in Daydreams, Guilt in Daydreams, and Hallucinatory Vividness of Daydreams, all subscales associated with a dysphoric mode of daydreaming. Somewhat lower positive loadings on dream length and Positive Reactions in Daydreams continued the trend of this factor, which clearly describes a Positive Fantasy Style including aspects of both waking and sleeping fantasy.

1.3. Study 3

1.3.1. Method. Ninety-nine college undergraduates, 49 males and 50 females, were asked to complete a questionnaire containing six subscales of the IPI and five additional scales developed for this study.

Each of the three daydream styles was defined by two appropriate IPI subscales; the new scales were those of Nightmares, Insomnia, Childhood Sleep Disturbance, Dream Recall, and Positive Mood. Items on the new scales took the same form as those of the IPI; each item was a statement about the relevant behavior followed by a five-point scale indicating the degree to which the statement is true for the reader. Phrasing was varied from positive to negative to avoid response sets, e.g., "Falling asleep is sometimes very difficult for me"; "I never have problems getting to sleep." All items were randomly assigned positions in a single questionnaire of 133 questions.

In addition to the questionnaire three sample dreams were presented subjects with the request to rate each on a five-point scale for the presence of positive affect, negative affect, bizarreness, vividness, and anxiety. This procedure was included to explore the possibility that a powerful response bias underlay the observation of daydream "styles," e.g., that persons appearing to be Positive-Vivid daydreamers merely respond more positively to experimental tasks involving fantasy, and would do so even when presented with other people's fantasies.

The request to "make up a dream" was included to obtain an actual sample of waking fantasy. That is, subjects were asked to construct and relate a "best possible" and "worst possible" dream, thus encouraging considerable affective expression in volitional fantasy. Such purposeful constructions cannot be considered spontaneous daydreams (Starker, 1974b) but may certainly be included in the broader category of waking fantasy. Subjects were also asked to report their most recently recalled dream. These three samples of fantasy life were rated as to length, positive affect, negative affect, visual quality, number of people, and presence of the "self" by a judge "blind" as to daydream scores.

1.3.2. Results. For both the Guilty-Dysphoric and Anxious-Distractible styles significant positive correlations were observed with self-reports of nightmares ($p < .01$ and $p < .05$, respectively), insomnia ($p < .05$ for each style), and childhood sleep disturbance ($p < .001$ and $p < .01$, respectively). The Positive-Vivid style bore no particular relation to the latter measures. Sex differences were negligible.

Correlation of sample dream ratings with daydream style scores yielded but two significant results out of 15 correlations, and one of these opposed the response bias interpretation. Hence, the presence of a powerful response bias toward matters of fantasy seems an unlikely explanation for the observation of daydream styles or for the continuities observed between daydream and other fantasy experiences.

Looking at the Made-Up-Dreams (MUD), high scores on the Positive-Vivid style were associated with the tendency to *include* the "self" in the "best possible" MUD ($p < .05$); high scores on Guilty-Dysphoric daydreaming were associated with *exclusion* of the "self" from this wonderful fantasy ($p < .01$). Even in this "best" MUD, Guilty-Dysphoric daydreamers tended to include negative affect ($p < .05$). On the "worst possible" MUD Positive-Vivid daydreamers tended to minimize negative affect ($p < .05$) and exclude the "self" ($p < .05$) from the terrible fantasy; Guilty-Dysphoric daydreamers produced longer "worst" fantasies ($p < .05$). Analysis of the last recalled actual dream was less profitable, but high Positive-Vivid daydream scores were associated with reporting more people in the dream.

Some interesting associations were observed between daydream styles and scales of positive mood and of dream recall. The positive mood scale contained such items as "Usually I'm in a pretty good mood" and "My bad moods are always short-lived"; it addressed itself to mood-in-general rather than mood-at-the-moment. High Positive-Vivid style socres were associated with more positive mood ($p < .01$), high Guilty-Dysphoric and Anxious-Distractible scores were associated with less positive mood ($p < .01$ and $p < .001$, respectively). Dream recall proved positively related to Positive-Vivid style scores ($p < .001$).

Factor analysis of the daydream style, sleep disturbance dream rating, and MUD scores, using the principal components method and a Verimax orthogonal rotation, yielded six factors that accounted for 51.7% of the variance. Two of the factors were purely instrumental, contributed by the MUD (6.8%) and dream-rating (6.0%) techniques, a third was clearly a dream-recall factor (11.4%). The other three factors are of greater interest and are displayed in Table I.

Factor A appears to describe a conflictual fantasy style that extends the Guilty-Dysphoric daydream style into additional realms of behavior. This configuration involves high scores on Guilty-Dysphoric daydreaming, the tendency to exclude the "self" from the "best" MUD, minimization of positive affect in the "best" MUD, reporting of nightmares, highly visual quality of the last recalled dream, history of childhood sleep disturbance, encroachment of negative affect into the "best" MUD, and the appearance of few persons in the "best" MUD and last nocturnal dream.

Loading highest on Factor B is the Positive-Vivid daydream style score, and the factor indicates extension of this style into other areas. Negative affect on the "worst" MUD is minimized and the self is excluded. Positive mood loads high. The "worst" MUD lacks visual quality and length. Sample dreams were rated high on vividness and frequent dream recall was reported.

TABLE I. Factorial Analysis of Daydream, Sleep Disturbance, Dream Rating, and MUD Scores

Factor A	Factor loading	% Total variance
Guilty-dysphoric	0.67	14.5
Best MUD, self present	−0.58	
Best MUD, positive affect	−0.54	
Nightmares	0.46	
Last dream, visual	0.42	
Childhood sleep disturbance	0.36	
Insomnia	0.36	
Best MUD, negative affect	0.34	
Best MUD, number of persons	−0.32	
Last dream, number of persons	−0.31	
Factor B		
Positive-vivid daydreaming	0.82	8.2
Worst MUD, negative affect	−0.62	
Worst MUD, self present	−0.62	
Positive mood	0.42	
Worst MUD, visual	−0.39	
Worst MUD, idea units	−0.37	
Dream rating, vividness	0.25	
Dream recall	0.25	
Factor C		
Anxious-distractible daydreaming	0.87	4.8
Guilty-Dysphoric daydreaming	0.46	
Childhood sleep disturbance	0.45	
Positive mood	−0.43	
Insomnia	0.37	
Last dream, negative affect	0.35	
Nightmares	0.34	

The Anxious-Distractible style of daydreaming is most prominent in Factor C. Associated with this style are the Guilty-Dysphoric daydream scores, childhood sleep disturbance, low scores on positive mood, reports of insomnia and nightmares, and negative affect in the last recalled nocturnal dream.

2. Discussion

Although there are methodological issues raised by the individual studies that are important in the planning of future research, these have been explored in detail elsewhere (Starker, 1974a; Starker, 1977; Starker and Hasenfeld, 1976). Therefore, we shall focus here on the results of the experiments and their implications for a general theory of fantasy.

The converging results of these three studies indicate that in addition to the interesting and readily observable differences between fantasy productions in waking and sleeping, there are important stylistic consistencies in fantasy that transcend the individual's state of arousal. These are seen most clearly in the realms of affect, anxiety, and bizarreness and may be observed at three different levels of functioning: dreaming, daydreaming, and volitional fantasy. They are consistencies in the "structure" of fantasy rather than the "content."

2.1. The Medium of Fantasy: Structural Considerations

Although our appreciation of the complexity of others may suffer for it, we frequently have occasion to describe our acquaintances in terms of broad affective dispositions. Thus, we may remark on someone's optomistic, pessimistic, introverted, extraverted, melancholic, sunny, brooding, or happy-go-lucky personality. Such generalities, however inadequate in describing a whole person, do succeed in capturing for us the tendency or predisposition of an individual toward a particular affective state. Similarly, the identification of a Positive or Conflictual "Fantasy Style" cannot be considered adequate to describe a personality but merely an indication of a predisposition toward employing the expressive capacities of fantasy in a particular way. Nor can Fantasy Styles claim the specificity of Singer's Daydream Styles, where a Guilty-Dysphoric pattern has been linked with particular sets of daydream content. At this point we can only identify affective disposition as a broad structural parameter, continuous across waking and sleeping fantasy, within which more specific contents are expressed.

That affective disposition colors an individual's dreams, daydreams, and other fantasy constructions is hardly surprising providing one takes a holistic, organismic view of human psychology. People constantly reveal their affective states in many different ways and "languages," e.g., bodily gestures, psychosomatic symptoms, reported mood, neuro-vegetative signs, distorted perceptions, etc. At the extreme, think of the depressed patient sitting with stooped shoulders, downcast gaze, moving with great difficulty, haltingly reporting in *sotto voce* his sad feelings and diminished appetites, seeing only the worst in his memories of the past and his perceptions of the present, and imagining only the most bleak future (if any). Thus exaggerated by the depressive, or conversely by the manic, it becomes clear that profound affective states can all but permeate the various expressive capacities of the individual. Are dreams and daydreams exempt? Studies of dreaming, daydreaming and depression have already indicated that this affect disorder can be discerned in both types of fantasy (Kramer, Whitman, Baldridge, and Lansky, 1966; Langs, 1966; Starker and Singer, 1975a, b; Schultz, 1976). The studies reported here reveal significant continuity of affect through waking and sleeping fantasy even in the absence of clinically extreme affective states.

Although it is simpler to think of mood states as the "cause" of the observed continuities across types of fantasy, the interactional models postulated by Feshbach (1967), Beck (1967), and Schultz (1976) in which mood and fantasy continuously influence one another via feedback channels seem advantageous here. Hence a positive presleep mood stimulates positive imagery and fantasy that, in turn, facilitate the calm, positive, relaxed mood until the occurrence of sleep. Dysphoric presleep moods yield conflictual fantasy productions that may elevate tensions and anxiety to the exclusion of sleep, causing mood to deteriorate further until total exhaustion may override the cycle. In sleep, the negative mood contributes to and is maintained by bad dreams or even nightmares.

It becomes necessary to consider, at this point, whether "anxiety" is a fantasy content (i.e., a specific affect) or a relatively nonspecific structural variable. Although it appears to have characteristics of both, it seems preferable in the present context to consider it nonspecific since it may be a common endpoint of a number of different fantasy contents. Inasmuch as anxiety is generally secondary to conflicts surrounding aggressive and sexual impulses, and because particular individuals may be made anxious by a great variety of dream and daydream contents, the "signal" or "informational" aspects seem more relevant here. Not only does it indicate a "danger" to the individual, it simultaneously effects a disruption of the very cognitive activities that have elicited the anxiety. Studies have documented the disruptive effects of anxiety on visual imagery (Starker, 1974c) and auditory imagery (Brett and Starker, 1977), and the particularly disruptive effect of anxiety on the emotionally valent auditory images of schizophrenic patients known to experience auditory hallucinations.

The three studies reported here indicate that level of anxiety, like affective polarity, is a general parameter of fantasy life that transcends state of arousal. In fact, it appears to have some important regulatory functions with regard to both fantasy and arousal. When present to sufficient degree in dreams it leads to abrupt awakening and experience of "nightmare." When present in waking it may prevent entry into the vivid hypnagogic reveries that facilitate the onset of sleep through its arousing qualities and its disrption of mental imagery. The anxious person seems predisposed not only to conflictual fantasy experiences, but to actual disruptions in the fabric of fantasy life whenever dreams or daydreams wander into "forbidden" areas or merely threaten to do so.

What of the stylistic consistencies in bizarreness of fantasy that have emerged in these studies? The measure of bizarreness involves scoring the extent to which content is highly unusual, strange, "crazy," in violation of the physical laws of nature. Experimental sleep researchers know bizarreness as the quality most frequently associated with REM-state dreams, a sleep state that also involves a high barrier to external stimulation (Adey, Kado, and Rhodes, 1963; Rosner, Goff, and Allison, 1963). Researchers in the areas of sensory deprivation, hypnogogic reverie, and hypnosis have also observed that drastic reductions in stimulation during wakefulness can lead to bizarre, dreamlike fantasy (Goldberger and Holt, 1961; Heron, 1961). Foulkes and Fleisher (1975) recently demonstrated bizarre fantasy to be a surprisingly regular feature of waking fantasy life in normals. Bearing all of these findings in mind, one possibility that emerges is that some people can more completely block incoming sensory stimuli than others, and this permits them more readily to escape the structuring effects of stimulus input and results in more bizarre fantasy productions. Such differences in stimulus blocking could reflect primarily physiological variations or the differential learning of cognitive controls or both.

One could also postulate that persons with elevated bizarreness of fantasy are just "crazier" than the rest of us, involved with more autistic, primitive symbols and thought processes. Attempts to link psychotic thought disorder with a bizarre style of daydreaming, however, met with little success (Starker and Singer, 1975a, b). Moreover, an implication of the Foulkes and Fleischer (1975) study is that normals are not less "bizarre" than psychotics in their fantasies but merely better integrated.

Thus far we have explored three structural parameters of fantasy: affective disposition, anxiety level, and bizarreness. Although they can hardly be considered independent of one another, these three factors currently seem most useful in describing those aspects of fantasy that transcend level of arousal. It is worth noting that Freud (1900) discerned the continuity of waking affects into dreams early in his clinical work, noting that affects, unlike impulses, do not appear to be transformed by the dream work.

Tart (1975) has applied the concepts of general systems theory (von Bertalanffy, 1968) to the phenomena of consciousness in a way that seeks to account for both its enduring structural continuities (styles) and the ubiquities of its various "states." He describes a "state" as "a unique, dynamic pattern or configuration of psychological structures, an active system of psychological subsystems," citing as examples "the ordinary waking state, hypnosis, alcohol intoxication, marijuana intoxication, and meditative states." He does not deal extensively with daydreaming and its position in the configuration called the "ordinary waking state" is unclear. Yet, the conception of discrete states of consciousness as complex configurations, gestalten, or systems that are essentially *transformations of other configurations* seems well suited to account for both the enduring components and the unique aspects of fantasy life in the individual.

Klinger (1971) appears to have anticipated Tart, noting that "neither waking fantasy nor dream experience is the exclusive domain of any but a very few ideational properties." Rather, he suggested that:

> . . . fantasy and dreams are part of a single continuing fantasy process which is subject to certain transformations imposed by physiological and stimulus events. It is unnecessary to sleep in order to generate dream-like ideation, and, apparently, it is unnecessary to be awake in order to produce relatively coherent, undream-like ideation; but the regular mutations of ideational structure and content observed in dreams are apparently the effects of physiological variations on a continuous fantasy process.

Viewed from this perspective, Guilty-Dysphoric daydreams and terrifying nightmares might be understood as highly related "state" phenomena, transformations of one another, whose manifest forms and rules of expression are shaped by fluctuating physiological and stimulus events but which nevertheless retain observable aspects of the underlying organismic continuity.

2.2. The Message of Fantasy: Content and Meaning

The discovery that even our most bizarre and seemingly unintelligible fantasy productions during sleep are in fact richly laden with meaning about our motives and feelings was enormously exciting to Freud (1900). His dream theory rapidly assumed a central position in psychoanalysis, with the mechanisms of the "dream-work" becoming the model for understanding symptom formation in the neuroses. The clinical problem, from the beginning, was to discern hidden and distorted meaning, to decipher the "rebus" (cryptic message) of the dream. Patients were educated to the task of associating at length to various elements of the dream so that the underlying contents might be unearthed. This rather demanding procedure required patient and analyst to pursue the several lines of association as far as possible and ultimately to determine some nexus of meaning that appeared at the convergence of the different routes.

I have chosen to emphasize the challenge of classically conducted psychoanalytic dream interpretation because it is relevant to our understanding of the experiments described here. Attempts to demonstrate experimentally the continuity of fantasy *content* across waking and sleeping states founder on some serious methodological problems, particularly that of defining appropriate criteria for identifying specific contents. In this regard the skilled psychoanalyst is in a far more favorable situation as he regularly can observe in detail the workings of a single patient's fantasy life and frequently succeed in deciphering more specific content messages from obscure dream data. The researcher is generally dealing with large numbers of individuals with whom he has extremely limited contact, so that he cannot be aware of the highly personal referents of many of their dream symbols.

Edelson (1972), in a brilliant comparison of Freud's dream and Chomsky's language theories, has demonstrated the highly analogous nature of the two theoretical systems. Each theory must formulate the transformational rules of a symbol system in order to interpret "deeper" levels of meaning from a manifest symbolic production. Freud's identification of condensation, displacement, and symbolization marks only an excellent beginning of this task. With our knowledge of the dream "language" still incomplete, with its transformational rules uncertain, with vast individual differences in symbolization the rule in fantasy, we cannot expect our experimental studies readily to discern such continuities of content as may exist.

Klinger (1971) suggests that fantasy life, waking and sleeping, is predominantly expressive of "current concerns." This point of view has the advantage of parsimony and is readily supported by clinical observations. The dreams reported by patients seem mostly to deal with their life situations. This includes dreams expressive of the transference experience, a particularly valent concern of psychoanalytic patients. Associating to their dreams may lead patients to a more profound understanding of the psychodynamic basis of their current concerns. This procedure, however, need not be seen as significantly different from the analytic approach to other than dream data. This is, manifest content (e.g., daydreams, overt behaviors) is examined along with associative links in a search for latent meanings that intersect a number of apparently disconnected phenomena is such a way as to seem illuminating or insightful. From this point of view the obscure nature of the manifest content of dreams may help or hinder the search for latent meaning. The very obscurity of the material insures that any motivated efforts to avoid (defend against, resist) particular classes of meanings are unlikely to succeed. Therapist and patient may then "sneak up" on such meanings by a very circuitous path. On the other hand, the same obscurity of content may frustrate the best efforts of patient and therapist to make sense of the dream.

If current concerns indeed comprise the major content of all fantasy productions, what of "infantile wishes" (Freud, 1900) or "deep structures" (Edelson, 1972)? The point of view expressed here in no way contradicts the significance of profound latent meanings to dream content. It does, however, suggest that these are specific (and particularly intriguing) instances of a more general rule, and that comparable latent meanings may emerge from all sorts of data. The extra "depth" and value accorded insight gleaned from dreams may be partly an artifact of the strenuous intellectual effort required to "dig it up."

Some of Freud's comments with regard to the continuity of waking and sleeping fantasy seem particularly relevant here:

> At bottom, dreams are nothing other than a particular form of thinking, made possible by the conditions of the state of sleep. It is the dream-work which creates that form . . . the fact that dreams concern themselves with attempts at solving the problems by which our mental life is faced is no more strange than that our conscious waking life should do so. (Freud, 1925, footnote to *The Interpretation of Dreams*)
>
> I cannot pass over the relation of fantasies to dreams. Our nocturnal dreams are nothing but such fantasies, as we can make clear by interpreting them. Language, in its unrivaled wisdom, long ago decided the question of the essential nature of dreams by giving the name of "daydreams" to the airy creations of fantasy. (Freud, 1908)

The experimental studies presented thus far indicate that certain structural parameters of fantasy are continuous through waking and sleeping, in particular, bizarreness, level of anxiety, and affective disposition. Continuities of content seem likely, particularly around issues of current concern, but the rules of expression in dreams are sufficiently unclear and the choice of symbols sufficiently individual to make this issue difficult to prove. At this point it will be helpful to broaden the scope of our discussion to include yet another aspect of fantasy: the hallucination.

2.3. Dreams, Daydreams, and Hallucinations

Striking similarities have long been observed between dreams and psychotic experiences, leading to the conception of hallucinatory psychosis as a "waking dream." Persecutory nightmares with their vivid, bizarre, and fearsome images certainly remind us of the waking experiences of some paranoid schizophrenic patients. Freud (1915) noted the resemblance of paranoid projection to the mechanisms of the dreamwork; Sullivan (1962) was particularly struck by the nightmarelike quality of schizophrenic experience. With the arrival of experimental sleep studies using EEG-methodology, it was inevitable that investigators should wish to elucidate and document the relation between the vivid dream experiences of the REM-state and the hallucinatory experiences of the psychotic state. Early research efforts testing the simple hypothesis that in psychosis the REM-state "leaks" into the waking state found this to be an inadequate explanatory model. Moving beyond "REM-leak" theory, it now seems more profitable to pursue the relationship between hallucinatory experiences in sleep and waking in terms of transformations of a fantasy continuum under differing physiological and stimulus conditions. That is, one can study the vicissitudes of imagic thought as it appears in dreams, daydreams, and hallucinations. The following collaborative studies represent our early efforts in this direction.

In studies conducted with Jerome L. Singer, the symptom patterns of newly admitted psychiatric patients were compared with their responses to questionnaires about daydreaming styles. One hundred and thirteen male patients were rated by interviewers for the presence and severity of hallucinations, delusions, anxiety, depression, and other symptoms. When a symptom cluster including auditory and visual hallucinations, delusions, and bizarre behavior was defined to yield an overall score for psychosis, it was found that patients with psychotic symptomatology could not be distinguished from others on the basis of daydream style. This finding held up, with one exception, when data on daydreaming was collected immediately following a series of introspective exercises rather than via retrospective questionnaires. The singular exception to this result was that psychotic patients reported a significantly greater incidence of fantasy "blocking" during introspective exercises, reporting either a lack of fantasy experience or nearly total lack of recall. A related finding was that psychiatric patients displayed significantly lower scores on the Visual Imagery in Daydreams subscale of the IPI than a comparison group of college students. These data are particularly interesting in view of the lingering popular conception of psychiatric patients, particularly psychotics, as persons who are lost in a world of vivid fantasy. Failure to unearth a psychotic pattern of daydreaming substantiates the view of daydreaming as a normal human process but leaves obscure the problem of hallucination. That is, it appears as if hallucinations in psychotics are neither "REM-leaks" nor particularly intense, vivid daydreams. A more complex model than these is required.

The final study to be described, conducted with Elizabeth Brett, provides one of the missing pieces for a more useful theoretical model. It focused on the vividness and controllability of volitional auditory imagery in hallucinatory and nonhallucinatory schizophrenic patients and in a comparison group of medical patients. Auditory rather than visual imagery was selected because of its clear predominance in the hallucinations of psychotic patients. Images of varying emotional content were elicited from sixty patients who subsequently rated their productions as to vividness and anxiety. A measure of controllability of auditory images was constructed based on the Gordon (1949) Scale.

Results indicated that when the content of imagery is ignored there are no differences as to vividness of auditory images among hallucinatory schizophrenics, nonhallucinatory schizophrenics, and medical patients. When dealing with emotional-interpersonal imagery, however, the hallucinatory schizophrenics produced significantly *less vivid* images in comparison to the other groups. Once again the simple enhancement-of-imagery model is shown to be insufficient in accounting for hallucinatory phenomena among schizophrenics. An additional result was that hallucinatory schizophrenics reported the least control over their affect-laden images.

There begins to emerge a picture of the hallucinatory schizophrenic as an individual whose basic image-forming and daydreaming apparatus is intact and functional regarding relatively neutral thought content but whose images and daydreams are severely interrupted by the introduction of emotionally valent content such that vividness and controllability are both markedly diminished. Hence a "discontinuous" model of the schizophrenic hallucination is suggested whereby the normal flow of imagery and fantasy is disrupted or blocked only to reappear in dissociated form as an hallucination. One important implication of this model is that the hallucination *per se* need not be considered a "defense" but rather *the inevitable return of the imagic flow following a defensive operation.* Of course, this does not rule out the possibility that the content of the hallucination is somehow defensively distorted from its origins in imagery and daydreams but the fact of having an hallucination need not be seen as a defense.

Why must the imagic flow return? This is an important and complex question regarding the basic fabric of consciousness. It seems likely that the stream of imagic thought provides a type of nonsequential information processing that is essential to human functioning. The imagic mode operates in a synthetic manner, integrating inputs from the different sensory modalities and from internal channels simultaneously. It enables us to express and retain meanings in terms of overall patterns of relations rather than separate elements. Like the "picture worth a thousand words" it carries a considerable amount of condensed information that can be rendered available in an instant, yet it far transcends any picture in its ability to represent auditory, visual, tactile, gustatory, and other stimuli simultaneously. The imagic mode is, in short, the most likely source of those relatively stable mental representations of ourselves and our complex environments that enable us to navigate our everyday lives. The stream of images during sleep probably represents the continuous processing of incoming and recent information into the more enduring mental schemata. We know that when the particularly vivid dream imagery of REM sleep is interrupted or inhibited by experimental intervention it will "rebound" as if "catching up." Perhaps the return of blocked imagic thought via hallucination is an analogous rebound effect based on some continuous pressure within the psycho-physiologic organization to produce the imagic flow of thought. The notion that imagic thought is an essential and continuous aspect of human data processing is congruent with the views of Singer (1966, 1975) on daydreaming, West (1975) on hallucination, Horowitz (1970) on imagery, and Ornstein (1972) on the differential functions of the two hemispheres of the brain.

3. Conclusions

The vicissitudes of fantasy have here been explored through the study of dreams, daydreams, imagery, and hallucinations. Results of these several experiments indicate that we are looking at related aspects of an underlying process whose formative and transformative rules are not yet completely understood. A holistic view is suggested in which fantasy of all kinds is intimately though complexly related to one's immediate "state of being," causing it and being caused by it, expressing it in a uniquely human form, and frequently transposing its expression in mysterious ways with results both wonderful and terrifying.

References

Adey, W. R., Kado, R. T., and Rhodes, J. M. Sleep: cortical and subcortical recordings in the chimpanzee. *Science,* 1963, *141,* 932–933.

Beck, A. T. *Depression: Causes and treatment.* Philadelphia: University of Pennsylvania Press, 1967.

Ben-Horin, P. *The manifestation of some basic personality dimensions in wakefulness, fantasy and dreams.* Unpublished doctoral dissertation, Univ. of Chicago, 1967.

Brett, E. A., and Starker, S. Auditory imagery and hallucinations. *Journal of Nervous and Mental Disease*, 1977, *164(6)*, 394-400.

Cartwright, R. D. Dreams as compared to other forms and fantasy. In M. Kramer and R. Whitman (Eds.), *Dream psychology and the new biology and dreaming*. Springfield, Illinois: Charles C Thomas, 1969.

Eagle, C. *An investigation of individual consistencies in the manifestations of primary process*. Unpublished doctoral dissertation, New York University, 1964.

Edelson, M. Language and dreams: the interpretation of dreams revisited. *Psychoanalytic Study of the Child*, 1972, *27*, 203-282.

Feshbach, S. Personal communication cited in Beck, A. T. *Depression: causes and treatment*. Philadelphia: University of Pennsylvania Press, 1967.

Foulkes, D. and Fleisher, S. Mental activity in relaxed wakefulness. *Journal of Abnormal Psychology*, 1975, *84*, 66-75.

Foulkes, D., and Rechtschaffen, A. Presleep determinants of dream content: Effects of two films. *Perceptual and Motor Skills*, 1964, *19*, 983-1005.

Freud, S. The relation of the poet to day-dreaming (1908). In *Collected papers*. Vol. 4. London: Hogarth, 1953.

Freud, S. A metapsychological supplement to the theory of dreams (1915). In J. Strechey (Ed.), *Standard edition of the Complete Psychological Works of Sigmond Freud*. Vol. 14. London: Hogarth, 1958.

Freud, S. *The interpretation of dreams* (1900). New York: Wiley, 1961.

Goldberger, L., and Holt, R. R. Experimental interference with reality contact: Individual differences. In P. Soloman (Ed.), *Sensory Deprivation*. Cambridge, Mass. Harvard University Press, 1961.

Gordon, H. L. A comparative study of dreams and responses to the Thematic Apperception Test. *Journal of Personality*, 1953, *22*, 234-253.

Heron, W. Cognitive and physiological effects of perceptual isolation. In P. Soloman (Ed.), *Sensory deprivation*. Cambridge, Mass. Harvard University Press, 1961.

Horowitz, M. J. *Image formation and cognition*. New York: Appleton-Century-Crofts, 1970.

Isaacs, D. *Daydreaming and mind-wandering: A construct validation*. Unpublished doctoral dissertation, City University of New York, 1975.

Klinger, E. *Structure and functions of fantasy*. New York: Wiley, 1971.

Kramer, M., Whitman, R. M., Baldridge, B., and Lansky, L. Depression: Dreams and defenses. *American Journal of Psychiatry*, 1965, *122*, 411-419.

Langs, R. J. Manifest dreams from three clinical groups. *Archives of General Psychiatry*, 1966, *14*, 634-643.

Ornstein, R. *The psychology of consciousness*. New York: The Viking Press, 1972.

Rosner, B. S., Goff, W. R., and Allison, T. Cerebral electrical responses to external stimuli. In G. H. Glasser (Ed.), *EEG and behavior*. New York: Basic Books, 1963.

Sarason, S. B. Dreams and thematic apperception test stories. *Journal of Abnormal and Social Psychology*, 1944, *39*, 486-492.

Schultz, D. Fantasy stimulation in depression: *Direct intervention and correlational studies*. Unpublished doctoral dissertation, Yale University, 1976.

Shulman, H. S. *Congruences of personality expression in self-conceptions, the Thematic Apperception Test, and dreams*. Unpublished doctoral dissertation, Western Reserve University, 1955.

Singer, J. L. *Daydreaming*. New york: Random House, 1966.

Singer, J. L. *The inner world of daydreaming*. New York: Harper & Row, 1975.

Singer, J. L., and Antrobus, J. A. A factor analytic study of daydreaming and conceptually related cognitive and personality variables. *Perceptual and Motor Skills,* 1963, *17,* 187-209.

Singer, J. L., and Antrobus, J. A. Daydreaming, imaginal processes and personality: A normative study. In P. Sheehan (Ed.), *The nature and function of imagery.* New York: Academic Press, 1972.

Starker, S. Autokinesis and attention distribution. *Perceptual and Motor Skills,* 1972, *34,* 743-749.

Starker, S. Aspects of inner experience: Autokinesis daydreaming, dream recall and cognitive style. *Perceptual and Motor Skills,* 1973, *36,* 663-673.

Starker, S. Daydreaming styles and nocturnal dreaming. *Journal of Abnormal Psychology,* 1974a, *83,* 52-55.

Starker, S. Two modes and visual imagery. *Perceptual and Motor Skills,* 1974b, *38,* 649-650.

Starker, S. Effects of hypnotic induction upon visual imagery. *Journal of Nerves and Mental Disease,* 1974c, *159,* 433-437.

Starker, S. Daydreaming styles and nocturnal dreaming: Further observations. *Perceptual and Motor Skills,* 1977, *45,* 411-418.

Starker, S., and Goodenough, D. R. Effects of sleep state and method of awakening upon Thematic Apperception Test productions at arousal. *Journal of Nervous and Mental Disease,* 1970, *150,* 188-194.

Starker, S., and Hasenfeld, R. Daydream styles and sleep disturbance. *Journal of Nervous and Mental Disease,* 1976, *163(6),* 391-400.

Starker, S., and Singer, J. L. Daydreaming and symptom patterns of psychiatric patients: A factor analytic study. *Journal of Abnormal Psychology,* 1975a, *84,* 566-570.

Starker, S., and Singer, J. L. Daydream patterns and self awareness in psychiatric patients. *Journal of Nervous and Mental Disease,* 1975b, *161,* 313-317.

Starker, S., and Starker, J. E. The terrifying world of children's dreams. *Marriage and Family Living,* 1976, *58,* 13-15.

Sullivan, H. S. *Schizophrenia as a human process.* New York: Norton, 1962.

Tart, C. T. *States of consciousness.* New York: E. P. Dutton, 1975.

Von Bertalanffy, L. *General system theory.* New York: Braziller, 1968.

West, L. J. A clinical and theoretical overview of hallucinatory phenomena. In *Hallucinations: behavior, experience and theory.* New York: John Wiley & Sons, 1975.

11

A Biologic Rhythm in Waking Fantasy

Daniel F. Kripke and David Sonnenschein

1. Introduction

One of Freud's early ideas was that the mental processes made vivid in dreaming have an influence on everyday waking thoughts and behavior. A problem with this concept has been the difficulty in measuring and confirming the action of any psychic agencies that Freud postulated, such as the unconscious, the libido, or the id.

The discovery of the rapid eye movement sleep state constituted an important advance, for rapid eye movement sleep seems to be a functional state of the brain that is an objective correlate of dreaming. Although the correspondence between the rapid eye movement sleep state and dreaming is statistical rather than exact (Hartmann, 1970), there is evidence relating individual eye movements to the scenario elements of dream stories (Roffwarg, Dement, Muzio, and Fisher, 1962). Since the rapid eye movement sleep state can be measured with electronic instruments and quantified, its discovery suggests an objective route to measuring dreamlike processes in waking subjects.

Several aspects of Freudian theory have been confirmed. For example, it has been demonstrated that the average adult dreams about 80 to 100 min each night, although most dreams are forgotten. It has also been shown that interference with the REM state is often followed by a rebound increase in the duration of Stage REM on

Daniel F. Kripke and David Sonnenschein • San Diego Veterans Administration Hospital; and Department of Psychiatry, University of California, San Diego, California. Mr. Sam Messin and Mr. Grant Wyborney participated in this study, which was partially supported by the Medical Research Service of the Veterans Administration and by Grant No. 1-KO2-MH00117-01 from the National Institute of Mental Health.

subsequent nights (Dement, Henry, Cohen, and Ferguson, 1967). Neurophysiologic explorations of the mechanisms and adaptive functions of Stage REM are not yet complete, but have tended to support the notion that Stage REM is a neuronal consummatory response resulting from some neurophysiologic or neurohumoral drive mechanism (Moruzzi, 1969). These concepts seem consistent with a drive or wish fulfillment model of dreaming, as well as the related concept that a dream or fantasied experience within the central nervous system might substitute for the behavioral consummation of a drive. Unfortunately, attempts to relate the minutes of Stage REM sleep to specific behavioral phenomena have been generally unrewarding. It is becoming clear that the duration of REM sleep is not in itself crucial to waking behavior, and that Stage REM in itself is not a "psychic agency" profoundly influencing waking life.

The quantitative relationship between waking psychological function and the REM state might be poor simply because functions occurring in the REM state also take place during wakefulness. This is equivalent to the idea that waking dreamlike processes as well as sleep dreams have influence. There is some physiologic basis for this. For example, the pontine-geniculate-occipital spike discharges characteristic of Stage REM may be recorded in nonREM sleep or during waking (Dement, Ferguson, Cohen, and Barchas, 1969). Genital arousal cycles normally associated with Stage REM persist during "REM deprivation" (Karacan, 1966). After Stage REM sleep has been interrupted, moreover, the rebound increase in subsequent Stage REM may be reduced if subjects experience waking fantasy (Cartwright and Monroe, 1968). Possibly, waking fantasies provide a consummatory release that reduces the same neuronal drive reduced by Stage REM. Evidence that consummatory functions like those of Stage REM may occur in waking life leads to a hypothesis that a physiologic state or physiologic functions like those of Stage REM should be identifiable in the waking state. The difficulty in confirming this hypothesis lies in showing that some waking physiologic process may be functionally equivalent to Stage REM when it cannot be identical.

It has often been observed that Stage REM (and dreaming) appear cyclically about every 90 to 100 min during normal adult sleep, expressing some form of oscillatory system. Although this oscillatory process is by no means as regular as circadian or even menstrual biologic rhythms, occurrences of Stage REM are certainly temporally nonrandom and to a considerable extent, statistically predictable (Globus, 1970; Kripke, 1974). Patterns of Stage REM occurrence resemble the discharge phase of a relaxation oscillator, a type of oscillator that is characteristically less regular than linear oscillatory systems

(Wever, 1965). One theory is that the REM–nonREM oscillator is composed of two groups of interacting pontine neurons (Hobson, McCarley, and Wyzinski, 1975). Other theories involve neurohumoral discharge. Such an oscillatory pattern is also consistent with a drive-release mechanism. Whatever its concrete nature, the REM state may be seen as one functional part of a broader oscillatory process. Since the cyclicity of Stage REM is less perturbable and better correlated with brain weight and life span than its measured duration (Hartmann, 1968; Zepelin and Rechtschaffen, 1974), this underlying oscillatory discharge process may be more functionally significant than the Stage REM state in itself.

If dreamlike processes are active in waking mentation, and given data that dreaming and Stage REM during sleep are part of an oscillatory system, once can predict there should be oscillations in mental function and its objective correlates during waking experience. Specifically, the intensity of fantasy in waking mentation might be oscillatory, if waking fantasy and dreams have similar underlying mechanisms. Although it may be farfetched to equate a brain oscillator system to a Freudian psychic agency, the limited and specific prediction that waking fantasy is cyclic is experimentally testable and can serve to support the broader hypothesis.

In this report, we present specific experimental observations of cyclicity in both waking mental functions and their physiologic correlates. Two experiments were performed. In the first experiment, rigidly controlled laboratory isolation was used to exclude any conceivable environmental biases. In the second experiment, no environmental controls were utilized, and the very presence of the experimenters was excluded, to see if the initial results might be generalizable to everyday experience.

2. Experiment 1

2.1. Method

2.1.1. Subjects. Eleven young adults were selected from a larger group of volunteers, because each expressed a willingness to report daydreams. Each gave written informed consent. Each was found healthy in the course of a psychiatric interview and a psychological screening examination (Minnesota Multiphasic Personality Inventory). Subjects were informed that the experimenters wished to relate EEG patterns to fantasy, but none were given any idea that the recordings would be analyzed for cycles.

2.1.2. Protocol. After breakfast, each subject was fitted with skin electrodes for recording a bipolar parieto-occipital EEG, horizontal eye movements, and a chin electromyogram. A BioSentry FM/FM multiplex telemetry transmitter was fixed to the scalp with collodion. Each subject then entered a well-lighted, plainly decorated 27 m³ room containing a bed and a reclining chair. Subjects were not permitted any timepiece, books, amusements, food, or water. They spent 10 hr in the chamber without communications from the outside. A masking noise obscured external sounds. Every 5 min, an alerting whistle was sounded until a button press was made. In part, this response was used to assure that subjects remained awake. The whistle also signaled subjects to write on a card a summary of what they had been thinking in the past 5 min, in order that their ongoing mental activity might be evaluated. Thus, one card was obtained each 5 min.

2.1.3. Physiologic Recording. EEG, eye movements, and chin EMG were recorded polygraphically. Each 20 sec of recording was scored separately for the seconds of EEG alpha activity and the seconds of rapid eye movement. Summations for each 5 min were then computed. Occasional high-frequency telemetry artifacts precluded systematic EMG scoring, although the EMG was useful in establishing that subjects remained awake.

2.1.4. Analyses. Several days after each experiment, each subject returned to the laboratory to review the cards reporting his mental content, which had been placed in random order. The subject ranked his cards on a fantasy scale that was defined as the following continuum:

1. Vivid dreamlike fantasies with bizarre or symbolic content and strong emotions such as wishes or fears.
2. Abstract and fanciful thinking, especially past or future.
3. Concrete, realistic, and present-time thinking or planning.
4. Awareness of present surroundings, thinking of what is happening, etc.
5. Present-time preceptual scanning and perceptual-motor activities.

An experimenter independently rerandomized and blindly reranked the same cards. Combined fantasy scores for each 5-min interval were computed as the mean of both rankings. In this manner, a relative measure of changes in fantasy over time was obtained.

Fantasy, alpha, and eye-movement scores each formed separate time series. The auto-correlation functions were computed for 18 lags (maximum lag = 90 min), and the hanned (smoothed) spectral transforms (variance spectra) were obtained (Jenkins and Watts, 1968). The variance spectrum partitions variability over time into several frequency components. If variability is random over time, the variance spectrum will be approximately flat; that is, variance will be equal among all frequencies. If there is a cyclic process in a time series, the spectrum will peak at the frequency of the cyclic process. Therefore, we prospectively predicted that fantasy variance would peak at 16 cycles/day (1 cycle per 72–120 min) if fantasy had a cycle similar to the REM–nonREM cycle.

Cross-correlation functions and cross-spectra were also computed between each pair of variables (Jenkins and Watts, 1968). These cross-spectra partitioned the covariance between two variables into several component frequencies, and the temporal relationships between peaks and troughs in two variables were expressed as phase-angle relationships. From the cross-spectra, coherence spectra were derived (Jenkins and Watts, 1968; Orr and Naitoh, 1976), which provide an estimate of the extent of covariation between two cyclic processes.

2.2. Results

All subjects reported occasional daydreams, characterized by vivid sensory imagery and bizarre, symbolic, or autistic content. Also common were memories of childhood, future plans, and vivid sexual fantasies. Subjects reported many thoughts concerning the experiment, but none hinted any awareness of our interest in rhythms. Retrospective interviews also confirmed that all subjects were blind to our hypothesis that daydreams are cyclic.

The fantasy scoring method was highly reliable. The mean Spearman Rank Order Correlation was 0.83 between fantasy rankings of subjects and experimenters. For each individual subject, this correlation exceeded 0.70 ($n = 120$, $p < .001$). In the mean fantasy variance spectrum for the 11 subjects (Fig. 1), the variance peak as predicted was at 16 cycles/day (1 cycle/90 min). Two contrasts were employed to examine if this variance peak could be a random result. First, variance at 16 cycles/day was compared with the mean variance at all other frequencies to see if the random expectation was exceeded, and second, variance at 16 cycles/day was compared with the mean variance at 8 and 24 cycles/day, to test whether the variance peaked at 16 cycles/day. In both contrasts, using either one-tailed t tests or the Wilcoxon Signed Rank test, the variance peak at 16 cycles/day was significant ($p < .01$). This indicates that there was a significant tendency for peaks and troughs in fantasy to occur about every 90 min. One-tailed tests were chosen prospectively because the experimental hypothesis could only be supported if the variance at 16 cycles/day were greater than random.

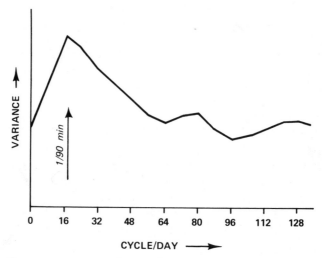

Figure 1: The mean spectrum derived from the 11 spectra of fantasy scores for laboratory subjects. Since fantasy was scored by a rank-ordering method, spectral variance was only a relative measure.

Due to telemetry problems, eye movement and alpha could only be scored for 8 subjects. Eye movement spectra peaked at 16 cycles/day, a peak that was highly significant by the first test ($p < .001$) but borderline by the second ($p < .06$). In the averaged spectra for alpha,

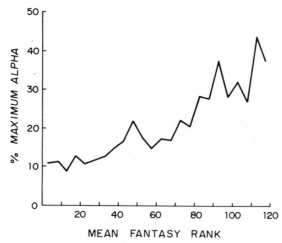

Figure 2: The mean relationship of fantasy to alpha scores expressed as a percentage of the maximal alpha of each subject.

the variance at 8 cycles/day exceeded the variance at 16 cycles/day; however, the variance at 16 cycles/day exceeded the mean of all other frequencies, that is, the random expectation ($p < .01$).

The most intense fantasy was associated with the most continuous alpha and the least rapid eye movement (Figs. 2 and 3). Fantasy and alpha were positively correlated (mean $r = 0.29$). Eye movement was negatively correlated with fantasy ($r = -.39$) and with alpha ($r = -.47$). These correlations were all significant ($p < .05$, $p < .002$, $p < .002$, respectively; two-tailed t tests of whether the mean value of r for the 8 subjects differed from zero). As might be anticipated from these correlations, the cross-spectra showed that at 16 cycles/day, fantasy was in-phase with alpha and roughly $180°$ out-of-phase with eye movement. Eye movement and alpha were $180°$ out-of-phase. The mean coherence spectra relating fantasy to either alpha or eye movement peaked at 16 cycles/day. This would suggest fantasy most closely covaried with alpha and eye movement at 16 cycles/day. The coherence of eye movement and alpha was slightly higher at the zero frequency (eg., the linear and circadian trends).

There were unusual small, rounded 0.2–0.5-sec excursions in some eye movement recordings during intense fantasies, but it was unclear whether these indicated eye movements, blinks, or perhaps orbicularis muscle contractions.

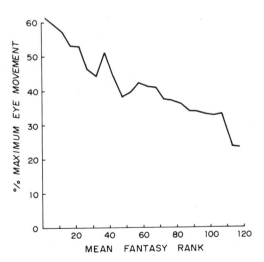

Figure 3: The mean relationship of fantasy to rapid eye movement scores, expressed as a percentage of the maximal score for each subject.

3. Experiment 2

3.1. Methods

To test if fantasy cycles were present in subjects who were not isolated, observations of fantasy were repeated in a new group of subjects who were studied in their habitual social environments.

Eight healthy young men and women, selected as in the first experiment, agreed to collect mental content reports throughout 12 hr of unrestricted daily activity. These subjects were instructed that we wished to measure how much daydreaming there was in ordinary life, but again, no mention of rhythms was made. Each subject carried a timer and a dictaphone that was used every 10 min to record ongoing mental activities. Later, these reports were transcribed and scored by subjects and investigators as in the first experiment. Physiologic recordings were not possible in unrestricted subjects.

3.2. Results

These subjects reported their ongoing thoughts during many and varied activities, such as working as a computer programmer, working as a hotel clerk, going to the beach, taking a shower, eating, watching television, etc. Fewer well-formed daydreams were reported than in the laboratory experiment, and the average interrater agreement was not quite so good (mean $r_S = 0.72$; minimum $r_S = 0.48$, $p < .001$).

The mean fantasy variance spectrum for these 8 subjects also peaked at 16 cycles/day. This peak was significant both contrasting 16 cycles/day with all frequencies ($p < .01$), and contrasting with 8 and 24 cycles/day ($p < .001$).

4. Discussion

In both the laboratory experiment and the field replication, the spectra for relative fantasy intensity peaked significantly at 16 cycles/day (1 cycle every 72–120 min), confirming the prediction that waking mental content is cyclic. Rhythmic environmental influences (apart from the 5-min whistle) were excluded from the laboratory study, while in the field, environmental influences were assumed to be random or unbiased, apart from a 10-min buzzer. Since about 90-min cycles were demonstrated in both settings, it is likely that these cycles were of endogenous biologic origin, and that they were expressions of an oscillation in brain functional state.

Even though we had intentionally selected volunteers who would be willing to report fantasies, and who were encouraged to do so, we were surprised how freely selected subjects could describe fantasies, and also, how reliably subjects and investigators could agree on the relative fantasy content of reported mental activities, using an unsophisticated scale, and rating blindly. We had excellent agreement with all subjects as to which mental content was relatively dreamlike. The validity of the fantasy scale as a gross indicator of brain functional state was confirmed by the significant and relatively linear associations among the mental content rankings and the alpha and eye movement scores (Figs. 2 and 3). The most intense fantasies were associated with about 4 times the alpha that was observed during the purest perceptual-motor states, but there was only 1/3 the rapid eye movement. Since statistically, 72–120-min cyclicity was better defined in fantasy than in eye movement or alpha, fantasy measurement seems to be a more favorable way of measuring the cyclic process than physiologic recording.

None of our subjects were aware of any rhythmic modulation in their mental functioning at the very moment they themselves were documenting their cycles in mental content. It is not obvious how so profound a modulation of experience might influence waking subjects without introspective recognition. Perhaps psychologic repression circumscribes our awareness of the daydreaming process, permitting us to recognize that daydreams occur without insight into their endogenous regulation. There is a similar circumscribed awareness of dream cycles, for even those subjects with excellent dream recall rarely report any sensation of periodicity in dreaming. Although suggestion may have influenced the overall quantities of fantasy observed, we are confident that suggestion did not produce the observed cyclicity, both because no awareness of the experimental predictions was expressed in the mental content recorded during the experiments, and because all subjects assured us that they had no idea we expected cyclicity when they were questioned after they had completed their participation.

The most intense daydreams probably occurred in an eyes-closed, drowsy state resembling hypnagogic revery. As in the hypnagogic state at sleep onset, there was very little rapid eye movement during the most intense fantasies, and muscle tone was generally maintained. Scrutiny of the recordings suggested that there might have been no rapid eye movement at all during episodes of intense fantasy, were the subjects not required to give button-press responses and write out their reports every 5 min. Thus, these results are consistent with the observation of Othmer, Hayden, and Segelbaum (1969) that rapid eye movement cycles continue during wakefulness, but our observations do not confirm the supposition that waking fantasies might be associated with rapid eye movement. To the contrary, we observed the most waking rapid eye movement during perceptual-motor activities. Because our observations do not support a notion that waking fantasy is physiologically identical to Stage REM, the findings do not argue that the "Stage REM cycle" is present in waking subjects. The oscillatory system observed must be more complex than the Stage REM phenomenon alone. _

We have conceptualized dreaming as a process or as a functional state of the brain, and we have hypothesized that some aspects of this process or functional state might occur cyclically during wakefulness as well as sleep. Whatever is being discharged during Stage REM and fantasy could be similar, be it conceptualized as neuronal or neurotransmitter discharge, ethologic consummatory response, or wish fulfillment. The demonstration that waking fantasy oscillates much like sleep dreaming tends to support the hypothesis that the underlying oscillatory processes are common, but it is not sufficient to prove commonality.

It seems there are actually numerous physiologic and behavioral functions that may be cyclic, for example, brain waves (Kripke, 1972), feeding behaviors (Friedman and Fisher, 1967; Lewis, Kripke, and Bowden, 1977), and hormonal release (Yen, Vandenberg, Tsai, and Parker, 1974; Lavie, Kripke, Parker, Huey, and Deftos, 1975). Some studies have suggested that the frequencies of these cycles may not be identical in wakefulness and sleep (Kripke, Halberg, Crowley, and Pegram, 1976). The spectral analyses reported here lacked sufficient resolution to detect any fine frequency variation, and higher resolution spectra would have been unreliable with our limited number of subjects. Hiatt and Kripke (1975) reported that there is a regular 100-min cycle of stomach contractions in waking subjects, but in results only published in abstract, Hiatt, Kripke, and Lavie (1975) found that stomach contraction cycles are unrelated to fantasy cycles, which could also be described in their subjects. They also found that during sleep, stomach contraction cycles are unrelated to Stage REM cycles. There seems to be more than one about 100-min oscillator in the human body, and thus, we cannot assume that the oscillator that produces a waking fantasy cycle is the same as that which causes periodicity in Stage REM.

To be certain that the cycles in waking fantasy and sleep dreams have a common mechanism, it might be necessary to show that their concrete biologic mechanisms are identical. Neurophysiologic research has not yet firmly established the concrete mechanisms of the REM-nonREM cycle, but very encouraging progress is being made. If similar techniques could be applied to the cycle of waking fantasy, we may eventually achieve a fully scientific approach to the role of dreamlike processes in waking life.

Whatever the physiologic origin of fantasy cycles, they are fascinating phenomena that may have practical import. Perhaps creative and imaginative work is modulated cyclically during the artist's day. Perhaps the fantasies of the neurotic and even their expression on the analytic couch are governed by an internal biologic regulator. Cyclic fantasies might also intrude upon the concentration of radar operators and long-distance drivers, and endogenous cycles might be one element controlling when failures of attention or performance take place. Although our crude fantasy rating method seemed to tap a cyclic mental dimension rather effectively, and was well-correlated with physiologic indices, much more work is needed to describe the specific psychologic alterations expressed in fantasy cycles, and their effects on everyday life.

References

Cartwright, R. D., and Monroe, L. J. Relation of dreaming and REM sleep: The effects of REM deprivation under two conditions. *Journal of Personality and Social Psychiatry*, 1968, *10*, 69–74.

Dement, W., Henry, P., Cohen, H., and Ferguson, J. Studies on the effect of REM deprivation in humans and animals. In Kety, S. S., Evarts, E. V., and Williams, H. L. (Eds.), *Sleep and altered states of consciousness*. Baltimore: Williams and Wilkins, 1967, 456–468.

Dement, W., Ferguson, J., Cohen, H., and Barchas, J. Nonchemical methods and data using a biochemical model: The REM quanta. In Mandell, A. J., and Mandell, M. P. (Eds.) *Psychochemical research in man*. New York: Academic Press, 1969, 275–325.

Friedman, S., and Fisher, C. On the presence of a rhythmic, diurnal, oral instinctual drive cycle in man: A preliminary report. *Journal of the American Psychoanalytic Association*, 1967, *15*, 317–343.

Globus, G. C. Rhythmic functions during sleep. In Hartmann, E. (Ed.) *Sleep and dreaming*. Boston: Little, Brown, and Company, 1970, 15–21.

Hartmann, E. The 90-minute sleep-dream cycle. *Archives of General Psychiatry*, 1968, *18*, 280–286.

Hartmann, E. Sleep and dreaming. Boston: Little, Brown, and Company, 1970, 405–422.

Hiatt, J. F., and Kripke, D. F. Ultradian rhythms in waking gastric activity. *Psychosomatic Medicine*, 1975, *37*, 320–325.

Hiatt, J. F., Kripke, D. F., and Lavie, P. Relationships among psychophysiologic ultradian rhythms. *Chronobiologia Suppl. 1*, 1975, *30*.

Hobson, J. A., McCarley, R. W., and Wyzinski, P. W. Sleep cycle oscillations: reciprocal discharge by two brainstem neuronal groups. *Science*, 1975, *189*, 55–58.

Jenkins, G. M., and Watts, D. C. *Spectral analysis and its applications*. New York: Holden-Day, 1968.

Karacan, I. The developmental aspect and the effect of certain clinical conditions upon penile erection during sleep. *Proceedings of the Fourth World Congress of Psychiatry: Excerpta Medica International Congress Series,* 1966, No. 150: 2356-59.

Kripke, D. F. An ultradian biological rhythm associated with perceptual deprivation and REM sleep. *Psychosomatic Medicine,* 1972, *34,* 221-234.

Kripke, D. F. Ultradian rhythms in sleep and wakefulness. In Weitzman, E. D. (Ed.), *Advances in sleep research.* Vol. I. New York: Spectrum, 1974, 305-325.

Kripke, D. F., Halberg, F., Crowley, T. J., and Pegram, V. Ultradian spectra in monkeys. *International Journal Chronobiology,* 1976, *3,* 193-204.

Lavie, P., Kripke, D. F., Parker, D., Huey, L., and Deftos, L. Pulsatile patterns of parathyroid hormone and plasma calcium during sleep. *Sleep Research,* 1975, *4,* 283.

Lewis, B. D., Kripke, D. F., and Bowden, D. M. Ultradian rhythms in hand-mouth behavior of the rhesus monkey. *Physiology and Behavior,* 1977, *18,* 283-286.

Moruzzi, G. Sleep and instinctual behavior. *Archives Italiennes de Biologie,* 1969, *108,* 175-216.

Orr, W. C., and Naitoh, P. The coherence spectrum: An extension of correlation analysis with applications to chronobiology. *International Journal of Chronobiology,* 1976, *3,* 171-192.

Othmer, E., Hayden, M. P., and Segelbaum, R. Encephalic cycles during sleep and wakefulness in humans: A 24-hour pattern. *Science,* 1969, *164,* 447-449.

Roffwarg, H. P., Dement, W. C. Muzio, J. N., and Fisher, C. Dream imagery: Relationship to rapid eye movements of sleep. *Archives of General Psychiatry* (Chicago), 1962, *7,* 235-258.

Wever, R. Pendulum versus relaxation oscillation. In Ascoff, J. (Ed.), *Circadian clocks.* Amsterdam: North Holland Publishing, 1965, 75-83.

Yen, S. S. C., Vandenberg, G., Tsai, C. C., and Parker, D. C. Ultradian fluctuations of gonadotropins. In Ferin, M., *et al.* (Eds.), *Biorhythms and human reproduction.* New York: Wiley & Sons, 1974, 203-218.

Zepelin, H., and Rechtschaffen, A. Mammalian sleep, longevity, and energy metabolism. *Brain Behavior and Evolution,* 1974, *10,* 425-470.

PART IV

Implications and Broader Perspectives

12

Attention and the Holistic Approach to Behavior

Mihaly Csikszentmihalyi

1. The Need for a New Approach

The fate of "consciousness" as a scientific concept is one of the most ironic paradoxes in the history of psychology. Once the central issue, the very essence of what psychology was all about, it is nowadays a peripheral concern, an antiquated idea about as useful as ether and phlogiston are to physicists. According to Murphy and Kovach (1972, p. 51), consciousness "has been a storm center in psychology for a century. Some regard it as an unfortunate and superfluous assumption. . . . Others regard consciousness as only one of many expressions of psychological reality; indeed many psychologists think that the recognition of a psychological realm far greater than the conscious realm is the great emancipating principle of all modern psychology ."

This quote hints at the two currents of thought that have displaced consciousness from center stage: behaviorism on the one hand, and psychoanalytic depth psychology on the other. It is not my intention to delve into the history of ideas to retrace the trajectory of the fall of consciousness. But a brief glimpse may be necessary to understand what went wrong, so the future study of consciousness may avoid past mistakes and be off to a fresh start.

Mihaly Csikszentmihalyi • Department of Human Development, University of Chicago, Chicago, Illinois. Research reported in this chapter was funded by PHS Grants RO1 HM 22883-01, 02, 03, 04 and by NHI Grant PO1 AG 00123-01.

From the very beginnings of psychological investigation, consciousness fell prey to the reductionistic tendency of the fledgling discipline aspiring to scientific rigor. The structuralists in the late nineteenth century had tried to analyze states of consciousness into elements of cortical structure. When this began to appear like an arid exercise, the functionalists substituted a supposedly more dynamic analysis that equated consciousness with the passage of neural excitation through sensory, cortical, and motor centers (Munsterberg, 1900; Washburn, 1908). Common to both approaches, and to contemporary studies based on them, is the assumption that to understand consciousness means to explain what it is made of, where it is located, and what makes it work. These are surely legitimate questions, of deep scientific interest. But neither the early classic studies, nor the current physiological research, deal with the phenomenon of consciousness directly, as an experiential given. They assume that we already know what there is to know about consciousness at the manifest level, and try to unravel its neurophysiological roots.

The dire epistemological state to which consciousness fell is probably due to this impatience of getting at "hard" evidence before enough was known about the thing that the evidence was supposed to explain. The whole point about consciousness is that it *is* conscious; that is what makes it interesting in the first place. Before there had been a chance to understand what it means to be conscious, that question was buried under reams of experimental data about sensory-motor pathways, and later under tons of reports documenting the wondrous ways of the unconscious.

A new approach to the study of consciousness may start from the simple assumption that the individual person, as an autonomous goal-directed system, manifests certain properties that are best understood in terms of total systemic functioning, rather than in terms of systems of lower levels of complexity (Campbell, 1973). There is no need here to get involved in the ideological dispute concerning reductionism. All that is being claimed is that processes that involve the total individual *as a system* are most usefully understood in a holistic context.

Consciousness is presumably such a process. The ability to reflect on one's inner states is a product of the total system in that phylogenetically it appears to have arisen only after other psychological functions like memory or reasoning were established (Csikszentmihalyi, 1970; Jaynes, 1976). More to the point, it is a total systemic process because however one defines consciousness, the definition must include a monitoring of inner states as well as outer environmental conditions, and thus represents the most complex and integrated form of information processing of which men are capable.

Consciousness broken up into its physiological components becomes meaningless at the level it is most interesting: the level of integrated human action and experience.

Psychology without a lively theory of consciousness is a rather lifeless discipline. To develop such a theory, however, much more thought and observation must be devoted to the study of consciousness at the holistic level. And the study must avoid the twin dangers of reductionism on the one hand, and introspective speculation on the other. Thus far the study of consciousness has tended to oscillate between the two poles of that dialectic. Is the time ripe for a viable synthesis? The most appropriate answer seems to be one of cautious optimism. The rest of this paper will try to point out some conceptual and empirical directions that a holistic study of consciousness may take, or is indeed already taking.·

The main assumption we shall be making is that attention is a form of psychic energy needed to control the stream of consciousness, and that attention is a limited psychic resource. From this assumption it follows that what one can experience and what one can do is limited by the scarcity of this resource. How attention is allocated determines the shape and content of one's life. Social systems, through the process of socialization, compete with the individual for the structuring of his attention. Tensions between various demands and the limited attention available is seen as the fundamental issue from which many of the most important problems in the behavioral sciences arise. If this is true, then attention has the potential of becoming a central concept in the social sciences because it provides a common denominator for resolving concurrently problems that up to now have been considered irreconcilable. Seemingly disparate issues in psychology, sociology, and economics become related once we use attention as the common variable underlying each of them. The purpose of this paper is to suggest directions that a synthesis based on the concept of attention may take.

2.   Consciousness and Attention

Attention is the process that regulates states of consciousness by admitting or denying admission to various contents into consciousness. Ideas, feelings, wishes, or sensations can appear in consciousness and therefore become real to the person only when attention is turned to them. Many claims have been made for the primacy of attention as a crucial psychological process. For instance, William

James had this to say:

> But the moment one thinks of the matter, one sees how false a notion
> of experience that is which would make it tantamount to the mere presence
> to the senses of an outward order. Millions of items in the outward order
> are present to my senses which never properly enter into my experience.
> Why? Because they have no *interest* for me. *My experience is what I agree to*
> *attend to.* Only those items which I *notice* shape my mind — without
> selective interest, experience is utter chaos. (James, 1890, p. 402)

The same point was made by Collingwood:

> With the entry of consciousness into experience, a new principle has
> established itself. Attention is focused upon one thing to the exclusion of
> the rest. The mere fact that something is present to sense does not give it a
> claim to attention. . . . Consciousness is absolutely autonomous: its deci-
> sion alone determines whether a given sensum or emotion shall be
> attended to or not. A conscious being is not thereby free to decide what
> feeling he shall have; but he is free to decide what feeling he shall place in
> the focus of his consciousness. (Collingwood, 1938, p. 207)

It was precisely the freedom and autonomy of consciousness that
James, Collingwood, Dewey (1934), and others stressed that was to be
denied by Freud. Although Freud (1900, p. 132) recognized "mobile
attention" as the psychical energy required to make thoughts and
sensations conscious, his whole life work was devoted to showing that
attention is not controlled by consciousness, and that mental processes
could go on below the threshold of consciousness. "The most complicated achievements of thought," he wrote (Freud, 1900, p. 632), "are
possible without the assistance of consciousness. . . . The train of
thought . . . can continue to spin itself out without attention being
turned to it again."

Demonstrating the power of the unconscious has been an essential step toward understanding behavior. It is unfortunate, however,
that further study of attention as the basic form of psychical energy,
clearly stated in Freud's own work, was soon and permanently
overshadowed by fascination with unconscious processes. "Psychical
energy" became identified with the libido. As such the concept fell
into disrepute: the notion that a finite amount of libidinal energy is
responsible for psychic processes was attributed to Freud's nineteenth-century "hydraulic" view of physics. Cybernetics had shown
that information processing does not depend directly on energy input;
hence, the idea of a reservoir of psychic energy that accounted
for psychic function and malfunction was widely rejected as being
antiquated.

Yet, if one identifies psychic energy with attention instead of
libido, as Freud himself did in his early writings, the objection that

the concept is an outdated analogy from mechanistic physics ceases to apply. If experimental research on attention has proven one thing, it is that attention is a finite resource (Binet, 1890; Bakan, 1966; Kahneman, 1973; Keele, 1973). Its intensity and inclusiveness have narrow limits. These limits are set by the relatively few bits of information that can be processed in consciousness at any one time. Each potential stimulus must be activated by the application of this limited resource if it is to become information available to consciousness. Allocation of attention is therefore a basic adaptive issue for any organism that depends on central information processing for its survival. What to pay attention to, how intensely and for how long, are choices that will determine the content of consciousness, and therefore the experiential information available to the organism. Thus, William James was right in claiming, *"My experience is what I agree to attend to. Only those items which I notice shape my mind."* The question, of course, is what determines one's agreement to attend to one stimulus rather than another, and hence the reasons for noticing one item instead of another.

Before considering such questions, it may be useful to consider more closely the phenomenology of attention. This can be done best by looking at mental processes that appear to be unaffected by attention. Dreams provide a good example of a mental process in which attention plays no part. We are conscious in dreams; that is, we experience emotions, visual images, and, to a certain extent, pursue logical thoughts. What is lacking, however, is the ability to choose among these elements of consciousness. I may dream of standing on a mountainside, and the picture that unfolds is as stunning as any I have seen when awake. The crucial difference is that I have no control over what I see: I cannot linger on a particularly pleasing view, or bring part of the landscape in clearer focus. The visual details pass through my consciousness at their own pace, and I never know what the next thing I "see" will be, or how long I will be allowed to look at it. A vista of startling beauty may open up in front of me, but no matter how much I try, the wish to keep it in my mind has absolutely no effect. What I see in a dream is determined by random (or unconsciously directed) associations among mental contents.

In dreams attention is paralyzed, unable to sort out and direct mental events; one experiences an uncontrolled drift in the stream of consciousness. By contrast it is easier to appreciate the "work" that attention accomplishes when it is able to function in the waking state. It channels the stream of consciousness; it gives the organism control over what information it may process.

It is interesting to note in this context that the paralysis of attention during sleep may not be an unalterable condition. There are apparently cultures in which either a few special persons (Castaneda, 1974) or the whole community (Stewart, 1972) are able to learn to control their dreams. This feat is said to require several years and great discipline. Those who achieve this form of control are held to gain extraordinary mental powers, which is not an entirely farfetched claim, considering the greatly increased power of shaping experience such a perfecting of attention would provide.

Other examples of conscious processes in which attention is impaired are clinical syndromes associated with schizophrenia and other mental disorders. In such states consciousness is flooded with an undifferentiated mass of incoming sensory data. Typical of such states are these accounts by patients: "Things just happen to me now, and I have no control over them. I don't seem to have the same say in things anymore. At times I can't even control what I think about"; or, "Things are coming in too fast. I lose my grip of it and get lost. I am attending to everything at once and as a result I do not really attend to anything" (McGhie and Chapman, 1961, pp. 109, 104).

The examples of what happens during dreams and pathological states suggests an answer to a vexing question, If attention controls consciousness, what controls attention itself? At the phenomenological level, the answer seems to be: consciousness. The argument is not circular, even though it seems to be. In dreams one is conscious of wishes or fears, and these direct one to actions or changes in consciousness. However, it is impossible to carry out these directions, because in sleep attention and consciousness are uncoupled. In waking life, the present content of consciousness initiates changes in its own state, which are carried out through the mediation of attention. Attention can be seen as the energy necessary to carry out the work of consciousness. One can conceive of consciousness as a cybernetic system that controls its own states through attention. Consciousness and attention appear as two closely linked systems, each controlling and being controlled by the other. The first contains information and provides direction, the second provides energy and new information by introducing unplanned variation into consciousness.

Let us assume that attention is indeed the central question of psychology. The point is, how can it be studied? What directions for research are possible? The directions I wish to explore are those in which attention is seen as a process that involves whole persons interacting in their usual environments. Most research on attention thus far has been conducted in laboratories, and its aim has been to establish the neurological mechanisms by which attention functions.

Thus, for instance, the work of Broadbent (1954, 1958) on the characteristics of stimuli that allow them to be filtered through attention into the cortical centers, or that of Hernandez-Peon (1964) on the arousal and stimulus-selection functions of attention in the reticular formation, focus on the physiological correlates of a physiologically established attentional process. This type of research is essential to the understanding of attention, but is not the only useful paradigm available.

To clarify the difference between the approach proposed here and the experimental approach, an analogy drawn from the biological sciences might help. There are essentially two ways biologists study animal species. One is by describing the anatomy, embryology, or biochemistry of its members, that is, by analyzing the animal into its components. The other approach consists in describing the animal's behavior in its natural habitat; this is the ethological approach that looks at the animal as a whole system interacting with other systems in its environment. Both approaches are legitimate and necessary to understand what an animal is and what it does. The situation is similar with respect to attention; one can study either the physiological processes that determine it, or one can study the phenomenon as a whole within a systemic context. We shall try to explore this latter course, in which attention is viewed as an adaptive tool of persons interacting in their environment.

When considered from this viewpoint, the empirical literature on attention is rather meager. A representative exception is the recent work of Klinger, Barta, and Mahoney (1976). Although they measure attention with rigorous laboratory techniques, they are interested in the relationship between persons' salient existential concerns and their allocation of attention, on the grounds that "psychological adaptation is a matter of responding appropriately to cues that bear on survival."

The purpose of this essay, however, is not that of providing a systematic review of the literature. (This can be found, in addition to sources cited earlier, in the following classic and recent works: Muller, 1873; Exner, 1894; Pillsbury, 1908; Titchener, 1908; Norman, 1969; Mostofsky, 1970). We shall develop instead a few of the implications of the perspective on attention just described and provide whenever possible hints on the operational means by which the questions raised could be answered.

Attention will be viewed as the common denominator in a variety of seemingly unrelated phenomena ranging from enjoyment, creative social contribution, alienation, and psychopathology to the issues of socialization, the maintenance of social structure, and the equilibrium between individual needs and the requirements of social systems. In such a short space it is obviously impossible to develop these relationships in any detail. We hope, however, to at least suggest the connecting links that bring together these disparate problems when they are viewed as manifestations of the same process of psychic energy exchange, all depending on the management of a limited supply of attention.

3. Attention and Optimal Functioning

It seems that every time people enjoy what they are doing, or in any way transcend ordinary states of existence, they report specific changes in attentional processes. To be conscious of pleasurable experiences one must narrow the focus of attention exclusively on the stimuli involved. What we usually call "concentration" is this intensely focused attention on a narrow range of stimuli. It is a prerequisite for making love or listening to music, for playing tennis, or working at the peak of one's capacity.

A few quotes from people in "peak experiences," or flow experiences as we have called them, illustrate the point. The excerpts are all from interviews reported in a recent study (Csikszentmihalyi, 1975). A university professor describes his state of mind when rock climbing, which is his favorite leisure activity: "When I start to climb, it's as if my memory input had been cut off. All I can remember is the last thirty seconds, and all I can think ahead is the next five minutes. . . . With tremendous concentration the normal world is forgotten." A composer of music describes her state of mind when she is working: "I am really quite oblivious to my surroundings after I really get going . . . the phone could ring, and the doorbell could ring, or the house burn down. . . . When I start working, I really do shut out the world." An expert chess player says: "When the game is exciting, I don't seem to hear anything. The world seems to be cut off from me and all there is to think about is my game."

The examples could be multiplied forever. Optimal experiences are made possible by an unusually intense concentration of attention on a limited stimulus field. As the three quotes above indicate, in such a state the rest of the world is cut off, shut off, forgotten.

But there are other experiences when the same focusing of attention occurs. This is when the organism must face a specific threat, when the person must resolve a problem thrust on him by the environment. What is the difference between the ·two kinds of concentration, between optimal and anxiety-producing experiences?

At first it would be tempting to answer that the difference lies in the quality of the stimuli that are being attended to. The optimal functioning of the flow experience would occur when the stimulus field provides stimulation that is objectively pleasurable or attractive, while anxiety-producing experiences would be produced by stimuli that are objectively aversive or unpleasant. It is true that there are some objective characteristics of stimuli that may be specified to produce optimal experiences, such as complexity, novelty, uncertainty, and so on (Berlyne, 1960). But ultimately this explanation fails to fit the facts.

In many cases people seek out stimuli that by any ordinary definition would be called unpleasant or threatening. Rock climbers and skydivers court disaster by exposing themselves to danger, surgeons concentrate on distasteful anatomical operations, ascetics deprive themselves of stimulation, yet they all continue to seek out such experiences and claim to enjoy them.

What is then the difference between optimal and aversive states of concentration? The only answer that fits appears to be a very simple one. Optimal experiences occur when a person *voluntarily* focuses his attention on a limited stimulus field, while aversive experiences involve *involuntary* focusing of attention. In other words, the individual's choice determines the quality of the experience. If, for whatever reason, a person chooses to pay undivided attention to a set of stimuli, he or she will enjoy the experience. We are led back to the relationship between freedom and attention suggested by the earlier quotes from James and Collingwood, and by the more recent work of White (1959) and de Charms (1968).

Our previously quoted work with flow experiences suggests that people voluntarily concentrate on tasks when they perceive environmental demands for action matching their capacity to act. In other words, when situational challenges balance personal skills, a person tends to attend willingly. For instance, a chess player will concentrate on the game only when the opponent's skills match his own; if they do not, attention will waver. This relationship between a balance of challenges and skills on the one hand, and enjoyable voluntary concentration on the other, has been found to exist not only in various leisure and creative activities, but in occupations like surgery (Csikszentmihalyi, 1975) and mathematical research (Halprin, in progress). Recently Mayers (1977) showed that high school students enjoyed those school subjects in which they perceived a balance of challenges and skills, and these were also the subjects in which their concentration was voluntary.

But why is voluntary focusing of attention experienced as pleasant? If attention is the means by which a person exchanges information with the environment, and when this process is voluntary—that is, under the person's control—then voluntary focusing of attention is a state of optimal interaction. In such a state a person feels fully alive and in control, because he or she can direct the flow of reciprocal information that unites person and environment in an interactive system. I know that I am alive, that I am somebody, that I matter, when I can choose to interact with a system of stimuli that I can modify and from which I can get meaningful feedback, whether the system is made up of other people, musical notes, ideas, or tools. The ability to focus attention is the most basic way of reducing ontological anxiety, the fear of impotence, of nonexistence. This might be the main reason why the exercise of concentration, when it is subjectively interpreted to be free, is such an enjoyable experience.

It is also reasonable to assume that the exercise of voluntary attention has a positive survival value, and therefore concentration has been selected out through evolution by becoming associated with pleasurable experiences, the same way that eating and sex have become pleasurable. It would be adaptive for an organism that survives through relatively unstructured information processing to enjoy processing information freely. Then the species would be assured that its members sought out situations in which they could concentrate on various aspects of the environment, and thereby acquired new information.

In any case, the arguments reviewed thus far warrant a generalization that could be useful to direct further research: *Subjectively valued experiences depend on the voluntary focusing of attention on a limited stimulus field.*

But there is another sense in which optimal functioning is a product of concentrated attention. Not only personal experience but also the more objectified patterns of human achievement depend on it. Worthwhile accomplishment is based on skills and discipline, and these require extensive commitment of attention to learn and to apply. "A science begins when we first of all restrict our attention and then define the limits of the region within which we seek to elucidate the operation of the constituent parts," says Chance (1967, p. 504). Thomas Kuhn has described how every science requires a drastic restriction of vision on the part of scientists: "By focusing attention upon a small range of relatively esoteric problems," scientists are able to delve in greater depth and detail into their investigations, and thereby advance their field (Kuhn, 1970, p. 24). The same holds true of art, according to Collingwood (1938). More generally, any field of creative accomplishment requires concentrated attention to the exclusion of all other stimuli that temporarily become irrelevant (Csikszent-mihalyi, 1975; Getzels and Csikszentmihalyi, 1976). It is rather obvious why outstanding achievement requires concentration. Since any scientific, artistic, or other creative effort depends on acquiring, recombining, or producing information, and since this process requires attention that is in limited supply, concentration must be the inevitable prerequisite of creative work.

One does not need to look at great accomplishments to realize this basic function of attention. More mundane work is just as dependent on it. In describing the workers that made industrialization possible at the dawn of capitalism, Max Weber commented on the relationship between puritanical religious beliefs and training on the one hand, and productivity on the other: "The ability of mental concentration . . . is here most often combined with . . . a cool self-control and frugality which enormously increases performance. This creates the most favorable foundation for the conception of labour as an end in itself" (Weber, 1930, p. 63).

It is perhaps less obvious that the focusing of attention required for superior achievement must also be voluntary. Only when a person chooses to get involved in an activity will he be motivated to sustain concentration long enough to bring it to fruition. It is an interesting fact that people can be forced to do practically anything, but their attention cannot be completely controlled by external means. Even slaves, labor camp inmates, and assembly-line workers cannot be compelled to pay undivided attention to their masters' goals (Frankl, 1963). The intense concentration required for complex achievement appears to be available only when given willingly. Of course, scientists or artists might be driven to their work by unconscious wishes, the need for money, or by greed of fame; what counts, however, is for the person to think of his compulsion as free choice. Of course, people can be convinced to devote attention voluntarily to tasks that are against their objective interests, as when workers are turned into their own slave drivers (Thompson, 1963, p. 357) through religious or moral indoctrination. These arguments lead to a second generalization: *Voluntary focusing of attention on a limited stimulus field is necessary to achieve socially valued goals.* Comparing this statement with the previous one, we see that both subjectively valued experience and socially valued accomplishment result from intense and voluntary investments of attention. If one accepts the equation between attention and psychic energy, one derives the rather obvious but terribly important conclusion that what is valued by individuals and society requires unusually high investments of free psychic energy.

What follows from this conclusion is that one of the major tasks in the development of human resources is the management of attention. If people are to lead a satisfying life and if society is to progress, we have to make sure that from childhood on persons will have a chance to develop their ability to concentrate. In schools, at work, and at home there are far too few opportunities for people to get involved in a restricted world of which they can be in control. Even when the opportunities are present—and to a certain extent they are always potentially present—most people do not know how to concentrate except under the most favorable circumstances, and so rarely experience the enjoyment that accompanies the flow experience.

In a research involving a group of adolescents who reported what they were doing and how they were feeling every time they were signaled with an electronic pager, during an average week (Csikszentmihalyi, Larson, and Prescott, 1977) it was found that the highest levels of concentration as well as enjoyment were reported when teenagers were involved in games and sports. The lowest concentration as well as the least enjoyment was reported when they were watching television. Yet, in a normal day these adolescents spent over three times as much time watching television as playing games or sports.

The use of electronic pagers to collect experiential samples promises to be a useful method for studying attention in its "natural habitat." One can tell, for instance, what situations and activities promote concentration, what are the emotional and cognitive correlates of high and low concentration, and so on. Presently we are studying groups of workers, on the job and in their homes, with this method. While the results are still being analyzed, certain trends are beginning to appear. When a person is doing something voluntarily, concentration is accompanied by positive moods; when the activity is perceived to be forced, the correlation is negative. When a person is doing something, and focusing his attention on it, that person's mood is in general more positive than when he is thinking about something else. For instance, a clerk who is paged while filing letters will report more positive moods when thinking about what she does than when her attention is somewhere else. Workers report feeling significantly more creative, free, active, alert, and satisfied when they are thinking about what they are doing, as opposed to thinking about something else, even when they are doing something they would not do if they had a choice. These are only trends so far, but they do show that there are fascinating things to learn about attention outside the laboratory.

Another connection between attention and optimal functioning is suggested by the work of Holcomb (1977). She has found that people who tend to be motivated by intrinsic rewards need fewer pupillary fixation points to reverse an ambiguous visual image. It seems that the ability to find enjoyment in any situation is correlated with the ability to manipulate information internally, with less reliance on external cues. If these results are confirmed, a whole new research field might open up in which laboratory and field observations would complement each other. In the meantime, the findings suggest that attentional processes should be studied in connection with other measures of autonomy such as field-independence (Witkin, Dyk, Faterson, Goodenough, and Karp 1962), body boundary (Fisher, 1970), and locus of control (Rotter, 1966).

4. Pathology and Attention

Optimal functioning at the individual and societal levels requires a certain kind of attention structuring; conversely, several personal and societal pathologies seem to involve inability to control attention. Studies of acute schizophrenia, for instance, have revealed a disorder called "overinclusion," which appears to prevent the patient from choosing what stimuli to attend to. It is defined as "perceptual experiences characterized by the individual's difficulty in attending selectively to relevant stimuli, or by the person's tendency to be distracted by or to focus unnecessarily on irrelevant stimuli" (Shield, Harrow, and Tucker, 1974, p. 110). Patients in this condition report experiences such as: "My thoughts wander round in circles without getting anywhere. I try to read even a paragraph in a book, but it takes me ages." "If there are three or four people talking at one time I can't take it in. I would not be able to hear what they were saying properly and I would get the one mixed up with the other. To me it's just like a babble, a noise that goes right through me." (McGhie and Chapman, 1961, pp. 109, 106). More recently the same condition has been noted in other psychopathologies as well (Freedman, 1974; Shield et al., 1974).

The role of attention is completely reversed in the enjoyable flow experience and the schizophrenic break. In the first case the structure of attention is strong, narrowly focused, and in control. In psychopathology it is weak, diffuse, unable to function. It is not surprising that another symptom associated with overinclusion is what some clinicians have called "anhedonia," which refers to a person's inability to enjoy himself (Grinker, 1975; Harrow, Grinker, Holzman and Kayton, 1977).

Clearly many important pieces of the puzzle will fall into place once we understand better the etiology of overinclusion, and its causal relation to psychopathology. It appears, however, that the extremes of concentration present in flow experiences and in schizophrenia lie on a continuum that has many intermediate points.

In a research on the effects of "flow deprivation" we have asked subjects to go through their normal daily routines, but to stop doing anything that was not necessary, any act or thought that was done for its own sake (Csikszentmihalyi, 1975). After only 48 hours of this regime subjects reported severe changes in their psychic functioning. They felt more impatient, irritable, careless, depressed. The symptoms were quite similar to those of overinclusion. Performance on creativity tests dropped significantly. The second most often mentioned reason for the ill effects of deprivation by the subjects was "the act of stopping myself from doing what I wanted to do." Apparently the experimental interference with the freedom of attention may have been one of the causes for the near-pathological disruption of behavior and experience.

The evidence reviewed thus far suggests the following generalization: *The inability to focus attention voluntarily leads to psychic disruption, and eventually to psychopathology.* It seems particularly important to research the intermediate stages of the continuum between flow and pathology. Many normal life situations are structured in such ways as to make voluntary concentration difficult, and hence are psychologically disruptive. Seventy years ago Titchener (1908) already noted the important role attention played in education. The current concern with hyperkinetic children and other learning disabilities will not reach a satisfactory solution unless we understand better the dynamics of attention involved. The problem is not how to control children in the classroom, but how to let them have control over their own attention while pursuing goals consonant with the goals of the educational system. This is part of the more general issue of socialization, however, and will be discussed in the next section.

The disruptive effects of the inability to control attention mentioned so far tend to be immediately experiential, or synchronic. They relate to proximate effects of a pathological nature. But it is possible to look at more long-range, dyachronic causes and effects that unfold throughout the life cycle of an individual.

It is possible, for instance, to reinterpret the notion of alienation developed by Marx in his early manuscripts (Tucker, 1972) as referring quite literally to the workers selling out control over their attention to the employer. A wage laborer in effect consents to focus his attention on goals determined by the owner of capital. It is true that the consent is voluntary, but one can argue, as Marx did, that when there are few other opportunities to make a living, the voluntary consent is not perceived as offering much of a choice. For a large portion of his life the worker must concentrate his attention more or less involuntarily on stimuli chosen for him by others. If attention is equated with psychic energy, and if one accepts the premise that experience is determined by what attention can process through consciousness, one is led to taking seriously the conclusion that wage labor indeed results in the worker alienating, that is, relinquishing control, over his psychic energy, his experience—in short, the energy and content of his life.

Of course this is an "ideal type" description of wage labor that only an orthodox Marxist would take to be literally true. The task of the researcher is to find out whether, to what extent, and under what conditions the predicted effects are true. It is clear, for instance, that much contemporary manual labor allows workers choice over the directionality of their attention. Blauner (1964), for instance, finds subjectively felt alienation to be less among workers in automated chemical plants than among workers on assembly lines, primarily because the former are able to schedule their own work, move around the plant, and change routines with relative freedom.

Our current unpublished work with factory and clerical workers also suggests that alienation of attention is almost never complete because the worker rarely needs his or her undivided attention to do the job. Among clerical workers, for instance, we find that when respondents are randomly "beeped" with electronic pagers in their offices, almost half of the time respondents report not being primarily involved with their jobs. The rest of the time is taken up with conversations, daydreaming, planning, or the kind of voluntary activities we have been calling "micro-flow." And even when the main involvement is with the job, the worker is more often than not free to think about something else.

This "inner freedom" is probably the last defense of people who for one reason or another are forced to alienate the focus of their attention. In a study already quoted, strong correlations were found between scores on an alienation test, and the proportion of time people reported talking to themselves, pets, and plants (Csikszentmihalyi, 1975, p. 152). While fantasy, daydreaming, and imagination are a vital part of any person's psychic life (Klinger, 1971; Singer, 1966, 1973), they probably perform an even more essential adaptive function for those who cannot concentrate voluntarily on what they are doing.

In any case, the study of alienated attention has barely begun. It seems that a great amount of useful knowledge could be derived from considering the various forms of attention disorders, ranging from actual pathologies to deprivations of voluntary concentration in work and schools, under the same rubric. The alienation of free psychic energy could then become a dyachronic construct that would provide a measure of how much control persons have over their consciousness, and therefore over their experience, throughout the life cycle.

5. Attention and Socialization

A domain of behavior in which attention plays a particularly clear role is socialization. Socialization can most broadly be defined as the changes an individual undergoes when interacting with others. These changes involve, before anything else, changes in the way a person structures his or her attention.

Research on socialization usually focuses on how persons modify their behavior, learn social roles, internalize norms, and develop identities as a result of interaction (Clausen, 1968; Goslin, 1969). But prior to and concurrent with these a more fundamental process, which underlies all the others, is taking place. To become socialized, one must first of all learn to pay attention to various cues, to process information according to established patterns, to respond appropriately to stimuli. These changes in consciousness require the acquisition of new structures of attention.

For example, one of the tasks confronting a child is socialization into sleep. Each newborn child has to learn to pattern its rhythm of consciousness on a sleep-wakefulness cycle that is not "natural," but adapted to its parents' cycle (Csikszentmihalyi and Graef, 1975). Every other learning task, from eating, toilet training, reading, to moral behavior, requires identification of relevant cues, the experience of appropriate emotions, and concentration on "correct" responses (Luria, 1973; Yarrow, Rubenstein, and Pederson, 1975). The same process continues in later socialization. Peer group members develop similar patterns of perceiving, evaluating, and responding to environmental cues (Becker, 1963; Sherif and Sherif, 1972). Eventually the building up of appropriate attentional structures results in the development of a whole "symbolic universe" congruent with that of the social system or systems with which the person interacts (Berger and Luckmann, 1967; Kuhn, 1970).

The other side of the coin is that in order to socialize a person—that is, in order to provide appropriate structures of attention—the socializing agents must invest some of their own attention to accomplish the task. As Bronfenbrenner (1970) and others have noted, a model has to attend to the socializee if he is to be effective. A parent or teacher will not know whether the child's behavior conforms to expectations unless they pay attention to what he is doing. Attention is needed to discriminate between behavior that needs to be rewarded or extinguished, and to provide the appropriate feedback. Moreover, unless the model pays attention to the socializee for its own sake, the socializee will not develop feelings of identification with the model. If the child feels that the model is paying attention in order to change his behavior, regardless of his well-being, the child will not contribute his own attention willingly to the goals of the interactive system.

Attention creates the possibility for exchange of information, and hence for systemic interaction. Without mutual attention, persons cannot experience the reality of being part of the same system, and hence are less likely to accept as their own the goals of the reciprocal system that evolves through socialization. When a mother pays attention to her child, the child knows that his actions will have a chance to affect the mother, and thus he is related to her; the two are a system. It is easier for the child to accept the restructuring of attention required by the mother when he feels systemically related to her; if the mother pays no attention the child experiences isolation, and thus is less likely to abide by systemic constraints she is trying to establish.

In short, *the prerequisite of socialization is attention investment on the part of the socializing agent, and the outcome of socialization is a change in the attentional structures of the socializee.* This formulation reveals very clearly the "psychical energy" aspect of attention. Any social system, in order to survive, must socialize new recruits into its attentional patterns (of perception, belief, behavior, and so on). This task requires energy, that is, attention. Thus, one might say that the survival of social systems depends on the balance in the ledger of attention income and expenditure. Conflicting demands for attention are a common source of stress in interpersonal systems. One of the most familiar examples is the mother driven to her wits' end by children who compete with other tasks for her attention.

This is just a first step in developing a theory of socialization based on the concept of attention. A workable theory will have to account for a great many other variables. For instance, it is obvious that some changes in consciousness are much easier to accomplish— require less attention—than others. A teenager may need little inducement to listen to rock music, but may have to be forced to learn trigonometry. Changes in consciousness that require great effort (i.e., great attention investment) are likely to be those that involve radical restructuring of information, or complex processing of new information. In general, the less predictable an attention pattern is in terms of the genetic programming of man, the more effort its acquisition will require. Patterns required by complex social systems tend to require considerable effort to acquire. By contrast it requires little or no effort to acquire patterns of attention structured around sexual stimuli or primitive musical beats. This argument is, of course, a very old one. Ribot's (1890) distinction between "spontaneous" and "voluntary" attention corresponds to concentration that requires little or much effort, respectively.

Despite the amount of work that needs to be done in order to give due weight to all the variables involved, it seems that a theory of socialization built around the concept of attention is a most promising one. It has the advantage of reducing to a common denominator the main dimensions of the phenomenon, which now are expressed in noncomparable terms, such as: the process of socialization, its outcomes, the characteristics of models, social costs, and benefits. All these concepts refer to transformations of attention, or to gains and losses sustained through its investment. The various forms of socialization—imitation, modeling, or internalization—can be seen as involving different patternings of attention. And, finally, such a theory establishes links between socialization and other processes based on attention, like optimal and pathological functioning, and the maintenance of social structure, which is the topic we shall turn to next.

6.   Attention and Social Systems

A social system exists when the interaction between two or more persons affects their respective states (i.e., thoughts, emotions, behaviors). In any permanent social system these effects are predictable and reasonably clear; we call them culture, norms, social structure, depending on the forms they take. To simplify matters they can all be subsumed under the general term: *constraints*. The constraints of a social system then are those changes in a person's states that are required for interaction with that system. A social system that fails to constrain the states of persons ceases to exist.

This brief and highly abstract introduction was necessary to point out that the existence of social systems is predicated on their ability to attract, shape, and maintain the structure of people's attention within specific limits. This is easiest to see in the case of the simplest social system, the dyad. A dyad survives only as long as the two people in it continue to pay enough attention to each other to make their relationship distinctly different from a chance relationship. For example, if two people do not agree to constrain their respective schedules so that they can meet at a common time, their encounters will be random, and hence nonsystemic. Unless two people synchronize their attentional structures to a certain degree by agreeing to common constraints, a relationship will be short-lived. Deciding to be at the same place, doing the same thing together, feeling similar emotions in response to similar stimuli requires restructuring of attention. Without it friends would not be friends, lovers would not be lovers. Even ordinary conversation between two people is only possible because each person abides by a complex set of constraints regulating when and how he should take the turn to speak or to listen (Duncan, 1972). If one were not to pay attention to the cues that structure conversation, that interaction would soon become random, or stop before long.

The same is true, only at increasingly complex levels, for the survival of larger societal systems. A university exists only as long as people are willing to constrain their thoughts, feelings, and actions in ways specific to that structure of attention that makes a university different from, say, a factory or hospital. "Private property" or "representative democracy" refer to patterns of constraint that remain real only as long as enough people agree to pattern their attention accordingly.

These rather obvious remarks acquire more weight when we recall that attention is in limited supply. It follows that the creation and maintenance of social systems is dependent on the same source on which individual experience depends. What one does with one's attention not only determines the content of one's life, but also shapes one's relationship with social systems, thereby affecting the existence of such systems.

The implications of this set of relationships has hardly been explored. In the empirical literature, about the only studies that even come close to it are ones that touch on the "cocktail party phenomenon" (Cherry, 1953; Keele, 1973), or the tendency in social gatherings to pay selective attention to some sources of information as against others. But the phenomenon is looked at purely from the point of view of a person's sensory filtering mechanisms, rather than in terms of how selective attention creates interaction, and hence social systems.

Studies that directly deal with the social-structuring effects of attention can be found apparently only in the ethological literature. Murton, Isaacson, and Westwood (1966) have observed that subordinate members of pigeon flocks eat less than more dominant animals, because they spend an inordinate amount of time paying attention to individuals of higher status. Kummer and Kurt (1963) have remarked that the social status of female hamadryas baboons is best revealed by the way they restrict their attention exclusively within their own group, and direct it primarily to its male leader. From these observations and the ones he himself collected, Chance concluded that

> attention has a binding quality. . . . The amount of attention directed
> within a group . . . will then reveal the main feature of the structure of
> attention upon which the relationships within the group are based. . . .
> The assessment of attention structure provides a way of describing and
> accounting for many features of dominance relationships in several differ-
> ent species. (Chance, 1967, p. 509)

This binding and structuring effect of attention is what needs to be studied in human groups. But in human social systems the phenomenon is much more complex. It is not enough to determine who pays attention to whom to uncover the underlying attentional structure that allows the system to exist. Human systems differ from other social structures in that they are largely based on attention that is objectified and stored in symbolic form. Perhaps the most effective of these symbols is money. A wage earner exchanges psychic energy for money by investing his attention in goals determined for him by someone else. The money thus earned can then be exchanged again for objects and services that are the result of someone else's investment of psychic energy. In contemporary societies, control over money directly translates into control over other people's attention. How the mediating function of money developed historically is discussed by Polanyi (1957), and Scitovsky (1976) presents a good case for the dangers inherent in taking the symbolic power of money too seriously. Thus, to understand the structure of human groups it would be misleading to simply measure the direction and duration of gaze among individuals, a procedure that might be satisfactory to reveal the structure of a baboon troop. It is necessary instead to determine the pattern of symbolically mediated constraints on attention. The major social institutions—economy, law, government, media—are all formalized structures of attention; they define who should pay attention to what.

This formulation allows us to restate one of the basic paradoxes about man and society. Every thinker who has dealt with the issue has recognized a basic conflict between individual needs and social constraints. The model of attention describes that conflict more economically than most theories. The point is that the psychic energy necessary to develop a satisfying personal life (i.e., *voluntary focusing of attention*) is the same energy needed to keep the social system in an organized state. Conflicting demands on the same supply of limited psychic energy cause the ambivalent relationship between man and society. An optimal social system is one that derives the psychic energy necessary for its existence from the voluntary focusing of attention of its members.

In a current study, we have begun to explore the way symbols attract attention, and how they serve to integrate personal experiences on the one hand, and promote social solidarity on the other. This involves interviewing families with questions concerning objects and events inside the home, the neighborhood, and the metropolitan area that have special significance for the respondents. Although this research is beginning to provide some basic information about the ways in which people objectify their attention in symbols, it is only the barest of beginnings. The field of possible research applications is simply enormous. An ideal first step, for example, would be a community study in which the psychic energy output from individuals would be balanced against the input of such energy in the social system. The main questions to be answered would be: How much of the total attention invested by individuals is voluntary? How much of it is structured by the constraints of the social system? What are the forms in which psychic energy is transformed before it is used up by the social system (e.g., voluntary work, taxes, church attendance, and so on)? How do the patterns of attention allocation discovered relate to personal development, and to community strength and stability? Only after systematic studies of this kind are conducted will we begin to understand more clearly how personal life satisfaction, personal and societal pathology, and the survival of social systems are related.

7. Summary and Conclusions

Attention provides the behavioral sciences with a concept that bridges a vast range of phenomena from the micro-personal to the macro-social. By recognizing the scarcity of attention, and its indispensable contribution to consciousness, one is able to use a powerful concept for the solution of a variety of seemingly unrelated problems.

Attention is required for a person to control what content shall be admitted to consciousness. The sum of all contents admitted to consciousness determine the quality of a person's life experience. A person who feels able to direct his or her attention freely enjoys the experience and develops a positive self-concept.

But social systems require highly complex attention structures. The pool of attention on which social systems draw for their continued existence is the same limited amount on which individuals depend to structure their own consciousness. Socialization is the process that mediates between the spontaneous allocation of attention by individuals, and the voluntary patterns required by social systems. Optimal functioning occurs when there is no conflict between spontaneous and voluntary demands on attention, that is, when persons voluntarily concentrate on goals that are in line with sociocultural constraints.

Therefore personal development and the development of sociocultural systems both depend on the economy of attention. How much attention is paid, to what, and under what conditions—i.e., voluntarily or under constraint—determine the characteristics of persons and social systems.

The main issues of a holistic behavioral science revolve around the question of how and where attention is allocated, and who is in control of this process. Research methods necessary to answer that question are beginning to emerge. Potentially it is not too difficult to determine how attention is allocated. Observation of gaze direction, records of involvement over time, time-budget records get at molar behavioral indicators that have a strong face validity. Such measures must be complemented by data on symbolically mediated attention, such as allocation and control of money, status, and other symbolic resources. To tap the inner movements of attention one must obtain records of fantasy, imagination, and other less obvious mental processes. "Experiential sampling" based on self-reports obtained through random electronic paging promises to be a useful technique for estimating attention structures in real-life situations (Csikszentmihalyi, Larson, and Prescott, 1977).

More crippling than the methodological lag, which can be overcome, is the theoretical disarray that presently surrounds the holistic study of attention. Until a consistent and coherent theory of attention is developed, research results will continue to be trivial, no matter how brilliant the techniques we devise. Only a new conceptual paradigm will be able to inspire new research, direct it along the most promising paths, and then relate findings to each other and explain them in a meaningful context.

ACKNOWLEDGMENTS

The author wishes to thank Barbara Rubinstein and Ronald Graef for suggestions and criticism in the editing of the manuscript.

References

Bakan, P. (Ed.). *Attention*. New York: Van Nostrand, 1966.
Becker, H. S. *Outsiders*. New York: The Free Press, 1963.
Berger, P., and Luckmann, T. *The social construction of reality*. Garden City, N.Y.: Doubleday, 1967.
Berlyne, D. E. *Conflict, arousal, and curiosity*. New York: McGraw-Hill, 1960.

Binet, A. La concurrence des états psychologigues. *Revue Philosophique de la France et de l'étranger.* 1890, *24,* 138-155.

Blauner, R. *Alienation and freedom.* Chicago: The University of Chicago Press, 1964.

Broadbent, D. E. *Perception and communication.* London: Pergamon, 1958.

Broadbent, D. E. The role of auditory localization in attention and memory span. *Journal of Experimental Psychology,* 1954, *47,* 191-196.

Bronfenbrenner, U. *Two worlds of childhood.* New York: Basic Books, 1970.

Campbell, D. T. "Downward causation" in hierarchically organized biological systems. In T. Dobzhansky and F. J. Ayala (Eds.), *The problem of reduction in biology.* London: Macmillan, 1973.

Castaneda, C. *Tales of power.* New York: Simon and Schuster, 1974.

Chance, M. R. A. Attention structure as the basis of primate rank orders. *Man,* 1967, *2,* 503-518.

De Charms, R. *Personal causation.* New York: Academic Press, 1968.

Cherry, E. C. Some experiments on the recognition of speech, with one and with two ears. *Journal of the Acoustical Society of America,* 1953, *25,* 975-979.

Clausen, J. A. (Ed.). *Socialization and society.* Boston: Little, Brown, 1968.

Collingwood, R. G. *The principles of art.* Oxford: Oxford University Press, 1938.

Csikszentmihalyi, M. Sociological implications in the thought of Teilhard de Chardin. *Zygon,* 1970, *5,* 2, 130-147.

Csikszentmihalyi, M. *Beyond boredom and anxiety.* San Francisco: Jossey-Bass, 1975.

Csikszentmihalyi, M., and R. Graef. Socialization into sleep: exploratory findings. *Merrill-Palmer Quarterly,* 1975, *21,* 1, 3-18.

Csikszentmihalyi, M., Larson, R., and Prescott, S. The ecology of adolescent activities and experiences. *Journal of Youth and Adolescence,* 1977, *6,* 3, 281-294.

Dewey, J. *Art as experience.* New York: Putnam, 1934.

Duncan, S. Some signals and rules for taking speaking turns in conversations. *Journal of Personality and Social Psychology,* 1972, *23,* 283-292.

Exner, S. *Physiologische Erklarung der psychischen Erscheinigungen.* Leipzig, 1894.

Fisher, S. *Body experience in fantasy and behavior.* New York: Appleton, Century, Crofts, 1970.

Frankl, V. E. *Man's search for meaning.* New York: Washington Square Press, 1963.

Freedman, B. J. The subjective experience of perceptual and cognitive disturbances in schizophrenia. *Archives of General Psychiatry,* 1974, *30,* 333-340.

Freud, S. *The interpretation of dreams.* New York: Avon Books, 1971 (1900).

Getzels, J. W., and Csikszentmihalyi, M. *The creative vision.* New York: Wiley Interscience, 1976.

Goslin, D. A. (Ed.). *Handbook of socialization theory and research.* Chicago: Rand McNally, 1969.

Grinker, R. Anhedonia and depression in schizophrenia. In T. Benedek and E. Anthony (Eds.), *Depression.* Boston: Little, Brown, 1975.

Halprin, F. Applied mathematics as a flow activity. The University of Chicago: Unpublished manuscript, in progress.

Harrow, M., Grinker, R., Holzman, D., and Kayton, L. Anhedonia and schizophrenia. *American Journal of Psychiatry,* 1977, *134,* 794-797.

Hernandez-Peon, R. Attention, sleep, motivation, and behavior. In R. G. Heath (Ed.), *The role of pleasure in behavior.* New York: Harper and Row, 1964, 195-217.

Holcomb, J. H. Attention and intrinsic rewards in the control of psychophysiologic states. *Psychotherapy and Psychosomatics,* 1977, *27,* 54-61.

Jaynes, J. *The origins of consciousness.* Boston: Houghton-Mifflin, 1976.

James, W. *Principles of psychology.* Vol. 1. New York: Henry Holt and Co., 1890.

Kahneman, D. *Attention and effort.* E-C. Englewood Cliffs, N.J.: Prentice Hall, 1973.

Keele, S. W. *Attention and human performance*. Pacific Palisades, Calif. Goodyear Publishing Co., 1973.

Klinger, E. *The structure and function of fantasy*. New York: Wiley, 1971.

Klinger, E., Barta, S. G., and Mahoney, T W. Motivation, mood, and mental events. In G. Serban (Ed.), *Psychopathology of human adaptation*. New York: Plenum, 1976, 95–112.

Kuhn, T. S. *The structure of scientific revolutions*. Chicago: The University of Chicago Press, 1970.

Kummer, H., and Kurt, F. Social units of a free-living population of Hamadryas baboons. *Folia Primatologica*, 1963, *1*, 4–19.

Luria, A. R. *The working brain*. New York: Basic Books, 1973.

Mayers, P. The relation between structural elements and the experience of enjoyment in high school classes. The University of Chicago: Unpublished manuscript, 1977.

McGhie, A., and Chapman, J. Disorders of attention and perception in early schizophrenia. *British Journal of Medical Psychology*, 1961, *34*, 103–116.

Mostofsky, D. I. (Ed.). *Attention: Contemporary theory and analysis*. New York: Appleton-Century-Crofts, 1970.

Muller, G. E. *Zur Theorie der Sinnlichen Aufmerksamkeit*. Leipzig, 1873.

Munsterberg, H. *Grundzuge der Psychologie*. Leipzig: Barth, 1900.

Murphy, G., and Kovach, J. K. *Historical introduction to modern psychology*. New York: Harcourt, Brace, 1972.

Murton, R. K., Isaacson, A. J., and Westwood, N. J. The relationship between woodpigeons and their clover food supply and the mechanism of population control. *Journal of Applied Ecology*, 1966, *3*, 55–96.

Norman, D. A. *Memory and attention*. New York: Wiley, 1969.

Pillsbury, W. B. *Attention*. New York: Macmillan, 1908.

Polanyi, K. *The great transformation*. Boston: Beacon Press, 1957.

Ribot, T. *The psychology of attention*. Chicago: The Open Court, 1890.

Rotter, J. B. Generalized expectancies for internal versus external control of reinforcement. *Psychological Monographs*, 1966, *80* (whole No. 609).

Scitovsky, T. *The joyless economy*. New York: Random House, 1976.

Sherif, M. and Sherif, C. *Reference groups*. Chicago: Regnery, 1972.

Shield, P. H., Harrow, M., and Tucker, G. Investigation of factors related to stimulus overinclusion. *Psychiatric Quarterly*, 1974, *48*, 109–116.

Singer, J. L. *Daydreaming: An introduction to the experimental study of inner experiences*. New York: Random House, 1966.

Singer, J. L. *The child's world of make-believe*. New York: Academic Press, 1973.

Stewart, K. Dream exploration among the Senoi. In T. Roszak (Ed.), *Sources*. New York: Harper & Row, 1972.

Thompson, E. P. *The making of the English working class*. New York: Vintage, 1963.

Titchener, E. B. *Lectures on the elementary psychology of feeling and attention*. New York: Macmillan, 1908.

Tucker, R. C. (Ed.). *The Marx-Engels reader*. New York: Norton, 1972.

Washburn, M. F. *Movement and mental imagery*. Boston: Houghton-Mifflin, 1908.

Weber, M. *The Protestant ethic and the spirit of capitalism*. London: Allen and Unwin, 1930.

White, R. W. Motivation reconsidered: The concept of competence. *Psychological Review*, 1959, *66*, 297–333.

Witkin, H. A., Dyk, R. B., Faterson, H. F., Goodenough, D. R., and Karp, S. A. *Psychological differentiation*. New York: Wiley, 1962.

Yarrow, L. J., Rubenstein, J. L., and Pederson, F. A. *Infant and environment*. Washington, D.C.: Hemisphere, 1975.

Author Index

Subject Index